# PROHIBITION'S PRINCE

The Bizarre Life of America's Millionaire Moonshiner

### GUY GRAYBILL

Foreword by presidential speech-writer James Humes

an imprint of Sunbury Press, Inc.
Mechanicsburg, PA USA

## CATAMOUNT PRESS

an imprint of Sunbury Press, Inc.
Mechanicsburg, PA USA

Copyright © 2010, 2011, 2024 by Guy Graybill.
Cover Copyright © 2010, 2024 by Sunbury Press, Inc.

Sunbury Press supports copyright. Copyright fuels creativity, encourages diverse voices, promotes free speech, and creates a vibrant culture. Thank you for buying an authorized edition of this book and for complying with copyright laws. Except for the quotation of short passages for the purpose of criticism and review, no part of this publication may be reproduced, scanned, or distributed in any form without permission. You are supporting writers and allowing Sunbury Press to continue to publish books for every reader. For information contact Sunbury Press, Inc., Subsidiary Rights Dept., PO Box 548, Boiling Springs, PA 17007 USA or legal@sunburypress.com.

For information about special discounts for bulk purchases, please contact Sunbury Press Orders Dept. at (855) 338-8359 or orders@sunburypress.com.

To request one of our authors for speaking engagements or book signings, please contact Sunbury Press Publicity Dept. at publicity@sunburypress.com.

FIRST CATAMOUNT PRESS REVISED EDITION: November 2024

Set in Adobe Garamond | Interior design by Crystal Devine | Cover by Lawrence Knorr | Edited by Lawrence Knorr.

Publisher's Cataloging-in-Publication Data
Names: Graybill, Guy.
Title: Prohibition's prince : the bizarre life of America's millionaire moonshiner.
Description: First trade paperback edition. | Mechanicsburg, PA : Catamount Press, 2024.
Summary: Prince Farrington, originally from North Carolina, was a prolific moonshiner and distributor during Prohibition in the Northern Appalachia region of Pennsylvania. Centered around Williamsport and Lock Haven, his ring of stills and accomplices are the stuff of local legends to this day.
Identifiers: ISBN : 979-8-88819-230-6 (paperback).
Subjects: BIOGRAPHY & AUTOBIOGRAPHY / Criminals & Outlaws | BIOGRAPHY & AUTOBIOGRAPHY / Cultural & Regional | HISTORY / United States / State & Local / Middle Atlantic (DC, DE, MD, NJ, NY, PA).

Designed in the USA
0 1 1 2 3 5 8 13 21 34 55

*For the Love of Books!*

This book is dedicated to the memories of Pauline, Pauline, Leo and Lee; our parents and the grandparents of our children.

# CONTENTS

Acknowledgments (2010)     vii
Foreword by James Humes     xi

1. Over Fourth Gap Mountain and Away!     1
2. Carolina Roots     12
3. From Tarheel to Keystoner     39
4. The Moonshiner, Revisited     54
5. The Politicians' Poverty     64
6. The Human Vortex     73
7. Moonshine and Mayhem     102
8. The Coterie of Cohorts     126
9. Other Major Players     166
10. "Moon Shine Farm": The Klobe Clan     178
11. The Clandestine Network     221
12. The Long Arm     262
13. The Bootlegger's Daughter     283
14. Days of Destitution     324
15. A Roadshow of Relics     336
16. The Legend Aborning     344

Bibliography     384
Index     386

# Acknowledgments (2010)

Gratitude is expressed to my wife, Nancy, who urged me to put this book on the front burner ahead of several other projects. That was an excellent suggestion, reinforced by other forms of support. Nancy also remains my first line of defense against sloppy observations and mistakes.

Among the many Pennsylvanians who shared precious stories or related information about the master moonshiner, I would like to thank Cheryl Bernard, Lou Bernard, Stanley Bitner, Mildred Bixel, Barbara Carter Blossom [now of New York state], Lynn Bowes, Hazel Brown, Darrell Byerly, Charles ("Bud") Coira, Margaret Coltrane, Pat and Phil Courtright, Edie Cox, Dolly Derr, Charles Dorwart, Daniel Doyle, Margaret and Harold "Bud" Drick, Beth Duck, Leroy Duck, Roy Duck, John Eastlake, David L. Eck, Leonard Embick, Dave Farrington, Tammy Farrington, Ken Feerrar, Kay Fetzer, Robert Fillman, Samuel Fuller, Wayne Fuller, Bill Gibson, Harry Glossner, Susan Glossner, Jacque Groce, Mary Groce, Gloria Schadt Harbach, John "Jack" Harbach, John F. Harvey Jr., Reverend Dean Hauser, Elizabeth Helsman, Dan Hills, Spencer Howard, Steve Hulslander, Clifford Johnson, Pauline Johnson, Nathan Jordan, Carol Kaler, Marjorie Bossert Kamus, Dorothy Knarr, Phil Landers, Lawrence Lebin, Linda and Ralph Lehman, Harry Lytle, James Matthews, Laura Matthews, Thelma Matthews, Frances McCormick, Lynn McCormick, Tom McCormick, Bill McCoy, Cliff Meixel, Jane Bubb Miller, Roseltha Lydia Button Miller, Kim Minier, Eugene Morris, Troy Musser, Charles Muthler, John Muthler, Harold D. Myers, Emily Packer, Leonard Parucha, Harold Pepperman, Mary Pepperman, Sue and Marvin Pontius, Beverly Fenton Porter, Chris Porter, Dave Proust, Dan Reinhold, Rene Rhine, Bill Rishel, Bob Rishel, Shirley Rishel, Freda Rockey, Tom Rockey, Charles Rosamilia, Ann Roush, Priscilla McCloskey Runk, Grace Sheddy, Bill Simcox, Theodore Simcox, Eugene Slegle, Ed Snook, Peggy Snyder, Charles Springer, Miller Stamm,

Patrick Steinbacher, Robert Stiver, Christopher Stoner, Bill Stout, Jodi Swartz, Charles Sweeney, Richard Thompson, Bill Tyson, David A. Ulmer, Patricia and Charles Ulrich, John Wagner, Nathan Walizer, Mary Washburn, Harold "Dutch" Washburn, Robert Weaver, Steve Weaver, Yvonne Weaver, Shaun Wolf Wortis, Kathy Zell and Dan Zell.

My brother, Lee, a computer expert, reduced my labors immensely by frequently sharing his abilities with his bumbling brother.

Wayne Welshans, of the Jersey Shore area knows the statistical and the colorful to a degree unmatched by anyone beyond Prince's family. He was a one-man resource library for this biography.

Among the many North Carolina citizens who helped me to expand and conclude this project, I thank Mary Anderson, Becky Farrington, Bunny Wright, Cindy Toomes, Dorothy Lee Highfill, Brenda Highfill, Ray Highfill, Tommy Farrington, Tony Hyatt, Jerry Highfill and Kelly Teague, all of whom visited with me in the very congenial atmosphere of Becky's house, where they tolerated my questions and provided me with solid information. Thanks, also, to Barbara Swindler for the unique information on Samuel Glenn. Thanks to Joe Porter and Dorothy Williams, both of whom gave me information on the moonshiner turned inventor Marshall "Carbine" Williams. Further, my work in North Carolina was made easier by the graciousness of Duilla and Dr. Paul Harkins of Greensboro, who hosted our visit to their state.

I am especially thankful for having had the opportunity given me, before their passing, of visiting and interviewing George Porter (P. D. Farrington's son-in-law), Gladys Rockey (not Gladys Porter, who is the principal subject of Chapter Nine), Charles Farrington Jr. (Prince's nephew, interviewed by telephone) and Leo "Chip" Taylor, who—as a youngster—was an occasional visitor to the Farrington home.

I also wish to thank the unknown courthouse employees of Guilford and Rockingham counties (North Carolina) and Clinton and Lycoming counties (Pennsylvania), all of whom quickly recognized an inept visitor and provided essential aid. My gratitude goes to Elizabeth Preston of the North Carolina archives office in Raleigh, who provided substantial long-range aid after I'd returned to Pennsylvania. Thanks, as well, to Bruce Daws of Cumberland County, North Carolina; Ed Dix of the Pennsylvania Bureau of Forestry; Mark Ternent, a wildlife biologist with the Pennsylvania Game Commission; Jonathan Stayer of the Pennsylvania Historical and Museum Commission; and the staff of the Soil Conservation Office in Lamar, Pennsylvania.

My special thanks go to G. Dave Porter and Dr. Robert Porter, grandsons of P. D. Farrington. This pair of direct descendants cleared many hazy misconceptions of mine and proved to be my best sources for the information needed to develop this biography properly. They patiently gave me the greatest quantity of the most reliable information of anyone consulted.

# Foreword

I first met Guy Graybill in the Spring of 2001. He was doing the Lord's work—teaching history in a rural high school in a town with unpaved streets in southern Colorado blighted by poverty and despair. Most of his students were from families on welfare in this nearby one-time mining area, which former presidential candidate George McGovern used as the subject of his doctoral thesis, writing on the violent strike in the early 1900s.

Guy Graybill is a gifted teacher with the innate talent of making history come alive by igniting his students' curiosity about events past and making them excited about study projects related to the assigned topic. Guy had invited me to share my experiences writing for five US Presidents with his students. We were both teachers in Colorado far from our commonly shared roots in Central Pennsylvania. (I was then the Ryals Professor of Language and Leadership at the University of Southern Colorado—now Colorado State University at Pueblo.) We both shared a passion for Pennsylvania's history and especially for the untapped lore of the Susquehanna Valley area. My first of 35 published books was *Sweet Dream—Tale of a River City* a history the City of Williamsport commissioned me to write for its centennial year. The title, *Sweet Dream*, I took from a Coleridge poem, "May we ever follow the sweet dream/Where Susquehanna pours its untamed stream." Coleridge, along with his fellow poets Wordsworth and Southey, was planning an artists' colony where the two Susquehanna branches—west and north—joined near Sunbury, close to Snyder County, where Guy grew up.

Williamsport, after the Civil War, became, for a time, the world's lumber capital. Pine trees felled in northwest Pennsylvania and were floated down the West Branch of the Susquehanna to lumber mills in Williamsport. Fortunes were made. The Williamsport High School team is still called the "Millionaires" because of the families made rich by the lumber trade.

I headed two historical societies, the Lycoming and Muncy, where I wrote articles on local history, such as rafting or the building of the West Branch Canal. But one thing that never came up in our love for Central Pennsylvania history was Prince Farrington.

I knew the Prince's daughter, Gladys, and her handsome son, David Porter. In fact, David was once in my Sunday School class at the Jersey Shore Presbyterian Church. I was introduced to them by my aunt, Margaret Humes Collins, my late father's sister.

The house in Jersey Shore became our home in the early days of our marriage when we worked in Washington, and Aunt Margaret became my surrogate mother, with both of my parents deceased. Because of her, I wrote two books: *The House of Humes*, on the Humes family and its pilgrimage from Scotland to Ireland to America, a thousand years. My aunt was fiercely proud of her Scotch Irish mountain roots. In her thirties, she moved to western North Carolina to build a school for illiterate mountain children. She published two books of poetry celebrating her love of Scots mountain people, their culture and their ways, *Plenteous Heritage* and *Four Seasons*. In the 1920s, she had traveled by rail across the country raising funds from D.A.R. chapters to fund schools to educate their illiterate kinsmen in the eastern mountains. Her favorite Jersey Shore Presbyterian Sunday School charge was David Porter, a darkly handsome and studious youth. His doting mother, the blowsy daughter of the Prince, would regale us with stories of how they played Monopoly with real one-hundred-dollar bills. Gladys adored her oft-absent father, not unaware of his faults. The "Prince" was no Robin Hood, stealing from the revenuers and giving to the poor. But he could be generous to his family and local churches. Until this book, I thought Prince was a name given to him for his princely purse (no, it was the name of the doctor who delivered him). My tee-totaling aunt, in a house that had never seen a drop of alcohol in its history spanning three generations, was enthralled by this prohibition Prince, but I remember her extracting a pledge from his grandson, David Porter: "Mrs. Collins, I swear to you I'm never going to touch a drop of liquor. I've seen too much of it in my family."

The Farringtons were Scots-Irish. There was no Irish blood; they were Scots who emigrated to Northern Ireland and then to America in the middle of the 17th century. The Scots had evaded and defied English revenue agents and then U.S. ones in the early days of the Republic. The Whiskey Rebellion of 1796 was just one example of Scots-Irish insurrection. The Scots gravitated to the mountains. The Appalachians from Pennsylvania to North Carolina, Kentucky and Tennessee became their home. They left the flat river land to the Germans, who were the better farmers. "The Scots," said Aunt Margaret, "were better talkers—preachers, lawyers and politicians." She said that, like Nixon, more Presidents were Scots-Irish than anything else—Jackson, Polk, Buchanan, Hayes, Arthur and McKinley.

In 1960, I was a Fourth of July speaker underneath the 300-year-old Pine Creek Tiadaghton Elm. My subject was "The Fair Play Men"—that Scots-Irish Presbyterian group who Henry Wharton Shoemaker (falsely) said governed themselves separately from Philadelphia and wrote, as mentioned previously, their own Declaration of Independence. One of them had been my forebear. A young listener, a student at Lycoming College, asked if it was difficult doing a talk when there were so few written records about the Fair Play Men. He was doing a college thesis on Prince Farrington and hoped to publish it as a book. I agreed to look over his material. I told him it was too sketchy and there was too little documentation for a book.

On the contrary, Guy Graybill has written a researched, carefully footnoted account with recorded interviews; and what's more, it does not read like some dry college thesis. It is a lovely, fascinating account that brings a figure of local folklore to life. History, as Guy Graybill has proved in *Keystone*, need not be a collection of dry statistics and dates. Just as he did in the classroom, he makes history a living thing and proves that local or regional history can reveal more about the culture, life and ethos of a people than a broader-scope national chronicle.

**James Humes**
Historian, biographer, Lycoming County native, and speechwriter to five U.S. presidents.

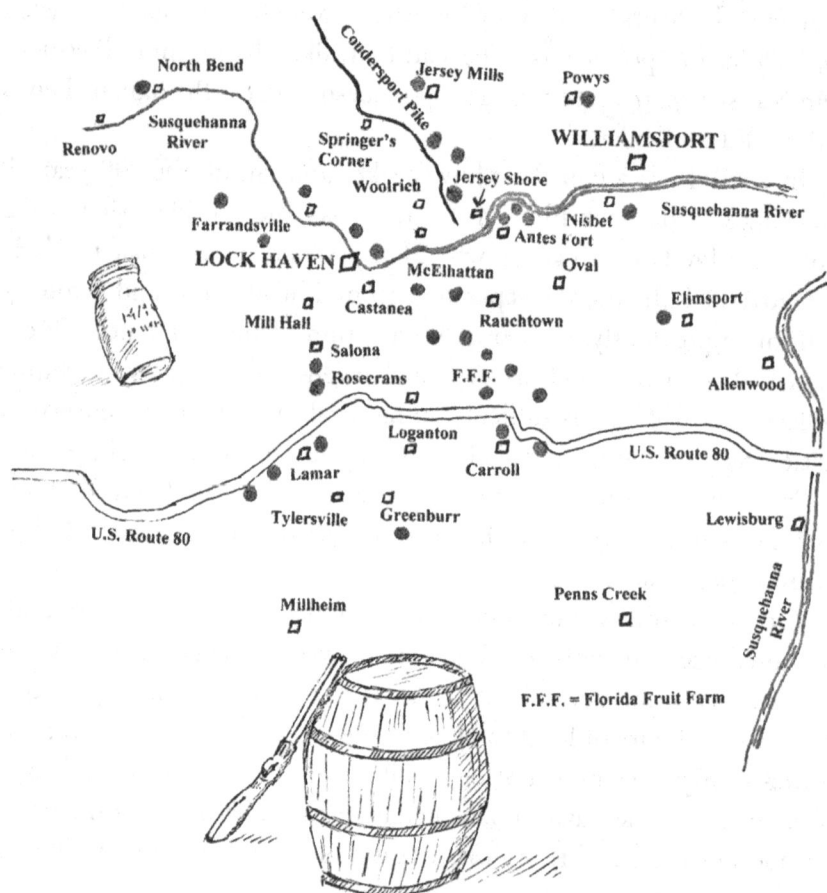

*A Map of "Farrington Country" in Pennsylvania. The approximate locations of known still sites are represented by black dots.*

FOREWORD xv

*Among the principal characters in this biography: genuine Farrington stock, owned by a resident of Jersey Shore, who received them as a gift many years ago.*

*Still worker with wheelbarrow at unidentified Farrington still site.*

*The two opponents - moonshiner and lawman - involved in the 1946 raid along the Tangascootac Creek, Clinton County, PA. (Farrington on left and Baxter on right)*

*A pair of photos of Farrington stills; not identified as any specific ones of his many sites.*

*The 19-year-old Prince Farrington, already active in the moonshine business.*

# · 1 ·

# Over Fourth Gap Mountain and Away!

**THE RAID ON THE "SCOOTAC"**
Prince David Farrington was no hillbilly, moonshiner. Farrington was a flamboyant rascal who planned and executed a vast illegal distilling operation. At one time or another, over the decades of the 1920s, 1930s and 1940s, P. D. Farrington had started and operated at least thirty stills in the isolated ravines and forests of Penn's Woods. At any given time, half or more of his secret stills were cooking away in the backwoods of Lycoming and Clinton counties about 100 miles and more north of the state capital in Harrisburg. His enterprise was producing an Amazonian stream of sour mash whiskey and was allowing Prince Farrington to amass a millionaire's fortune. Lawmen raids were rather common, but none threatened his career as a master moonshiner and bootlegger until the fateful raid of August 26, 1946.

August 26, 1946, was the night that this skilled and innovative criminal joined one of his workers for a middle-of-the-night visit to one of the finest and most productive of his many hidden distilleries or 'stills.' That summer night, several hours after midnight, as he drove his truck through an isolated creek valley, Prince. D. Farrington was blissfully ignorant of the recent activity of state and federal officials, who were planning a joint operation to catch him in the illegal act of working one of his sylvan moonshining operations.

Many geographical entities in the region carry names provided by the American Indians. This creek valley was no exception. The name of the creek is Tangascootac (assumed to mean 'small, swamp creek'). Locals refer to the stream and the valley as the "Scootac." The waters of the Tangascootac wind out of the hills northwest of the town of Lock Haven,

Pennsylvania, and flow for about eight miles before joining the Susquehanna River a few miles upstream from the town. Lock Haven is the county seat of Clinton County. It remains an important town because of its state university and some paper mills. The town has a regular county museum, plus another museum that reminds folks that Lock Haven was once home to the main factory manufacturing Piper aircraft.

Today, despite the fact that the Tangascootac has a drainage area of nearly 50 square miles, virtually no one lives in the *Tangascootac* valley, although, in an earlier century, there was active bituminous (soft coal) mining among the creek's headwaters. As the richer veins disappeared, the mining camps—Peacock I, Peacock II, Revelton, Bear Swamp, Tangas and Eagleton, disappeared as well, to be replaced with a like number of ghost towns. Today, the few remaining structures have been converted to hunting cabins. There is also a promise of future activity to be spurred by timbering and by the search for natural gas. Those two activities were not a factor shortly after the end of World War II. The splendid isolation of the Eagleton site struck Farrington as being an ideal location for a moonshiner's still.

Farrington hadn't been the first to appreciate the seclusion of the Scootac. During the Prohibition era, an Italian immigrant and miner, Andrew Zanella, did some moonshining on the site of the former Bear Swamp property. He bought peaches from local orchardists and distilled a highly-regarded peach brandy. Thus occupied, Zanella thrived and earned his nickname, "Peachy."

In 1944, Prince Farrington had a still operating in the Tangascootac Creek valley. That one had quickly been raided, but Prince liked the site and decided to try using it again. So, in 1946, working by night, Farrington again established a still in the *Tangascootac* valley at the ghost town of Eagleton. It was one of Farrington's most ambitious operations. The still on the 'Scootac' was estimated to have cost $10,000 in the currency of the time. A tent provided shelter for the workers, but that was just the beginning. Of this still site, Farrington's son-in-law, George Porter, recalled, "It was like a city up there. They had their own power plant, with lights strung around. They had a steam boiler, where they cooked their mash and cooked the mash out." Closer to the valley's entrance, "they had something like a road check. The trucks would come down here and stop by. They'd have this [distinctive] odor as they'd go by." His distilling complex was hidden within a ravine and at the terminus of an unpaved road that had stretched for eight miles from the nearest roadway. The still site, on the upper waters of the Tangascootac, had been costly, but it was a superb operation. P. D. Farrington, as usual, had planned for everything with one exception. The aging moonshiner was about to encounter a young nemesis.

## PRINCE'S BEST-KNOWN NEMESIS: AGENT RICHARD BAXTER

Prince David Farrington had been born in Guilford County, North Carolina and had risen to near-legendary status in the Clinton/Lycoming counties of Pennsylvania. After a quarter-century in Pennsylvania, Farrington, or "Prince," was an established 'celebrity' in the above-mentioned pair of counties. One man who was about to bring grief into Farrington's life was Richard Baxter. Baxter (September 11, 1908—December 2, 1988) was a native of Fannettsburg (Franklin County) in southern Pennsylvania, but he spent his childhood in Allenwood, a riverside town of several hundred people, along the Susquehanna. Allenwood is situated just outside Lycoming County in northern Union County. Richard Baxter's father, Reverend Thomas George Baxter, was a veteran of the Spanish-American War who ministered to the congregation of the Washington Presbyterian Church in Allenwood. Facetiously, one might mention that Richard Baxter was blessed with some 'emmanent' relatives (his mother was named 'Emma' as was his sister. Eventually, he married. His wife was a teacher, named Emma Cross Baxter.

After completing the two-year high school program in Allenwood, Richard attended the nearby Milton High School until his graduation. In 1928, Baxter graduated from Susquehanna University in Selinsgrove, Pennsylvania. He now had a degree in Secondary Education. He continued his formal education at New Jersey's Princeton Theological Seminary, but he left the seminary in 1931 without a degree. While the Baxters were living in Allenwood, the Baxter family and Harry Jamison's family were "very good friends," according to Elizabeth Jamison Helsman. She remembers him as "Dick" Baxter, and she also remembers that "Dick's" father was deeply disappointed when Richard decided not to become a minister.

While Prince David Farrington was edging into his 50s, Richard Baxter—almost two decades younger—was becoming active in the investigative duties of the Liquor Control Board. As a young man, Baxter had served as a motorcycle cop with the Pennsylvania Highway Patrol and in 1933, when he stopped a car near Smethport, Pennsylvania (McKean County), he was shot in the arm by the unknown driver. Later, he joined the Pennsylvania Liquor Control Board. Baxter was working with the Liquor Control Board in Philadelphia when he left that position to enter the U.S. Navy during the Second World War. Perhaps inspired, in part, by his having been shot while on duty, Richard Baxter taught himself to be an expert in the use of his service weapon. He had trained to the point where he expressed confidence that he could handle almost any armed confrontation. During his military service, he was stationed in Chicago, serving with the shore patrol and being an instructor in the use of the pistol. Following his military service, Richard Baxter returned to his home area (and to what some might identify as "Farrington Country"). He and Emma lived in Williamsport, where he rejoined the Liquor Control Board. Baxter's off-duty hobbies were pistol shooting and the reloading of ammunition for his large collection of firearms.

Richard Baxter was quoted as saying that, as a youth, he stumbled on a Farrington still. Baxter told his father of the find, and his minister/father cautioned, "Better stay away from there, or something might happen to you."[1] However, once Richard Baxter reached adulthood, he became a 'revenuer' and, after many years in law-enforcement and military service, he found himself pursuing Prince Farrington, the moonshiner. Baxter, the lawman, it turns out, caused more trouble for Prince than Prince did for him. While Baxter was in the act of apprehending Prince Farrington at one of his stills, his father's words of caution may have crossed Richard's mind. Baxter, having seen deer tracks near the still, asked his prisoner, "If I came back here to hunt, would you shoot me?" Prince reassured his young pursuer, "Never shot nobody yet, son. Don't suppose I ever will."

As noted in the opening pages of this biography, Richard Baxter was the primary agent involved in the tracking and apprehension of Prince Farrington at his sprawling Tangascootac operation (August 27, 1946). Baxter was the assistant supervisor for the Liquor Control Board in Williamsport from 1946 until 1960. He also served in the well-known

---

1. Stone, April 9th, 1950.

Pennsylvania town of Punxsutawney, as well as in Pittsburgh, before moving to the Erie office about 1966. In 1968, long after Prince Farrington had died, Baxter was the district supervisor for the Pennsylvania Liquor Control Board in Erie. Now, a long way from anything related to Prince—in time and space—he had another unsettling experience. It was in Erie, one evening, that he made a late-evening departure from his office. While unlocking his car, someone—in a hushed voice—called "Baxter." As he turned, a shot was fired, and the bullet whizzed past his shoulder and hit the window of his car door! His unknown attacker escaped, but the ballistics study indicated that Baxter had the good fortune to have been missed by a bullet fired from a .38 or a .357 magnum. He was still residing in Erie when he died on December 2, 1988.

If one were to visit the old Gamble Farm Inn, now owned by Troy Musser, he or she might be allowed to view the old, unopened whiskey bottle that was once at the Lycoming County Courthouse. Somehow, that lone bottle escaped from the county building and traveled from owner to owner before Musser, a local contractor, through private purchase, became the historic bottle's latest keeper. As mentioned below, in Chapter Eight, that particular bottle was among the illegally stored booze confiscated for trial from the farm of Frank and Hazel Kreamer. The official tag attached to the bottle mentions the names of the two accused owners, plus the date of the confiscation, etc. At the bottom is the very clear signature of the lead agent in the raid who first took possession of that particular bottle of illegal liquor and took it to the courthouse as trial evidence. The 1948 signature is that of Richard Baxter, at the time, the thorn in Prince Farrington's side.

For some time, in 1946, Richard Baxter had been closely monitoring the Tangascootac operation.

Baxter knew that timing, in the making of sour mash whiskey, was critical. When he saw that a new batch of moonshine was almost ready for working, he went to his office in Williamsport and notified his boss, Leonard Owens. A team of state and federal agents was put together. That night, harassed by rain and mud, the agents sneaked through the wet brush to the still site. There was no one there to work the still, but the agents were prepared to wait. Eventually, when no moonshiners appeared, the agents, still waiting, returned to their car to run the engine and warm themselves. They moved their car to a less conspicuous place.

It was nearly 4:00 in the morning when they finally saw the headlights of an approaching truck. The agents quickly laid flat on the wet forest floor and watched Prince Farrington and a helper, Harry McGonigal, drive past. The agents continued waiting before making their move. They were awaiting daybreak, knowing that darkness would favor the moonshiners.

Leaving a couple of agents behind to stop any other vehicles that might arrive, Owens, Baxter and two other lawmen sneaked toward the still. When they saw Farrington's unoccupied truck, Richard Baxter pulled the keys from the ignition and uncapped the spark plugs. Then, the agents moved in and arrested the two men. Prince Farrington had been cleaning the firebox. Farrington, who had been arrested enough times to find the process more annoying than alarming, simply dozed while the agents destroyed his costly distilling equipment. It was noted that P. D. Farrington had almost $1,000 on his person when apprehended. He was then driven the fifty or so miles to Lewisburg, Pennsylvania, to be charged in the Middle District of Pennsylvania.

As noted above, the August 1946 raid was actually the *second* raid on this site. Farrington had been arrested here in 1944 but had been fined and released. This arrest was more serious. The huge inventory of equipment was dismantled. Some of it was destroyed, and some was hauled to Wilkes Barre. The raiding officials also noted the presence of 1,500 one-gallon syrup cans and more than a ton of soft coal.

On January 21, 1948, an indictment was handed down, with bail being set at $1500. After a friend posted the $1500 bail, Prince Farrington was free to await trial. Prince already had more than a dozen arrests in his background. He had already seen the inside walls of prison cells on many occasions and in many locations. Now, in the late spring of 1948, the walls again loomed before him.

Prince Farrington was likely the only person who ever knew the number of stills he had established in the narrow ravines or disguised buildings of Lycoming and Clinton counties of north-central Pennsylvania. He was likely the only person, as well, who had a hint of the number of secret storage places that housed his considerable output of moonshine liquor. Other amorphous statistics would have included the number of local people who worked for Farrington and the number of farmers and merchants who would sell him grain, sugar and other commodities needed for his nocturnal endeavors. Similarly, no one knew the number of local men—and at least one woman—who drove delivery routes in order to peddle Farrington liquors, or the number of women this philanderer may have bedded or the number of people to whom he loaned money with no record and with the odds against repayment. Nor would anyone have numbers for the subterfuges he used or the methods he devised in order to elude the law. Of course, regarding the law, no one could have stated the number of revenue agents or others whom he bribed to keep his 'rap sheet' from expanding. And not even he could likely have kept a tally of the tens of thousands of gallons of moonshine liquor he distilled or the mountains of money his booze had generated. Even without solid statistics, it was easy to understand why U.S. Attorney Arthur A. Maguire had identified Prince as "king of the bootleggers!"

Harold "Dutch" Washburn related a story. It has been related by others as well. Several men, all now dead, from Clinton County, Pennsylvania, were visiting Canada on a fishing or hunting trip. These "locals" had long heard that Canadian whiskey was better than that produced in the United States. When they went into a Canadian bar, they told the bartender that they wanted a bottle of his very best whiskey. The Canadian bartender reached beneath the bar and brought out a bottle of whiskey that had been cooked by a man named Prince David Farrington. This story, apocryphal or not, is alive in north-central Pennsylvania. Thus, while there were many unknown facts about Pennsylvania's premier moonshiner, a legend was already circulating about one 'invariable': P. D. Farrington's sour mash whiskey was among the very best because, according to the *Lock Haven Express*, Farrington was "a great moonshiner."

Ironically, the hapless agents who dealt with this moonshiner could not have imagined the scope of his work. Their work uncovered but a small number of the sites where Farrington or his associates operated stills, a fraction of the people who were involved with his illegal enterprise, and only a fraction of the quantities of moonshine produced and the monies generated. Metaphorically speaking, what the agents exposed was merely the tip of the keg.

Once Prince Farrington was no longer in their midst—due to prison, illness or death—all of the above data would be open to speculation or verification. And Farrington—on the verge of another prison term in the middle days of 1948—was able to observe the sprouting seedling of a robust legend, as will be shown in Chapter Fifteen. That seedling would later be nurtured by hundreds of people, locally and beyond. The fascinating events of his career—usually told in colorful, little smidgins—would make his life story the most popular in Clinton County and among the more popular in Lycoming County. However, on that June day in Lewisburg, Pennsylvania, in 1948, his trial was about to begin, and a conviction and sentence seemed certain. If convicted, it was the role of the court to impose a lengthy sentence on Farrington and to get him situated, once again, in a federal prison cell. Then Prince D. Farrington would stop making moonshine, and the popular review of his colorful and often bizarre career could begin.

At last, on June 8, 1948, officials and others met at the courthouse in Williamsport, Pennsylvania, for Farrington's latest sentencing. The plaintiff was the U.S. government. Farrington, the 56-year-old, long-time moonshiner, was the accused. Once again, this stocky, balding, and genial quinquagenarian was facing the probability of an extended prison term. A friend of Farrington, Lemuel C. Groce of the Castanea area of Clinton County, had paid the $1500 bail money. This allowed the former convict to remain free until the trial.

If those with criminal backgrounds ever compare resumes, P. D. Farrington's resume would have created envy. Farrington had a criminal record going back more than four decades. His record of arrests—on both state and federal charges—began in 1905, when Farrington was barely sixteen years old, and might be concluding now, in 1948, with his anticipated sentencing to another term in a federal penitentiary. Prince was to be represented at this trial by Lewis Shapiro, a Williamsport attorney.

When agents went to P. D.'s last home, a cabin on Antes Creek, they found that "the nest was warm, but the bird had flown." Coffee and scrambled eggs, both still warm, sat on the kitchen table. When the court session finally opened, at ten o'clock that morning, in the Post Office Building in Williamsport, the defendants' names were read. Lemuel C. Groce, the bondsman for both defendants, was there. So was the co-defendant, Harry McGonigal. So was Prince Farrington's attorney. Farrington's name was read, but there was no answer. Minutes passed. Prince's name was read a second and a third time, as Groce must have seen his $1500 slipping away. As the minutes passed, Richard Baxter—one of the revenue agents involved in the incriminating raid—told those present in the courthouse that he had earlier seen Farrington driving a small, green truck and heading south over Fourth Gap Road.

The little green truck was already familiar to government agents. Earlier, someone had tipped them to the fact that P. D. Farrington had the truck rigged to hold containers of bootleg liquor under the fenders. The agents had then visited and perforated the containers so that the contraband flowed from beneath the fenders. Further, Farrington's grandson, David Porter, recalled watching his grandfather work on that truck. Sometime earlier, something heavy had fallen on the little green truck, damaging the cab area. Dave recalled watching his 'Pawpaw' cutting away the cap, then pounding the damaged area back into some semblance of its former shape before welding the roof back onto the truck body. That is the truck that Agent Baxter had seen bouncing along the mountain road near Ravensburg State Park in lower Clinton County. It was also reported that P. D. Farrington had, on the back of his green truck, a Plymouth or Dodge coupe. The passenger seat was also believed to have been occupied by the fugitive's wife, Martha ("Mattie"), who, according to the later FBI report, had, at that time, no known criminal record and, according to Lycoming County records, was no longer his wife.

The location of the trial's subject on the gravel Fourth Gap Road meant that he had got on the mountain road near Ravensburg State Park, near the village of Rauchtown. It was soon decided that those present for the notorious moonshiner's latest encounter with the justice system may as well disperse since P. D. Farrington was going to be absent from this, his latest of many court appointments.

The next couple of years saw no developments in the status of the case. Authorities hadn't located the moonshiner. In fact, no one seemed to be *trying* to locate him. Only a few close-mouthed family members seemed to have known his fate. Finally, in the spring of 1950, Richard B. Stone, a writer for the Williamsport (Pennsylvania) *GRIT*, began researching and preparing a two-part report on Farrington. It was published in April (April 9th and April 16th editions) of 1950 and recounted the story of P. D. Farrington's colorful career. That feature mentioned the fact that Farrington's whereabouts remained unknown. Stone closed his account of P. D. Farrington by observing that "He may be riding still . . ." Prince Farrington, once one of the nation's richest, most colorful and busiest moonshiner, had vanished.

"Nubbin Ridge," the Farrington farmstead near Greensboro, North Carolina, painted, as a birthday present for his wife, Rebecca Tucker Farrington, by Prince's nephew, the late John Alexander Farrington Jr. Used through the courtesy of Rebecca Farrington.

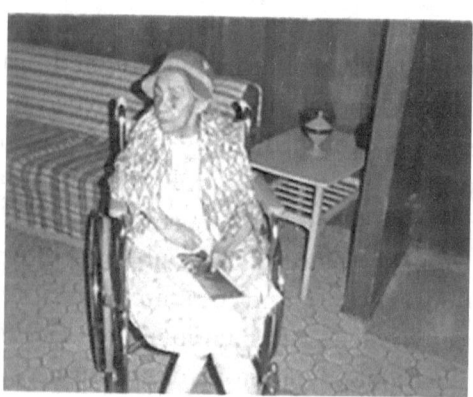

Nannie Herbin Glenn who, as a young woman washed and ironed clothes for the neighborhood, including the Farringtons. Her husband, Samuel, collected and delivered the clothing until his untimely death along a Carolina highway. There is no known photo of Samuel Glenn.

*A family portrait. Prince and Batie are not present. Seated in the middle, front row, with an infant, are Thomas Beverly Farrington and his second wife, Sarah. Beside Sarah is Thomas' sister-in-law through his first wife, Betty Elizabeth Williams Farrington. The two sons in the back row are Charl (left) and George Hobson (Hob). Tom's three daughters are (left to right) Zenadah (Nade), Phoebe and Elsie. Seated beside Tom is his son-in-law, Alonzo Rayle, Phoebe's husband.*

*Prince's mother, and Thomas Beverly Farrington's first wife, Betty Elizabeth Williams Farrington, who died in 1904, while Prince was a young teen.*

*Prince's older brother, Batie, in his World War I uniform.*

*W. Nunery King, a co-conspirator of Prince David Farrington. Both had their portraits taken at the same studio: the Atlanta federal penitentiary.*

# · 2 ·

# Carolina Roots

The Farrington name appears to come from southern England, perhaps through Ireland. The name is derived from the combined Old English words for *fern* and *settlement*. There is a town, Farrington Gurney, in Somerset County, about ten miles southwest of Bath. The "Gurney" portion of the name is unrelated to the wheeled beds and is believed to come from the name *Gournay*, the name of the family that once owned the land where the town now sits.

The Farringtons who inhabit our biography were in North Carolina, at least from the early 19th century. The parents of our subject, Thomas Beverly Farrington (1861–1922) and Betty Elizabeth Williams (1866-1904), were married a couple of days before Christmas in 1886. Her side of the family has a clearer view of the earlier branches of their family tree, with links going back several generations to George Washington Williams, who was born about 1819 and who arrived from Belfast, Ireland, in 1849.

Prince Farrington's dad, Thomas Beverly, was the child of John Alexander Farrington, whose name was also given to Tom's and Betty's fourth child and, eventually, to a grandchild. From about 1914, the Tom Farrington family lived on a farmstead, later known as Nubbin Ridge, on the bank of Deep River, near High Point, in Guilford County, North Carolina. Thomas Beverly bought the farm at auction on the steps of the Guilford County Courthouse. Nearby businesses in the days of P. D. Farrington's childhood would have included an ice plant and a grist mill. Corn was an abundant crop on the Nubbin Ridge acreage. It was there that Tom Farrington farmed, fathered a small brood and distilled liquor.

In later years, the family members decided that the whiskey-making tradition—which was followed by some family members—likely devolved to Tom and his male offspring from Betty Williams Farrington's Irish-born father, George Washington Williams.

Batie, the first child of Tom and Betty Farrington, was born in 1887. On June 3, 1889, they again became parents. This child was a premature male infant—a *preemie*. It is doubtful whether a doctor was present for the actual birth since many in the Farrington family were born only with a family member present as a 'midwife.' During the next generation, for example, one of Tom and Betty Farrington's daughters, Phoebe Farrington Rayle, was an active area midwife. However, the family believes that a Dr. Prince came to the family's aid regarding the care of the premature boy. Since the use of an incubator for maintaining warmth and moisture for the under-developed baby was unavailable to the Farringtons, family members believe that Dr. Prince had the parents place the swaddled neonate behind the kitchen stove in order to improve his chances of survival. The baby survived, and the grateful parents now had a name for their new arrival. The baby was named for the doctor who likely saved its life. Thus, the second child of Tom and Betty Farrington was named *Prince* David Farrington.[2]

Prince's son-in-law, George Porter, once asked a visitor if he thought that photographs of Prince suggested that Prince had American Indian features. Porter said that the story was that the Farrington's ancestors "went inland and bred with the Indians." Regarding Prince's appearance, Porter noted that "He had a very dark complexion, with coal black hair, when he had hair. He was a strong man, a very powerful man."

Others in the family also saw possible Indian lineage by noting that several family members, down to the present, have had the signature Oriental, or epicanthic, folds over the inner corners of their eyes. Prince himself added to this conjecture about Oriental ties by telling the family that a Farrington had run off with the Indians at Roanoke, the 'lost colony.' Prince's grandson, Dave Porter, says that he found no Farringtons on the manifest of the ship that brought the people who

---

2. Much has been made, by various Pennsylvania writers, of the 'Prince' moniker. Although Prince's given name might well have been something as mundane as those of his male siblings—Batie, Charles, or John—Keystone-state writers have repeatedly preyed upon and played upon the regal aspect of the name. The author firmly believes that overemphasizing the subject's given name damages the integrity of the biography, so the use of the name 'Prince'—in something other than a straightforward usage—is minimized in this work. –G.G.

populated the initial Roanoke settlement, nor is it known today if anyone from the 'lost colony' at Roanoke Island even *survived*. This doesn't mean that the Farringtons of Nubbin Ridge had no American Indian genetic material from other early encounters. Again, Dave Porter also tells of seeing a North Carolina relative whose appearance convinced him that she was Native American. A factual curio: When Prince David Farrington moved to Pennsylvania, he became the close friend of an authentic Chippewa Indian.

Betty Elizabeth (nee Williams) Farrington provided Tom with heirs at a near-annual rate, bearing a total of ten children between 1887 and 1903. Prince was in his fourteenth year when, on January 6, 1904, his mother died.

After Prince's mother, Betty Williams Farrington, died, Tom, the widower, had an African-American man named Sam Glenn helping to care for his children. The Farringtons liked Mr. Glenn. He appears to have been an important influence on their lives during his time with them. Glenn was married to Nannie Herbin Glenn, and they were the parents of seven children: four sons and three daughters.

Nannie helped Sam support their family by doing laundry and ironing for area families. Her customers were many of the White families along Route 220, south of Greensboro. About two weeks before Christmas (December 10th) in 1938, Sam walked from his house to the Farrington's and delivered Nannie's ironing. While returning home, walking along Route 220, Sam was run over and killed! He died from a crushed chest, caused—said his death certificate—by an "auto accident." The certificate lists his father's name as Joe Glenn, while his mother's name was "unknown." Glenn, who was once an important part of the Farrington household, was buried (December 10, 1938), according to his death certificate, in the Stony Hill cemetery. More formally, his burial was in the churchyard of the Bethel AME church just east of U.S. Route 220. His burial site is marked by a homemade stone with his name and the words, *born* and *died*. Dates were never added.

Tom Beverly Farrington married again. His second wife was Sarah March Dillon, who died of illness. Sadly, her tombstone lies in pieces, and little can be gained from her grave marker. Thomas Beverly married yet again, with his last wife being Mary Alice Tinsebloom. The marriages of Prince's three sisters, Phoebe Ellen, Zenadah ("Nade") and Elsie, added the family names of Rayle, Coltrane and Osborne, respectively, to the clan.

Prince's oldest brother, Batie, left home to enter the military during World War I. He was said to have suffered from 'shell shock' (post-traumatic stress disorder?). Batie never returned to Nubbin Ridge. Why not? "I don't have a clue!" declared a family member. A life-long bachelor, Batie lived in a small 'shack' at Rehoboth Beach, Delaware and worked as a salvage diver for the United States government. Eventually, he moved to the area of Richmond, Virginia, and lived there for four or five years, not far from his sister, Elsie Farrington Osborne.

One cannot evaluate the story of Prince David Farrington without noting the unique settlement to the south of Guilford County, that was known as Black Ankle. The name Black Ankle is thought to refer to the people who worked in the valuable turpentine trade, an occupation based on the once-abundant long-leaf pines of North Carolina. The term *Black Ankle* is also suspected of being the origin of the state's nickname, the *Tarheel State*. Black Ankle is an unincorporated community within the scenic area of the Little River and the Uwharrie Mountains, barely 30 miles due south of Nubbin Ridge. The original occupants of Black Ankle were members of the Oldham family (now spelled in a variety of forms) who arrived in the 18th century and who have been known during the ensuing two centuries as a unique group. Although they are now becoming somewhat assimilated, they were long thought to be a clannish community that preferred moonshining to mingling. Nor did they see the need for hunting licenses for shooting at wild game or nosy strangers. The attitudes of the Black Ankle folk were matched, if not adopted, by other independent-minded rural North Carolinians, especially its moonshiners.

Prince Farrington matured and learned to farm as well as to distill quality whiskey. He rarely attended school. "I attended school only on days when it rained," Farrington said repeatedly over the years. For any part of rural America, in that day, such limited formal education was common. The primary newspaper for Guilford County, North Carolina, was, and remains, *The Greensboro Record*. The *Record's* edition of May 15, 1905, offers revealing educational statistics that put schooling's limited popularity into perspective. The superintendent announced that the total amount spent that year topped $23,000 (which amounted to slightly more than $8 per pupil. The 1905 graduation ceremony for the Greensboro High School commencement was held in the local opera house, with just twelve diplomas being awarded. Ten of the twelve graduates were girls.

Prince also had no interest in attending church. However, he was developing a passion for making whiskey, as his father was doing. His dad, too, had a skill at whiskey making and an aversion—prevalent among many Americans—to paying taxes on the liquor that he nursed into a highly-regarded whiskey. Since Tom Farrington was known to have been bonded, he must have avoided his tax obligation on the part of his production. A neighboring farmer, Isaac Stanley, was a prohibitionist who appears to have accused the Farringtons of being bootleggers. The *Greensboro Record* said that Tom Farrington, his sons Batie and Prince, and a friend, Fred Ozmont, retaliated. Neighbor Stanley's granary, barn, and several other outbuildings were torched. This was Prince's first encounter with the law. He was 15 years old.

Fred Ozmont agreed to testify against the other accused arsonists. He was sentenced to five years of labor on the county roads. In the September 1905 session of the Guilford County Court, the jury failed to reach a verdict regarding the patriarch, Thomas Beverly Farrington. However, a guilty verdict was returned (September 27th) against Batie and Prince Farrington (now just a few months into his 16th year). The solicitor's motion for judgment resulted in a finding that "the defendants Batie Farrington and Prince Farrington each be imprisoned in the County jail for five years and assigned to work during imprisonment upon the public roads of Guilford County."

A broader picture of 1905 justice in Guilford County appears in the same September court record. There, one reads, in the report of the Grand Jury, that they found both the County Home and convict camp No. 1 to be "well kept." They also found that "Convict camp No. 1 is composed of 43 male and 1 female prisoners. The inmates of County Home are as follows: White males 5, white females 14, colored males 11, colored females 7." The report also lists numbers for the inmates who were insane: "1 colored male and 2 white females."

In the term of court begun on June 18, 1906, the record declares, "State vs. Prince Farrington, Batie Farrington, Fred Ozmont: Off." Prince, then, was freed from the Guilford County jail system after having served nearly nine months of his five-year sentence.

## PRINCE, MARTHA, AND ALGERNON BARBEE

Many years after both Prince Farrington and his wife, Martha, had died, Prince's niece-in-law (brother Charlie's daughter-in-law) Emily, recalled Martha White Farrington. One part of her recollection: "She [Martha, known to most of the family as "Matt"] was quite the berries; that woman. Where in Hell Prince ever found her, I don't know."

If *found* is the correct verb, Prince seems to have *found* Martha White in one of the towns to the east of Nubbin Ridge. She was one of the children of Henry and Julia White. She had two sisters who lived most of their lives in the Greensboro/High Point area. The Whites were among North Carolina's more prolific families. The index of deeds in nearby Alamance County Courthouse, for example, runs to 56 pages of entries under "White." Martha's obituary lists her date of birth as being August 9, 1895. Therefore, she was just 17 when she married the 23-year-old Farrington in a ceremony conducted by a Justice of the Peace, Algernon Barbee, in Chapel Hill, North Carolina (Orange County). On that document, both Prince and Martha list their residence as Orange County. They also avoided the need for parental consent by listing Martha's age as 20 years, a fudging factor of three. The date of their nuptials was the 4th of October, in 1912.[3]

The newlyweds began their marriage and their family in Chapel Hill. At some point in their early marriage, they were living closer to the family homestead at Nubbin Ridge when they lived in a house near Burnett's Chapel. Their first child, Tom, was born about 1914. Gladys was born in 1918. Gayle Randall was born about 1921. Their fourth and last child, Prince David Farrington Jr. ("Whitey"), arrived about 1925 after they had relocated to Clinton County, Pennsylvania.

George Porter said that his mother-in-law, Mrs. Martha Farrington had been a good-looking young woman. Martha was a wisp of a woman,

---

3. Phoebe Ellen Farrington's name appears as Phoebe, Phebe, and Pheoby. Unable to reconcile these spellings, this book will use the P-H-O-E-B-E spelling throughout.

weighing less than 100 pounds. Regarding the compatibility of Prince and Martha, "They fought like cats and dogs," in the opinion of one family member.

There was a time after they had relocated to north-central Pennsylvania when they were visiting North Carolina and staying at the home of Alonzo and Phoebe Ellen Farrington Rayle. Some family members approaching the house were surprised to see feminine clothing hanging from a balcony and from the branches of a tree. When Prince was asked about the scattered garments, he explained that Martha had threatened to leave him—so he was simply helping her.

There was another incident recited within the family. Martha had cooked a meal and had all the food on the table when Prince arrived. Something sparked his anger. Prince grabbed the tablecloth, gathered it into a bundle with food and tableware inside, and tossed it from a window.

Her descendants identified Martha White Farrington as being from a deeply religious family. That might explain her troubled life with Prince Farrington, and it might explain why she spent much of her time in upstairs isolation, where she wrote Biblical verses directly onto her bedroom walls. She also used photographs to express her pain. She would take a red-inked pen to draw crude outlines around people or objects on the black-and-white print of the photographs.

In 1985, when the newspapers interviewed Gladys regarding her plans to write a book about her father, there was little mention of Gladys's mother, Martha. Descriptions of Martha, or "Matt," show her as being, at the least, a bit beyond eccentric. One can only speculate on whether or not her peculiarity was brought into her marriage or whether it was nurtured during a marital relationship with a spouse who pursued a very public criminal career and who had a proclivity toward marital infidelity. "Prince loved women," as a couple of family members acknowledged. Martha didn't like his livelihood, and she brooded over his philandering. When her father, Henry White, chided Prince for his infidelity, Prince's retort was blunt but clear. "You sure as hell can't expect me to get by on what Matt gives me! She can't satisfy me."

The ink on the marriage license of Martha and Prince Farrington had barely dried before he was back in court. He and a confederate, Nunery King, were charged with four counts—the illegal making, hauling, hiding and distributing of alcohol. The date of their illegal activity, as identified in the statement of charges (June 1913), was May 2, 1913. Therefore, we know that Prince was barely into his seventh month of marriage (October 4, 1912) before being collared once more.

In August 1914, Prince and his dad signed a bond for $1000, guaranteeing Prince's appearance in the December session of federal court for the Western District of North Carolina in Greensboro. Thomas Beverly Farrington was listed as assuring his son's appearance at the December court session, showing sufficient property.

Another court order, also from June of 1913, ordered the arrest and confinement of Nunery King for the December session of the federal court (Greensboro) on an indictment for the "illegal distilling, etc." of "Spirituous Liquors" as part of the case against "Prince Farrington et al., Guilford County." The accompanying envelope has a notation that King was said to have family at Randleman and to work at the Naomi Cotton Mills. It also notes that the marshal failed to locate the defendant.

On December 12, 1914, papers were signed that pledged a $300 bond on Nunery King for his appearance in federal court in Greensboro. That document shows the legend, "his mark," on the line above Nunery King's "X," suggesting that Prince's early cohort was illiterate.

Less than a week later (December 18, 1914), Prince faced three local (Guilford County) bootlegging charges, resulting in a fine, a suspended judgment and the payment of a bond ($200) tied to his "good behavior" appearance in each county court term for one year.

Earlier (January 26, 1914), Prince's father, too, was back in court. Thomas Beverly Farrington pleaded "no contest" to a charge of manufacturing liquor and was ordered to pay a $250 bond and to appear in court periodically for the next two years to show good behavior.

When the June session of the federal court opened in 1915, Farrington and King both pleaded "not guilty," but to no avail. Both were found to be guilty. Thus, on June 10, 1915, an unlettered Nunery King, whose fine had been suspended, began his sentence of a year and a day in the United States prison in Atlanta, Georgia. Prince Farrington's fine was also remitted, but his sentence was for 15 months in Atlanta, beginning, as well, on June 10, 1915.

The penitentiary's new-inmate processing procedure has also given us a look at the other process—the aging process—and lets us see Prince's features about one week after he celebrated his 26th birthday. Here we see the 26-year old criminal whom the processing agent describes as having the appearance of a 35-year-old and with "Hair thin on top." His home was listed as Chapel Hill, his occupation as "farmer," and it was noted at that time that he had no aliases. The form also makes one realize how active this outlaw has been. He was now facing more than a year in a federal penitentiary at 26, and he already had two prior jail terms.

## "AND HIM SAFELY KEEP"

First arrested in 1905 and again in 1913, Prince David Farrington saw the courtroom again in 1914 and 1915. On this last occasion, two criminals with royal titles, Prince Farrington and a confederate, Nunery King—also of Guilford County—were tried in the Federal District Court for the Western District of North Carolina (Greensboro). Their crimes involved violation of the Internal Revenue laws. The court found Prince guilty of "Distilling, Concealing, Removing, retailing Spirituous Liquors." On June 10th—just a week after his 26th birthday—Prince was sentenced to a term of fifteen months in the federal prison in Atlanta, Georgia. King's sentence was for one year and one day in the same Atlanta facility. The court remitted the fines for both. In each case, the marshal of that federal district was ordered to "take into custody the said prisoner and him safely keep and deliver to the Warden of the U.S. Prison for the execution of the sentence." Farrington became federal prisoner #5832, a number that he would hold for a full year before gaining early release on June 11, 1916. Similar numbers lay in his future. While his several prison sojourns may seem harsh, one might also suggest that they were part of the experience Prince Farrington would have by the time (January 28, 1919) that the nation created a new climate in which Farrington would still experience arrests and imprisonment; but in which he would thrive, financially. That new climate came with the adoption of the 18th Amendment to the U.S. Constitution and the onset of Prohibition.

## THE FATE OF THE CONFEDERATE

Nunery King had a walk-on role—a bit part—in the grand drama that was the life of Prince D. Farrington. However, for one who was willing to leaf through the packet of 59 pages that reveal the prison life of Nunery

King, he became a real person; one who was fated to be arrested for working with a young moonshiner and sharing a trial and a federal prison term with that young moonshiner. A King's criminal collusion with a Prince would cause both to be sentenced to serving a prison sentence at the region's major prison, the federal penitentiary in Atlanta, Georgia.

Nunery King was sentenced to a year and a day, along with a fine and costs of $100. The fine was excused, and on June 10, 1915, his sentence began. So King, inmate #5830, began serving a sentence that ran parallel with that of inmate #5832, Prince David Farrington. Within King's papers, one can compare the nearly square 'rolled' fingerprints with the plain fingerprints. There are no missing digits, but the note below the plain prints, over the line awaiting the "Prisoner's Signature," are the words "Can't Write."

Upon his arrival, King's property was recorded. He possessed a coat, a shirt, a pair of shoes, a comb and its case, shoes, socks, suspenders, trousers, a tie, an undershirt, a hat, two handkerchiefs and one leather pouch. The pouch was likely for tobacco storage since he later received shipments of tobacco and cigarettes from family or friends. The only item submitted to officials was an unidentified "key."

The Atlanta pen's photography equipment was excellent. These two 1915 'mug shots' are remarkably clear. The processing officer noted, with the pictures, that King's complexion was "sallow," his height was 5 feet 7½ inches, and the bridge of his nose was convex. He was identified as being a native of the state of North Carolina and was a 37-year-old laborer. Unlike Prince Farrington, whose 'apparent age' was well beyond his actual age, Nunery King's 'apparent age' matched his appearance. Both of Nunery King's parents were natives of North Carolina, and both had lived to see their 37-year-old son go to Atlanta. This illiterate inmate also left, beyond the prison walls, a child and a wife.

Penitentiary records show that, within a week after his incarceration, a letter written on his behalf was mailed to Randleman, North Carolina, to Nunery King's wife, Nannie. Letters to his wife were mailed on a weekly basis throughout his time in Atlanta. There are very few other letters sent from King during his nine months in prison. Conversely, Nunery King got letters from his wife roughly twice weekly and from his mother on a monthly basis or more often. He also got a few letters from nieces, a brother, a cousin and a few friends. Existing forms indicate that permission for most outgoing letters had to be approved by the warden. The flourishing signature of Warden Fred G. Zerbst appears on several such permission forms.

A closer look at life in the early 20th century might begin with a list of items received by Nunery King shortly before Christmas (December 13th) in 1915. The sender or senders are not identified on the standard prison form for recording articles received by convicts, but the list includes a box of chocolates, a cake, two packages of candy, a package of dates, 13 apples, 5 oranges, 4 tangerines, a box of 4 apples, 2 oranges, a pack of chocolate, four packs of Stud smoking tobacco, 11 packs of Piedmont smoking tobacco and some Chiclets. Several smaller shipments arrived shortly before Christmas in that same year and within a week after Christmas. After the year-end flurry of foodstuffs, tobacco, etc., no packages were arriving for Nunery King. Then, in mid-February 1916, he received three valentines.

Responding to a request from the Justice Department in Washington while it was reviewing King's status for a pardon, the prison physician noted that Nunery King had "gained fourteen pounds in weight since his arrival here and that his condition is good." While a pardon had been "denied" in September 1915, King was granted early parole in March 1916. On March 30, 1916, W. N. King walked through the gates of the Atlanta Penitentiary and slipped from the pages of Prince Farrington's biography.

Prince David Farrington's debt to society, *this time*, was paid by June 11, 1916, when he was discharged from the U.S. Penitentiary in Atlanta and supplied with transportation to Chapel Hill, North Carolina.

Prince and Martha and their growing family eventually took up residence near the old Farrington homestead in Guilford County. They lived close to Burnett's Chapel, the church that became the center of the spiritual life of the Farrington clan. Prince was careful not to break into that circle. Today, the plot that was once home to Prince and Martha is part of a housing development.

During 1917, as the United States government mobilized to engage in the war that had been raging in Europe, Prince Farrington was among those registering for consideration for military service. Prince's registration form indicated that he was married and the father of one child. It also affirmed that he was a natural-born citizen as well as a self-employed farmer. So far as military service was concerned, Prince did not break into that circle either. In late 1918, the First World War drew to its finale. As troubled peace sessions were underway in Paris, Prince Farrington was reflecting on his own peace.

In that decade of his life that extended from 1905 to 1915, Prince had appeared in court many times and in prison multiple times. A young man with the criminal record of Prince David Farrington may well have longed for a place where the landscape was more desolate, and his record was unknown to the law. Enter Jim Wilson.

## CALL OF THE WILD

By 1920, Prince Farrington had criminal records in at least two counties in North Carolina, as well as a federal prison record that resulted from an arrest in one of those counties. The combined stories from family members indicate that while Prince and Charl were in prison in North Carolina, a man named Jim Wilson occupied an adjoining cell. Their conversation indicated that Wilson was in jail for smuggling dope from Cuba through Greensboro and that Charl and Prince were jailed for making moonshine. Wilson's hometown was Salona, in rural Clinton County, Pennsylvania. Salona was, and remains, a one-street town, with the southern end of the street coming out of a heavily wooded mountain gap along the banks of a creek named Long Run, while the northern end of town is but a few hundred yards from another mountain gap, through which Salona's residents must travel in order to reach the employers and emporiums of the college town of Lock Haven.

When Prince groused about the ever-present law officers, Jim Wilson—who could have been a tourism spokesman for Pennsylvania's rugged splendor—suggested that Prince come to the Keystone State if he wanted greater privacy, pristine mountain streams and an abundance of isolated ravines. In addition, he pointed out to Prince that the area of Sugar Valley, south of Salona, had farmland where one could buy all the corn needed for moonshine operations. Obviously, an operation that would be located in the Sugar Valley of Pennsylvania would put a moonshiner's bigger markets (New York City, Pittsburgh, Philadelphia, etc.)

within much easier reach. The place described by Wilson seemed to be a moonshiner's paradise. Prince was enthusiastic about taking his family, friends and fervor and relocating to Pennsylvania.

The magic chariot that would take Prince to this rustic paradise was the old Ford automobile owned by Prince's friend, Joe Gardner, who was to become one of Prince's best confederates. That chance meeting in a Guilford County jail cell was to lead to a pivotal change in the life of Prince Farrington. He and his young family—along with brother Charl and friends Joe Gardner and Lemuel Groce—were emigrating from North Carolina to the Keystone State. The year was 1921. For the remaining years of his life, Pennsylvania would be home for Prince Farrington. However, Prince still maintained family and criminal ties with the Tarheel State.

## RETURN OF THE PRODIGAL

Prince David Farrington would return to Guilford County from time to time. Actually, he still had a criminal trial to attend in Guilford County. He and his brother Charl both had appearances in the same county's court in December of 1923. The docket for December 1923 shows that a warrant was issued for Prince on December 17. Again, in the January 21 session of 1924, the warrant is repeated. In both cases, *retailing* is the charge. For perspective, one might note that, on the same court record,[4] four other cases—none involving Farringtons—had *retailing* as the charge. Prince's trial was held in March of 1924 before Judge Henry P. Lane. It appears that Prince Farrington, who moved to Penn's Woods to get a fresh start, was still—three years after departing—involved in the justice system of Guilford County, North Carolina.

Within the many memories held by the North Carolina part of the family, Bob Caudle's experience was well known. Caudle had gone north to work for Prince. While there, he served time in prison in Prince's stead. His daughter was told that her father was suffering from tuberculosis and was spending a year in a sanitarium. That's how one family hid the stigma of a father in prison for his support of Prince Farrington. When Caudle was released, Prince built him a large house in Level Cross, North Carolina, where Caudle opened a store. Even in that capacity, Prince

---
4. Guilford County, North Carolina, January, 1924, p. 33.

must be considered to have 'used' Bob Caudle. Bob's nice new house was built with secret compartments as places for Prince to hide money and booze. Prince's building of the Caudle store/residence in Level Cross may or may not have been coincidental since Level Cross was locally referred to as "Whiskey Junction."

Regarding Prince's return visits, his North Carolina relatives expressed both acceptance and resentment, depending on the reasons for his visits. But, the real heroes, to those who stayed in Guilford County and the nearby areas of North Carolina, were not the returning moonshiner and his wife; a couple who sometimes flashed wealth with their costly clothes and changing cars or who sometimes flashed poverty, as when he needed money for legal fees. The heroes to Prince's North Carolina siblings and other relatives were another brother, John Alexander (1893-1977), who never left Nubbin Ridge, and Prince's sister, Phoebe Ellen Rayle (1891-1949), who was a mother and a midwife.

It was John Alexander Farrington, about four years younger than his brother, Prince, who bought the land rights to their father's homestead from his siblings, Prince, Hobson (Hob), Charles (Charl) and Zenadah (Nade). And, when John Alexander Farrington, Prince's younger brother, married Cora Grace McCandless, he was reuniting the homestead with an earlier proprietary family since the Farrington property had once belonged to Cora Grace's grandfather.

John Alexander had a razor strap prominently displayed, the threat of which brought order among the many young who lived with or visited with him and his wife, Cora Grace (nee McCandless). However, the memory of the razor strap was nearly lost among the many pleasant and positive remembrances of John Alexander. A grandchild, Norma Jean Smith Briggs, wrote a memorial to John Alexander when she learned, in far-off Rigby, Idaho, of his passing in February of 1977. Her "remembrance" was written so that others could "share in the esteem and admiration in which John Alexander Farrington was held in the minds of admirers and descendants." Norma Jean wrote of John's "love—for his fellow man. He was always willing to help others, and he let them know he really cared." For example, the family's experience with racial interaction was not limited to Mr. Glenn [mentioned earlier in this chapter]. Family members declare that John Alexander Farrington, Prince's younger brother, hired

Blacks to help with the farm work and then insisted that they join the family for meals.

Dorothy Lee Highfill, one of John Alexander's children, emphasized that her father was a moderate drinker who embraced Christianity in his later years. Another granddaughter, Bunny Hyatt Wright, didn't offer recollections from across the nation as Norma Jean Smith Briggs had done but from a property adjoining Nubbin Ridge. Still, her observations were basically the same. "My grandfather, John Alexander Farrington, was an *awesome* man. I lived beside him until his death."

The farm operated by John Alexander supplied bountiful crops of corn needed to feed the family and the farm animals. He also raised tobacco for sale. The animals on his farm included cows, pigs, horses and chickens. One of his horses, a riding horse named Dan, served as amusement for young family members.

Hiding liquor was common, and being able to bluff was a major skill for those involved. Once, when government agents came to brother John Alexander Farrington's North Carolina farmhouse, they searched the entire house and found nothing. Beside the house, among the other buildings, was the kitchen, a normal arrangement in a clime where using a cooking stove in the house left the rooms much overheated. When the lawman asked John Alexander if he might check the kitchen, John told him that if he wanted to check it, he certainly could, but he rented that to his daughter-in-law and son. The lawman declined, and the kitchen went unchecked, leaving John Alexander's son and daughter-in-law to dwell in peace—among their landlord's supply of stored moonshine.

John Alexander didn't only hide liquor from federal agents. He hid it from an even stricter authority figure: Cora Grace. Since John Alexander enjoyed the occasional 'nip,' he might have a bottle hidden anywhere among his several satellite buildings. Then John would offer a half dollar to a grandson, Tony Hyatt, to keep his bottle location secret from Cora Grace, but she bumped Tony's wealth up a notch by giving him a second fifty-cent payment to tell her where John Alexander kept a bottle hidden.

Eating was a well-recalled activity involving John Alexander. He caught a large snapping turtle by the river and made a tasty turtle soup. He enjoyed cottage cheese and Coca-Cola. He often ate fiery green peppers with his meals. When neighbors joined him for tobacco harvesting, he'd pull ripe watermelons from his patch. Sometimes, the watermelons were simply dropped on the ground to break them open for sharing. As fishermen returned from the river, John Alexander invited them, without regard to *color*, to stop for a drink or a bite to eat. One relative remembered John Alexander stealing a bite from Cora's biscuit when she stepped away from the table. On another occasion, he emptied a milk carton and filled it with fresh cow's milk in order to educate one of the children who imagined that he didn't like fresh milk.

One last *eating* anecdote: Despite having had a dozen offspring of their own, John Alexander and Cora Grace adopted children. Once, a social worker delivered a trio of boys to John Alexander and Cora Grace. The youngest was several years old and was too shy to join the family for meals. He went unfed for several days. One night, when the family had retired, John Alexander went into the kitchen for a snack. Soon, he saw the little boy standing in the kitchen doorway. A hearty invitation from John Alexander, "Well, come on. Let's eat." brought the youngster running to the table to join his adoptive father. He ate heartily and then became a regular at mealtime.

What the FBI did not learn but would have appreciated knowing was that Prince's brother, John Alexander, and John's son-in-law, Joe Hyatt, delivered food to the fugitive Prince while he was hiding in North Carolina. But, for all their support, Prince's Tarheel relatives were reluctant accomplices. In fact, one of Prince's sisters, Elsie, married and moved to Clayville, a small town near Richmond, Virginia, in part, the family believed, to get away from the inordinate influence of alcohol in the life around Nubbin Ridge. Also, a niece of Prince, Hilda Coltrane (*see* Chapter 8) spent some time with her family in Pennsylvania. She and the family left Prince's Keystone State sphere and returned to North Carolina, where she lives today, with mostly negative thoughts of her Pennsylvania years.

Eventually, John Alexander Farrington sold some of the land to help Prince cover legal fees.

Later, again, Prince became even more audacious. He arrived with a lawyer, asking John Alexander and Cora Grace to sell the home and a few remaining acres. Prince's pressure was wasted. John Alexander and Cora Grace reminded Prince of the long-standing agreement that the

Farrington homestead would not be divided. Their refusal was adamant. They had saved the homestead.

Another of Prince's family who the North Carolina Farringtons highly regarded was Prince's sister, Phoebe Ellen Farrington Rayle (1891-1949), whose husband was Alonzo Rayle.

The Rayles, at that time, had no electricity. However, Alonzo had a huge tank buried in the lawn. That tank was filled with carbide, a chemical which, when wet, produces a flammable gas. That gas was piped into the house where the jets could be ignited for illumination. If the flame weakened, Alonzo would walk outside and adjust the flow of the flammable gas.

Phoebe was the midwife for the family and the neighborhood. Phoebe Ellen's daughter, Cindy Rayle Toomes, recalled her mother repeatedly telling her children, "I might be gone for the night, but I'll be back." During Phoebe's years as a midwife, she was said to have brought every neighborhood baby into the world.

Phoebe Ellen and her family were just one more group of individuals whom Prince imposed.

While in North Carolina, Prince filled the Rayle's living room with five-gallon brown jugs of the booze that he would be selling. His sister told her children, "Don't go in there!" Since their living room was unheated, there was no incentive to visit Prince's illegal stash. He'd park his truck in the woods behind the Rayle's house. While it sat behind their house, Prince would repaint it to make it unfamiliar to authorities. Once, his niece, Cindy Rayle Toomes, reported, Prince painted lettering on the truck. The words she could recall were "Blue Ridge . . ." something or other.

Prince brought gifts for members of the Rayle family. He once brought a hornless Brown Swiss cow. Brown Swiss were unknown in the area, but the Rayle's appreciated it as a good dairy cow. Prince also brought Christmas gifts for the Rayles. Phoebe Ellen's daughter, Cindy Rayle (now Toomes), accompanied her family on a visit to her Pennsylvania relatives. She was just three or four years old. While there, Cindy recalled, Prince and some of the family went shopping. "Prince knew I loved red." He bought his little niece a white dress with a red collar. But, these displays of generosity did not reduce the pain suffered by his sister,

Phoebe Ellen. As Cindy remembers, "My Mother—it broke her heart what he was doing, but she'd never say 'No' to her brother."

Prince's niece, Dorothy or "Dot" (Mrs. Ray) Highfill, told of getting a bit cheeky while a young girl and being in a car with several adults, including Prince. Dot said that Prince, crippled and on crutches at the time, wanted a beer. Little Dorothy admonished, "You should be drinking milk." Prince's unsurprising reply, "Drinking milk is like kissing your wife. There's no kick in it!"

## "YOU KEEP SWEET"

Along with the gifts that Prince would bring on his return trips to North Carolina, Prince brought his wife, Martha (Aunt Matt or Aunt Mattie). The presence of Prince's whiskey tainted his visits. So did the presence of Mattie. Mattie had a way of antagonizing some of the in-laws of Guilford County. Aunt Mattie didn't associate with the kids, nor did she have much interaction with the adults in the house. No matter the time of day or night when Prince and Mattie arrived, Phoebe Ellen Rayle fed them a full meal. Mattie, who was remembered as being 'germophobic,' "would sit behind the table on the bench all day and never offer to help, while Phoebe Ellen would be cooking or doing dishes." The family would complain, "Martha was all concerned about Martha!" The North Carolina relatives were unimpressed. Still, "My mother [Phoebe Ellen] was a wonderful wife and mother," recalled Cindy. "She put up with Aunt Mattie, and she was always kind to her."

Thanks to her fugitive husband, Mattie (Martha White Farrington) garnered several mentions in the FBI reports during the Bureau's 1949-52 manhunt. One such mention is quoted in the agent's report of February 20, 1951. The agent quoted a woman, Georgiana Fiorini of Mildred, Pennsylvania, as offering the opinion that Mattie "was a mental case." An agent also reported that a Jersey Shore policeman, William J. Messner, told the agent that Martha Farrington was "very peculiar," although he didn't think that she was "mentally unsound."

In addition to Martha White Farrington's strange behavior, she was remembered for always having very fine clothes. "When Mattie died," added Cindy Rayle Toomes, "she had a 50-gallon drum—*filled with new shoes!*"

Mattie Farrington's grand-niece, Debbie, emphasized, "Aunt Mattie would dress in layers of clothes. It would be nothing for her to have six or seven layers of clothes on when she arrived here."

Leo "Chip" Taylor was close to the drama surrounding Prince David Farrington while Prince was living across the Susquehanna River from Jersey Shore, Pennsylvania. Taylor's recollection of Mattie: "Prince's wife never was around too much. She'd be down in North Carolina a lot. She didn't like the idea of Prince working with whiskey. She was back and forth."

While Prince was in the Lewisburg (PA) penitentiary, Mattie was receiving public assistance from the office of the State Department of Public Assistance in Williamsport.

One of Martha White Farrington's grandchildren, Dr. Robert Porter, has remembered her—peculiarities and all—in verse. To Robert, his grandfather, Prince Farrington, was "PawPaw," and his grandmother, Martha, was "Gram." With Robert's kind permission, we offer this gem:

GRAM (Martha Farrington)

"It happened so long ago it isn't true anymore,"
my grandmother said
when we asked her why she married PawPaw.
Maggie and Jiggs, we called them.
The oddest couple;
He, the sly, burly bootlegger,
Back from a long, sweaty day at the still:
"Goddammit, Matt, where's my supper?"
"You old hog, you had three squares yesterday!"

She, a Pentecostal sneak drinker,
Hated dust, hated housework even more.
Sat in the same chair most of the day,
Dusting only what she could reach
Without standing up, thinking of ways
To bribe us to do the rest.
Our reward was a bundle of change in a toilet paper twisty:
"Go getcha a creamsicle and bring me Anacin and a Coke!"

She chewed it like candy, tin after tin,
Washing it down with big swigs
And soft rumbling belches.

"She'll never die; she'll just rust away," Dad said.
"And she's got Jesus all wrong,
'Cause she keeps changing my liquor to water!"
Once, she hid a bottle of Coke in the oven
It exploded just after Mom peeked at the roast,
Mom hollering loud enough to peel wallpaper
And you'd'a thought the cussing out would take,

But Gram did it again days later
Out of pure meanness, we guessed.

On hot summer days, she'd bundle up for a blizzard
Cranking up the big porch rocker,
Her plastic ukulele plinking out mountain tunes,
Songs of young love, ghosts, and early death
Jealousy, murder, six white horses, O Susanna,
And the moon shines tonight on pretty Red Wings.

We begged her to yodel some more,
Her one great trick, next to plopping out her false teeth
And hot peach pies with butter crust and cinnamon syrup
Exploding summer in your mouth.

Years later, a midnight phone call.
Gram had died in the nursing home, Mom said.
She was stubborn to the end,
refusing the feeding tube.
"You know I had to raise two sets of kids,
My own, plus Matt was a set unto herself."

There were too many irons in the fire,
Grad school, two kids, and an eight-hour drive,
So, instead of funeral memories

Other ghosts come haunting now,
Piercing pictures, clear as yesterday,
So strong I don't have to think
About what I'm feeling.

Yes, there were positive views of Mattie, if few. Two undated letters exist that were written to Martha Farrington by individuals who obviously liked her. The first is from a surprising source: her husband's sister, Elsie. Even a critical reader can detect the warmth and sincerity of Elsie's letter. Elsie was the youngest Farrington daughter—there was a last child, George Hobson Farrington, to follow a couple of years later. When Elsie Farrington was 19 years old, she married James Carl Osborne. They chose to live near Richmond, Virginia, about 250 miles from the Farrington homestead at Nubbin Ridge. Elsie and James Carl lived in the country, taking their mail on the rural delivery route of the little town of Clayville. While much may be forgotten, today, her letter is packed with information. Given here, in its fullness, is a handwritten letter written from Elsie Farrington Osborne to Martha White Farrington. A reference to Elsie's daughter, Betty, seems to be saying that Betty was visiting with John Alexander Farrington for a weekend. Elsie's thoughts were written on a five-hole sheet of notebook paper.

*Clayville Va*
*Route 1*

*Dear Sister and Family*

*Sure was glad to get your letter and to know you were O.K. except for lonelyness Sure hope you can pull your self together and feel better some times I get the Blues so Bad I cant hardly stand it all my children are here in Va but some times I don't see them very often altho I havent got but 9 children and 4 grand children one of my girls Betty went down to Alex this week end they had got the letter from you all looks like Bate would come Back to some of his people wonder if any one would know who to notafi if anything was to happen to him. Well this leaves all as well as usual and sure is dry here we don't have any crop not even a garden. We have a store and* gas station. Am making a living Louis and Tommy are the only two at home right now

Well Mat I did wish we could have been together longer But as you said, we couldent have talked But if you have the chance come down and stay as long as you like would be glad for you to come Well guess I will close tell Gladys and the children and all the rest Hello for me and write again soon

With love to all
Your Sis Elsie.

The reader might observe that Elsie mentions "Mat," her sister-in-law, along with her niece Gladys, two of her sons and one of her daughters, plus two of her brothers, Battie and John Alexander. Not specifically mentioned was her brother (and Martha's husband), Prince David Farrington.

Also providing a more positive view of Mattie was her adoring niece, Artis Caudle. Artis' letter—also undated—is excerpted here:

*Dear Aunt Mattie,*

*Appreciated your letter more than you will ever know... There's not a day goes by that I don't think of you... and wish that I could have another chat with you...*

*Sure would like to hear you pick the banjo and sing some. You will just have to come to see us sometime.*

*How are all your children and how's Prince? I hope they are O.K. ... and for yourself, I do hope your doing good. I do love you and wish I could see you more. There's quite a distance between ... tho.*

*"You keep sweet" and let me hear from you again real soon ...*

*Love,*
*Artis*

The phrase that Artis put in quotes seemed to provide a fitting title for this sketch of Martha ("Mattie") White Farrington. Also, no matter what sort of reception Mattie and Prince received on their return trips to Guilford County, Prince Farrington was quickly becoming a household name in two counties of Pennsylvania.

*Brungard School, Rosecrans, where Prince's and Martha's (Mattie's) children had early schooling.*

*Granville Elementary School (now a museum and township offices), Antes Fort.*

*Daughter, Gladys.*

*Heavily forested ridges a few miles southeast of Loganton (northwestern Union Co.).*

## 38 PROHIBITION'S PRINCE

*The World War II draft registration card of Prince Farrington; the reverse is not shown; but it carries a date of April 27th, 1942.*

*Posing for posterity in Antes Fort. Third from right is Leo Taylor, fifth from right is Taylor's friend and Prince's nephew, B. W. Coltrane. Also in picture: a '35 Plymouth.*

## · 3 ·

# From Tarheel to Keystoner

**A MOONSHINER'S PARADISE?**
If one could remove the three-tiered level of legal authorities from the picture, Prince David Farrington had found a moonshiner's paradise. *Even today*, nearly a century after Prince Farrington's arrival, the area that lured him north is largely undeveloped. The tree-covered ridges still hide the many small streams that cut through rocky ravines en route to the mother of Pennsylvania waters, the Susquehanna River. Despite the great growth rate of much of the nation, Lycoming County today remains 75 percent wooded land, with Clinton County's wooded area exceeding 82 percent! Although the copper equipment and some other evidence are gone, the modern land developers had left most of the secluded still sites about as pristine as when they were abandoned by the fugitive named Farrington.

Prince, Martha and their young family settled on a ridge near Loganton, Pennsylvania, in the area known, since Colonial times, as Sugar Valley. It was suggested that Sugar Valley was so-named because of the trees known as sugar pine (*Pinus Lambertiana*). This is a misconception. Ed Dix of Pennsylvania's Bureau of Forestry notes that no evidence has been found of any planting of sugar pine, a common tree in the American West, anywhere within the state. The valley, with villages named Booneville, Greenburr, Carroll, Rosecrans, Tylersville, Eastville, and Loganton, had and continues to have the sugar *maple*, from which the American Indians got the syrup that they boiled to make a naturally sweet snack: maple sugar.

Sugar Valley had a memorable lifestyle. The common occupations were virtually all tied to the land: farming, lumbering and quarrying. The people of the valley were known to be a close-knit group. Ed Snook spent his childhood in the small community of Rosecrans, a town named for the Civil War general W. S. Rosecrans (1819 - 1898), under whom a local man had served. Snook says that the valley folk were naturally helpful to their neighbors. Snook cites an example of such support: If a man died, leaving a widow and young children, men of the town would spend a Saturday cutting and hauling firewood to fill the family's woodshed for the coming winter. They also, as a community, offered meat and other essentials. There was nothing saccharine about the sweetness of the people of Sugar Valley. Prince David Farrington, the new resident in the valley, bought land that had once belonged to a man named William Purman (or Poorman).

William Purman's journey to Sugar Valley began just a short distance away in Millheim (Centre County) but involved a long stay in Florida en route. Purman was born in Millheim, April 11, 1840. He took his schooling locally and studied law in Lock Haven prior to the US Civil War. His service in the Union Army led to an assignment in Florida (1865). Purman chose to stay in Florida, where he was admitted to the bar in 1868. His busy political career in Florida included serving in the Florida legislature, chairing the state's Republican Party and serving two terms in the U.S. Congress. In 1878, he returned to his hometown, where he pursued an agricultural career that included the purchase of land in Sugar Valley.

Purman had envisioned a great plantation-style farm in Sugar Valley, which he named the Florida Fruit Farm. Purman planted thousands of apple trees, creating productive orchards of more than a half-dozen apple varieties. The 1880 census shows William Purman living on the sprawling farm with his wife, three children, a mother-in-law, a sister-in-law, four servants, and nine hired hands. In 1883, Purman moved to Boston, Massachusetts. Later, he moved to Washington, D.C., where he lived in retirement until he died in 1928. Purman's plantation/farm was both bountiful and beautiful. The Lock Haven *Express* (December 2, 1939) stated that William Purman once had "an apple orchard numbering ten thousand trees, a never-to-be-forgotten scene in blossoming time." That same publication had claimed (November 2nd, 1912) that the Florida Fruit Farm was "the largest apple orchard in the state." After several intervening owners, the Florida Fruit Farm became the home of

Prince David Farrington, his family and his plans for a moonshiner's mountain fastness.

While Prince Farrington owned the farm, there were—according to Lester Seiler's memory—a hundred acres of apples and fifty acres of peaches. Seiler, who sometimes worked on that farm, specifically cited the *Northern Spy* variety. Seiler also identifies potatoes as an excellent cash crop for the *Florida Fruit Farm*. "There wasn't any year that I was there that we didn't have over 9,000 bushels of potatoes and most generally anywheres from 2500 to 4500 bushels of apples."

Thanks to William Purman's legacy, a law-abiding farmer should have prospered. Today, a few of those fruit-bearing trees remain.

The Florida Fruit Farm also had wooded areas where one might hide a still or two. With large purchases of equipment and supplies from nearby businesses, Prince quickly began making moonshine. How long was the future millionaire moonshiner in the Keystone State before being arrested?

If Prince Farrington had hoped for a respite from the law, once in Pennsylvania, he misjudged badly. It would only be a slight exaggeration to say that Pennsylvania authorities had a welcoming party for Prince, awaiting his arrival. He hadn't yet had the time to learn which local officials were bribe-able and which were honest. Only a few months after moving his family and his moonshining business to the Keystone State, government agents conducted their first raid at the Florida Fruit Farm. More would follow.

## THE WELCOMING PARTY—1922

In the spring of 1922, 'dry' agents raided the Florida Fruit Farm but found little more than part of an old still. However, they soon had plans coordinated for a return raid in early July. This second raid was under the direction of John B. Ernst and S. R. Campbell. Others involved in the July raid included three agents from Philadelphia: George Vogt, James Gibbons and Vincent Martin. Two local agents—Morton B. Reeser and W. R. Lockard—completed the roster of the July raiding party. This party was organized at Jersey Shore and descended on Farrington's farm at about 1:30 on a July afternoon. This raid was, said the Lock Haven *Express* (July 7th, 1922), "one of the biggest and most important raids ever conducted in the state of Pennsylvania." The newspaper might have saved some typesetting time by putting aside that plate for several later reports that they would be running.

Although the raiding party had been warned that men armed with high-powered rifles were watching the farm, the *Express* wrote that the officers "were undaunted" as they sought and destroyed the alcohol and the distilling equipment. Stored liquor was found in fence corners, stone piles, wood piles, underground and elsewhere. The agents also collected bottle labels and government stamps that were counterfeit.

Prince Farrington was not on the farm. The news account said that he was thought to have gone south about a week before the raid. This meant that his friend, Joseph ("Joe") Gardner, also of North Carolina, was in charge of the farm, but he, too, was absent during the raid. Luther Self, one of Farrington's workers, was the only person found to be present on the farm. He was also the only one apprehended by authorities.

At least two other men were also present—but hidden—when the raid began. Those two (apparently armed lookouts with high-powered rifles) had a running gunfight with agents Ernst and Campbell before escaping. The agents were armed with heavy-caliber revolvers. No one was injured in that four-man battle. Apparently those same two men did not leave the area. They were believed to be the same pair of lawbreakers who were hiding within sight of the raiding activity and who, from hiding places, fired at the raiders' cars as they were leaving at the end of the afternoon. The raiding agents could not see the attackers; but still returned some shots in the general direction. Since no one appears to have been hit, despite the use of top-quality firearms and despite two episodes of gunfire having been exchanged, one might *speculate* that Prince Farrington had instructed his cohorts not to hit anyone but simply to attempt to scare the interlopers.

The *Express* noted that the Florida Fruit Farm contained 240 acres "and is laid out with innumerable fruit trees stretching as far as the eye can see and all showing signs of neglect on the part of the present owners, who had discovered a much more lucrative business."[5]

As the agents departed, neighbors appeared and—perhaps in jest—loudly expressed their sorrow over the confiscated alcohol that was so close yet so inaccessible. "There it goes!" was the common cry of the spectators.

---

5. Edition of July 7, 1922.

At this stage of Prince Farrington's career, the people of Clinton and Lycoming counties clearly thought of Prince, his relatives and his fellow moonshiners as outsiders from the South who were in Pennsylvania on a temporary basis. This view was reflected in the *Democrat*'s newspaper accounts that referred to "threats of being shot by the gun-toting southern guards." There were also the comments of John Ernst, immediately following the raid.

Ernst, head of the raiding force, was quoted as opining, "I am thoroughly convinced, however, that the whole quartet was brought to the Lock Haven vicinity for the sole reason because they were experts in the moonshine whiskey business."

How significant was that 1922 raid? The *Clinton County Democrat* (July 14, 1922) identified the raid as "one of the biggest and most important raids ever conducted in the state of Pennsylvania."

The Lock Haven *Express* of the previous week had carried much the same report.

The tally? A full 22 barrels of whiskey, valued in the deflated currency of the time at about $15,000, were loaded on trucks for hauling from the site. At the site itself, two stills, each of 300-gallon capacity, were destroyed by the agents. They also collected thousands of bottles, plus labels. In addition, they gathered three 44-caliber Colt revolvers, plus shotguns and Winchester rifles. Evidence studied, but not removed, was the mash itself, from which the whiskey was being distilled. Ernst's judgment: "The men were masters in their business. They certainly did not waste any mash!"

The newspaper accounts refer to the destruction of two stills but also claim that *three* stills were located in a nearby woodland. The agents' investigation revealed two wells that had been dug at the stills, plus an additional pipe that was also supplying water from an old pump closer to the house. When the farm's distilling apparatus had been in full operation, with Gardner working the day shift and Self the night shift, it was estimated that they were producing about three large barrels of moonshine daily.

The writer for the Clinton County *Democrat* (July 14, 1922) became almost rhapsodic in describing how the image of a still in the mountains near Loganton, Pennsylvania, was similar to a scene in the then-contemporary American South:

The raid is one of the most important of any made in Pennsylvania. It was also one of the most difficult, owing to the location of the stills in the mountains. In fact, the scene very much resembled that of a southern moonshiners' camp, and the gunplay gave it a very realistic Kentucky setting.

With the moonshining and bootlegging career of Prince David Farrington still stretching another quarter-century into the future, there was destined to be a whole series of "very important raids" to be witnessed by the folks of Clinton and Lycoming counties.

## AFTERMATH

The first great raid on Prince Farrington's operations in Pennsylvania resulted in arrest warrants being issued by W. D. Crocker, U.S. Commissioner. The warrants were issued, wrote the Williamsport *Sun-Gazette* (July 12, 1922), for "Prince Farrington, owner of the Florida Fruit Farms near Loganton, and the others associated with him in the conduct of mammoth moonshine operations which were raided—last week."

Another result of the June 1922 raid: Wilbur Lockard, a Lock Haven patrolman who had participated in the raid, was suspended from his post for 30 days for having joined the raid without his superiors' permission. However, he was reported to have been offered a federal law-enforcement job, which would also have increased his income.

Whether a modern observer would find it newsworthy, the local newspapers saw newsworthiness in the mere transporting of illicit booze through their town. The Lock Haven *Express* of 1922 reported that "Another truck carrying five barrels of moonshine whiskey from Florida Farms in Sugar Valley to the Lycoming County Jail in Williamsport made its way through Lock Haven." The paper also tallied the haul for its readers, telling them that "This makes 57 barrels with an average of 35 gallons to the barrel." That tally let readers know that nearly 2,000 gallons of Prince Farrington's moonshine had been confiscated and removed to the jail.

Thus, the county jail had—at one time or another—held the moonshine and the moonshiner. Coincidentally, the Lycoming County prison was already famous, or infamous, for being the last residence of

Catherine Miller and George Smith. This prison housed the same yard in which Catherine Miller was hanged back in 1881. Catherine Miller and her lover, George Smith, hatched a plot as old as David and Bathsheba (c. 980 BC). Catherine and George killed her husband, Andrew Miller. It appeared that Andrew hanged himself in a neighbor's barn. It also appeared that he gave himself severe head wounds and left bloody straw nearby. It also appeared that he got his wife's paramour to wear bloody trousers when authorities came to investigate. The lovers were sentenced to hang. Their hanging took place in the old prison yard in February of 1881. Catherine Miller, fiercely shrieking, became the last female to be hanged within the commonwealth of Pennsylvania. Eight years later, a North Carolinian was born who was destined, someday, to sleep within the walls of that same prison. Today, that great lithic structure has been converted into a business. Now called "The Cell Block," the former Lycoming County prison has morphed into a nightclub.

## HIS NEIGHBOR, HIS PARTNER

Turbit Seiler farmed a farmstead that was neighbor to Prince Farrington's Florida Fruit Farm. John Wagner, who also lived near the Florida Fruit Farm, remembers his grandfather, Turbit Seiler. Turbit bought sugar from Prince Farrington and used it in his moonshining operation. This brought the inevitable raids by government revenuers. Turbit had a small brood that included Lester, Margaret, Edna, John and Raymond. Lester was interviewed in 1983, but the tape was unpublished and never circulated until Dan Hills, its current owner, offered to loan the tape to the author. From that tape, we can experience the anxiety caused by an anticipated raid, as well as a handful of genuine raids, as recalled by the late Lester Seiler, Turbit Seiler's son:

> One time, they raided us—in the winter or fall, after we had it hidden in the manure pile in the barnyard, in the milk shed, right where we threw the straw down. The bull [kept] them in the barn purtin' near a whole half a day! After they were in, the bull wouldn't let them out. Every time they come to the door, he'd come for them, and they'd head back into the barn. They didn't know it; they coulda got out the back door. We had

a little door on the barn door. A lot of them didn't [have the secondary door], but we had a little door on the barn door. The bull kept them in there for, oh, a coupla hours. I don't know just how long.

Anyways, we talked to a [judge]. He was a lawyer at the time. He and Dad were pretty good buddies. Dad told him about [the bull intimidating the revenue agents]. He [the judge] said, "Well, it's a good thing they didn't find any evidence. If they had found any whiskey in the barn, they could have shot the bull, and you couldn't have done anything about it." But they didn't have no evidence. They had nothing on us, so they wouldn't dare.

One time, too, I got scared after it [the raid] was all over. They come there, and we didn't have any [moonshine]. We didn't have any whiskey, and we didn't have anything running. They come and said about searching, and Dad said, "Go ahead. We ain't got nothin'." After they were gone—It must have been an hour or so after they left, it just dawned on us. Up there at the silo . . . the empty one . . . back in behind the silo, there laid the whole still! We never thought about it being in the barn. Whether they didn't open the door—they never found it, anyhow!

Ann Roush, however, did. But that was years later. She tells us that her family later moved onto the Turbit Seiler farm. Ann recalls seeing copper tubing and a large vat hidden beneath straw in the former Seiler barn. Seilers hadn't bothered removing that moonshining apparatus before the farm was sold. That farm, where the Seilers once lived, was one of three or four farms that are now gone completely. Today, those farms sit beneath the waters of a large mountain-top reservoir that is part of the Lock Haven municipal water supply.

Returning to Lester Seiler's account:

One time the revenue guys come there to our place in the spring of the year. I'd say not quite as late as this. We had the window open, you know. They came in on the porch. Came in like that. Anyway, Dad met 'em outside. They showed up with badges— They were revenue men and searchers. Well, my sister, Edna, was in there, and she was washing dishes. There was a pint bottle [of moonshine] on the sink, right next to the drain sink. Edna grabbed that pint bottle and smashed it on the cast iron drain sink, and turned the water on! They woulda took her for destroying evidence, only she wasn't of age, so it didn't matter. They couldn't do nothing about it.

I guess we was raided about four times, or five. One time, Lester Fiedler (c. 1901–1953) was on the tower.[6] We put our still out in the field, after haymaking, that was. We had two stone piles in the field out from there. And we were away from the road on that side, and we laid the still up against the stone pile in the field, so it wouldn't show; but, in the tower, they had field glasses and, of course, from that side, they could see it [the still]. They seen this here still and tried [in vain] to locate it. Boy! As soon as they left![7]

Lester Seiler also related the account of another raid, in which the still owner, Adam Stabley, rather than admit that it was his still, helped the agents to destroy his still: "Did I give you Ad Stabley's story on moonshine? Did you know Ad at the 101 Ranch?"

The interviewer recognized the name. "I remember that. It was a whorehouse—" It should be noted, however, that Lester Seiler in no way acknowledged the "whorehouse" designation. The 101 Ranch was owned throughout part of the 1920s and 1930s by Adam Stabley, who ran a brothel and speakeasy from his house along Rockey Road. Stabley also did some of his own whiskey making, with his still hidden higher on the ridge, above his establishment. Although the 101 Ranch was just a few miles from Prince Farrington's Florida Fruit Farm and about two miles from a property owned by Farrington's associate, Joe Gardner, none of the older citizens of the area recall any sort of ties between Ad Stabley's house of ill repute and the Farrington/Gardner pair.

---

6. Seiler is referring to the nearby state-operated fire tower. The towers were built on Pennsylvania mountain tops, with workers manning the towers and looking for possible forest fires, in order to send crews to handle the fires before they became dangerous or destructive.

7. Lester Seiler, when he starts narrating some of his accounts, has a voice not unlike that of the late actor, Walter Brennan, including the occasionally high-pitched voice inflections.

> Anyway, you know Ad was making [moonshine] right up over the hill from his place, you know. That there was called the Bear Swamp, where them huckleberries are. You see, there's two places out there are called the Huckleberry Swamp, on top there. One comes out the pond road—That's where Ad had his [still]. It was lucky Ad was going out that day and had his bucket along. He was going to pick huckleberries. So, the revenue men caught him. They thought he was going up there to his still. And they told him about finding [it]. And he said, "Boy, I wouldn't know anything about that." He went along and even helped to smash up his own still!

Seiler's recounting of Adam Stabley's involvement in smashing his own still led one of the interviewers to ask Seiler, "What would they cost? Those stills?" and "Where would you buy them?" To which Seiler replied that they'd not cost much. Where could they be bought? Seiler explained that they could be bought from any tinsmith, an occupation that barely exists today.

> Oh, any tinner. Any tinner. You might take and give him maybe $5 extry, and that's all, and you'd never hear nothin' about it.
>
> ["Did he make them out of copper?"]
>
> Yup. Any tinner. I'll tell you, old Prince was the one to solder. Old Prince would take—I don't know how he done it. He'd rub that [hot] old soldering iron on his cheek. He'd touch it [the cheek], too! And he'd say, "Well, it ain't hot enough" or "Too hot." Then he'd rub it on his pants a couple of times—then he'd rub it on his cheek again. When he'd start [soldering], it was just like water falling—that's the way the solder'd just fall from that soldering iron when he started, and it wouldn't be all in big chunks—it was nice, just like he painted it on.
>
> ["He'd use an acid first, would he?"]
>
> Yeah, he'd put an acid on.
>
> ["What was this, an electric iron?"]

No, this was just one he put in the fire. He had a pretty good-sized iron—He'd take and wipe it on his face, and if it was too hot or too cold, he'd wipe it on his pants . . .

Lester Seiler seemed to enjoy the interview, and he volunteered the information that the interviewer never solicited but which certainly illuminated the moonshining process.

Another bizarre incident that occurred on the Turbit Seiler farm involved the 'rummy' (or hard drinking) dentist of Lock Haven, Dr. Robert Shaffer. [This account is from the recollection of a living witness, John Wagner, a relative of the late Lester Seiler]. Dr. Shaffer visited Turbit Seiler because of the availability of whiskey, a commodity craved by the dentist. On this particular visit, Turbit Seiler was complaining to his visitor about a nagging toothache. The issue was addressed. With farmer Seiler lying on his back, on the ground between the corn crib and the barn, Dr. Shaffer sat on Seiler's chest, took huge pincers and yanked the troublesome tooth. Everything about this procedure was extreme. The ground replaced the dental chair; the barnyard replaced the office; horse pliers replaced the dental tool, and, says Wagner, both patient and dentist were patently drunk.

In 1926, Prince moved his operation from the Florida Fruit Farm to the bottom lands along the Susquehanna River, across from the town of Jersey Shore. He and his family moved into a large home on the river bank. Jersey Shore was on the opposite side of the riverine island known as Long Island. A smaller town, a similar distance from Prince's house, but to the south and on the same side of the Susquehanna as Prince's home, is Antes Fort. As the name suggests, Antes Fort is on the site of a private colonial-era fort. It had been erected by Colonel John Henry Antes, for whom the local creek is also named.

While Prince Farrington's name has become the most-recognized name throughout Sugar Valley and Clinton County, the individuals who created the valley's 1965 commemorative booklet and those who compiled the 117-page sesquicentennial booklet in 1990 failed to mention his name or anything about the man.

*The very young Farrington children, Gladys and Prince Jr. The picture was taken at the Florida Fruit Farm.*

The Caldwell United Methodist Church, north of Rosecrans. This was just one of several area churches that were said to have repairs made from the funds donated by Prince D. Farrington.

*Prince in a snapshot, posing beside the new automobile.*

*Martha (Mattie). She, too, is posing beside a marvelous riding machine.*

*The World War I draft registration card of Prince David Farrington. Note that it lists, for June 6, 1917, a wife and one child.*

# · 4 ·

# The Moonshiner, Revisited

**NOT EXCLUSIVELY A MOONSHINER**
Prince Farrington, the nearly life-long moonshiner and bootlegger, had several forms of legitimate employment. Foremost among these would have been his farming. His farming lasted through much of his lifetime. However, during his early years in Pennsylvania, he also made deliveries for a soft drink distributor, and during World War II, he worked in a defense job in the Allenwood-Alvira area.

Prince's involvement in his job at Allenwood was interesting for a couple of reasons. For one, Allenwood was the town from which Richard Baxter emerged. Baxter was the revenue agent who successfully pursued and apprehended Prince Farrington at his elaborate distilling operation on the Tangascootac Creek on August 27, 1946 (see Chapter 1). A second interesting fact about Prince Farrington's Allenwood-area employment: He had a legitimate form of employment during the 1940s in which he worked at a pump house, at Spring Garden, a settlement midway between Allenwood and Alvira. However, if local rumor is reliable, Farrington used that legitimate operation as a cover for operating another illegal still!

**SOME VERY EMINENT DOMAIN!**
In 1940, the village of Alvira sat about three miles northwest of Allenwood. The town consisted of a couple of dozen families, a pair of small stores, a blacksmith shop, and four churches. Beautiful farms surrounded this charming village. The road that passed through the town was known as the Culbertson Trail, and it was known to be a cross-country shortcut for shipments of Prince Farrington's whiskey that were being sent from Jersey Shore to Allenwood and the thirsty markets beyond.

In early December of 1941, an act of war occurred nearly five thousand miles from Alvira. The Japanese warlords decided to attack a militarily unready giant: the United States of America. Few towns or cities in America would feel the impact of that war more than the town of Alvira, Pennsylvania. No one in Alvira could have imagined that the distant war would obliterate their lovely little town in Union County, Pennsylvania. However, two town meetings—in February and March of 1942—were held in the Christ Lutheran Stone Church. These meetings confirmed that the United States was going to buy about 8,000 acres in Alvira and the surrounding lands. The federal government was exercising the right of eminent domain and buying all the lands needed. The lands were to be purchased; but for prices that the landowners found to be pitiful. Even more stunning was the time frame. From the date of that second town meeting, all residents had to be gone from their Alvira homes within six weeks!

What had happened? The citizens of Alvira were quickly uprooted because the area, about 8,000 acres worth, was to be transformed into one of several sites to be used for creating mountains of TNT (trinitrotoluene) explosives for use against the three countries against which the United States Congress had declared war. The demands of war called for the quick destruction of the town, including the dynamiting and burning of buildings that had been businesses, schools, homes and two churches.

Within a few weeks, government agencies and private contractors were creating the buildings and concrete bunkers that were required for a major manufacturing complex. Many miles of roads and rails were built. Until huge trailer towns were established on the grounds, buses brought *defense workers* from Williamsport to their critical jobs in the Pennsylvania Ordnance Works. The explosives could now be made in gargantuan quantities and stored in the 150 new beehive-shaped bunkers. The Ordnance Works did not make bombs. The Pennsylvania Ordnance Works simply made the lethal ingredient that would be inserted elsewhere.

Alvira's corpse was never revived. Most of Pennsylvania's authentic ghost towns were the result of economic swings related to natural resources such as coal, lumber and oil. Alvira was unique. Instead of former landowners returning, different government entities carved the pilfered turkey. The U.S. Bureau of Prisons, in 1950, was given more than 4,000 acres, while the Pennsylvania Game Commission was granted more than 3,000 acres. The remaining acres went to numerous recipients of small tracts. Thus, instead of driving northwest from Allenwood and catching a sign saying "Village of Alvira," one reads a sign informing him or her that they have arrived at Pennsylvania's State Game Land # 252. The unfamiliar motorist cannot know the tragedy behind the sign.

Strangely, even this operation involved Prince Farrington. When a resident saw a man (Huddy and Metzger, p. 32), hard-at-work, laying pipe into the Pennsylvania Ordinance Works, the man told the curious local that he was laying pipe and fixing the pump house. That seeming interloper was a hard-working Prince Farrington. Years later, former resident Robert Russell recalled (Huddy and Metzger, p. 33), "You know who ran the pump house down there at Spring Garden (a small settlement between Alvira and Allenwood)? Prince Farrington! They were having trouble with the pump there by the old iron bridge, and he got it going. What they didn't know was that he had a still set up in the pump house, too . . . made a nice fifth of whiskey; the man did . . . Well when they finally closed him down and he went to trial at the courthouse up in Williamsport, guess what . . . all the evidence had 'run away.'"

## FARRINGTON'S METHODS OF OPERATION

Prince Farrington used a variety of skillful and innovative approaches to hiding his stills and their addictive distillate. Some failed, and some were successful. Here are two such attempts.

Scientific advances are embraced with equal enthusiasm by the law-abiding and the lawless. Kerosene was processed, and so named in Canada in 1854. It was found to be a non-volatile liquid that furnished light. Eventually, kerosene also became a source of heat. At some point in his career, Prince Farrington began using kerosene to supply the heat needed for his distilling operations. Why kerosene? There was no telltale smoke to rise above the treetops. Science unwittingly supported moonshining.

Another Farrington method of deception was his loading of the perimeters of a truck-bed with crates of chickens, within which was a stash of whiskey. This specific mode was identified by Amber Keene, a native of Sugar Valley, as well as the 93-year-old genealogist of the Rishel and related families. She now resides in historic Boalsburg (Centre County). Amber was also a descendant of the Poorman family that originally developed the lush orchards of the Florida Fruit Farm. Ms. Keene has related a specific, non-Farrington Sugar Valley incident worth recording. She tells of an aunt, Harriet (Hattie), who was married to Henry Karachner (the Karchners now omit the second 'a' from their family name). One day, while Henry was away, their house caught fire. "Aunt Hattie" quickly laid the baby daughter, Helen, in a basket, picked up the basket, took her son, Clair, by the hand, escaped the burning house and ran across the field to a neighbor's house.

Even for Prince Farrington, the chance of being apprehended at a still was a real concern. Prince approached this dilemma by moving some stills; but he also used an increased number of stills and bribery as ways to increase his productivity. Prince might also have had others run stills for him. Even with Prince's several incentives, many individuals had their own stills. James Segraves has noted that phenomenon, with slight exaggeration: "Wherever there was running water, they made whiskey. They also kept moving the stills to try to keep ahead of the revenuers."

## PRINCE AND PRIME REALTY

For the past half-century, Dora and Leroy Wenker have been regular patrons of the farm market in Lock Haven, but Leroy's story goes even further back in time. As a young farm boy attending a tiny, rural school, Leroy shared one of the wide desks with young George Helvly. The Helvly's had a farm as well, just east of the Swissdale church, but their barn's hay mow (rhymes with 'cow') served a different function. Under the Helvly's hay mow, there was also a stash of Prince Farrington's whiskey.

The young student, George Helvly, got diphtheria. Soon after, his desk mate contracted it too. The Helvly boy never recovered. He was buried in the Swissdale churchyard. But Leroy Wenker's body was fighting. The doctor had asked Leroy's family if they had whiskey. He wanted Leroy to be given whiskey as a medication. They had none, so the Helvlys gave some whiskey to the Wenkers for young Leroy. With Helvly whiskey, the doctor's orders were followed. Leroy, given a tablespoon of whiskey each morning, survived the diphtheria.

The Wenkers lived along the Susquehanna, between Lock Haven and Farrandsville. They owned two farms on the south side of Bear Mountain, near Farrandsville. They also owned a tract of timber, containing almost 150 acres, on the north side of the mountain. One day, around the year 1940, Leroy Wenker was in the barn where he and his dad, Carl Wenker, were milking the dairy herd. Raymond Bauman, a friend of Carl and Prince Farrington, appeared at the barn door. He told Carl Wenker that Prince Farrington would like to talk to him. Leroy's dad told Raymond Bauman, "As soon as I get finished milking, we can go in the house and talk." Farrington and Bauman visited with Carl in the old farm kitchen. He had heard stories, both negative and positive, about Farrington. Young Leroy was impressed. Prince Farrington was visiting at *his* house. Leroy still recalls seeing Prince sitting in the old wicker rocking chair and brushing his hand back over his balding pate as they talked.

Prince Farrington explained his interest. He wanted to buy the timber tract from Carl Wenker. Carl said that he had no interest in selling the land to Prince. Instead, he planned to sell the timber. Leroy observes today, "Dad knew why Prince wanted to buy the land."

Another interesting picture of Prince came from his former personal driver, Sam Fuller. Sam says that Prince knew where every spring was located. While driving someplace, Prince instructed Sam to stop. They were at a roadside spring that Prince knew was there. Then Prince would have a swig of whiskey before turning up the brim of his hat. He'd put spring water into the brim and drink it as a chaser.

There was the constant threat of Prince or his helpers being caught. Despite the risk, people still went directly to the Stewart/Courtright farm to buy alcohol. Once, in 1933, Tom Bauman and his mother spent the night visiting different relatives in Lock Haven and close to Queen's Run, north of Lock Haven. When they telephoned for Raymond Bauman to come to get his wife and son, Raymond drove to the temporary bridge to cross the Susquehanna and enter Jersey Shore. The temporary bridge was actually the old bridge, which was being replaced. That temporary bridge was shifted slightly on railroad ties to one side. Then the new replacement bridge had been completed; but it had not yet been opened. Cars were allowed on the temporary bridge one at a time. As Raymond waited for his turn to proceed, just one car was ahead of him. Bauman knew that the three occupants of the preceding car had been buying liquor from Prince. That car proceeded onto the bridge, which suddenly collapsed into the ice-swollen river. Raymond Bauman saw one of the men get out of the car and cling to some ice briefly, but all three drowned. Tom and his mother had to walk across the new and as-yet unopened bridge in order to rejoin Raymond Bauman for the sad trip home.

## DOWN BY THE RIVERSIDE

At one point in time, Prince invited relatives to occupy his large farmhouse that was the centerpiece of the Gheen (today Courtright) property (see Chapter 11). These relatives were Prince's sister, Zenadah ("Nade") Coltrane, her husband, Kyle Coltrane and their three children, Hilda, B. W. and Wade. Tom Bauman, a neighbor boy in those days, recalls many visits to that farm. Memorable to the lad was the presence of large letters painted on the side of the tobacco shed. It was the name of one of the former owners: GHEEN. That name was visible from the highway across the river. However, Bauman was more impressed with the matron of the house, although he never knew Zenadah Farrington Coltrane's real name. He says simply: "Nade was a beautiful woman." He explains: "I used to take my dog, and we'd walk down between our farm and the Gheen farm. I can always remember this: Nade would see me coming, and she would always have southern biscuits baked. *Always*. When I'd go in, she'd have one of them cut in half with butter and blackstrap molasses on and a glass of milk. "My mother later told me that Nade had cancer. She had an operation, and they took her one breast, but it had already spread into the other one as well as into her bone structure. The cancer cut short the life of this fine lady. She was still living on the Gheen farm when she died; I think it was in the Williamsport Hospital. She was the first person I was around whose passing away really upset me."

PRINCE DAVID FARRINGTON was a child of the era. He had charm and generosity, with an untroubled knack for breaking laws. His reputation as a womanizer is also secure. Ethel Klobe Quiggle often mentioned her impression: Prince liked women. He had an eye for women. Velma Williams (now Wolfe) was the sister of Prince Farrington's daughter-in-law, Martha (Mrs. Tom Farrington). Velma recalls having once been told by Prince, "You're a fine-looking young lady." Her friend, Tammy Farrington, observes that Velma, now in her tenth decade of life and after bearing nine children, remains "an attractive lady."

## MARTHA WHITE FARRINGTON ("MATTIE")

As mentioned earlier (*see* Chapter 2), Martha ("Mattie") White Farrington (1895–1972), when visiting with Prince's sister in North Carolina, would sit for hours at a table and never offer to help with cooking or dishes. One might guess that this behavior was borne from her reluctance to associate with Prince's relatives. But, her grandson, Robert, reinforces the image in his verse (*see* p. 31), saying Mattie "Sat in the same chair most of the day, dusting only what she could reach . . ." Likewise, Tom Bauman, a young neighbor of the Farringtons when they were living on a farm near Jersey Shore, Pennsylvania, related, "The Farringtons never called me *Tom*. It was always *Tommy*. All except Whitey. All of them: Gladys, Tom, Gayle, and Prince . . . even Matt (Martha). I remember her. She'd sit behind the kitchen table for hours and hours on end. Maybe she'd get up to go to the bathroom. When she came back, she'd sit right there again. I never saw her do anything so far as cooking was concerned. We'd come in from the fields, and if we had a little ground on our shoes or anything, 'You hogdogs!' That was her favorite saying: 'You hogdogs!' She'd kind of give us all hell. Prince's favorite saying was 'Hell's bells!' if something went wrong. I can remember Prince saying that a good many times.

"Prince did all the cooking. He was a good cook. My favorite: For breakfast he made milk gravy on toast. And he always kind of burnt the flour before he put the milk in it, you know, and it was kind of brown. Geez, I could eat a good bit of that. Then he had a thing he would make; he would call it *succotash*, but my mother would call it *vegetable soup*. I remember he used a pressure cooker and had that on the stove. He'd have a chunk of boiling beef in it. When it got done, you know, we'd get in there . . . and he'd get that piece of beef out, and he'd slice it. He'd slice that down, and then he'd put it on bread. He bought Italian bread all the time. He'd cover that with beef. While he was eating that, he had these hot Mexican peppers—about as big as your little finger—on a little dish, and he would pick one up from there. I tried to eat one, one time. Oh!

Oh! But, in all the time that I knew Prince, I never saw him eat a piece of pie . . . a piece of cake . . . or any candy. I never saw him eat any of those. He had no fascination for sweets."

Several individuals expressed a hint of Mattie's peculiar behavior in Chapter 8. One day, recalled Ed Carothers, Prince and Mattie were going to a midsummer affair. Mattie came downstairs wearing a mink coat. Echoing similar remembrances was Tom Bauman, who mentioned an oddity of Mattie's regarding clothing. "She always bought the best of everything. She would wear a dress for maybe three or four days; then she'd take it off, turn it inside-out, and wear it for another three or four days. She was eccentric like that, you know."

## SIDE-BY-SIDE BURIAL PLOTS

There was considerable interaction between Prince, his wife and children and Prince's siblings and their families.

There was some contact between Mattie's family and Prince's family through Mattie White's sister, Hazel, who married Scott Anthony. They were parents of two children, Bernice and Lobby. Bernice married Howard Dodson, a very wealthy businessman from the Greensboro area of North Carolina. She died in 2011. Lobby's tragic fate is discussed in Chapter 9. Although many people interviewed described Martha White Farrington as being, at best, eccentric, her sister, Hazel White Anthony, was described as decidedly levelheaded and easy to be around. A legitimate question might be: Was Martha White naturally eccentric or 'odd,' unlike her sister, Hazel, or did her choice of mates weigh more heavily on Martha than her fragile personality could bear? We must remind readers, again, that in 1929, Martha succeeded in obtaining a Lycoming County divorce from Prince Farrington, a divorce decree that never fully divorced them since they still more-or-less remained as estranged partners right through their declining years and directly to their side-by-side grave plots at Burnett's Chapel in Guilford County, North Carolina.

## THE GRAND HOLIDAY OF DECEMBER 5, 1933

Prince David Farrington was determined to be a moonshining outlaw. While the 18th Amendment (1919) outlawed the manufacture, transporting or sale of alcohol, Farrington had already been making untaxed and illegal liquor before the amendment was passed. During the ensuing 14 or so years, while Prohibition was in effect, Farrington was defying the 18th Amendment and its supporting laws by moonshining. Finally, when the 21st Amendment replaced the 18th Amendment, Farrington briefly tried the legitimate route but soon returned to the secluded stills of the moonshiner.

Those addicted to alcohol and those who simply loved to consume it were 'chompin' at the bit' for the end of Prohibition. From the sots to the social drinkers, the return to legalized alcohol could not come fast enough. Obviously, imbibers spirits (pardon the pun) were lifted when, in 1932, Franklin Delano Roosevelt promised that if he were elected to replace President Herbert Hoover, he would push for repeal of the much-trampled 18th Amendment. When Congress, in early 1933, issued the text of the proposed 21st Amendment, it allowed a seven-year period for the required two-thirds of the states to accept it. Seven long years? They needed less than ten months!

The way many people celebrated December 5, 1933, one would have thought that the nation had just won its independence or that the First World War had just ended. Instead, great hosts of the American public were celebrating the passage of the 21st Amendment to the U.S. Constitution. One by one, the states had voted to ratify the proposed new law. On December 5, 1933, at 5:32 P.M., Utah approved ratification. The requisite number of ratifying states had been reached. Less than two hours later, President Franklin D. Roosevelt issued the proclamation damning the 18th Amendment to perdition. The grand celebration that followed was in observance of the end of legally enforced temperance. The 21st Amendment, passed on December 5, 1933, was ratified, presumably to end the lawlessness and mayhem of the 1920s. It was during that era of anti-Prohibition lawlessness that Al Capone, Dion O'Banion, Benjamin "Bugsy" Siegel, Joseph Kennedy, Prince Farrington and many others made their fabled fortunes. Still, that lawlessness was replaced by the mayhem of drunken driving that takes thousands of American lives annually. However, the temperance advocates were properly chastened, never to raise their lemonade-drenched voices again. The proclamation of December 5, 1933, acknowledged the triumph of the lawless minority. They had regained their booze! All was right with the world.

The end of Prohibition posed a real dilemma for Prince David Farrington. People could now legally buy their spirituous liquors. They could also pay normal market prices. Still, after Prince tried, unsuccessfully, to do some legal distilling or brewing, he fell back on his skills and on his reputation for making superior quality whiskey. He re-entered the misty haunts of the moonshiner.

## · 5 ·

# The Politicians' Poverty

**WHEN *REAL POVERTY* STALKED THE LAND**
Two Biblical spokesmen for Jesus, his apostles Matthew (Chapter Twelve) and Luke (Chapter Twenty-one), tell of Jesus observing a widow putting two of the land's tiniest coins into the temple collection. As Jesus explained, the widow's contribution was far greater than the larger sums given by the wealthy since it was virtually all that she had. *That* was poverty.

Charles Dorwart, also mentioned in Chapter 13, recalled his mother feigning a lack of hunger when there was insufficient food available for the evening meal. Dorwart could readily identify with the Biblical accounts of the widow's mites since he remembers his mother giving each of her children a penny to put into the collection plate in Sunday School. Living within the poverty that was aggravated by a father who had an unabated "lust for booze," young Charles Dorwart worked on farms for a small pay and a meal, but sometimes the strenuous farm work provided only the meal. While the town of Antes Fort, where Charles lived, had few substantive jobs, he earned small amounts of income from the farm jobs, plus lawn mowing and, as a teen, from staying overnight with elderly individuals. In that last line of employment, Dorwart several times had to run to one of the only two households in Antes Fort that had telephones, in order to place emergency calls. The accumulation of an extra dollar became the entertainment portion of his income. This was used for a movie at Jersey Shore's Victoria Theater for 15 cents, plus a hot dog and a milk shake. Charles Dorwart, who later organized the Antes Fort museum in the old school building, has a vivid memory of the time when the ticket seller told him that he appeared tall enough and old enough to pay the 25-cent adult ticket price. One other aspect of the economic life of young Charles Dorwart matched that of the poorest folks across America: Charles helped his mother to take in the washing and ironing of other families, with the washing being done in a tub on their back porch.

## HAND ME DOWNS AND NATURE'S HARVEST

Geraldine (Bower) Wynn was born (1923) in the Rosecrans area of Sugar Valley and lived there, on Rockey Road (*see* Chapter 7) until she was required to move into the extended care facility in Lock Haven Hospital for the last three years of her life. Mrs. Wynn told her interviewer her family consisted of her parents, two siblings and herself. Although poor, she said that they always had enough to eat and to wear, as well as a warm place to sleep. Her dad, Harry Bower, worked in the early lumber industry, cutting timber. Her mother, Maggie (Duck) Bower, helped tend their cow and chickens. An occasional pig, purchased from a neighbor, would be butchered for the additional meat. A neighbor would bring his horse and plow to prepare their land for planting. When Harry borrowed a team of mules, on one occasion, young Geraldine got experience in harrowing the fields. Here, again, the age-old practice of gathering brought the family extra food from their haul of huckleberries, chestnuts and 'honeysuckle apples' (the small, light green and tart fruit of the wild honeysuckle bush). Her dad also supplemented the family's diet by hunting and fishing. Bear meat was also on their menu, and Geraldine remembered a lady guest asking for an onion that she could eat in order to modify the taste of her bruin feast.

Mrs. Wynn also observed that those neighbors who didn't own tillable land suffered much more from poverty than those who had truck patches or gardens. Geraldine's berry picking helped to finance her clothes. Hucksters, buying and selling to rural folk, visited locally. There was also the 'ragman' who would gather old clothes, papers and other unwanted items. Fortunately for Geraldine, the ragman stored some things in her grandfather's shed. This arrangement allowed the inquisitive girl to look at his stock. It was there that she found some hymnals that she was able to give to an impoverished, nearby church group that was meeting in a tent. The storage shed was where she also spied an attractive dress which she asked for and which she was given. From their own accumulated rags, the Bower family quilted bedding and braided rugs.

Geraldine Wynn said that they walked wherever they went, including the one-room elementary school where she and her siblings studied. That was a one-mile jaunt. Her teacher also took the students to one of the larger farms to teach them how to square dance. Then, as now, Memorial Day was the occasion for a parade and ball game in Loganton. An even-more-special day was when a circus came to Loganton. Geraldine and her mother walked the two miles to that event, although the youngster had trouble staying awake for the long walk home.

The creation of the Civilian Conservation Corps as a federal work program put young men to work in many areas far from home. Many of the CCC projects involved building woodland roads. CCC workers were paid $25.00 per month, with $20.00 being sent home, and the worker was allowed to have the $5.00 to squander as he wished during the upcoming month. How many romances were kindled by the presence of Civilian Conservation Corps camps in an area? How many young CCC workers were enchanted by attractive local girls, or, conversely, how many local females' hearts fluttered at the sight of the neatly uniformed stranger to their area? Apparently, a solid marriage resulted from the meeting (*see* Chapter 6) of the local girl, Thelma Witmyer, and the CCC member from Texas, Milburn Matthews. Here, too, another Sugar Valley romance: Geraldine Bower and a CCC worker from the Rauchtown area, named Arthur Wynn.

Although it was thought that her dad's family had some dealings with the valley's noted moonshiner, Prince Farrington, Geraldine Bower Wynn's maternal side of the family had little or nothing to do with Farrington. Geraldine did recall, however, that her mother never said anything critical of Prince Farrington. To her mother, Farrington was a benevolent man who helped people who were in need.

Although Geraldine Bower Wynn died in the hospital in Lock Haven in early 2011, her body was returned for burial at the Mount Pleasant Cemetery at Rosecrans, about three miles from the home where she had been born.

## WHEN THE LESS TYPICAL WAS TYPICAL

Like Charles Dorwart and the late Geraldine Bower Wynn, many of the older citizens of Lycoming and Clinton counties in Pennsylvania remember living through or hearing parents graphically describe what *real poverty* was like. Real poverty involved extending the lives of badly worn leather shoes by putting strips of rubber automobile inner tubes or pads of newspaper pages inside. Similarly, the Depression-era generation remembers clothing being handed down, altered to fit, and then being handed down once again. Clothing that became too worn to wear was cut into pieces to become the makings of patch quilts or coverlets. Feed mills became the boutiques where poor folk bought used and patterned cloth feed bags to be used for clothing, curtains, etc. Plain feed bags, on the other hand, were sewn into bedding and kitchen towels. Bed sheets— once they became too worn through the middle—were cut and re-sown, with the edges now seamed to form the middle. Cloth that, seemingly, had reached the end of the line simply assumed a new utilitarian form: the dust cloth. Today, the only folks wearing threadbare clothing are the millionaire country singers!

It may be difficult for most citizens of our gluttonous nation to remember shortages of food or the lack of choices even when food was available. When beef, pork or poultry was served at the dinner table, the bones may already have been extracted in order to boil for a weak broth. If there was no meat available, a poor-person's gravy was made by browning flour in a pan of simmering water. Some families used the dried root of the common chicory plant to create a substitute coffee. Coffee grounds, where used, were often saved to be dried and used another time, while eggshells and vegetable parings were scattered in the family garden to enrich the soil. School lunches were often sparse, with the poorest youngsters carrying only an unbuttered sandwich spread with lard. The more fortunate students carried sandwiches spread with home-made fruit preserves. There might also be seasonal fruit or a hard-boiled egg. Farm youngsters might enjoy a lunch that includes watercress sandwiches. Many rural family members helped fill the family dinner plate by gardening, hunting wild game, fishing the creeks, gathering the seasonal harvest of wild nuts and berries or hunting wild game. Richard Grugan has observed that "They didn't hunt for fun as much then. They hunted for food." Another example of successful scavenging for food: dandelion, a despicable weed today, was a welcome dish, served with a savory bacon dressing, on many Depression-era dinner tables.

For rural folk, the preservation of food was a natural activity. Bernard Wynn, the grandson of a Sugar Valley farmer who also did both driving and hiding of Prince Farrington's moonshine, mentioned an activity rarely seen today: the smoking of meats. The wood to be burned for the smoking process would be dead chestnut mixed with either sassafras, maple, or hickory. Other types of wood might smoke or 'cure' the meats, but they wouldn't enhance the flavor. Add to the home-style preservation of foods the order in which foods had to be consumed, with perishables eaten quickly and the other foods smoked or, with produce, stored in underground bunkers or within cellars. From the proper preservation and storage came the feasts of fall and winter. On the other hand, Marie Segraves was remembered for the canning of venison.

## A FUEL WORTH STEALING FOR

When the train stopped at Antes Fort, it was common for local citizens to wait for a compassionate engineer to toss down a few chunks of coal in order for those below to gather the welcomed fuel for their homes. One can imagine this happening many times in many towns across the country. In fact, Harry Barner told of something similar occurring in nearby Jersey Shore. There, we're told, there was a slight grade in the railroad tracks. So, someone would grease those tracks. While the engineer struggled to get his train off the greased slope, locals would climb onto the more isolated coal-laden cars and unload some of the precious chunks of carbon fuel.

One childhood incident related by Bob F. Johnson of the McElhattan area: As a youngster, he and his father, George Johnson, cut a lot of lumber with a crosscut saw. His father also farmed for others. Robert, as a boy, climbed onto a car of an idle coal train and tossed a small pile of coal to the ground. After the somewhat lighter train chugged from the area, he went home and told his father what he had done. The father first scolded him for the theft and then hitched his horse to a wagon and went to gather the booty.

Bob Miller's memories were interesting for his remembrances of little improvements that came into his family's life. He remembered the addition of electricity to his life in 1942 and the purchase of a used Farmall 8 tractor with its stud wheels.

## GLEANING

The public recognition of 'charity' has roots as old as the Old Testament of the Christian Bible. There is the specific admonition (Leviticus: 19:9-10), "And when ye reap the harvest of your land, thou shalt not wholly reap the corners of thy field, neither shalt thou gather the gleanings of thy harvest. And thou shalt not glean thy vineyard, neither shalt thou gather *every* grape of thy vineyard; thou shalt leave them for the poor and stranger. I am the LORD your God."

Further, one of the great pastoral tales in the Bible, as well as its most romantic story, is the one found in the second chapter of the book of Ruth. Here, the reader is treated to a love story, the story of a celebrated marriage between a Hebrew and a Moabitess, and the story of fulfilling one's obligation to the poor. The gleaning field was the setting for the meeting of Boaz, the land owner, and Ruth, the widow and barley gleaner who was to become his wife.

Rural Americans, during the era of the Great Depression, experienced the phenomenon of gleaning. John Muthler adds a local view to the picture of gleaning. John was a young man when Prince Farrington lived on the adjoining farm between Antes Fort and Jersey Shore. Muthler recalls having relatives who lived in Cogan Valley, off Route 287, in the area of White Pine and Brookside. Those relatives raised peas for a cannery. This was just one of many places where one could see the Biblical tradition of gleaning still being observed. Local people, Muther remembers, were allowed to come into those Cogan Valley fields to gather peas that the machines hadn't harvested.

## PRINCE: A WELCOME PRESENCE

If a new plant moved into an area, everyone recognized its economic potential immediately. When the new moonshiner moved into Clinton and Lycoming counties in Pennsylvania, the realization was slower to happen. The economic impact of this entrepreneurial moonshiner was assured but not obvious. The acceptance of Prince Farrington and his fellow outlaws came about slowly, helped by his liquid assets and his cash on hand. A stranger who wanted to give money to people who would help him cook and carry his liquor wouldn't remain a stranger for long. An equally enthusiastic welcome came from those people who craved the alcoholic drinks that were, from 1919 until 1933, illegal to make, market and consume. Many local people were eager to bend and break stifling laws in order to help Prince by working for him or by buying his superior quality whiskey for their superior quality thirst.

A hint of Prince's economic impact would be found in the comments of Dave Ritter's dad. Dave noted that his dad had a saying, "It didn't take too much to know who was running moonshine for Prince because they usually drove a fairly new car." This couldn't be better illustrated than by viewing the photo of the three members of the Meixell family who worked with Prince Farrington. All had new cars!

One image of Prince is as an employer of children. He hired people to work for him. Older teens might be given an advance in order for them to be able to buy a bicycle. This would give them transportation to his farm. He was also known for hiring younger, local Antes Fort-area children. They were usually less than ten years old. He'd pay about eight cents an hour. Then he led the toddlers to the field to hoe corn. They were also admonished to *stay out of the rye*! They were then left to labor unsupervised. He'd return to find them playing "hide and seek" in the rye. Prince would chastise them and fire them! But, the next day, Farrington would be back, hiring the same urchins in an on-going effort to get a good corn crop. While his methods may seem harsh, he still paid slightly more than other employers of young folk.

## AN ISOLATED FARM TALE

Charles Dorwart, whose memory has repeatedly given readers glimpses of early 20th-century life of the Antes Fort/Jersey Shore areas of Lycoming County, also recalled another personal incident. As a youngster, he worked on the tenant farm of the Fox family. That farm was located just east of Antes Fort. While Dorwart was working on the wagon behind the baling machine, he swung the large hook used to capture the emerging hay bale and pulled it onto the wagon. At that instant, the baler lurched, and young Dorwart got a severe gash in his ankle. Also revealing the special strength of childhood ties: Dowart notes that today, there are no members of the Fox family living in Antes Fort, yet several family members still drive the extra miles in order to return to the town's United Methodist Church for Sunday worship.

## A MODERN SPINDLETOP?

During the latter half of the 1800s, Pennsylvania was the premier oil-producing state. However, the Keystone State was replaced as the nation's great oil center with the discovery of the rich quantities of petroleum that lay beneath the surface of Texas and Oklahoma. Near Beaumont, Texas, on January 10, 1901, the discovery of an incredible bed of oil ushered in the modern age of oil drilling and retrieval. The site was known as *Spindletop*. It was after the discovery at Spindletop that oil finally moved past coal as a national fuel source. The abundance of oil also helped produce the nation's proliferation of automobiles and trains.

## A SIMILAR STORY, REPEATED

Prince David Farrington's moonshining and bootlegging had little impact on the environment. Purists would have trouble even locating his work sites; much less seeing any environmental harm resulting therefrom. However...

As the early 21st century unfolded, many were, once again, lamenting hard economic times. While the economy of the Clinton/Lycoming counties' area was far richer than it was during Prince Farrington's heyday, employment had become harder to find and harder to keep. Once again, a new source of wealth appeared. This new 'moonshine' was also produced in the hinterlands, such as the forests north of Lock Haven and Swissdale. Trucks could be seen, at almost any hour, driving into and out of the mountains. New money was arriving in what was once "Farrington Country." The name of the new commodity was not "white lightening," however, and it was not hidden in false fenders and gas tanks. This was natural gas and it was turning the area into "Marcellus Country." This fuel comes from a gas-rich geological phenomenon known as Marcellus Shale. The gas is found in a stratum that lies about 8,000 feet beneath our own feet. A mixture of water and chemicals is pumped into the earth in a process identified as 'fracking' so that the gas is primed for removal or for capping for future extraction. Today, Pennsylvania is one of a quartet of states that sit astride this trillion-dollar treasure.

The number of new wells involved in this boom is expected to shoot past the 100,000 figure eventually! Williamsport, some are predicting, will become the state's third great economic hub, forming a triangle with

Pittsburgh and Philadelphia. The companies that are among the energy giants of America are now drilling into the region's rich beds of Marcellus shale gas. The purchase of mineral rights and the tapping into the local economy are creating wealth for distant entrepreneurs as well as for local landowners, business owners and field workers. As happens with many technological advances, there is a mix of culture shock and bulging wallets. In a single day, one can observe the many noisy, road-mangling trucks hauling water from the Susquehanna to the new drilling sites while also noticing the men in hard hats who are carrying boxes of meals from the local eateries. Modern terminology has been developed to help people express their rejection or acceptance of the new mix of woe and wealth. Opponents declare, "NIMBY" ("Not in my back yard!"), while others might proclaim "PROWL" ("Please ravish our woeful lawn!"). The new 'moonshiners' are among us.

## · 6 ·

# The Human Vortex

Prince David Farrington lived in a world where the law was flouted, and a narcotic nectar was created and marketed. Prince used charisma and cash to draw countless others into his operation. And wherever Prince induced someone to work for him, that individual's family members would likely have their lives greatly altered. At first glance, one could mistake Prince Farrington for a moocher, but he was much, much more. He was one of those people who can best be described as a human vortex, an all-consuming whirlpool.

Prince needed you. He needed you to do one or more of the huge catalog of chores to be done in order for him to be able to make his moonshine whiskey, hide it, haul it, and market it. He also needed people to inform him, hide him from pursuers, feed him when he was a fugitive, mislead his pursuers about where he might be, and so on.

First among those who were willingly or reluctantly allied with the moonshiner was his wife. Martha was followed by their children and his early criminal comrades. For example, Prince brought in his brother, Charles ("Charl"), in part with the gift of a house in Lamar. Charl, his wife and their extended family members were also involved. Eventually, even though he was living and working in Pennsylvania, he managed to involve some of his relatives in North Carolina. For benefit or loss, dozens swelled to hundreds. Whether relatives, friends, associates, businessmen, or government officials, all who ventured too close were sucked into Prince Farrington's lawless vortex.

## A MOONSHINER'S JOB DESCRIPTION

What was the process that was so critical to Prince Farrington and other moonshiners or legitimate whiskey producers? Before a single drop of moonshine could be distilled for sale, the distilling equipment had to be secretly secured and secretly assembled. A natural water supply was needed, and if not available, water had to be acquired through pipes or some other system. Then the supplies for the actual distilling had to be secretly obtained and taken to the sight, undetected. These supplies would include grain and sugar.

Avoiding detection was a major goal. Considerations included secretly securing the materials for all the distilling apparatus, then getting it into the area and to the site or sites of the stills.

There are many versions of the moonshining operation in print. Here is one more. It is the version given to us by Lester Seiler, in his own words, during the 1983 interview (see the bibliography). Seiler regularly worked in the moonshining trade with his father, Turbit Seiler, and sometimes worked directly with Prince Farrington. While his interview is certainly informative, the reader is reminded that this was only one young man's occasional glimpse of Prince Farrington and may not reflect properly on Prince's career in moonshining. His taped interview is not always clear. As nearly as we can understand it, it is as follows.[8]

> No. No. That [boiler] was steel. He didn't use a copper still. He used all steam. His still was one of them hogshead barrels. What did they hold—a hundred and some gallons? The second barrel (he had hooked on a second barrel that was maybe higher than the refrigerator that sets there). It would hold a four-foot square box one time. Now, he could do it with his [steel] still when he run, but he couldn't do it with a copper still. You see, he could put all his mash and everything in it because there was no fire there. He cooked his by steam. He never had no fire under the mash.
>
> With a copper still, you've got to put your fire under that, and then, if you had too much stuff in, it would aburn it; stick to the bottom sometimes. If you were monkeying around and let the fire die down, you kind of quit boiling a little bit, or, if you wasn't quite near enough boiled, then you. You see, you stirred

---

8. Question marks indicate an unclear phrase or two.

it until it was just about boiled, but if it don't start boiling quick enough and, sometimes, you can burn it that way.

I'll tell you: your first steam that comes out is your strongest alcohol. That's purtin' near [almost pure] alcohol. You want to try and keep that as much as you can 'cause the longer you cook it, the less strength it has. We used to take and always run eight to ten gallons, depends on how much time we had. That's called 'backins.' You put that back in. It had a different taste. It would taste kind of woolen-like. It might have been maybe 40, 50, 60 proof; you know, that way. You could get drunk. It wouldn't be as strong as beer is, if you wanted to drink much of it. We'd take and run that again. That's called backins, you understand. Prince did, too. For a long time, Prince had a barrel of it [backins] that he'd take and run back in.

[Interviewer questions: "How big was the boiler that made the steam?"]

Well, I don't know, like for respecting horsepower. The only thing is, it wasn't put onto a motor. I'd say it was about three foot across the boiler where the—was in. He'd run four of them boxes a day, four of them four-foot boxes a day. One of them boxes oughta make about 30 to 40 gallons.

["He had this near the Florida Farm?"]

In answering this question, Lester Seiler describes a moonshining building that reminds one of a famed Frank Lloyd Wright structure in Fayette County, Pennsylvania.

Yeah, down there's what they called "the Barner piece." [More descriptive lines follow, then—] There's a spring right down over the hill. That's where he [Prince] had his building, you know—right across [spanning] the creek. The creek run right through the building. He had it fixed up that they never carried no water. The water was pumped into the boiler from there, and it was high enough up above the spring—piped in—that they could take hold and clear to wash the boxes or anything like that there without carrying! That's the same way when they run that stuff out. Oh, I don't know; Prince had 150 pigs out there in that pen. Still, they'd eat the mash. Clean it up. They'd run it out there in the lot. That way, they had kind of a trough. Then the rest of it—that didn't stay in the trough—run over and just run down through the woods and green briars.

["How much would they get a gallon, for a gallon of whiskey?"]

Well, around, I'd say, seven, eight dollars for the average. The first we ever made, we got 16 for it. We got 20 for applejack. He had a couple barrels of cider. We run it off.

We had a little still in the cellar—our cellar. And we took, and we run these barrels of hard cider off and made apple jack. Dad and them got $20 a jug for that. Then you'd get ten, twelve for whiskey.

["Why would you get so much more for that?"]

Well, apparently more of a scarcity of drink. And another thing: it went mostly to high-class people. I'll tell you, old Jake Heimer [1853-1937] got about half of what we had. That old barber over there in Lock Haven. He'd take and buy whiskey from us for years and years. Why, he bought enough whiskey from us that we coulda bought a farm if we had kept it (brief chuckle).

## A DIGRESSION

Lester Seiler wandered from his subject on one occasion to tell the interviewer about hunting information he was eager to share.

You know, a bear will tramp every time in the same place when they tramp the road. Like, he will come in here to drink, he'll put that foot over there. He comes in here tomorrow or next week, he'll put that foot over there—the same place. And I'll tell you another thing: You can chase six bears down a trail and I'll bet you there will only be one set of tracks. Yes sir!

His listeners seemed doubtful. Was this the claim of some rustic windbag? Not Mr. Seiler. Here's a learned observation: "Black bears do, in fact, have the peculiar behavior of stepping in the same footprints made by previous bears when traveling on a trail—These trails might lead to seasonal food sources, like a productive berry patch or cornfield, wallows (where they roll in water to keep cool) or through thick cover. I've seen bear trails with these distinctive depressions in Clinton County, among other places in Pennsylvania."[9]

## ... AND THE PAUPERS!

Prince Farrington was a man of several talents. Among the finer ones was his organizational ability. Not only did he organize the workforce and the manufacture of illicit whiskey, but he also organized the construction of numberless stills in countless locations. He also organized the sale and distribution of the moonshine. He organized the purchase of huge quantities of sugar and other ingredients. Likewise, Farrington organized the stashing of the finished whiskey in countless hiding places. He also organized his schedule, employing the full 24-hour cycle to his needs. Lastly, he organized the system for acquiring his main ingredient, the corn . . .

Farrington paid inflated prices for the corn provided by area farmers. Some of these farmers had several sources of Farrington farthings. In addition to the inflated prices that they received for their corn, they could get extra income from the presence of a still somewhere in the wooded lands therein and yet another payoff for hiding a stash of whiskey and, perhaps, nurturing it, as recalled by Thelma Matthews. This income was a powerful factor when farmers' support of Prince Farrington was needed. For example, this money would be a major influence when Prince was looking for shelter from pursuing revenue agents. Local lore says that he and his vehicle would suddenly disappear into a farmer's barn until the pursuers left the scene. We've cited at least one case that was supported by testimony.

There was another strong tie between Prince Farrington and some of the farmers: His whiskey. The delivery system involved a Farrington helper making the rounds of certain farm customers. The Farrington

---
9. So writes Mark Ternent of the Pennsylvania Game Commission (July 16th, 2010).

worker would see the empty mason jar that had been placed where he could locate it. The mason jar would be sitting on a one-dollar bill. Farrington's agent would fill the jar with the juice of the moonlight and take the dollar. While most cases of the farmers working with Prince Farrington seem similar, all had unique developments. Consider the case of George and Gladys Rockey of Rockey Road, a couple of ridges east of the Florida Fruit Farm.

In later years, George and Gladys Rockey were honored as top farmers, but that didn't erase their record of support for Prince Farrington. They had allowed a still to be constructed on their land, just off Harbaugh Road, a short distance from their house. And when Boyd "Duke" Greak was shot while working that still, he was allowed to recuperate in an unknown location—right on their property. Both of the Rockeys—husband and wife—liked Farrington and the money he provided to them. George Rockey was quoted as proclaiming, "We never knew the Depression."

Nor did the Farringtons.

## FUNDS BEYOND COUNTING

> My sister she works in the laundry,
> My father sells bootlegger gin,
> My mother she takes in washing,
> My God! How the money rolls in![10]

Prince Farrington not only sold bootlegger liquor; he manufactured it as well. He had money coming in from both ends of the operation. No one doubted that Farrington, at his career peak, was worth millions. The reader is reminded that a $20 bill was a small fortune to the average citizen of the era.

Harold "Dutch" Washburn of Sugar Valley remembers when he and his family lived as neighbors to Prince Farrington while the Farringtons still lived on the Florida Fruit Farm near Loganton. Another neighbor, and friend of Washburn, John Wagner, also spent his childhood in a

---

10. Early song lyrics, quoted in Bailey, p. 776.

ramshackle old farmhouse, a neighbor to Prince. The outside appearance of the old dwelling belied the occasional wealth that was funneled through its rustic doorway. Wagner recalled that when he was a child, he saw Prince, Joe Gardner, and several of the moonshiners gather at the Wagner house after another batch of whiskey had been marketed. His parents' kitchen table would be stacked high with money, awaiting friendly division. Although Wagner still lives in the Loganton area, the old hovel is gone. That property now rests beneath the waters of the Lock Haven Water Company Reservoir.

Some folks enjoy telling of their childhood poverty when they claim they had *everything* but money. Farrington's children seemed to have had *nothing* but money. Stories have been told of Farrington's children playing with $20 bills. They had spending money when most children had but pennies available to purchase the commodities of kinder-hood. Leonard Parucha, another nonagenarian with a very clear mind and strong voice, described one facet of Prince's wealth at its height. "His kids played with silver dollars." Cindy Toomes, a niece of the moonshine magnate, saw her cousins playing with stacks of paper money, some tied in rolls and used for play, pretending that the rolls of bills were toy cars. She also remembers seeing Prince's son, Prince Jr. ("Whitey"), driving a toy motorized car. Prince's children were envied rarities in their generation, unlike the current generation, when nearly all children have small fortunes at their disposal.

As mentioned in Chapter 8, Prince had a close relationship with the owner of Thompson's meat market in Jersey Shore. A businessman with a different attitude toward Prince, but a cooperative businessman, as well, was Dan Hills' grandfather. Dan remembers that his grandfather, O. B. Hills, owned a coal and lumber yard in Mill Hall. While Dan's "granddad was all against alcohol," he accepted Prince as a reliable customer. Prince would sometimes stop at the business office to declare, "O. B., I'm going to get raided." and he would name the date, benefiting from having informants in high places. Prince would then settle his account with O. B. Hills before disappearing for some time until things quieted again.

Prince Farrington obviously loved moonshining. He also relished opportunities to spend.

Although Farrington wasn't paying taxes on his moonshining and bootlegging earnings, he had heavy expenses, as many entrepreneurs would know. Prince Farrington paid huge sums for the equipment for his network of stills, as well as their maintenance. As centenarian Miller Stamm related, he was once summoned to weld some damaged pipes. The damage had occurred when a still attendee let the fire get too hot, melting some of the couplings.

Farrington also paid large sums for the corn, the source of which was area farmers. By paying inflated prices for the corn, Prince was buying a farmer's grain and his silence. For a moonshiner with the vision of a Prince Farrington, developing and cultivating workers and sympathetic neighbors was a vital part of life. He needed farmers who would sell him the corn, understanding merchants[11] who would sell him large quantities of sugar, workers for running the stills, workers who would transport the finished fluid, and people who were willing to hide the whiskey at its several stages of aging and processing, as well as those folks whose only involvement was to avoid reporting a felonious neighbor, or a willingness to allow him to hide on the property if being pursued. Robert J. Weaver now lives in Booneville, in Sugar Valley. That's about seven miles from his birthplace, just north of Rosecrans. While still a youth, Robert Weaver recalled an incident when revenue agents were pursuing Prince. Farrington stopped and asked Robert's dad if he could park briefly in Mr. Weaver's garage. He was fully concealed when a car full of agents drove past. Having lost their quarry, they soon drove back in the other direction. Soon after that, Farrington thanked Mr. Weaver and drove away. Later that evening, Robert J. Weaver recalls, someone brought his dad a gallon of moonshine whiskey and a $20 bill.

As critical to Prince's success, as any person on his support list, would be those who were willing to trade favors—those law-enforcement officers, at several levels, who would avoid action against Prince Farrington's criminal activities or delay action for a critical length of time. Their bribes might include money or some of the forbidden liquor. These corrupt law-enforcement officials are discussed further in later chapters.

Martha Farrington regularly complained about Prince's "dirty money." This led to a bizarre interlude involving their youngest son. That

---

11. Such as the owners of Thompson Meats, who are discussed in Chapter 8.

son, Prince D. Farrington Jr. ("Whitey"), wrote an account in 1994. The younger Prince Farrington wrote of a childhood incident that occurred when his father, Prince Sr., was hunting and when Whitey's mother, Martha, was upstairs and—as was often the case—not inclined to venture downstairs. Whitey saw an opportunity to impress his mother, whom he frequently heard condemning the 'dirty' money that Prince brought home. Whitey knew that a large supply of gold certificates lay beneath some blankets in a closet. He lifted one of several bags of 'dirty money' and carried it to the pantry.

In the pantry was a sink with drainboards on both ends. He put water into the sink and dumped the money. It floated, he recalled, like "leaves of lettuce." Whitey washed several hundred certificates in soapy water, then rinsed them in clear water and hung them "all over the place, lamp shades, couches, etc." The newly cleaned money was still drying when Prince returned from hunting. He had several friends with him and all came into the house to get warm and enjoy a drink. When Junior announced to his dad how he had cleaned the bagful of dirty money, the prosperous and genial moonshiner simply observed, "You sure got it good and clean. That's all I can say." Prince's hunting buddies, who may also have been impressed with Whitey's effort, included an unnamed state senator, plus Tom Buckley, a highway patrolman, and Tom Little, the sheriff.

## SMOKE IN THE BOTTOMLAND

On March 4, 2009, the author interviewed Thelma Witmyer Matthews at Manor Care Health Services of Jersey Shore. With the support of Thelma's daughter-in-law, Laura Matthews, we were given a charming glimpse of a past period of rural American life. Thelma told of a childhood during which her family farmed and "killed lots of rattlesnakes." The small farm on which she grew and matured was located east of Loganton and about a dozen miles southeast of the Florida Fruit Farm of Prince Farrington. Because Thelma's father was crippled by rheumatism, he was unable to handle much of the normal farm work. This situation meant harder work for Thelma and her siblings.

Beyond the regular chores, the family did extra work to gain some income. Mrs. Witmyer, Thelma's mother, raised flowers and did a splendid business of selling the bouquets in Williamsport. They also picked huckleberries. "I always always wanted to pick more huckleberries than Mom," she joked. Her mother and the children walked for several miles to get into huckleberry country. Once there, the children were sent to pick from the fullest bushes in order to keep them working while their mother picked around the edges of the patches. Once, a brother, seeing a rattlesnake nearby, called to their mother; she grabbed a heavy stick and broke the snake's back. By that time, Thelma also shouted. There was a second rattler. That day, Thelma recalled, they killed five rattlers and a lone copperhead.

The berries were picked and put directly into small buckets in which *True Blue* brand tobacco had been sold. Once filled, the buckets of huckleberries were carefully poured into larger baskets. Picking into the small buckets was a way to prevent the accidental spilling of a large quantity of the berries. Once picked, the berry harvesters trod the long walk home. Thelma said that her mother always carried a collapsible cup made of aluminum. If they passed a spring, her mother took the cup, filled it with cool water, and slowly poured it over the inside of the wrist as a way of cooling the body. Their harvest of huckleberries was then loaded onto a spring wagon and pulled by horse to Williamsport, where they were marketed for 26 cents a quart.

Thelma also related her extreme sadness when she and her husband sold their 16 head of dairy cows to a farm near Watsontown, about 25 miles to the east. "I bawled like a baby," she said. Then, she told of visiting that farm some years later. When the farm wife told a son to bring the grazing cattle for milking, Thelma said, "Wait! Wait!" Then, her eyes shining and her voice becoming animated, she told of walking toward the herd and calling, "Come oo . . . on! Come oo . . . on!" She soon had the cattle walking to the barn for milking, just as she had coaxed them to do years before.

If her father hadn't been crippled, she suggests that he'd not have agreed to hide liquor for Prince Farrington. However, it was done, in this case, "to put food on the table" or to get some needed article of clothing for one of the family. In any case, the Witmyers did store illegal liquor for Prince Farrington. It was stored in their attic and beneath the straw in the barn. They also took care of the kegs by lifting and shaking them daily. This was done to help the aging process. "That," she declared, "makes muscles!" While Thelma Witmyer Matthews' family used little alcohol, they did dig a huge hole in the floor of the barn. There, the Witmyers hid their personal keg of whiskey. They had a bicycle tire pump that was used to pump air into the barrel in order to draw liquor from the embedded keg for family members. All this sequestering of liquor also added a fearful aspect to her parents' lives.

Among her most vivid memories was one that involved their hidden cache of Farrington whiskey. One day, she saw one of Prince Farrington's cronies, Jake Kohberger, rushing toward their house. He jumped the picket fence and shouted, "Hide the whiskey! Hide the whiskey! The revenuers are coming!"

Thelma recalled, "That was a scramble!"

The kegs had to be carried down two flights of steps and rolled across the floor for loading onto a spring wagon. The valuable cargo was then driven down into the wooded part of the bottomland. There, it was quickly stacked among the laurel and other thick, concealing growth. Despite Jake Kohberger's alarmed state, the alarm was false. No revenuers appeared.

Upon reaching womanhood, Thelma Witmyer married Milburn Matthews, a Civilian Conservation Corps worker from Texas. They stayed on the family farm.

More than one family maintained stills in the heavily wooded acres south of the farm of Thelma and Milburn. Once, the Witmyer cows' behavior became very erratic after they had wandered into some of the discarded mash from a nearby still. Thelma also recalled mornings when she and Milburn would stand on their front steps and look across the bottomland to the south. Their sweeping gazes would spot four or five columns of smoke rising into the morning sky, each indicating the location of someone's secluded still.

Thelma Witmyer Matthews, a vibrant daughter of the land, assured the visitor, "Hard work never killed anyone!" One would be unwise to try to refute her observation. Several months after the interview, Thelma died. She was in her 100th year.

## PRINCE, CHARMING

Prince was a man of modest height and a muscular frame. Balding began while Prince was in his late teens. His physical description, as related by Douglas Clyde Parker, seems to show a bit too much influence from his interviews with Prince's daughter, Gladys. This impression is gleaned from the parts of the Parker article that tell readers that Farrington "had a— hide—as tough as an elephant's" and was "built square like a bull and that strong." As discussed further in Chapter 16, such exaggeration isn't needed. Farrington was a real person with genuine positive and negative attributes. Is he worth embellishing as a moonshining myth? Of course not. Is he worth remembering? For that, Prince Farrington is highly qualified.

## PHYSICALLY SPEAKING

Prince David Farrington was of average height and weight, with a marked change in his physical appearance as the years and lifestyle took their toll. The aging Prince was described by reporter Richard B. Stone as being "massive and muscular,"[12] with a chubby and tranquil face, scarred on the nose, requiring glasses on occasion, walking with a limp and nursing a diabetic condition that was exacerbated by his drinking. A glance at Prince's portrait, when he was in his 24th year, shows a seemingly intense and handsome young man, similar to Stone's description above, but nattily dressed and with a modest cleft in his chin.

## SARTORIAL CONTRADICTIONS

On his husky frame, according to Stone's observations, Prince Farrington wore the shirt, overalls and (sometimes) the jacket of a farmer. Stone noted that, while the clothes were not ragged, his shoes were cut by the aging moonshiner himself in order to accommodate his diabetes-deformed feet. As mentioned in the preceding paragraph, Prince in formal attire would fit comfortably in the most formal circles. His grandson, Dave, reflected on his years of seeing his grandfather in informal clothes. Dave tells of his being stunned by the formal appearance made by Prince on the occasion of their having attended the movie *Carbine Williams* together. "That was the only time I ever saw him dressed up. In my memory, Prince always wore khaki-like work clothes. I was surprised to see pictures of him in his heyday. He was always dressed up. Like a clothes horse, almost, but I knew him as an older man."

Prince Farrington seems to have thought a magnificent automobile was also part of one's wardrobe. He loved new cars. As "Chip" Taylor

---
12. *GRIT*, April 9, 1950.

observed, "Most of the time I knew Prince, he had a big car, a Nash. They made the Nash big at that time, and it had a big trunk in the back and Prince would use that for himself."

Prince seemed to be comfortable in the kitchen. Perhaps his occasional tantrums drove Martha from the kitchen; but we learn of Prince sometimes cooking for his dysfunctional family. Lester Seiler observed,

> It would be nothing for him to take a chunk of meat from the stove, like a beef—something like that. That's the way they did. They didn't sit down at the table. Really, I'd been at their place a lot—and I never seen anybody sit down at the table and eat, you know, like a family—There was purtin' near always sumpin' on the stove.[13] You know, at that time, they didn't have electric stoves like we have now. They had these here wood stoves. There was purtin' near always sumpin', a kettle of some kind, and a pretty big one. I'd seen Prince go over there, with a fork that way, and take a chunk of meat in his two hands—and eat that. No bread; nothing else!

## THE BUSINESS PRINCE

Prince Farrington had no time for keeping track of money. If he wasn't going to obey the tax laws, why keep cumbersome financial records? For most of his adult years, he had an abundance of money, far more than needed to avoid financial worries.

In 1924, Prince Farrington had a building constructed in Randleman for Bob Caudel. It was large enough for Caudel to use for a home and store. Cindy Toomes felt that it was done as a way to repay Caudel for the months that he spent in prison in Prince's stead. As mentioned in Chapter 2, Prince used the construction to his advantage by having it built with hidden compartments where money and liquor could be hidden.

Prince had a knack for making accommodations. Despite the several major raids and several arrests, he also seems to have had arrangements that allowed him some flexibility in his illicit enterprises. He was able to

---

13. Lester Seiler's truncated phrase, meaning almost, was purtin' near, or pretty nearly.

convey to some members of the legal establishment the understanding that there was enough profit for him to share if he was just given some space to operate and the time to conduct even a partial program.

The way he approached his moonshining suggests that he realized that he couldn't keep the existence of every still a secret, but if he had enough stills operating, the several undetected ones would pay richly.

## THE REVENUERS

In 1999, Alan Jackson recorded a song, "Revenooer Man," that had been written by another country artist, Johnny Paycheck. The song has surprising lyrics since the theme of much country music is anti-government, suggesting that an anti-government attitude is typical of American 'rednecks.' However, Jackson's song, "Revenooer Man," seems to favor the usually-reviled revenue agents, those government workers who had to push into the widespread moonshine lands of America, such as the lands inhabited by Prince Farrington and his friends.

The marvel isn't that Prince David Farrington served jail terms in many different prisons. The marvel is that, with many stills operating and many people being involved, for more than 40 years, Farrington didn't spend much more time in prison. Reasons that one might offer for Prince's *relatively* few episodes behind bars would include:

- The sympathy of many people for his defiance of local and federal laws.
- The skill which he exhibited in hiding so much of his operation.
- The lack of law-enforcement resources needed to properly pursue the nation's vast number of moonshiners/bootleggers, including Prince Farrington.
- The power of the bribe.

During the 1930s, government agents were supposed to be dedicated to the enforcement of laws that would prevent the making, transporting, selling and consuming of alcohol. They were supposed to police one of the world's longest boundaries as well as all the homes and hollows within those lengthy borders. This dedication, during the thirties, got those agents an annual salary of less than $3,000. Bribes were a common form of supplemental income.

In the life of Prince David Farrington, the long arm of the law was often found to have mutated into an outstretched hand. It appears to have been common for Prince to offer—and to have accepted—bribes for some service in return. He successfully bought critical favors from many willing individuals, from farmers to federal agents.

It has been recorded that once, a moonshining acquaintance of Prince was raided. Prince quickly distributed $12,000 to the raiding agents, who left the scene empty-handed, except for the generous bribes they had just earned. Prince reasoned that if the agents demolished his friend's still, they would soon want to raid his. While many citizens might cringe at the thought, it was a normal arrangement. Bribery benefits all parties—except the law-abiding.

Quoting Prince: "I got so many months to make liquor at this site." This was how he explained to his family the dynamics of bribery. He let the right (meaning the 'bribed') authorities know of a new operation. Then, he'd get all the production he could from a still for a set period of months. Then, Prince would notify the authorities, who would get considerable publicity while destroying a moonshining operation, one which they should have been raiding months earlier.

## A MEMORABLE TERM IN PRISON

In the 1930s, P. D. Farrington spent some time in the Northeastern Penitentiary in Lewisburg, Pennsylvania.[14] He was, while there, prisoner #5784. His prison card from that incarceration also indicates that he had no aliases. This is not surprising. Farrington was a moonshiner and bootlegger for many decades. He had once said, to his son-in-law, "A person's a damned fool for having pictures taken," yet he didn't seem to hesitate to pose for family pictures, and he seemed to enjoy the publicity that was growing in its coverage of Farrington as a celebrated outlaw.

When asked, one time, if he preferred the local people in Pennsylvania or those of his childhood home in North Carolina, Prince observed, "I like these closed-mouth Dutchmen."

Of course, a high percentage of his 'close-mouthed' neighbors were also Scotch or Scots-Irish. While the Pennsylvania Germans gravitated toward the state's better farming areas, it was common for the Scotch

---
14. July 12th, 1937 to September 27th, 1939.

and Scots-Irish to go into the Keystone State's more mountainous frontier areas. The most common names in the Williamsport/Lock Haven telephone directory are those beginning with the "Mc" designation. That designation, alone, from Mc Andrew to Mc Williams, exceeds 1,100 entries. Many other Scotch or Irish, or the combined Scots-Irish, family names appear, with hundreds of entries for each.

The ease with which cooperation occurred in the effort to bypass the law is found in the account of Prince Farrington's son, Prince Jr. (known as "Whitey" to family and friends). He said that his father was asked to provide the illegal whiskey for an event being held in the Harrisburg area. Prince asked his son, Prince Jr., to deliver the booze. All was arranged. Young Whitey drove a truck carrying the illegal liquor to the area's main highway, Route 15. There Whitey met a pair of State Police motorcycle patrolmen. He slowed long enough for the two troopers to pull in front. Then, with an impressive police escort, a very nervous Prince Farrington Jr. drove the truck south on Route 15 to the Harrisburg area, where he delivered his contraband cargo to the annual picnic of the Pennsylvania State Police.

## ENOUGH TESTIMONIALS TO QUALIFY FOR SAINTHOOD?

Frances Farrington Gardner, who lives in Bellefonte today, was Prince's niece (Charl's daughter) and Joe Gardner's sister-in-law. She observed the moonshining culture from within. "I lived with Prince," she recalls today. Frances mentions—in particular—her recollection of Prince's family covering for Prince when revenuers came calling. The family's stock answer when asked about Prince's whereabouts: "They're down making apple butter." This, she remembered, was enough to satisfy the agents, who then ended their visit, seemingly satisfied that they had done their duty

Frances thought "very, very, very highly" of her uncle Prince, says the Reverend Dean Hauser, her pastor today. Pastor Hauser's recollection is based on many of Frances Farrington Gardner's accounts; but is summarized in her claim that Prince "was a wonderful uncle and a giving person."

Ed Snook, mentioned several times elsewhere, made this telling observation.

"The big thing about Prince was everybody made money off Prince."

Of course, Ed's reference was to those who helped produce, deliver, provide ingredients, or fulfill many other roles in the Farrington enterprises. Many people profited financially. While some suggested that Prince was very secretive about his 'recipe' for quality whiskey, he apparently shared it with several individuals who used Prince's formula to make moonshine, which Prince bought from them.

John F. Harvey Jr. is a plumber from Castanea, one of the towns in the heart of Farrington country. He relates an account of Floyd Shaffer, an earlier plumber from the same town. Floyd Shaffer says Harvey was jailed for installing plumbing for some of Prince Farrington's moonshining apparatus. Mr. Shaffer was, according to Harvey, "a very respected man." In fact, says Harvey, "Almost everyone who was in bootlegging was respected around this area." His other observation is, "I've never heard a derogatory thing about Prince."

In 1938, when Prince was hoping to be placed on parole, letters attesting to his character were submitted by more than 30 gentlemen, primarily from the towns of Williamsport and Jersey Shore. That list included businessmen, government officials, a deputy sheriff, and one sheriff.

Lynn Bowes, of Jersey Shore, whose family once owned the Jersey Shore *Herald*, remembered that his dad and several other investors bought the land from Prince, near the Stewart/Gheen farm, for the Jersey Shore airport. His recollection: "Prince was well thought of. My father knew him. He probably bought liquor from him."

The Dorwarts of Antes Fort had numerous encounters with Prince Farrington. Among them was a singular incident that left a strong impression on the Dorwart children. An aunt came to visit the Dorwarts. While there, she became sick. Mr. Dorwart told the aunt to rest while he went for a remedy. The dad went to see Prince and explained his problem. Prince excused himself, then returned with a small bottle. Mr. Dorwart returned home and gave some of the bottle's contents to the aunt, who then retired for the night. The next morning, she was fully recovered. The passing of three-quarters of a century since that 'treatment' has not diminished the positive image that the incident imprinted into the minds of the Dorwart children.

We need to address one of the popular local collections of folk tales from the area of Clinton and Lycoming and another half-dozen nearby counties. These stories, related by James York Glimm, are charming; but of doubtful reliability. Here's an example: In this Glimm story (*see* Chapter 3), set in Loganton (Clinton County), Glimm identifies a man named Bill Morris of Milton as being a moonshine-making farmer. Morris had been independently making moonshine over his young daughter's protests. Once, Morris took a couple of five-gallon jugs of moonshine to Loganton, planning to sell them to Prince Farrington. Instead, in Loganton, Morris encountered revenue agents. They wanted to see what was in his jugs, and he was as shocked as the agents to learn that the jugs contained buttermilk! According to Glimm's tale, Morris's daughter had shown her concern for her father by substituting buttermilk for booze. This tale, and many others in Glimm's book, are just a bit too cute to be believable. The most telling quote from Glimm, and one worthy of memorization, says, "The more widespread a character's renown, the more likely it is to be a media creation." That, to a degree, applies to Prince David Farrington Sr.

Among the people whom Prince Farrington encountered in his normal day, or night, he appeared to be readily trusting and an easy-going individual. As a man whose primary role was as a moonshiner/bootlegger, that may have been risky, but it may have created a similar trust in some of those who came into his presence. The first encounters between the late Leo "Chip" Taylor and Prince Farrington demonstrate Prince's easy-going trust. Leo Taylor was a classmate of Prince's future son-in-law, George Porter. While Taylor and Porter were attending high school in Jersey Shore, Taylor also became acquainted with B. W. Coltrane, Prince's nephew and son of Kyle Lindsey Coltrane and Zenadah "Nade" Farrington Coltrane. B. W. and Chip became lifelong friends. Taylor described his first meeting with Prince.

Chip was still a preteen when B. W. Coltrane invited him home. The Coltranes were living with Prince's family at the time. Later they would move to a farm that was owned by Prince and was farther from the Antes Fort/Jersey Shore highway. When B. W. and Chip entered the house, Prince and several others were relaxing and drinking. An open gallon jug was present. When Prince saw Taylor, he wanted to know if the new kid could be trusted. B. W. answered.

"Yeah, Uncle Prince, he can be trusted. If I couldn't trust him I never would have invited him home with me."

Prince said, "Well, that's alright."

Turning to their young guest, Prince asked, "Do you want to drink some of our whiskey? Do you want to try some of our whiskey?"

Leo Taylor suspected that Prince was kidding, but he wasn't sure. His response:

"No. I don't think that I would like it."

"Prince," Taylor recalled, "got a big kick out of that."

Then Farrington told the lad, "Well, I'll tell you. I hope you never start."

Taylor was impressed that "a bootlegger would tell anyone not to start drinking."

Then Prince became even more friendly with Chip Taylor.

"You downed [disparaged] my whiskey. I hope you don't down my cooking. I'm making spaghetti for supper for all of us. When it's ready, I'll call you, and you come in."

"Of course," Taylor remembered, "Prince was real nice that way."

Taylor also recalled witnessing another example of Prince's style. "I only ever met Prince about three or four times. I remember one time that I was there at the house, and Prince came driving up in his big car and he had a fellow with him who acted as though he wasn't too smart. Anyway, Prince said to him, 'Say, how about you taking my car up to Charles, my brother? You know where he lives.' and the man said, 'Oh, yeah, up in Lamar.' Prince said, 'He wants to borrow my car. How about you taking it up?'"

"'Oh, yeah, yeah, yeah,' he said. 'I'll take it.'

"Boy, he was all anxious, doing something for Prince. So he went up there. Prince had told him that somebody would bring him back down. Of course, they did. They brought Prince's car and him back down. Anyway, he came rushing in to Prince and said, 'Prince, you didn't tell me that there was whiskey in that trunk! I was hauling whiskey up there!' Prince said, 'I'll tell you, if I would have told you that there was whiskey in there and the police would have stopped you for anything, you'd have given yourself away right away. Anyway, I wasn't going to tell you there was whiskey in the trunk.'

"We all laughed about that," Taylor continued. "We thought it was pretty funny."

During Prince's later legal, financial and health tribulations, he could bring a smile with the right remark, such as this complaint to his daughter, "Well, Gladys, they've torn up another one of my playhouses!" Similarly droll was this lament: "I wish they'd bring back Prohibition so a fellow could make an honest living again."

Just as Prince David Farrington expressed the wish that Chip Taylor would never begin using alcohol, he also showed concern that his children avoid it. Prince's grandchildren tell of Prince offering his own sons money if they wouldn't drink, apparently with mixed results. His youngest grandson, Craig Porter, over whom Prince had fawned while the boy was yet an infant, died in a drunken driving accident of his own making.

There's also one rather pathetic account regarding the aging nephew, B. W. Coltrane. Leaving a married brother, Wade, in Pennsylvania, the Coltranes[15] returned to North Carolina. B. W. returned to Pennsylvania periodically to visit. On one visit to Pennsylvania, B. W. had dinner at the house of his old friend, "Chip" Taylor. Later in the evening, the Taylors and B. W., along with B. W.'s local lady friend, went to visit George and Gladys Porter at Porters' tavern in Jersey Shore. Later, B. W. excused himself to say 'goodnight' to the Porters. After he left the table, his girlfriend said that she was leaving without waiting for B. W. to return. She exclaimed: "I'm not going to put up with this, the way he drinks!" Having witnessed some problem drinking in her own family, she was unready to face it again with her evening's date. Taylor followed her from the building, vainly trying to change her mind, but she continued hurrying down the street toward her home. It was, Taylor believed, B. W.'s last visit to the state.

"Whitey" Farrington penned a few paragraphs of a 'memoir' in 1994. Here, he related two incidents: the delivery of booze to a state policemen's picnic, cited above and a second memorable incident involving his father and his father's new, four-door, blue 1936 Ford automobile, one of several cars that he owned at the time. Prince Jr. told of being with his father and a friend of his father, Tom Weidler, a lanky and husky Dutchman who spent years working in the railroad shops. The two

---

15. Prince's sister and her husband, along with their son, B.W.

men and "Whitey" were returning from visiting the town of Espy, near Bloomsburg, Pennsylvania. On the return trip, along an isolated, snowy road, Weidler asked, in an anxious tone, for Prince to stop the car quickly so that Weidler could relieve his bowels.

Prince said, "Tom, there ain't a bathroom within twenty miles of this place."

However, Prince stopped the car and Tom Weidler hurried to get out of the car and climb over a snowbank. Then Weidler called, "Do you have any toilet paper or newspaper or anything?"

"Jesus, Tom," Prince called back, "this is a new Ford, and I ain't got no stuff in it like my other cars!"

Weidler pleaded again, asking Prince what he should do. "Whitey" ends the account with Prince calling back, "I don't know, but we've got to get going. Be a sport and just pull your pants up!"

While he was being interviewed in 1983, Lester Seiler was asked, "Well, what kind of man was Prince? Was he a likable person?" Seiler responded, "He never made trouble. He was an easy-going fellow. If he had anything and you needed it, it didn't matter how much he needed it; he'd give it to you—One time, our car wouldn't work. I don't know what was the matter with it. And he come in there. My brother had [already] gone, and I was supposed to go. And he (Prince) up and said, 'Here, take mine.' He walked home across the field. That's all there was to it."

Prince Farrington's easygoing manner was displayed during a government raid. While agents smashed his equipment, Prince dozed. When he awoke, the agents were tallying the output of the illegal still. When Prince heard them refer to the 50-gallon capacity of the barrels, he interjected, "I never saw them barrels before in my life. But, I'll bet you $100 that they don't hold more'n 40 gallons."

## A READY WIT

Before sound bites were in vogue, Prince Farrington's wit was making great sound bites for reporters for otherwise drab news articles. Regarding his illicit occupation, he once observed, "It's a hard way to make an easy living."

A humorous observation that may seem confusing today could have been appreciated in a day when people made clothing from the large cloth bags in which animal feed, sugar, salt, etc., were sold. When he was walking along a street, taking a young boy for a stroll, a friend remarked about the sweet child, to which Prince replied, "He ought to be. He's been wearing sugar sacks for diapers!"

Prince apparently spent so much time in the courtroom that he was even comfortable expressing witticisms in replying to the judge. Thus, the quote, when the judge reprimanded Prince for his tardy arrival, "Yes, sir. I knew it. But I figured a hearing is like a funeral; you can't do nothin' without the corpse." When, as mentioned above, the assistant U.S. attorney, Arthur A. Maguire, said that Prince was "the king of the bootleggers!" Prince said softly, "I think Maguire's beginning to admire me."

## PRINCE, THE PHILANTHROPIST

At least two churches are tied to stories of Prince's generosity. One was the United Methodist church in Antes Fort and one was the Caldwell United Methodist Church just north of Rosecrans near his Florida Fruit Farm. At one time or another, each solicited a donation from Prince in order to replace the church roof. Both received enough money for the job. Of the $400 given to the one congregation, only about half was used for the roof. Then, local legend tells us, Prince refused the offer to return the unused funds, suggesting that it be given to the preacher. The preacher agreed to keep the surplus, reasoning that God needed the funds more than Prince needed them.

Another lingering story tells of Prince giving money to a church on several occasions until some of the church women expressed concern that it might be money from his criminal activity. Prince asked if they didn't consider the possibility that it was money earned by his farming. The ladies still expressed concerns, so Prince told them to suit themselves. That money source ended.

As with many Farrington incidents, the details are lost, but the point is evident. For example, there was a house fire on Godtchall Road, near Rockey Road. The house was destroyed, and a family was homeless. By morning, Prince had arranged for the trucks to begin arriving and the materials for a new home to be delivered.

Similarly, Frances Farrington Gardner recalled the time that a fire destroyed a home in Jersey Shore, and her uncle was on the scene the very next morning. He had already ordered, at his expense, the supplies needed for the rebuilding of the destitute family's new home. The supplies also began arriving that morning. While Prince's charitable gestures were common, it was such incidents as these that guaranteed the late moonshiner/bootlegger Prince David Farrington the "Robin Hood" label that is permanently attached to his name in Clinton and Lycoming counties of Pennsylvania.

Decades later, Mrs. Selinda Fritz had not forgotten the time, during the Great Depression, when her neighbor, Prince Farrington, had given her a large supply of beans for her own planting.

Many years ago, the late Dave S. Ulmer farmed along Pine Creek near Torbert. He passed to his grandson, Dave A. Ulmer of Jersey Shore, an account of having gone to Farrington's house near Antes Fort. He hoped to get some pipe from Farrington. The man answering the door told Ulmer that Farrington was not home but that he should state his interests. Ulmer carefully explained his need for some pipes to supply the watering trough used by his horses. At that point, a man, previously unseen, arose from a nearby chair. It was Prince Farrington who was silently monitoring the conversation.

"Mr. Ulmer," he said, "you just take what you need."

Dave Ulmer, of Jersey Shore, also tells of hearing his grandfather, Dave S. Ulmer, recall an incident where the grandfather, Dave S. Ulmer, and his wife were driving downstream alongside Pine Creek on their way to market. At the railroad bridge in the area known as The Narrows, they were stopped by federal agents, one sticking a machine gun into the car window, upsetting both occupants. The agents were looking for Farrington. As the younger Ulmer remembers the account, Farrington was thought to be sitting on a nearby mountain and laughing at the agents' fruitless efforts. The elder Ulmer also expressed amusement that many church congregations of the area solicited money for church projects (new roofs, etc.) from Prince D. Farrington before attending Sunday morning services where they sometimes heard sermons that condemned his illicit activity.

Another opinion that matched the majority was that of the late Thelma Witmyer Matthews, who found Farrington to be "a nice man."

Hazel Brown, visiting with Gladys Rockey during Gladys's interview, added, "He gave people money."

Leonard Parucha observed, "He was good friends with everybody." and "He was a very generous man."

At one time, Prince planted a large crop of tomatoes to sell to the local cannery. At harvest time, Prince had no system for gathering the tomatoes, so he hired local boys, including Charles Dorwart, for the harvesting. They simply walked through the fields, pulling the ripe tomatoes and putting them into baskets. They worked on a very hot day. The foreman told them that he wanted them back for a second day. He also promised that during the next day, if the heat was so troublesome again, the boys would be taken into the house for drinks. When Dorwart told his mother, Ruth, about the offer of going into the house of Prince Farrington for drinks, she said that he should be" damned careful" about what he was drinking! Sure enough, the next day was another scorcher, and the foreman had them troop into the house for drinks. There, in the kitchen, Prince Farrington was sitting in a large, galvanized washtub, bathing. He unabashedly pointed to the kitchen sink and told the boys to help themselves to the cold water from the spigot.

"I never met Prince," Don Cowfer admitted, but I was told that he was a helluva nice man. He gave to the poor. If he met a kid on the street who was ragged or something, he'd take the kid and buy him a new set of clothes."

Ed Snook, who was born and raised in Rosecrans, just a few miles west of the Florida Fruit Farm, tells a similar story of Prince's generosity toward poor children. As Snook relates, Prince took delight in sending shoeless boys to Hauser's shoe store on Allegheny Street in Jersey Shore. The clerk always knew the routine. The barefoot or poorly shod child, or a parent, informed a clerk that Prince Farrington had sent him. Then, the clerk fitted the child with a new pair of shoes, for which Hauser's salesperson added the price to Prince's ongoing credit tab.

Prince Farrington also hired boys to work for him. At least one, said Ed Snook, was an eight-year-old. Prince paid boys better wages than most area employers. Prince also advanced the money to some of the boys so that each could buy a bicycle to ride to his job with Prince.

Dave A. Ulmer has lived in the Jersey Shore and Pine Creek (Toomes Run) area all his life. The sum of all the comments he heard: "There's nothing he wouldn't do for people."

Among the younger generation, including those people whose only knowledge of Prince Farrington has been through earlier writings or hearsay, Larry Sheddy's declaration rather nicely summarizes the widespread opinion of the people of Farrington country, "He was a good guy, who helped a lot of poor people."

Gladys Rishel Rockey, on whose farm Prince Farrington had a still (*see* Chapter 11), said that Farrington was "a great man." With growing insistence, she added: "He was, he helped a lot of people." She also suggested another aspect of his personality by observing, "He was a great talker, too."

After decades of hearing Prince Farrington being discussed, Dan Reinhold of Mill Hall had the impression that "Everybody liked him. That's why he never got caught!" That false impression, of course, is corrected with a glance at Farrington's record of arrests, as cited in Chapter 12.

The penury of the Dorwarts was typical of most families of the time. Charles and Dorothy both related actual incidents that happened to their large family. That may have been one of the reasons why Charlie, even today, praises Prince Farrington's concern and generosity. Charles repeats the oft-told story of Prince Farrington paying for repairs to a church. In Charles' case, the building was the United Methodist Church of Antes Fort. There were others. Also, each year, when the school opened for the new term, needy children were each given a new pair of jeans, a new shirt and a new pair of shoes.

Dave Poust, a Jersey Shore area resident throughout his eight decades, did know Prince personally. His spur-of-the-moment evaluation: "Prince was a hard-working individual who loved to make moonshine—the best around. If he knew you and liked you, he'd help you. He was a very generous person. He bought windows and glass, etc., for the church in Antes Fort."

Students from the seventh grade of the Granville School in Antes Fort would take an annual field trip to the town of Hughesville to attend the Lycoming County Fair. Charles Dorwart remembers Prince Farrington going to Hughesville to the fair on the day that the Antes Fort children were attending. There, Prince provided money for the Granville students to have rides and refreshments.

Despite the traumatic firecracker incident related in Chapter 7, Harry Lytle's memories of the moonshiner/bootlegger are strongly positive. A lot of moonshiners were making whiskey, but much of that liquor could cause alcohol poisoning, but not that of Prince Farrington. When poverty gripped the valley and the nation, Prince offered help. "We were poor. He came to our house with boxes and bags of groceries. No one in Hopples Hollow that I ever heard of would testify against him." People in Hopples Hollow, says Lytle, were very serious about referring to Prince as "Robin Hood."

In assessing the community's admiration or dislike of Prince David Farrington, vehemence must be weighed to appraisals, whether positive or negative. The vehemence of one of his former personal chauffeurs, Sam Fuller, must account for something. His unsolicited evaluation: "Be sure you say that he was a heck of a nice guy—because he *really* was!"

It's easy to get the impression that the flow of positive testimonials is endless, but there is a minority report to offer.

## THE NEGATIVE RECOLLECTIONS

Marjorie Kamus (*see* Chapter 8) remains, to this day, unimpressed. She says that one shouldn't "make him out to be a folk hero. He was anything but. He was a crook." She also denigrates the popular thinking that Prince Farrington was "*our* crook." The exceptional aspect of this crook's life, she concedes, was that he was known for making "excellent moonshine." She was told that when Farrington's illegal stills were raided, they never dumped the product; but took it to Harrisburg, where it was reputedly served at events, including a gubernatorial inauguration. While he remains a much-admired man for his generosity, it was still, Marjorie Kamus notes, "illegal income" that he contributed to organizations and individuals.

Also among the disenchanted was Art Decker. The Deckers were from Brookside, a town in the mountains north of Jersey Shore and Antes Fort. Art's brother, Torrence Decker ("Diz" to friends), was born in 1915 and died in 1994. Some of that life span was spent behind bars, the result of his ties to Prince Farrington. That stirred Art's anger. Art's vituperative condemnation: Prince and his kind were "white trash." One might have reminded Art that his brother, "Diz" Decker, had willingly joined that "white trash."

One more negative view, penned by a local newspaper editor, appears in Chapter 13.

*The late Thelma Matthews of Sugar Valley who recalled, from her busy 100 years of life, a number of violent incidents.*

*Prince's brother George Hobson, who died of acute alcoholism.*

*A posed scene at a Farrington still. The picture is a phony representation of trouble.*

*The old Faith Yarrison house in Rosecrans. The house saw its share of mayhem.*

*Prince, in one of his many newspaper portraits.*

## · 7 ·

# Moonshine and Mayhem

**THE CLAWS EXPOSED?**
Despite a normally calm and tolerant demeanor, Prince could exhibit a more bellicose approach, depending on the provocation. The degree of his bellicosity is impossible to assess since some of the violence that occurred within his area and his time could not, with certainty, be attributed to Prince David Farrington.

In fact, one of the area's unsolved cases happened just a few years before Prince's 1921 arrival in Clinton County. Harry and Clara Humpstead Hauser lived with their half-dozen children (five sons and a daughter) along the old dirt road that was then (early 1900s) known as Lower Pine Run Road, north of what is now Route 220. His grandson, Reverend Dean Hauser, says that his grandfather was a good provider, with a number of small, water-powered, steam-engine-driven sawmills scattered throughout the neighboring hills. On Saturdays, "Grammy" Clara would bake a half-dozen or more pies. Then, on Sundays, they invited local folks, including several local invalids, to join their own large family for a Sabbath Day repast.

We've heard the saying too many times: "He was the nicest person until he was drunk." That's part of Pastor Hauser's evaluation of his grandfather, old Harry Hauser. Of course, there was one other thing that could stir the emotions of Harry Hauser. The checkerboard. No matter the game, too many players love to play but hate to lose. This was Harry's attitude. More than one late-night game with the hired hand ended when a frustrated Harry grabbed the checkerboard and slammed shut the board's two halves with the pieces caught inside. Then he'd grab the metal lifter, raise the stove lid and slide the checkers to their fiery fate. Clara would arise the next morning to find that Harry was already outside and, from a broom handle, was sawing off and painting another set of checkers.

Harry Hauser was also considered to be a "horse trader" or a "wheeler-dealer." That is to say, some family members felt that it was the drinking and 'horse trading' side of Harry Hauser that led to the fateful evening sometime around 1916. Harry was leaving, likely for another night of drinking. So one of his sons, Lester, overtook Harry and begged him not to go drinking. Harry wasn't dissuaded, and a disappointed Lester walked, alone, the mile or so back to their home. Harry Hauser's family was convinced that the patriarch was at one of the taverns along the old route known as Antlers' Lane. Son Lester, an eleven-year-old, spent some of the late hours of that same evening sitting on the porch and playing checkers by lantern light with the hired hand, John Kline. Sometime after midnight, the checker players were unnerved by the sound of a horse galloping through the night toward the house. When the horse and its rider stopped at their gate, Lester noted that the horse was lathered from the ordeal. The stranger called, asking if he was at the Hausers' home. When he was told that he was, indeed, at the Hausers' home, the man called, "I have some bad news for you." Lester's mother was summoned from the house, and the rider announced that Harry Hauser had been beaten to death along Antlers' Lane.

Revelations about a tragedy can sometimes magnify the event's tragic aspects for the victim's relatives. Other results of an investigation might simply add further shame. With the Hauser family unwilling to pursue the case, Harry's killing was left unsolved. Burial was in the large Wildwood Cemetery along Lycoming Creek Road, near Williamsport. Clara ("Grammy"), Harry Hauser's widow, left the farm and moved to the town of Linden. Eventually, Clara became a highly-regarded live-in housekeeper and cook for several of the wealthy families along Williamsport's street of millionaires, Grampian Boulevard. The Hauser homicide is an important reminder: No one can ever claim that the arrival of Prince David Farrington (1921) was Clinton and Lycoming counties' harbinger of lawless violence. Nor did Prince's arrival inaugurate any sort of *peaceable kingdom*, either.

## THE POSERS AND POSEURS

Prince Farrington's still operators were great posers and greater poseurs (pretenders). That is to say, they assumed positions at the secluded stills where they worked, sometimes sporting rifles and revolvers, in order to be photographed while pretending to be dangerous moonshiners waiting to exchange gunfire with revenuers or with innocent local hunters. Those who worked at Prince Farrington's outlawed stills should have adopted Prince's observation: "A person's a damned fool for taking pictures in the business I'm in," as his son-in-law, George Porter, once recalled. Whether or not any of these pictures ever caused the 'models' any trouble is unknown. However, they eventually were reproduced many times over and several of them got into newspapers. One set of these photographs is still prominently displayed in the Restless Oaks restaurant at McElhattan. While the fellows in these photographs appear to be 'hamming' for the camera, real events described in Chapter 3 and in this chapter suggest that *real* dangers did accompany the moonshine trade.

## A POTPOURRI OF PUGNACITY

Prince Farrington's eldest grandson, Dave Porter, recalls beginning to attend another school near Jersey Shore in a neighboring township. There, he encountered some older boys who began to torment him. Complaints to his grandfather brought this advice: "Fight like hell. You may not win, but they won't bother you anymore."

Leo "Chip" Taylor was a companion of Prince's nephew, B. W. Coltrane and he was an occasional visitor in Prince's home. When asked if he ever saw Prince in an angry mode, Taylor had this to offer:

"Yes, there was one time. Prince Farrington's three sons and one daughter were attending grade school at Antes Fort when the oldest son, Tom, and a friend of his came to school wearing work shoes. At that time, they had things called hobnails.[16] They put those in their shoes, you know, and they cut up the nice, wooden floor in the school.

"The school teacher, Mr. Bull, was his name, told them, 'You boys are in trouble. I'm going to have you clean up the floor and sand it down and everything.'

"Tom went home and told Prince about it. He lied to his dad and said that he didn't do that.

"Then Prince came to the school and the teacher, Mr. Bull, was ringing the bell for all of us to come into the school at the end of the one

---

16. Nails, with heavy heads, that were driven into the soles of shoes or boots in order to prevent slipping and/or wear.

o'clock break. Mr. Prince Farrington verbally tore into him something terrible! Mr. Bull was becoming upset and nervous and ordered all of us kids back inside and to go to our rooms. We went, but we came part way back out—it was something we just couldn't miss.

"Anyway, Prince, he was strong, and this Mr. Bull—at that time, they wore suits with a vest. Mr. Bull wasn't very big. Prince grabbed hold of him by his vest, gave a half-twist, and picked him up right off the floor.

"Mr. Bull pleaded for Prince to look at the floor; but he refused until one of the other sons told their dad that Tom gave him the wrong information. Prince looked at the floor and then asked Tom and his friend for the truth. Both boys owned up to the wrongdoing and apologized to the teacher and Prince.

"Prince promptly apologized to Mr. Bull. He said that he would contact the school directors about fixing the floor and that he would pay for it. Prince also said that, for punishment, the boys would stay after school for a week or two and clean up the room—which was the teacher's job each day after school. Prince also said that he would contact the parents of the other boy involved since he knew them and that the boys would start cleaning the school that day. It ended up that when they cleaned the schoolrooms, several of the local boys came and helped them because they liked the way the two boys apologized to their teacher and took the punishment."

## LATIMER'S LITTLE TALE

In 1986, Robert Latimer of Muncy, Pennsylvania, had a paper entitled "Whiskey Steal" published in the April issue of the Muncy Historical Society's bulletin. It was written with a particular writing style bordering on the picaresque and evincing the author's natural humor. It is mentioned here because it also cited a carefully-tempered threat from Prince Farrington. The paper mentions fifteen local family names for the people involved in the account, all 15 of which are family names to be found in the local telephone directory today.

Latimer's tale begins by telling of the common theft of pre-prohibition liquor that was stolen from warehouses that were guarded by men who might well have been friends of the thieves. He then mentions the early days of Prince Farrington. Russell Vermilya is the main character in this story and the one who learns of a barn full of Farrington's whiskey in kegs and barrels. When Vermilya decided that the opportunity was, indeed, golden, he enlisted the help of two other men and his girlfriend. Then, he borrowed a couple of trucks from his dad's gristmill and visited the barn. There, the conspirators loaded the equivalent of about 17 barrels of booze and left. The first person whom they asked to store their treasure—a farmer—chased them away.

Prince Farrington had little trouble tracking the stolen liquor and learning the name of the culprit behind the theft. Soon, Muncy was abuzz with rumors and questions. What might Farrington do when he caught the thief? What would become of the liquor? Where was the liquor being stored?

A trio of men from the town finally located the stash, along with Russell Vermilya and two other men, in Muncy's old slaughterhouse. Ten gallons of whiskey each was enough to bribe the three outsiders to leave. Vermilya got his remaining kegs and barrels moved to an area greenhouse, with the exception of the barrel that fell off the transporting truck and broke open. Part of the broken barrel's liquid assets were salvaged and put into other containers. Within a few days the haul of moonshine had been further subdivided for more bribing. What remained was again hidden in several Muncy-area locations.

For several days, Prince Farrington was snooping around the town of Muncy. Within a few days, he encountered Russell Vermilya, the thief who robbed the bootlegger. Prince admitted to Vermilya that he couldn't have him arrested but that he'd see that Vermilya would get a 'whipping' whenever he left Muncy. However, Prince also said that he wanted whatever whiskey the inept Russell Vermilya had left, except for one barrel that he'd leave for Russell's use. Russell agreed; Prince regained seven of the original 17 barrels that he had lost, and Robert Latimer's account reached its bloodless conclusion.

## LEE SNOOK'S WELL-FINANCED VACATION

About eight miles east of Loganton, near the town of Carroll, stands an old barn that was once used for the storing of some of Prince Farrington's moonshine. The owner was Lee Snook. At some point, Lee and his wife sort of 'embezzled' a good quantity of the hooch and sold it. The couple left on a booze-financed cross-country vacation. Shortly after returning from their memorable trip, several unidentified assailants attacked Lee. He was severely beaten and spent considerable time recuperating and reflecting.

## DAMNING TESTIMONY?

As quoted in William Rombach's paper (*see* Chapter 1), an unidentified friend of Prince broke an agreement, and Prince approached him with a loaded shotgun and threatened to kill the man.

Martha (Mattie) White Farrington was frail and fearful. Rombach states (*see* Chapter 1) that when she filed for (and was granted) divorce from Prince in 1929, she told the court that Prince would constantly come home drunk and would beat her at least "once a month." His wife's damning testimony was corroborated by another pair of witnesses and was left unanswered by Prince Farrington, who failed to respond to the subpoena. Prince's absence removed the need for any tough decision-making by the judge. As mentioned above, in Chapter Two, Mattie won her divorce; but failed to pull free from the Farrington vortex.

It might be well to return to the raid that was made on the Florida Fruit Farm in the summer of 1922. During that raid, agents gathered a small arsenal that included Colt revolvers, shotguns and Winchester rifles. That raid also had a pair of Prince's lookouts firing shots at the law enforcement officers when they first arrived and again while they were departing. While Prince may have tempered his show of violence as he aged, the warning of the agent who led that raid must be given some weight. That agent, John B. Ernst, was saying that it was Prince who had created for himself the reputation of being a "killer" and had convinced the farmers of the surrounding section and numerous others of his readiness to shoot if the occasion justified it."[17] Still, it must be emphasized that within a couple of decades, that evaluation had been greatly tempered by local individuals when describing Prince Farrington.

## THE COOPER HOLLOW PURSUIT

Because Turbit Seiler was in the moonshining business with his neighbor, Prince Farrington, Turbit's son, Lester, had an active history as a youthful

---
17. Clinton County *Democrat*, July 14, 1922.

moonshiner who lived near Prince's Florida Fruit Farm. Another of Lester Seiler's several taped recollections:

> We ran a couple of times that they [revenue agents] was after us. One time, they chased me down Cooper Hollow—and never got me. They woulda got me that time if they'd minded their business, but they didn't do that. They were in there—I don't know how many there mighta been before I come in. I come in, oh, around about ten o'clock, I guess.
>
> Earl Moyer lived down where Lou Snook lives, down below the road, down there by the white church. Down there in the hollow, you know. Well—I used to put sugar down there. Well, he [Earl Moyer?] was in with us that way, in the barn. And I'd take a 100-pound bag of sugar and carry it right up over the hill and back into Cooper Hollow, right out through the cemetery down there. I didn't mind it then, but now I couldn't carry one-half that far.
>
> I had this hundred pound of sugar when I came in [Into the area of the neighbor's still]. As soon as I came in, I seen that stuff was tore up. I knowed there was somebody strange in there for this reason: Anybody, like Ern Cooper or any of them that went in there—know'd where the whiskey was. They always had whiskey in there, and if anybody wanted a little or to borrow a jug of it that way—it wasn't tore up like that.
>
> We had a canvas, a personal canvas—sewed together to make two. It was about 18 foot wide and 24 foot long. We'd take and put poles up, you know. We'd come out here about eight feet, and then we'd drop the other end back down. That way, we had it fastened down at the ground. Then we had our stuff under there—You could take it and keep them dry. And it come right out, [to within] a couple of feet of the fire, you know; right at the still. You could set under there and put fire in if it was rainin' while you were running [cooking mash].
>
> We had a burlap bag where we put straw in where you could lie down. We had two fellows there and one fellow could sleep awhile while the other'n [tended the still]. Anyways, I seen

everything was tore up. I just took and threw my bag of sugar on the bed and went out the back and started down the hollow. I didn't start uphill. I started downhill.

Pretty soon they give a whistle on both sides and all around! I seen 'em coming down the sides, and I went through between them. They hollered, "Halt!"

I had a .32 automatic, one of them 7.55 mm—in my hip pocket. They shot first. I pulled that out while I was running—I don't know how I got it out of my hip pocket, but I got it out. I just held it back like that and shot about three shots. They started cursin' and swearin' to beat the band! But they stopped!

I went across the creek and waited. Nobody come, so I went home then. We didn't come back that night. But, the next night—oh, about four o'clock. We went in and got Ray, and we run [made moonshine], and nobody came in and bothered us. That was the only time that they raided us at that one there.

It should be mentioned that a number of people in the Farrington circle used 'salty' language, which the author dutifully relates, but Lester Seiler, who recorded many incidents, as offered here and elsewhere in this book, used no vulgarity or profanity. While that may seem unique, it likely presents a more accurate portrayal of rural speech patterns in Clinton County than some readers would be willing to concede.

## SOME MEMORIES, WITH INTEREST

Harry Lytle went to the eight-grades, one-room Brungard school, which was also the school attended by the young Farrington brood. As a small boy, Harry lived in the area between Salona and Loganton known as Hopples Hollow. His maternal grandfather was Scott Currin, who, at 18 years of age, was the publisher, editor, reporter, etc., of the Loganton *Journal.* At that time, Scott Currin was recognized as the youngest newspaper publisher in Pennsylvania.

In July of 2010, Harry dipped deep into his 87-year-old memory to recall, as he was just reaching school age, going to his aunt Faith's local store north of Loganton and just a few hundred yards north of the Rosecrans church.

Harry Lytle's aunt (his mother's sister) was Faith Currin Masters Andrews Yarrison (born in 1894), with her last three names coming from three marriages. She bore a son with each of her first two husbands. Faith Yarrison—with several stills scattered through the rural area near her store—did some of her own moonshining in cooperation with Prince Farrington. Harry, the spindly youngster, was trained in the ways of the moonshining community from his earliest memories. When revenue agents stopped at his Aunt Faith's store, they may mention their orders to raid a nearby Farrington still. Then the revenuers would relax for a few minutes, with a soda pop or some candy. This gave Faith the time needed to send little Harry hurrying into the woods near the store. He would notify the appropriate still workers who were operating there. The still workers quickly hid what they could and retreated deeper into the woods and beyond the range of the revenuers. When another resident, John Harbach, was told, in the summer of 2010, of the claim that Faith nurtured and hid alcohol, he said, "I wouldn't be surprised because she was a very sneaky person."

Gloria Schadt Harbach told a similar account of local support for Prince. It was, she says, her grandfather, William L. "Bucky" Schadt, who worked at the Castanea Brewery before his marriage. Although he did not use alcohol, he was not opposed to the moonshine concept. Gloria's grandfather later owned a Mobilgas Service Station on Bellefonte Avenue in Lock Haven. Now, he knew the members of the local police. Those law officers would confide in William Schadt about their upcoming raids on Prince Farrington. William would then pass along word of the impending raid to be sure that Prince was forewarned.

Harry Lytle also tells of his Aunt Faith removing a small rug from the floor behind the store counter. This revealed a trap door. When the trap door was raised, young Harry Lytle, carrying a kerosene lantern, scurried into the hidden basement room to dump burned sugar into the clear moonshine that Aunt Faith was aging. Thus, with Faith's homemade caramel, Harry changed her 'white lightening' to a rich, amber-colored whiskey.

When Harry was 17 years old, he worked for some time with the Civilian Conversation Corps, stationed at Elimsport and working in nearby forests. He later served in the U.S. Army. It was after his discharge from the military and his return home that Harry's uncle, Aunt Faith's brother, came to Harry to tell him that the bank in Loganton had a small bank account in the name of "Bud" Lytle. The account had been idle for years and no one knew to whom the account belonged. His uncle wondered if the dormant account might belong to Harry. For Harry Lytle, the unclaimed account brought back an old memory.

When Harry was a youngster, playing in front of his aunt's store, he had a sandbox and pail. One day, Prince Farrington and several other men came to the store to get some whiskey. It was around Independence Day, and the fellows had firecrackers. They sat Harry Lytle's overturned sand bucket on top of one of the lighted firecrackers. The bursting firecracker carried the sand bucket high into the air and left it dangling on the cluster of wires that were attached to the large utility post. Harry sent up a wail. Aunt Faith appeared and berated Prince and his friends. A collection was taken and given to Faith Yarrison for her nephew. Faith used the money to open an account in the name of her nephew, whom she referred to as "Bud" Lytle. So, about two decades after the event, Lytle reaped the modest profits of the boisterous behavior of Prince David Farrington and his friends.

Ann Roush, Faith Currin Yarrison's granddaughter, also remembers the family's story of her grandmother, partly as she received the accounts from her dad, Evan Andrews, son of Faith Currin Yarrison. Faith kept a '38 revolver with her and slept with the weapon beneath her pillow. Ann remembers seeing the gun. Also, Evan related to his daughter how he slept by one of the windows. He was asleep one night when a gunshot awakened and startled him. It was Faith, firing over his prone body at some men who were trying to steal the moonshine that they knew was stored beneath her porch.

On another occasion, as Faith was closing the store/speakeasy, a customer coaxed for more booze. Faith refused and locked the store for the night. However, the thirsting customer broke into the downstairs. He was stumbling or crawling up the stairs toward the second floor. From the top of the stairs, Faith shot! The unscathed intruder hastily declined further Faith Yarrison's hospitality! The next morning, the bullet hole was clearly visible in the door on the first floor. The bullet's location in the door revealed a trajectory that would have hit her intruder if he had been upright and sober while trying to get some service!

For the proper perspective regarding Faith Yarrison, it must be noted that she also adopted two sons; sons that she raised to be good citizens. Millie Bixel, who knew the adopted boys and attended school with one, affirmed that Faith Yarrison, a distaff moonshiner, speakeasy operator and occasional gunslinger, raised "good kids."

## THE SAGA OF ROCKEY ROAD

Rockey Road runs east-to-west for only about seven miles along the northern ridges of Sugar Valley. It is not known as Rockey Road because of its stony surface; but because members of the Rockey family lived along its once-dusty lane. Strangely, although it measures barely seven miles in length, it had enough social activity to fill its own book. The problem: Much of its fascinating past has not been recorded. Tom and Freda Rockey are the only Rockey family members, so named, who still live on the road that was named for Tom's great-grandfather. The saga of Rockey Road would have to incorporate the events that occurred in the adjacent roadways and hollows. Hopple Hollow, for example intersected with Rockey Road close to Loganton. Hopple Hollow has been largely obliterated by the great causeway that is Interstate 80. That hollow is named for the several Hopple families that lived within its natural ravine. 'That was a rough area. They were out in the country with no law," according to the judgment of John "Jack" Harbach, an area native. Rockey Road, with its wild environs, contained bear-frequented huckleberry bogs, a speakeasy/bordello, a couple of one-room schools, a 1930s-era Civilian Conservation Corps camp, a church campground, a modern recreational campground, a secluded sylvan waterfall, a sprinkling of hidden still sites and several hardscrabble[18] farms The Rockey Road swath, with a mile on each side being studied, shows a 75 percent figure for such soil; hence the term. The other 25 percent qualifies as very good or prime farmland.] There was a day during the Prohibition years that an encounter with a bear in the Rockey Road neighborhood, may have been one's safest encounter.

Prince liked women. Several in the family admitted that. Still, we don't know his exact role, if any, in the 101 Ranch, an old house on

---

18. The term *hardscrabble* is an early 19th century combining of the English word, *hard*, and the Dutch word, *scrabble*, (to scratch). The word is used here to denote barren, substandard farming soil.

Rockey Road, in the basement of which illegal liquor was stored. "The moonshiners used that. They had the call girls there." Thus, says "Dutch" Washburn, a lifelong resident of Sugar Valley, who remembers that the place had operated in the 1920s and, he believes, closed in the late 1930s. Miller Stamm of Loganton said (April 2010) that "Back then it was a whorehouse." The income generated by the 101 Ranch would have come from two primary commodities: the whiskey in the basement and the women in the garret. Some members of the Kulp family lived there later, but when it sold flesh and moonshine, it was owned by Adam ("Ad") Stabley, who was first identified in Chapter 3. Stabley's bordello, known as the 101 Ranch, was located less than ten miles from Prince Farrington's Florida Fruit Farm.

There was always the veiled threat of violence connected to the moonshining/bootlegging trade. During the 1920s and 1930s, violence in American society was a given. People who lived in Clinton and Lycoming counties during those two decades, which happen to coincide with the time and location of Prince Farrington's primary activity, learned of ugly crimes; but sometimes with no names being attached to the perpetrators. The reader may confront the accounts; but with the understanding that their time and location cannot incriminate. They can only confound.

It was in 1925, while Prince David Farrington still lived with his family at the Florida Fruit Farm, that two schoolchildren made a gruesome discovery.

In 1877, the Knarr[19] School was opened on the extreme western end of Rockey Road, on the edge of the farm of a Knarr family. The architecture is similar to that of the other 19th-century valley schools. It had one large classroom and, outside, had a school-wide porch that was under roof. The roof was marked with a gable in the middle, so that a triangle broke the straight line of the porch roof.

The school was closed in 1953. The property was transformed into a residence and changed hands several times. Tom Rockey bought the property at a recent auction. He sold it to a nephew. The nephew and his wife—the current owners—have enlarged and transformed the historic old schoolhouse into a rustic log home.

---

19. The 'K' is pronounced so that the school's name becomes kuh-NARR.

Mildred (nee Knarr) Bixel has seen more than 90 years of history unfold in the Sugar Valley area. Mildred (Millie) tells of going to the Knarr School, on the corner of Rockey Road and Route 477. That site, today, is just a few yards from Route 80 and directly behind a mini-mart. As mentioned above, the school building is now a modest residence. Millie's family lived on the adjoining farm. As happened on many days, Millie and her sister, Flora, were the first arrivals on one school day in 1925. They were stunned to find the schoolhouse porch and step spattered with blood. A trail of blood led across the schoolyard and to the edge of the country lane. Frightened by the sight, the girls nervously awaited the arrival of others. When another student, Stewart Geyer, got there and said that it appeared that someone had been killed there, the children began shouting for help. As soon as the teacher, Mr. Russell Douty, arrived, he postulated that the blood may have come from an animal being killed. Douty had some schoolboys get buckets of water and scrub away all the blood. Millie helped with the scrubbing. On the following Sunday evening, Millie's brother, Harry Knarr, attended church services. On the way home, he stopped to visit friends, where the group sang hymns to organ accompaniment. When Harry left his friends' home, it was nearly midnight.

As he walked along Rockey Road, the road where the school was located, he discovered a small, recently lit, unattended fire burning in the middle of the road. The flames were consuming a pile of clothing. A couple of days later, according to local accounts, Lee Rockey, who lived on the road that bears his family name, was fishing at nearby Rauchtown Creek when he discovered a girl's body. The body was about five miles northeast of Knarr's schoolhouse and about three miles from Stabley's stable, the 101 Ranch. However, contradicting the local account about Lee Rockey, the Lock Haven *Express* reported that the woman's body was discovered under some brush by some campers. Nearby, the paper noted, a woman's coat, full of holes, was found. The paper doesn't offer the reader any insight regarding the origin of the holes. Nor does the paper, or anyone else, suggest any connection to the Maxwell automobile that was recently wrecked by running down over the bank near the body of the murdered woman. It doesn't even tell the reader who owned the Maxwell.

Related news articles about the discovery of the murder victim and the ongoing investigation into the victim's identity were offered by the Lock Haven *Express*. Clinton County District Attorney William Hollis soon had two major candidates for the murder victim. The first was 23-year-old Teresa Stabley, whose family owned the 101 Ranch brothel along Rockey Road. The second was Grace Martz, of an age similar to the age of Teresa Stabley.

Henry Martz, the father of the Martz girl, was reported to have gone to Newark, New Jersey, because it was learned that Grace Martz was in jail in that city. He returned, saying that he had been able to speak with his daughter without being in her presence and that she was now in New York State, although he explained nothing. A few days later, reported that Grace Martz was now living with a brother in Albany, New York.[20]

The other person whom authorities thought might be the murdered woman was Teresa Stabley, who had had no contact with her family for many months. Teresa was married to Floyd Klobe, a major figure in another murder investigation in 1927 (*see* below, this chapter). However she had split with Klobe and left the area. When the woman's body was found, Teresa had been out of contact with her family for months, placing Teresa at the top of the list of likely victims.

The case was made that much more puzzling because the newspaper accounts even suggest no cause of death. Yet, the face of the victim must have been made unrecognizable by the killer or killers since Teresa's family had been unable to say whether or not the victim was their daughter.

The August 8 issue of the *Express* mentions the opinion of those who had seen the body before burial. These folks said that examination of the teeth showed the wearing pattern of someone over thirty and, perhaps, as old as the early 40s.

Finally, during the following January, Teresa returned home. She had been utterly unaware that she was considered to be a possible murder victim.

The most recent person questioned by the author, about this was a decades-long resident of Rauchtown. He repeated the local story: The

---

20. *Lock Haven Express*, August 3rd, 1925

body was found near the Rauchtown dam, and the corpse was said to have been of a young woman from New Jersey.

The bloody schoolhouse porch, the midnight blaze on a country lane, and the discarded corpse were all within a chilling distance of the 101 Ranch. Although never verified, local talk tied the hapless lass to Stabley's brothel. Whomever she was, her obituary was limited to a few whispered rumors.

## A PATRIARCH DISPATCHED

For the Farringtons, the Meixels, and the Seilers, moonshining was a family activity, with more than one member being involved. This was also the case with the Klobe family, which lived at Carroll, just a few miles southeast of Prince Farrington's Florida Fruit Farm. The Klobes operated some of their own stills and they also worked with Prince Farrington. In fact, George Mayes of Antes Fort, who was a young man in Prince's last days, remembers one of the Klobes as being "father of a lot of his [Prince's] operations. He set them up."

Late on the summer evening of August 16, 1927, Thelma Witmyer Matthews and her husband, Milburn, walked to the farm of Charles and Maggie Klobe to make arrangements for the threshing of their grain. On the return walk, they found another neighbor, Charles Klobe's dad, Herman Klobe, lying by the road. Klobe was still alive, but the back of his head was brutally gashed by an axe! He appeared to have crawled to the side of the road from the scene of the attack. He was rushed to the hospital in Lock Haven, where he died at 7:55 on the morning of August 22nd. Klobe said local rumor, still had several hundred dollars in a wad of bills in his pocket. Herman Klobe's son, Floyd, was injured in the same altercation but soon recovered.

Within hours of the attack, Louis B. Huntingdon [or Huntington] was apprehended and charged with the assault.[21] The alleged attacker was a former policeman in Scranton, where—years earlier—he had been acquitted in the death of a prisoner who had tried to escape. He had once been involved, as well, in an attack on a young man who worked

---

21. Throughout the ensuing months of legal developments and newspaper accounts, Huntingdon's given name was listed as Joseph. It was only late in the trial, as his attorneys began to present his defense, that Huntingdon informed the world that he had been using a phony given name.

for him in a saloon in the town of Plymouth, near Scranton. Lastly, he was currently wanted on a charge of aggravated assault and battery for an alleged stabbing at South Danville (the railroad designation for the town of Riverside) in Northumberland County, about 30 miles east of Carroll. Thus, it was not surprising to find that Huntingdon had taken an assumed name, Joe McWilliams, when he arrived in Sugar Valley and started working for the Klobes.

Huntingdon, 57, and a younger man, Earl Knepp (or Knept), 22, lived in the old house owned and once occupied by Herman Klobe, 72. Herman, a stroke victim, had reduced use of the right hemisphere of his body and was now living with a son, Charles. The Klobes and their two tenants all lived in the area of Carroll. Knepp and Huntingdon were hired for one principal duty: the making of moonshine whiskey for the Klobes. Herman Klobe's two sons, Charles and Floyd, had originally done the haggling involved with the hiring of Huntingdon. At the same time, trial testimony suggested that the elder Klobe and his tenant, Huntingdon, developed a close relationship, with Huntingdon referring to Herman as "Daddy" and often shaving the elderly Klobe patriarch. Over the next few months, Huntingdon and Knepp helped produce about 70 barrels of whiskey.

On the night of August 16, 1927, three men, none of whom would likely qualify as being sober, became involved in a tense encounter. Earl Knepp, the younger hired man, was not directly involved, but Louis B. Huntingdon demanded payment for his work, while Floyd Klobe insisted on giving him only a few dollars. The two men fought fiercely, with Knepp as their witness. Huntingdon was badly beaten. Then, defense testimony claimed, Floyd Klobe attacked Huntingdon with a butcher knife. While Huntingdon was backing away from Klobe, he managed to grab a two-bitted axe and swung at Floyd Klobe, leaving him crippled and on the ground. Somehow, in the ensuing minutes, Herman Klobe arrived and was hit—with an axe—so forcefully on the back of his head that it pierced the brain.

Charles Klobe and a passing neighbor took the two injured Klobes (Floyd and Herman) to the hospital in Lock Haven. Floyd recovered nicely, but his father, Herman, died. A physician witness testified that the Klobe patriarch died from meningitis caused by the infected wound.

Meanwhile, Louis B. Huntingdon had grabbed a traveling bag, got into Charles Klobe's *second* car, and began driving east. However, he only drove the purloined vehicle as far as a cooper mill, a distance of about two miles, before the car struck a stone and overturned. Huntingdon then continued going east on foot. He was apprehended by authorities near the town of White Deer, about 20 miles from the crime scene. Because of Huntingdon's severe facial injuries, he was examined by Dr. Robert Schaffer, the prominent dentist and drinker from Lock Haven. Dr. Schaffer said that Huntingdon appeared to have been in a train wreck. He also noted that Huntingdon, who had lost two teeth, could hardly open his mouth. He had a badly swollen upper lip and a swelling around one eye that looked "like an egg."

Louis B. Huntingdon spent the next five months in the Clinton County prison, awaiting trial. With Herman Klobe's death, Huntingdon faced a murder charge. Judge Harvey W. Whitehead of Williamsport presided over the selection of a dozen of Huntingdon's peers. Finally, on the 24th of January, 1928, Judge Whitehead called the court into session, and the trial commenced. The people of Clinton County packed the courtroom to enjoy one of the county's most sensational trials. Several sessions would have overflow crowds, with some would-be spectators being turned away.

At 9:00 A.M. on the first day of the Herman Klobe murder trial, the crowd waited to see the defendant. Louis B. Huntingdon's background had preceded him. Members of the Clinton County community had already learned much about Huntingdon's checkered past. That's why it was critical that his 'first impression' be positive. It was.

Louis B. Huntingdon's daughter and son-in-law were present for the trial, having come south from their home in Auburn, New York. When Sheriff C. I. Wenker led Huntingdon into the courtroom on January 24, 1928, the defendant was wearing a properly fitted gray suit. He was cleanly shaven and wearing tortoise-shell-rimmed glasses. The reporter from the *Renovo Record* was moved to observe (January 25th, 1928) that Huntingdon "had the appearance of a business or professional man." The Lock Haven newspaper simply noted Huntingdon's "pleasing appearance."

Attorney S. L. Gilson and District Attorney William Hollis presented the commonwealth's case. Much of their case was testimony by the only witness to the events who was not directly involved, the youthful moonshiner's assistant, Earl Knepp. His testimony, later labeled as unreliable by some of the jurors, was that Huntingdon was the instigator and the person who attacked both Floyd and Herman Klobe with an axe. Henry Hipple, who would later become a local judge, was the main counsel for the sartorially resplendent defendant. Attorney Hipple conceded that Huntingdon struck Floyd Klobe in self-defense but denied that he harmed the elder Klobe.

Oddly, from the trial's beginning, there seemed to be little effort to hide the duties of Huntingdon and Knepp or the considerable involvement in the moonshining of the three Klobes. The entire case swirled around the making of moonshine, the disagreement about Huntingdon's compensation, and the evening confrontation of Floyd Klobe and Louis B. Huntingdon, both of whom had done some heavy drinking prior to their violent encounter.

Initially, ten jurors favored acquittal. Once the other two were persuaded to join the majority, the verdict was rendered. Louis B. Huntingdon was free. He joined his daughter and son-in-law, returning with them to their home in Auburn, New York.

The conclusion of the Klobe murder trial came and went with no answer to the question of who dealt the fatal blow of a double-bitted axe if it wasn't the defendant. In fact, if the newspaper accounts are comprehensive, the trial ended without the question ever having been posed.

Today, the current owner of those mash-enriched acres has a sign honoring the land's colorful past. Painted on a rock are the words that identify the Klobe property as the Moonshine Farm.

## A BULLET FIRED

When Prince had a still operating on the Lee Rockey farm, the apparatus was situated just off Harbaugh Road. Boyd Greak, known as "Duke," was handling the still. Gladys Rockey recounted the shooting that once occurred at the still. She remembered, "They raided it and shot one of the guys, but he lived. It was during the Depression, before George and I got married." Greak saw revenue agents arriving. He fled into the trees. These agents were already exploring the area when Greak realized that the pressure in the boiler was building. He hurried to the still and cut the pressure.

With in imminent explosion avoided, Greak again attempted escape. As he ran from the site, a lawman fired, with the bullet hitting Greak in the back. The bullet barely missed his heart. The officers took him to the Lock Haven hospital. With his emergency medical care finished, he was resting. Later that night, said Don Cowfer, "Prince stole him out." Prince took Boyd Greak to the farm of Prince's friend, Lee Rockey. There, just a few hundred yards from the scene of his injury, Boyd "Duke" Greak was hidden. Prince had a friendly doctor from Williamsport treat the injured man. Prince also hired a nurse to care for Greak, who recovered and had many decades to reminisce.

Bob Stiver is troubled by a couple of stories of local killings, including the story told locally of Lemuel Groce. Groce, local storytellers say, changed his name to Jack Carter in order to help people forget a shooting in which he was involved. Unfortunately, the author was unable to get details regarding that shooting.

After learning of the several stories of local killings, one is reminded of what is commonly known: Prince Farrington had armed guards at both ends of Ireland Road while he was moonshining whiskey in a house along that road. Then there is the old *Clinton County Democrat* newspaper account, cited in Chapter 3, that told of Farrington's men shooting at the officers involved in the 1922 raid at the *Florida Fruit Farms*. That article mentioned the 'arsenal' that agents confiscated during the raid. And there is the gallery of pictures of Farrington still workers sporting guns and even posing with them. What provocation would have turned those guns from props into lethal weapons?

A significant testimonial comes from Lynn Bowes, whose father, Lee Marshall Bowes had once owned the Jersey Shore *Herald*. As Lynn remembers the account, some men from outside the area were visiting with Prince Farrington when the raid of 1934 occurred. The visitors were eager to "shoot it out" with the agents. Prince, however, poured sand on the fire by declaring, "No! No shooting. We're not going to shoot anyone."

Perhaps it was Prince Farrington's admonishment of "No! No shooting" that led to the snappy reaction when these two men were caught in the 1934 raid. When they were told that they were under arrest, one, in reference to Prince Farrington—snapped, "Why don't you see the boss?"

## 'JUICE' FOR A JUDAS

Prince Farrington's grandson, Dave Porter, remembers opening a bureau drawer in the presence of his grandfather and seeing a leather-bound chunk of lead—a blackjack. This happened when Dave was about five years old, and it took place in an old farmhouse near where the Jersey Shore airport now stands. Prince's casual reaction ended the experience, leaving the boy with little more than a lifelong image of a common weapon of the period. Another relative, however, witnessed Prince in the act of using another period weapon.

A close relative recalled accompanying Prince to Williamsport. Prince was delivering his periodic jug of sour mash whiskey to one of the lawmen who gave Prince his loyalty and his silence. On this trip, however, Prince was delivering his liquid payment to a man who, Prince had just learned, had betrayed him to the law. Arriving at the man's home, they found him sitting on his front porch. Prince was there to end their relationship. Prince summoned him to the car for his regular payment for 'protection.' While the man walked toward the car, Prince removed a pair of brass knuckles from the glove compartment. With the weapon in place, Prince waited until the man leaned in toward the moonshiner. In an instant, the powerful arm of Prince Farrington swung—his fist smashed the Judas in the mouth! Blood and teeth spattered as the man went reeling to the ground! Before putting the car in motion to leave, Prince tossed a jar of whiskey from the car and snapped, "Here's your payment!"

The lawman never pressed charges, but both he and the Farrington family member who had accompanied Prince were now among the few people who were aware that Prince David Farrington wasn't always and ever an easygoing moonshiner.

*Four moonshiners at tent site. From left, they are "Pud" Hill, Col. Segraves, Charl Farrington and Lemuel Groce. Date and location are unknown.*

*Debbie Farrington and her mother, Emily Farrington Packer, who was a Farrington moonshine driver.*

*The stone of Virgie and Charl Farrington of Lamar.*

*Joe Gardner's house in Lock Haven.*

*"Fuss" Schaffer entertaining from a wheelbarrow at a Farrington still site.*

# · 8 ·

# The Coterie of Cohorts

> Never A Christmas Morning,
> Never the Old Year Ends,
> But Somebody Thinks of Somebody,
> Old Days, Old Times, Old Friends.
>
> —Prince Farrington

The above verse and printed signature are taken from an undated Christmas card. They are a rhyming reminder to the card's recipient that Prince Farrington wanted to assure them of his friendship. They are a gentle reminder to the reader that Prince consciously developed valuable friends. The "old friends" of the verse might easily refer to Prince's friends from North Carolina: his family members, his brother's family, and friends Lemuel Groce and the Gardner brothers.

A measure of Prince Farrington's people skills is the large number of good friends he cultivated. Here, we suggest a septet of truly valuable friends who were crucial to Farrington's work in Pennsylvania. Three were from the North Carolina friends and four were from among the many that he cultivated in Pennsylvania. The seven emphasized here include Prince's brother, Charles Farrington, as well as Joe Gardner, Lemuel Groce, Henry Sampson, Clair Thompson, Jacob Kohberger and Colonel Henry Shoemaker. Prince found the latter four in the Keystone State.

The Tarheel trio eventually settled in three different area towns—brother Charles ("Charl") went to live in Lamar, to the west. Joe Gardner resided in Lock Haven. Lemuel Groce moved into Castanea, a small village near Lock Haven. Prince settled near Loganton before finally settling in Antes Fort, near Jersey Shore. Let's briefly look at each, beginning with Prince's brother, Charl, by far the most bizarre.

## A. Charles ("Charl") Farrington

Charles Archibald Farrington was known to the family as "Charl," the name we'll employ for this account. He was the hard-working and harder-drinking younger brother of Prince David Farrington. Of Prince's nine siblings, Charl was the one who would share in Prince's plans to prosper in Pennsylvania. Once Prince had decided to try life in the Keystone State, it was he and Charl who were first to arrive from North Carolina before sending for their families. The two brothers would remain close and supportive throughout their lives. Although Charl, too, was arrested and jailed several times, he got none of the notoriety that went to brother Prince. These siblings had many similarities, including their compelling love of whiskey and their satisfaction with distilling their own without legal authority.

Charl was born in 1897 in Yadkin County, North Carolina. He was eight years younger than Prince; but he played a major part in the successful portion of Prince's career of nearly five decades. He, too, was involved in the moonshining business before he left North Carolina. He recited an incident that Lester Seiler recounted many years later. As Seiler told it, Charl said that the family would cook mash for whiskey in some isolated North Carolina woodland. However, they would wait to assemble the still until the mash was fully prepared for distillation. By using that method, the revenue agents, should they find the unfinished mash would not have the Farrington still to destroy. One afternoon, Charl went to dismantle the still. He told his father, Thomas Beverly Farrington, that if any strangers came around, Thomas should fire a shot as a signal to Charl. Thomas forgot. Rather than a stranger arriving, a chicken hawk appeared and got one of the peeps. Thomas shot at the chicken hawk. Poor Charl heard the shot and reacted. "I grabbed that old still, and I run for an hour!"

In 1919, Charl married Virginia Tinsebloom. Virginia's nickname was "Virgie," the name that now graces their tombstone. She was four years older than Charl and was the daughter of his dad's third wife.[22] As a part of Prince's effort to keep Charl in Pennsylvania, Prince bought Charl and Virgie a large, Victorian-style house on Silver Avenue in Lamar, a small town to the west of Prince's Florida Fruit Farm and, today, a stop

---

22. This marriage meant that Charl was married to the daughter of his step-mother and his wife was married to the son of her step-father.

on Interstate 80. Charl and Virgie were the parents of Juanita, Shirley, Mildred, Frances, Thomas (Tommy), Robert and Charles Jr., whom his dad addressed as "Buster." Frances married Joe Gardner's brother, George "Sugar" Gardner. Fran and George Gardner lived in Bellefonte. Fran was very close to her cousin, Gladys Farrington (later Porter). Fran and Gladys both agreed were more like sisters than cousins.

The mental image of Charl Farrington that is carried by a granddaughter, Tammy Farrington, is one of a red-cheeked and smiling man in bib overalls, with a toothpick in his teeth. She also recalls him as a working man who tended a garden and raised donkeys. He also raised and butchered pigs and cows. The family's image of Prince's younger brother includes many Prince/Charl similarities. Both were witty, rustic storytellers and private distillers, as well as the owners of a hearty laugh and an ingrained contempt for authority. Both were skilled jerrybuilders. Charl, for example, had, as a cistern, a barrel that sat in an upstairs bathroom. It was rigged so that it could be slid outside during rainfall. Then, it was pulled back into the bathroom, where an attached hose allowed the rainwater to flow to the downstairs washing machine. Also, at the time that Charles Archibald Farrington and his family lived in the large house on Silver Avenue in Lamar, one of its features was a hidden passageway, resembling a rope-driven dumbwaiter, that extended to the third floor. This device was used for hiding whiskey.

Charl's house in Lamar had extensive porches and stained glass windows. Above the entrance to the front porch, there was a decorative panel depicting a sunrise theme. [Interestingly, there is also a sunrise scene filling the upper part of the tombstone of Thomas M. Farrington, who died in 1986 and whose grave lies a few yards from that of his parents, Virgie and Charl.].

Among the North Carolina Farringtons, it was Charl who was more fondly remembered. Dot (Dorothy Lee) Highfill, a niece, complained that Charl was the only one who would come and visit "Granny and Grandpa Farrington (Charlie's and Prince's brother, John, and his wife, Cora)." There exists a brief letter written on the personal stationery of Miss Juanita Farrington of Lamar, Pennsylvania. At first glance, it is confusing. Then one realizes that it was written by Charl, on his daughter's stationery, to his brother, John Alexander. It says:

*Lamar, Pa. Mar. 17, 1952*

*Dear Brother*

*Just a few lines to let you know we are all well Hoping to fine you all the same I Havent Hered anything from any one Down there for some time. Just wrote to P. D. Havent Hered anything from Him for some time the last I Hered he was not very good He is in Springfield, Mo. in a Hospital He said He was getting the Best of treatment and Doctor care*

*We Have Had a pretty Rought winter up Here and is cold and windy now it was 28 Below Zero in jan. I Havent Had much work since Xmas. I think I will get a job this week*

*What are you doing are you Still in the Sand Business Well that is all for this time.*

*Pleas ans. Soon and let us Know How the People are down there. How is Lonzo and Kylee gting alone tell him to wrigHt*

[No signature]

Charl Farrington also acted as an unlicensed physician in the Lamar neighborhood. If a neighbor suffered a flesh wound, he or she would be brought to Charles Farrington. Charl would cleanse the wound with whiskey, give the patient a shot of whiskey and down a shot of whiskey himself. Then, he would thread a large upholstery needle and repair the wound.

Emily Mateer Farrington (now Packer) was married to Thomas M. Farrington, and she lived for years with her in-laws, Charl and Virgie, whom she addressed as "Pap" and "Grandma." She relates vivid memories of the impact of alcohol on the household. It extended far beyond whiskey's application during Charl's repair of neighborhood wounds.

The alcoholism of Prince, Charl, and a younger brother, Hobson, made it into some members of the next generation. Charles' son, Tom, mentioned above, avoided alcohol, according to his family, until he was 29 years old. About that time, he joined a plasterers' union. Following union meetings, they would stop to drink. Tom began drinking at the post-meeting social events and was soon buying whiskey by the gallons. By the age of 51, it had killed him.

Another recollection of Emily Mateer Farrington Packer: "Grandma told me that, back in—it must have been '32 . . . '34 . . . or sometime, when they raided down there, they threw it out the third-floor window. Some of the kegs busted. Grandma said, 'We couldn't even drink our well water.' She said, 'You could get drunk off of it!'"

Charl was a very *immoderate* drinker. He needed regular trips to the well of booze, which, in Charl's case, was of the artesian variety. His visits to the Nittany Inn of nearby Snydertown or the VFW in Lock Haven were almost daily rituals for Charl, who had his own bottle opener in the Nittany Inn. In the earlier days, when he rode a horse to the Lock Haven VFW, others would help him onto his horse. Thus, he was assured a ride home since the horse could do what its besotted rider couldn't do. Far worse were Charl's attempts to get home when he drove his car to the club. His granddaughter, Tammy Farrington, told of seeing him leaving the VFW. He "backed out, and he'd hit one car, went forward and hit another car, and then just proceeded—but he made it home. It was shameful."

Tammy, Emily's daughter and Charl's granddaughter recalled her grandfather being in the basement for days at a time. "My mom would say, 'Do you know what he is doing down there? He's making whiskey.' But he was also getting drunk. He just didn't come out for days."

On one hot summer day, Lee Rossman, the driver of a truckload of chickens, stopped at Charl's place in Lamar. Charl invited the fellow to join him for a drink. The pair disappeared into the cellar. The family would not disturb them. One makes due with what is available, and all that was available was the unfinished, or *green*, whiskey that Charl had been tending. They drank it. They stayed in the basement, boozing, into the next day, sleeping in the coal bin. On the third day, they emerged from the cellar. The man climbed back into his truck, with whatever chickens were still alive, and left. Both men had emerged in a filthy state from the coal on which they had slept. Charl's return to the world of the sober was even less impressive. He had, before leaving his green whiskey, "beshit himself."

Charl also hosted Saturday night parties in Lamar. He had a jukebox and booze, two essential ingredients for partying, 1940s-style. His Saturday night parties might be attended by Joe Gardner, "Sugar" Gardner

[Joe's brother, George], Jake Kohberger and others. Stanley Bitner, a hard drinker in his youth, is now a nonagenarian, sober in Salona, although he still appreciates the occasional drink. Bitner went to some of those parties at Charl's home in Lamar. "I drank a lot of beer up at his place. I spent the whole weekend." Asked if the parties were upstairs or in the basement, Bitner recalled that "The house was wide open. How he got away with it, I don't know—he must have been paying off the neighbors," Bitner joked. Stanley Bitner also saw whiskey in the basement. "He had jugs of it down there. It was great whiskey."

During the late 1950s, Leonard Embick of Greenburr, in Sugar Valley, worked for a large contractor as a laborer. He and others would drive north from Lock Haven on Route 120 to the town of Renovo, cross the vast rail yards of that town and arrive at the Green Lantern beer garden. Turning right, they would drive into the mountains to the village of Tamarack. There, Embick worked on the construction of a large natural gas storage facility. A number of times, the car that Embick was in would follow another car, headed for the same work site. Two carpenters occupied that other car, one of whom was Charl Farrington. This pair of skilled carpenters would build the wooden forms into which Embick and the others in his crew would pour concrete. The trip from Tylersville or Lamar to Tamarack was more than fifty miles, a long drive for an alcoholic. The young Embick and his companions would often see Charl and his co-worker, both en route to work and on the return trip, drinking from a brown paper bag.

The back steps of the house in Lamar were a place where Prince and Charl relaxed and drank. "Prince and Charlie—whiskey," Emily remembered. "So you knew that if you saw them drinking, that *that's* what they were drinking. Well, Pap [Charl] and Grandma always had cats around, and Prince and Charlie put whiskey in a pie plate for them cats—tied their tails together and let them go until they killed themselves—They just sat there and laughed like goddam fools . . ."

Martha White Farrington also stayed with Charl's family sometimes, where they found her to be both vexing and entertaining. Mattie would join her brother-in-law, Charl, for 'jam sessions' of bluegrass and other country music. She could play the ukelele, guitar, banjo, violin and piano. However, her eccentricities are even more memorable. Charl, who had his own alcoholic demons, would become very angry with Mattie's drinking while at his house. Mattie was "a little, old, frail thing. Very frail. She might have weighed 90, 95 pounds," recalled her grandniece. After Charl's wife, Virgie, became senile, Mattie would sometimes stay at Charl's home in order to support Virgie. She also stayed at Charl's house the time that Charl fell off the roof and was admitted to the hospital. However, Mattie's drinking made Charl very angry.

Tammy, who was Charl and Virgie's granddaughter, related how Aunt Mattie (Martha) would send her to the store "for four cents worth of Dutch loaf [luncheon meat], a bottle of Bayer aspirin and two bottles of Coca-Cola." Tammy believes that there was something in the Coca-Cola at that time that has since been removed; but that interacted with the aspirin, causing a cheap 'buzz'. Mattie was also known to have, on at least one occasion, stolen a drink from Charl's aftershave lotion.

"She was hilarious. She would argue with him—fight with him. He used to get so mad. But, you know, back then, there was no education on alcoholism. There was very little known about it."

If her drinking wasn't troubling enough, her dressing habits were. Martha wore several layers of clothes, even during the summer months. Here is Emily's account of a time that Martha stayed overnight at Charles and Virgie Farrington's home. She was assigned to sleep with her niece, Juanita.

"We were sitting here in Virgie and Charl's living room watching television. That was in the time when you couldn't afford the damned thing! Anyhow, Juanita went up to bed—well, Mat had gone up . . . Martha had gone up—upstairs. [Martha] was staying with Virgie, and them—Oh, Virgie hated her. But, anyhow, Juanita went up—and she hollered—Juanita came out—it's an open stairway—and she hollered.

"Daddy—Daddy!"

Pap said, "What the hell do you want?"

Juanita said, "Will you get the hell up here and make Aunt Matt get out of my bed!" She added, "She has her clothes all on—her fur coat, her hat and her shoes!"

So, I went upstairs because we[23] lived up there. Juanita had a bedroom there, too, and there come Aunt Matt. She was just a little woman.

---

23. Charl and Virgie's son and his wife, Emily, and their daughters.

Mattie offered, "I didn't mean to do no harm."

"Well, I said, 'Aunt Matt, you can't sleep with your coat and hat and shoes on." I said, 'No wonder Juanita gets mad at you.'"

Mattie said, "Well, can I sleep on your couch?"

Emily consented, so Aunt Martha slept on the couch—still wearing her hat and coat and shoes.

Emily recalled more.

"She was a honey. She used to dig the centers out of pies! Still, you couldn't help but like her . . . oh, she was lazy. She didn't do nothin! I don't know how Prince ever got tangled up with her. Well, Virgie had to nurse (Mattie's) kids . . . she was too darned lazy! As little as she was, she probably didn't have any milk, but Virgie had to nurse Mattie's kids when Mattie had them 'cause Virgie had some about the same age . . ."

"You know," Emily Mateer Farrington Packer continued, "laying all jokes aside—looking back—they were good people. They *were*. They would do anything for you. And, I said to my kids, 'If it wouldn't be that we lived there with Pap Farrington—with him raising beef and pigs and stuff, we wouldn't have had meat to eat. Pap would give it to you."

Dave Porter, one of Prince's grandsons, offered this evaluation of his grand uncle, Charles: "Charl spent some time in jail. He was kind of a second fiddle, in a way. I think that his children were probably ashamed of the fact that their dad spent time in jail and things like that, but they were probably more normal than Prince's children! You know—the definition of normal—straight-laced, I guess."

Charl's family was aware that he, too, had whiskey-making skills and made some of the whiskey for Prince's market. Law officers were equally aware. Some of Charl's encounters with the law follow:

- October 1926—For the unlawful possession of alcohol, sentenced to a fine of $1,000 and six months imprisonment in the Clinton County jail.
- January 1930—Petitioned and was allowed to offer his Chrysler sedan as surety on a $1,000 bond.
- May 1930—The court granted him "the privilege of giving bond for the payment of [$200] fine and such within two days.
- June 1936—Fined $300 for a violation of the state's liquor laws.

- June 1942—After he plead guilty to liquor violations: "You, Charles Farrington—shall pay a fine of $300, the costs of prosecution and undergo imprisonment in the common jail of Clinton Co. for and during the term of three (3) months.
- November 1942—Sentenced to a fine of $300 and three months in the Clinton County prison.
- November 1948—For the manufacture and possession of illegal liquor and with the use of an illegal seal. The sentence: A fine of $100, plus costs plus confinement for 30 days.

Between Charl's two 1942 court sentences, Charl's long-suffering mate, Virginia Tinsebloom Farrington, endured the pain of arrest and trial. She pleaded "guilty" to violation of the liquor control and beverage license laws. In October of that year, she heard her sentence being pronounced: A $100 fine and, in default of payment, a 30-day stay in the same county-run hostelry that occasionally served her husband.

Prince and Charl, says Prince's grandson, Robert Porter, were obviously "affectionate brothers." By way of illustration, there is this account: Late one evening, after another session of drinking, Prince Farrington was ready to leave for home. Charl decided that Prince was too drunk to drive home, so he did the driving. However, when Charl was ready to return to Lamar, Prince showed the same sibling concern. So Prince drove back to Lamar to deliver his brother. That night, the same process—the bombed leading the bombed—was repeated several times before it ended.

Two of Charl's grandchildren, Debbie and Tammy Farrington, had been warned about possible raids. Grandma Virgie had told them: "If you kids ever come home from school and see black cars, guys with black suits and black, shiny shoes, you don't tell them nothing!"

Seemingly, the bootlegging families recognized a type of 'uniform' being worn by their revenue-agent tormentors. That style of dress—some sort of 'revenuer blacks'—set them apart from the world in which the moonshiners worked.

One day, the warnings came flooding back as the two young girls got off their school bus and walked toward their home, where they lived with their parents and their paternal grandparents, Charl and Virgie Farrington. Debbie and Tammy exited their school bus and walked toward their home. Debbie related:

"So we got part way, to where we could see all the cars, and I said to Tammy, 'Do you know what . . . we've got company.' She said, 'In black cars?' I said 'Yes,' and we could see the guys. I said, 'Do you think we should go home?' She said, 'I don't know—Where are we going to go?'

So they went home. When they walked into the house, they asked their mother: 'What's going on?' and she said, "You just never mind what's going on!"

Inside the house, there had been a lot of activity, as Charl's daughter-in-law, Emily, recalled:

"I'll tell you a quick story: One cold day . . . I mean, it was cold. I lived upstairs on the second floor of that big house down here on Silver Avenue. My husband, four kids, and I lived there. And I was out at the clothesline hanging up clothes. I had gloves on and they'd stick fast . . . and I looked over at the right—all these cars were pulling in.

I thought, 'What the hell'? I saw these men in suits getting out, carrying long flashlights. I thought, 'Oh, God!'

"So, I went in the front door, and I heard them talking to Virgie out in her kitchen. And I had two gallons of the stuff upstairs! [Short laugh] I thought, 'What the hell am I going to do?' [Apparently, they had] a search warrant! So, until I got out back to where my kitchen was, there was one of these revenuers going through my cupboards, and I said to him, 'What the hell are you doing?' and he said, 'If you're a Farrington, you know what the hell we're doing!'

"I said, 'I'm not a Farrington!' I said, 'I'm a Mateer' [her maiden name]. He took the lid off the vanilla and off the vinegar and he was smelling. I thought, 'Go on, but just don't go in my bedroom!' So I thought, 'Well, the only thing I can do is go back out to the clothesline.' I thought, 'If they come after me, I'll just take off down into the woods!" (Chuckles). So, anyhow, they left, I said to Grandma (that's what I called Virgie). I said, 'Grandma, did they all leave?' You had to know Grandma. She was a Southerner, and she talked real fast. You know, most Southerners talk slow, but she talked fast. And she said, 'I believe so.' She said, 'Let's go down in the cellar and look.' So, she got a flashlight, and we went downstairs and looked around. Nobody. I said, 'Grandma, I have two gallons of that up in my bedroom closet.' 'Oh, Lordy,' she said, 'We've got to get rid of that.' I said, 'What are we going to do with it?'

She said, 'We're going to pour it down the commode!' I said, 'Down the commode!'

"And, see, they had picked up 'Pap' Farrington [Prince's brother] . . . Charlie. They stopped him down here by the yellow church and made him go with them. They took him down to Lewisburg. He said they stopped at all the beer joints down the way. (Laughs).

The federal revenue agents had taken Charl Farrington to a number of taverns, buying him drinks. After Charl was drunk, they asked where they could get more liquor. Charl obligingly took them to a well-concealed still hidden beneath an old sawmill. Once he revealed it to them, the agents proceeded to shoot it full of holes while a dumbfounded Charl looked on. Daughter-in-law Emily mentions the deception in her account.

"They had found his still and shot holes in it. [It was] over at the old sawmill, at the railroad . . ."

"So, anyhow, they brought 'Pap' back . . . oh, it must have been about eleven o'clock at night. And Tom, my husband, said, "Daddy, where were you?" He [Charl] said, 'Where wasn't I?' He said, 'Is there any of that stuff here?' Tom said, 'Ask Emily'. That's me. I told him. I said, 'Pap, we poured it down the commode.' 'Oh, Jesus Christ!' he said. 'Give me a straw, I'll go out to the cesspool and just suck it out!'"

The revenue agents had used Charl's special weakness to trick him into revealing his still. And, although the revenue agents earned Charl's vocal damnation by leaving his handsome still perforated and ruined, they didn't arrest him. He and Virginia lived for another decade or more in the grand old house on Silver Avenue. Charles Archibald Farrington outlived his older brother, Prince, by about 15 years, dying in 1971. His grave is in a small, rural churchyard just north of Lamar. He is buried beside Virgie, who also died in 1971. Their shared headstone carries their names and vital dates, along with the Biblical phrase, "Blessed are the pure in heart, for they shall see God."[24]

## B. Joe Gardner

Joe Gardner had a picture hanging in his Lock Haven parlor for many years. The sharp old photograph depicted a moonshining operation at some undisclosed and unrecognizable woodland site. The overall size

---

24. Matthew 5:8.

of the picture slightly exceeds ten by thirteen inches. The photograph reveals piles of kegs, barrels and giant wooden bins sitting in the vicinity of a couple of large tents and a lean-to type of shelter that protected a large still. Posing amid all the moonshiners' paraphernalia are three men. The middle figure, too professionally dressed for this setting, is Joe Gardner, Prince Farrington's close friend. Prince Farrington would be furious about his outlaw cohorts posing for pictures. No matter. The men sometimes let their likenesses be recorded, thankfully for those of us today who wish we could have been witness to some of those unfolding events.

Gloria Schadt Harbach, of Williamsport, writes (August 22nd, 2010), "It does seem strange to me that there is no mention of Joe [Gardner] in any of the articles on Prince F. Prince F. may have protected him." She also offers the opinion that Joe Gardner was Prince's associate and "one of Prince Farrington's closest friends." Gloria also remembers that Joe and his second wife, June, visited Gloria's parents in the town of Castanea, where stories of Prince Farrington were exchanged. Her grandfather, William L. Schadt, was also involved with Prince, as mentioned in Chapter 12.

Joseph H. Gardner was born December 28, 1894, in Oakdale, North Carolina. He served in the military during World War I. In 1922, Gardner and his first wife traveled to Pennsylvania with Prince Farrington and lived in a house that was close to Prince's Florida Fruit Farm. Joe, his sister, Thomasina ("Tommy") and his brother George ("Sugar") were all involved with Prince Farrington, but Joe was his close friend as well. Joe Gardner, who sported a couple of gold teeth and was considered to be a "very nice person," managed to avoid the legal problems of Prince Farrington. He lived in the Loganton area for some years before moving to Lock Haven. He became a legitimate businessman, selling coal and owning a trucking company. In both businesses he was able to provide help to Farrington in the areas of storing and transporting the moonshiner's illegal liquor. The basement of Gardner's home in Lock Haven was said to have been used for the sequestering of moonshine while his trucks hauled hooch to many distant markets. Since their contraband was hidden beneath coal, that whiskey was always in kegs rather than the fragile glass jugs. John Wagner of Sugar Valley remembered being a driver for Gardner. Although he wasn't present when the trucks were loaded, he learned that several had kegs of moonshine stashed under his cargo of coal.

Joe Gardner's other illicit activity involved a romantic link to a local woman, June Kreamer Fleisher, who was born in the small town of Greenburr, off the northern slope of Nittany Mountain and across Sugar Valley from the homes of Joe Gardner and Prince Farrington. June was two decades his junior. Joe and June rendezvoused at a house that he owned just a short distance east of the Florida Fruit Farm on Spruce Run Road. One of their trysts at the house on Spruce Run Road was interrupted shortly after they, when Joe's spouse, the wife of his youth, entered the house with a shotgun. Mrs. Gardner found the couple upstairs. They raced into a closet and shut the door moments before Mrs. Gardner blasted the door with gunshot pellets. Neither of the lovers was injured, but the door, says "Dutch" Washburn, went un-replaced for years.

Joe later got divorced. Joe and June then married in a Williamsport parsonage in 1938. After a honeymoon visit to High Point, North Carolina, they resided in Lock Haven. His ex-wife, rather than returning to her North Carolina family, remained in Lock Haven, living in a house that was less than two blocks from the newlyweds. Unlike Prince, Joe became an active member of the community. He was a member of the First United Methodist Church of Lock Haven, a member of the Veterans of Foreign Wars and a life member of the Elks Lodge of Lock Haven.

After Joe died in 1980, he was buried in a local graveyard in Dunnstable Township. As a widow, June remained active. She was employed for some time at SusqueView retirement home. After she died in 2000, June Gardner was buried beside Joe, the moonshiner's partner, beneath a tombstone that is labeled "Together Forever."

## C. Lemuel Groce

In 1946, when Prince Farrington was arrested—again—and awaiting trial—again—it was Lemuel Groce who proffered the $1500 that allowed Prince to remain free until his trial. Groce lost that $1500 when Farrington skipped his trial and drove over Fourth Gap Mountain Road and into obscurity. Groce and his family nearly lost their house, but it was a gesture that he would likely have repeated even if he had known the decision that Prince Farrington would make. After all, he was one of the men who followed Prince into Penn's Woods and who, for some years, helped Prince in the moonshine business. Lemuel lived in Castanea (pronounced *kas TANE uh*, locally), a Clinton County town first settled by Italian immigrants (hence the Italian name for the chestnuts that were then abundant in the area).

The impression, still held today, by David L. Eck of Jersey Shore was that Lemuel "Jack" Groce was the 'right-hand man' of Prince Farrington. This might remind the reader of the fact that there are two Lemuel's in American whiskey making. That is a whopping coincidence. Lemuel Groce was once in the illegal distilling trade, working for a man who was far more prominent than himself, Prince Farrington. The other Lemuel in the distilling trade, but legally, was Lemuel Motlow, who also worked for a man who was far more prominent than himself. However, Lemuel Motlow's name is still on the label, and the more famous man for whom he worked was Jack Daniel of the Jack Daniel's distillery. Also, it seems likely that both Lemuel's got their uncommon name from an obscure Biblical king mentioned in the Bible's book of Proverbs (31:1-9). The Biblical Lemuel was advised by his unnamed mother to concentrate on wise rule and to avoid chasing women and using strong drink.

Lemuel Groce was another Tarheel by birth, having been born in tiny Worthville (Randolph County), a few miles southeast of Randleman and about fifteen miles from Nubbin Ridge, the farmstead of Prince Farrington's family. Lemuel's parents were Herbert and Ollie Jenkins Groce. His mother, Ollie, was a full American Indian who was killed while she stood behind a coal truck, guiding the driver toward the unloading area when she was accidentally crushed against the building.

While there are more than two dozen entries in the Lock Haven/Williamsport telephone directory with the spelling of G-R-O-S-S, only two have the G-R-O-C-E spelling, Lemuel's daughter, Jacque and his widow, Mary. He was still a young man when he came north to work with Prince David Farrington. Once here, he married Venetta Mader, a local girl from Jersey Shore. With Venetta, Lemuel Groce fathered three daughters. Venetta eventually left Lemuel and became an elementary teacher in Maryland, where she died of cancer while still a young woman. Lemuel, known among his Pennsylvania neighbors as 'Jack,' not only worked with but was a close friend of Prince Farrington. Jacque Groce is one of the three daughters of Lemuel and Venetta; Jacque recalled an occasion when she was with others in the car when her father was driving along the isolated road that linked her hometown, Castanea, with the next town to the east, McElhattan. Her father stopped, she remembered, "in the middle of nowhere" and walked into the nearby wooded area. Soon, he returned to the family, carrying a paper sack containing a bottle of moonshine whiskey. The moonshine was the object of his stop.

Jacque remembers just one visit to the Lemuel Groce house by Prince Farrington. Near the end of his career, Jacque recalled, Prince stopped by just one time, and he was "apparently drunk."

Jacque also remembers, when, as a child in the Robb Elementary School, she told the class her father's line of work. While her teacher may have enjoyed her description, Jacque thought that she was merely identifying an innocuous occupation. Her daddy, she informed all, was a bootlegger. While the FBI was hunting Prince David Farrington as a fugitive, the special agent in Philadelphia filed a report (PH 115-4), in which he informs the Washington bureau that Lemuel Groce was "a former bootlegger," who now (1950) "operates a slaughterhouse in Castanea, Pennsylvania, south of Lock Haven." Actually, Lemuel Groce was also plagued by a rumor that he was involved in a shooting where someone died during a raid on a still. My informant was uncertain just who it was who was shot and just who it was who did the shooting. In any case, it caused Lemuel Groce to begin identifying himself as "Jack Taylor." While working as a bartender at Shirk's hotel in Jersey Shore (mid-to-late 1950s), few people knew his real name.

Lemuel Groce wed for a second time, marrying Mary Thompson, whom Jacque says had a very positive influence on her father's behavior, particularly in convincing him to avoid heavy drinking. "She saved his life," according to Jacque's respectful assessment.

## D. Henry Sampson
TWO NATIVE AMERICANS?

During an interview, George Porter, Prince Farrington's son-in-law, said that his father-in-law had the appearance of a Native American. As the interviewer was recording their talk and was also looking at photographs of Prince, Porter described Farrington as having "a very dark complexion, coal black hair, when he had hair. He was a strong man, a very powerful man. He wasn't one to have pictures taken. He said, "You know, a person's a damned fool for taking pictures." George Porter explained his father-in-law's seemingly Native American features by observing that the early settlers of the Carolinas "went inland and bred with the Indians...." Prince also claimed to have been descended from survivors of the so-called "Lost Colony" who intermarried with the Native Americans. Such a claim might be impressive if it wasn't such a popular claim in North Carolina.

Two of Prince's three sons, Thomas and Gayle Randall, also had swarthy complexions and high cheekbones. Also, like his father, Gayle was stocky, barrel-chested and strong, traits considered to be common among some of the Native American groups of the American Piedmont. A family tradition tells of Gayle transferring from Jersey Shore High School to the high school in Lock Haven in order to get into a school with a wrestling team. Gayle Farrington made the wrestling team and went on to defeat the reigning state champion before promptly quitting the team.

It seems strangely ironic that this man, Prince Farrington—who might have been part American Indian—became close friends with Henry Sampson, a man who was a known American Indian and one who had come through the rigors of the Carlisle Indian Industrial School as well.

The Indian Wars in the American West ended with one hellish decade of conflict. That decade began June 25th and 26th, 1876, in the Montana hills along the Little Big Horn River (known to the Native Americans of the area as the Greasy Grass). Here occurred the smashing victory of American Indian warriors over the golden-haired and vainglorious Lieutenant Colonel George Armstrong Custer (who also held the honorary rank of major general) and the ill-fated troops under his command. The decade ended on September 4, 1886, when the Apache war chief, Geronimo, surrendered to the U.S. military in Skeleton Canyon in the Arizona Territory.

Long before the Indian Wars concluded, 'reformers' were pondering the most appropriate way to assimilate the Native Indians into the more 'civilized' culture of the intruder Americans. Sincere reformers would have included Henry Laurens Dawes (1816-1903), who sponsored the Dawes Act of 1887, which gave land ownership to many Indians. Another major reformer was General Richard Henry Pratt (1840-1924). Pratt's notion of reform involved the assimilation of the Native Americans by taking their youngsters from the reservations and putting them into distant 'Americanizing' boarding schools. It was the boarding school concept of General Richard Henry Pratt that brought an Indian boy to Carlisle and, indirectly, provided a future friend and cohort to Prince David Farrington.

General Richard Henry Pratt was very successful in creating off-reservation boarding schools, where large numbers of Indian boys and girls—with the acquiescence of tribal leaders—could be shipped for enforced assimilation into the 'white' way of life. General Pratt's crusade for assimilation went forward when he was able to open the abandoned barracks of a former cavalry post in Carlisle, Pennsylvania, near Harrisburg. This opening occurred in 1879, and the school, under Pratt's inflexible leadership for its first quarter century, operated until 1918. This was the first and largest of the off-reservation schools, and it altered the lives of more than 10,000 American-Indian children from nearly 150 tribal groups.

At the Carlisle Indian Industrial School, thousands of bewildered American-Indian children were indoctrinated into the ways of White America. Hundreds of miles from their tribal homes, they were required to change their clothing styles, hairstyles, language and other native ways of living. Most of these Americanized youngsters returned to their tribal families after their several years of cultural shock were completed.

Henry Sampson came to General Pratt's Carlisle Indian School from the Saginaw Chippewa people. His parents were John and Mary Sampson. He was born on the 21st day of June in 1882. His birth date tells us that he was about seven years older than Prince Farrington. That age difference did not prevent them from forming a strong and long-lasting friendship. Sampson had a home address listed as Kawkawlin, Michigan, near Bay City, on the shores of Saginaw Bay, in Lake Huron. He was twelve years old when he arrived at Carlisle on September 5, 1894. Records indicate that he re-enrolled in 1903. The institutionally-generated newspaper reports Sampson's having returned in March of 1907 from the Bloomsburg, Pennsylvania area, where he had been staying with an unnamed family. Shortly after that (May 1, 1907), Henry Sampson finally separated from the school, leaving at "his own request." He had been affiliated with the school for more than a dozen years. Henry Sampson had two sisters—Anna and Jennie—who were at one time enrolled in the Carlisle Indian School as well. However, both girls returned to their tribal relatives on the shores of Saginaw Bay in Michigan. Anna became Mrs. Isaac Cook of West Bay City and Jennie is known to have lived, at one time, in Kawkawlin.

Apparently, Henry Sampson, the full-blooded Chippewa, chose to remain in the east. In 1917 (December 17), a letter written by a person named R. B. Rhone indicates that a somewhat homesick Henry Sampson was then working on a farm near Bloomsburg, Pennsylvania, just outside the village of Rupert. Mr. Rhone, writing on the letterhead of the Freight Agent for the Delaware, Lackawanna, and Western Railroad, was writing to the Carlisle Indian School to ask for someone to communicate with a lonely and forlorn Henry Sampson. The petitioner describes Samson as being "worthy of confidence, and his employer [Stanley E. Ruckle] is very interested in him and holds him in high esteem." A letter (December 19, 1917) from the superintendent thanks Mr. Rhone for the letter and informs him that if Henry Samson sends fifty cents, he will receive the weekly newsletter from the school. The letter also includes the last known addresses (both in Michigan) for Henry's two sisters who had attended the Carlisle institution. The letter concludes by saying that the school officials would be glad to have Henry "come to Carlisle sometime."

Several people who came into contact with Henry Sampson would remember his stature but not his name. Prince's grandson, Dave Porter recalled, as a child, living in Prince's rented farm in Mackeyville while his father, George Porter, was serving in the military. He remembered Sampson as a small, brown-stained person who told fascinating stories. He also recalled a time when he joined "the Indian" in the following of some wild animal tracks down a lane near the farm. In his 1983 interview with Richard Brown, Lester Seiler told of when he and Henry Sampson shared a menial chore:

> [Potatoes] that we shipped out were in 100-pound (burlap) bags. I've got a couple of them [large needles] here now. Yeah.

> That there Indian and I were down there under Joe Gardner, you know. I don't know if you ever heard about him [Henry Sampson] or not. He was down there at Spruce Run. He was a purebred Indian—a little fellow. I don't know how long he was down there, a couple of years, at that lower place. He came up there. Him and I, well, we sewed a hundred and fifty 100-pound bags that Joe took down into the Carolinas.

Records don't answer the major question: How did this full-blooded Chippewa meet and become friends with Prince David Farrington, the North Carolina native whose son-in-law suspected that Prince, too, was part Native American? From the mid-1920s to the mid-1940s, Sampson would be one of Farrington's loyal workers in the moonshine trade. He, too, succumbed to the allurement of alcohol. One Farrington family recollection was of Sampson getting drunk and spending a winter night on the open back of a pickup truck with a bag of frozen potatoes for a pillow. George Porter often saw Prince and Henry, each hiding their supplies of alcohol from the other, with each trying to locate the other's stash when his own was depleted. Porter also remembered when George Slifer, Jersey Shore's police chief, informed George that two men were seen intoxicated and trying to negotiate the streets of Jersey Shore on a tractor. The two rounders were Henry Samson and Prince Farrington. Slifer told Porter that he didn't want to arrest anyone and that George had "better find them and get them out of town damned quick!"

Henry Samson, Native American, was one more person from the Farrington vortex to be arrested.

In May of 1944, Farrington and Samson were arrested. They were brought before Judge Henry Hipple and the two associate judges, Charles Dunn and James F. Bridgens. The pair was charged with the illegal manufacture of liquor. Henry Samson, who had no prior criminal record, was fined $75 and half the court costs and put on probation. Prince Farrington was fined $250 and half the costs. Prince was also released after pleading for leniency because he had a 200-acre farm and two of his sons were away in military service.

In the mid-1940s, when Prince's fortunes had taken a sharp downturn, there was no longer work for Henry Sampson. Eventually, he began working for Joe Gardner on a Gardner-owned farm near Loganton. In mid-July of 1946, Gardner had Sampson working on a farm near Salona. It was there that Sampson fell from a hay wagon. He was rushed to a hospital, where he was found to have suffered a concussion and three broken vertebrae. Henry Sampson was paralyzed. Prince visited his old friend in the hospital, where Henry lamented that he did not want to live in that condition. The 63-year-old alumnus of the Carlisle Indian School died a few days later. Mrs. W. J. Shoemaker, the coroner, ruled out an inquest.

### E. Clair Thompson

The town of Jersey Shore sits on the north bank of the West Branch of the Susquehanna, about 200 miles from the river's far-away source in Cambria County. After Prince Farrington moved from Loganton to Antes Fort, the latter's neighbor, Jersey Shore, became the principal municipality in his life.

Clair Thompson's father, Lydie Curtin Thompson, was among the most successful entrepreneurs of Jersey Shore. In the early 1890s, he started a meat market. Soon, he was operating three markets in town. When automobiles hit the general market, Lydie Thompson opened a Chrysler/Plymouth dealership, which also offered Reo trucks. While Lydie operated from the central meat market, his two sons operated his outlying markets, with Lee at the West End Food Market and Clair at the market that was housed in an annex to the Victoria Theater. When Prince Farrington moved into the large home across the Susquehanna River from Jersey Shore, he became a close friend of Clair Thompson.

Clair Thompson was among the several businessmen who helped Prince Farrington get the supplies he needed. Clair Thompson got huge supplies of sugar for Prince, the sugar that was delivered by night to the places where Prince would use it. The sugar was mixed with rye or corn to create the mash from which the bourbon or whiskey was distilled. Clair also passed along, to his son, Dick, the understanding that, while Prince Farrington chose to move north to Clinton County, Pennsylvania, because of the secluded gullies and streams—ideal for sequestered distilling—he also wanted to be closer to New York City and the other large clusters of thirsty Prohibition violators.

The Thompsons owned a cabin along Pine Creek, several miles north of Jersey Shore. They hosted weekend parties at the cabin, where food from Thompson markets and liquor from Farrington stills were abundant. Lee Thompson recounted a story of his brother, Clair, getting drunk at one of those cabin parties. Needing the toilet facilities, Clair staggered toward the outhouse, reached the proper location and tumbled into the open cesspool! Several of the party-goers had moved the outhouse a few feet farther from the cabin in order to play a trick on poor Clair. All those sober enough to see the humor in the situation laughed heartily. Then, Clair was fished from the sewage and washed with buckets of water. Still besotted and besmeared, Clair fell asleep in the back seat of his handsome, big sedan. One of the other party-goers braved the stench in order to drive the drunken Clair back to Jersey Shore. The car, with Clair still dozing inside, was parked in Clair's garage, to be found the next morning.

Dick Thompson, who heads Jersey Shore's Thompson Meat Market today, recalled the ugly, wintry weather of one particular night when he was a child. The night was "colder than hell," and his parents had gone to the Jersey Shore Elks Club for the evening. Prince Farrington was out of the area, serving a sentence in prison. There was a rapping on the door of the Thompson household. When he and his brother opened the door, they were momentarily startled by the strange, ice-covered figure before them. "It looked like a ghost!" Dick remembered. When they finally realized that it was Henry Sampson, they invited him into the house and gave him food. Henry Sampson told them that he had been watching one of Prince's stills for several days with no one relieving him or bringing him food. So, Sampson had walked the several wintry miles to Jersey Shore to the one place where he knew that Prince Farrington had friends. When the boys' parents returned, their dad, Clair Thompson, let Sampson eat and stay the night. The following morning, he took Sampson back to the briefly-abandoned still site.

## F. Jacob "Jake" Kohberger

"They were buddies," said Miller Stamm of Loganton about the relationship of Jake Kohberger and Prince Farrington. Stamm has lived all of his 100 years in Sugar Valley and has recalled, as well, joining his father (1934) in moving an old plank house from Rosecrans into Loganton, where Stamm and his bride were to live. Stamm also recalled the general store that Kohberger had near the town of Carroll, in Sugar Valley, about five miles east of Loganton. The store was attached to a two-story house where Kohberger and his wife, Mary Jane (nee Overdorf), lived.

The Kohbergers had several children, including a daughter who died as a young mother, another daughter, Geraldine and a son, John J., who was somewhat estranged from his father and who, as this is written, is in his nineties and living in Williamsport. After Jake and Mary Jane separated, she remained at their home in Carroll. Jake lived elsewhere and owned a number of businesses, including a nightclub, the Minnequa Club across the Susquehanna River from Williamsport, and the Buffalo Inn near present-day Woolrich. The Minnequa Club was at Duboistown, and most patrons arrived from the Williamsport side of the river by boat. Daughter Geraldine (1920-2009) worked—as a teen—at her dad's Minnequa Club. She later inherited the Buffalo Inn.

Jake Kohberger was one of Prince Farrington's early financial backers. Farrington saw a wealthy return if the initial investment was large enough to buy the equipment needed to produce large quantities of illegal whiskey. Kohberger, who also sold grain to Prince, was convinced. He and the other early investors in Farrington's plan reaped where they had sown. Despite his increased financial fortune, not all in his family were impressed. It is Jake Kohberger's granddaughter, Susan Glossner, who has a less-than-sympathetic attitude toward her late grandfather's ties to the illegal trade in alcohol. Ms. Glossner's caustic observation: "If people want it and there's a lot of money involved, someone will provide it."

Jake's Minnequa Club was near the southern entrance to the Duboistown bridge, near South Williamsport. This was a large, 'classy' nightclub, reached by boat. The name of the club, Minnequa, is a name made from Indian sounds rather than from actual Indian words. It matches the name of a small town in Pennsylvania's Bradford County. According to one source (Donehoo, 1928), the sounds that form the name Minnequa loosely mean "to drink together."

At one time, Kohberger also ran the Buffalo Inn near Jersey Shore. While involved with the Buffalo Inn, he was said to have had a still hidden in the tobacco barn across the street, as well as a black bear, "Inky," in a cage behind the inn. That particular bruin had been on display, even earlier, at Kohberger's store at Carroll. Jake's daughter, Geraldine, later ran the Buffalo Inn. The Buffalo Inn was an authentic attraction for passing travelers since Kohberger also had a herd of a dozen or so imported buffalo grazing in an adjoining pasture. Eventually, the Buffalo Inn was licensed to serve alcohol. It also served buffalo burgers, an exotic food in those days and in that part of the nation. One of Prince's grandsons felt that local people were unimpressed with the bison burgers, which they found to be chewy and have the taste of boiled shoe leather. The Buffalo Inn was demolished in the early days of the 21st century.

In his later years, Kohberger drove to Alaska. The trip gained local publicity for the former bootlegger. It also gained some broader notoriety, as the Nash Corporation ran some ads featuring the "noted sportsman" and his Rambler station wagon on the highway to Alaska.

Jake Kohberger was well-known locally for being generous to people who needed some work or other assistance. Locally, "A lot of people worshiped him," recalled a family member. That same moment of recollection included the thought that some few were not so enchanted.

All but one of the several buildings long associated with Jake Kohberger no longer exist. His house and store in Carroll are long gone, razed by the bulldozer to make room for Interstate 80. His Minnequa Club in South Williamsport no longer stands, and his Buffalo Inn on Route 150 was recently demolished. Only his house in Avis remains. But, so long as the Prince Farrington legend lingers, so will the memory of brother Charles, as well as the memories of Joe Gardner, Lemuel Groce, Henry Sampson, Clair Thompson, and Jake Kohberger.

On the other hand, Colonel Henry Shoemaker has been a legend in his own right. His name was already very well known in Pennsylvania before his friendship with Prince Farrington. Colonel Shoemaker was a popular storyteller whose books and other writings had already made him prominent even before Prince Farrington had arrived in the area.

## Colonel Henry Wharton Shoemaker, Friend and Fabulist

Colonel Henry Wharton Shoemaker (1880-1958) was a fabulist or folklorist, or some less printable descriptor. He wrote baseless stories that state historians mostly discredited. He lived less than ten miles from the Farrington home in Antes Fort. Shoemaker of McElhattan must have considered it quite fortuitous that the area's most successful moonshiner had moved but a "stone's throw" from his home. Shoemaker "was known to pal around with Prince and his cohorts," according to Bob Porter, who also pointed out that "almost all of Farrington's friends and coworkers were serious imbibers..." During Prohibition, Shoemaker apparently suffered through the agony of abstinence, along with many other alcohol lovers, so he became one of Prince Farrington's steady customers as well as a close friend. Prince's son-in-law, George Porter, related that Shoemaker "was a frequent caller over the bridge, you know. He liked his whiskey..." As a popular writer of folklore, a former minister to Bulgaria, and the owner of several newspapers; Shoemaker had enough political influence to be appointed (1948) Pennsylvania's first—and last—state folklorist, a post that was promptly abolished when he finally left the position in 1956. The Farrington family members feel that Shoemaker used his political clout in Prince's favor. As one family member stated, "It's more than likely that Shoemaker paved the way for Prince's whiskey to be delivered to highly placed officials in Harrisburg and Washington."

### H. Faith Currin Yarrison

Faith Currin Yarrison was the only female who qualified as a Prince Farrington cohort. However, because of her willingness to use a gun to defend her illegal booze from thieves and actually use it on multiple occasions, her account appears in the preceding chapter.

### NO BOURBON MYTH

The phenomenon of whiskey runners becoming stock car drivers was immortalized in Robert Mitchum's 1958 motion picture, "Thunder Road." The portrayal was typical of 1950s life among the moonshine runners. While the movie's song mentions mostly Kentucky/Tennessee towns, the lasting impact of whiskey hauling transforming some drivers into auto-racing stars transpired in Prince Farrington's native area in North Carolina.

It's no coincidence: Prince Farrington, the nation's master moonshiner, as well as a major player among the nation's bootleggers, was born in rural Guilford County, North Carolina. This is just about 70 miles from Ronda, the 1931 birthplace of Robert Glenn Johnson Jr., known to racing fans as Junior (without the quotes). Junior Johnson is now recognized as one of the all-time great race drivers, a NASCAR champion who honed his skills in the Carolina hills. Junior Johnson does not hide the information about his youthful years—including his eleven months term in prison—as a driver hauling illegal booze on the byways. Johnson says radio host Eli Gold "epitomizes NASCAR . . ." and is "the embodiment of the moonshine days, which obviously begat the sport."[25]

It's the truth. Several of the top stock car race drivers began their 'leadfoot' careers as speed-loving bootleggers in rural North Carolina. Before they became legendary track stars of the old dirt race tracks, they sped through the Tarheel countryside, carrying moonshine whiskey to the saloons and salons of North Carolina and neighboring states.

Today, NASCAR is a sports phenomenon. It has grown since its 1947 founding into a continent-wide activity. It is now America's fastest-growing sport. One might observe, tongue-in-cheek, that if our foreign oil sources were ever denied us, we'd likely go to war in order to keep our racetracks roaring.—

What is, or was, stock car racing? Today's racing cars are prebuilt, expensive, high-speed machines known as sprint cars. Although very costly, most sprint car drivers keep a spare race car. Such was not the case in the early days of racing; days when young drivers took standard (or stock) automobiles and modified them as their automotive skills and finances allowed. Here is one example that appears to be typical: Around 1950, Glenn Walter, who lives about 20 miles from Clinton County in Penn's Creek, Pennsylvania—spent $50 for an old Ford coupe. He invested another hundred dollars or so into 'building' his stock car, including the addition of galvanized water pipes that formed his protective 'cage.' This was his own money. He then began competing in the races that were held at a local dirt track in Selinsgrove. Today, both of Walter's sons are sprint car drivers, with one of his sons still racing in Clinton County, where the track sits about three miles from one of the old Prince Farrington still sites.

There were modest connections between Prince Farrington and the early stock car racers. Prince and other young men regularly hauled illegal whiskey at breakneck speeds over the byways of North Carolina,

---

25. *American Profile*, April 18-24, 2010, p. 14.

delivering contraband liquor. As mentioned, several of those drivers, whose driving skills were honed by hauling hooch, became the earliest stock car champions of the 1940s and after. Prince David Farrington lived in the very heart of what later became NASCAR country before he sought the imagined solace and solitude of north-central Pennsylvania. As mentioned above, while in North Carolina, Prince had lived about 50 miles from the hometown of Junior Johnson, who spent nearly a year in jail as a young man, for bootlegging; before going on to become an auto-racing legend. Prince also lived less than twenty miles from what is now the Richard Petty Museum at Randleman, North Carolina.

There are actually two family ties between the Pettys and the Farringtons. The first: Richard Petty's mother, Lib (Elizabeth) Toomes Petty (b. 1917) was a cousin to Prince's sister-in-law, Cora McCandless (Mrs. John Alexander) Farrington. The second link also involves Richard Petty's mother. Lib Toomes Petty, was also a cousin to the man who married Prince's niece, Cindy Rayle Toomes. Cindy has recalled how her late husband, Blease Toomes, and Richard Petty's dad, Lee—whenever they met—would go barreling down the open highway in reckless but friendly competition. Cindy was with Blease for one of those utterly unsanctioned races. Lee Petty (b. 1914), also a moonshine hauler as a young man, became an early champion race driver. As did Junior Johnson and others, Lee Petty eventually left the moonshine run to become a champion race driver. Lee had a stellar record until it was eclipsed by his son, Richard Petty. Junior Johnson and Richard Petty, Lee's son, became (May 23, 2010) two of the first three race car drivers to be inducted into NASCAR's Hall of Fame, which is located in another North Carolina town, Charlotte. To further thicken the plot: As recently as 2010, Cindy Toomes and Patricia Petty (Richard Petty's sister-in-law) vacationed together at Holden Beach in North Carolina.

There was yet another slight connection between Prince Farrington and stock car racing. Sam Fuller of Jersey Shore, was a personal chauffeur for Prince. Fuller was mentioned in an FBI report (February 20th, 1951) as one who drove used cars for Prince. Fuller did considerable driving while taking Prince on local trips. He also drove one of four pickup trucks the 1500 or so miles to Oklahoma City when Prince was delivering the four trucks that he'd sold to a party in the Sooner State. Did the four trucks also carry some precious contraband cargo? "Maybe, maybe not," says Fuller, who also says that if moonshine was being hauled, he was unaware. He does remember driving back to Pennsylvania through North Carolina, where he and Prince spent three weeks visiting members of the Farrington clan. Sam Fuller, who still resides in Jersey Shore and now dabbles in the flea market trade at the Antes Fort flea market, owned and maintained a stock car but had another individual do the driving. The car was a three-window Ford coupe sponsored by Prince's son-in-law, George Porter. Fuller modified the car for racing purposes by removing the manifolds and installing makeshift roll bars. Fuller says that his car and its driver raced at the Riverview Speedway. The track was a one-half-mile dirt oval located in the Williamsport suburb of Newberry. Yes, Fuller informs us, the Porter-Fuller coupe won some races. While Sam Fuller did not drive in stock car races, he is a former moonshine-era driver who once sped through the night to deliver hooch and then owned a car that sped through the afternoon to deliver thrills to stock car fans.

## THE TRAVELING TAVERNS

When Prince's moonshine was to be shipped in large quantities, trucks were employed; but smaller shipments could be made by using large automobiles. Fortunately for the bootleggers, the cars of the 1920s and 1930s were ostentatiously large. Models designed to appeal to the affluent offered more potent engines, with roomier bodies on longer and larger chassis. Whatever was not essential for the operation could be converted into storage space for moonshine.

On a far, more modest scale, it was mentioned in Chapter 1 that Prince concealed liquor beneath the fenders of his little green truck. That was but one of many modified vehicles owned by Prince.

Charles "Bud" Coira Sr. bought a 1929 or 1930-model Pierce-Arrow sedan automobile from Prince. Coira's son, Charles, Junior, now an attorney in North Carolina, recalls, "I remember distinctly, my dad bought a 12-cylinder Pierce-Arrow, with wooden-spoke wheels. It was the first car with headlights in the fenders." Mr. Coira Jr. also recalls the radiator ornament: an unclad man kneeling and aiming a bow and arrow down the highway. The bottom of that metal bowman would change color if the car were overheating. The Coira family used the car, once owned by Prince Farrington, to attend the World's Fair in Chicago in 1933. This Pierce-Arrow reinforces the notion, expressed elsewhere, that Prince Farrington loved big cars.

Charles Coira's wife, Mary Dempsey Coira, was the principal character in another of those stories about Farrington country that involved someone connected to Prince Farrington through his illicit liquor. As Clinton County Museum curator/historian Lou Bernard recites the tale, Mary, a native of Scotland, had a secret recipe for making meatloaf. The dish became a community favorite. Various organizations solicited her culinary specialty, and she willingly obliged. When the local chapter of the Women's Christian Temperance Union sought her favor, she unhesitatingly provided the meatloaf. Then came the quandary. Some of the WCTU members requested copies of her recipe. The problem? The Coira's regularly bought Prince Farrington's bootleg whiskey and Mary always added a quantity to her meatloaf. As her family later admitted, this daughter of Caledonia provided her neighbors with the recipe, but without a key ingredient, an ingredient that would have riled the local members of the nation's staunchest anti-alcohol force.

A Packard automobile that Prince owned once served as a model for moonshining modification. Lester Hauser worked for a while at the River Front Chevrolet garage in Jersey Shore. One day a large Packard automobile was brought in for some repair work. As automobiles go, it was a gem, with its wooden spoke wheels, powerful engine and boat-like length. The shop foreman told Hauser to fix the gas tank. Hauser slid beneath the large vehicle, found the gas tank and examined it fully. Then he slid out again and told the foreman that the tank was completely intact. The foreman's response: "Lester, I said the *gas tank*!" Eventually, Lester Hauser was made to understand. The Packard's *real* gas tank did not leak. Nor did it have any gas. *That* tank was loaded with booze. There was, however, a homemade gas tank mounted beneath the back seat. That smaller tank was the one that held the gasoline. Lester removed that tank, got a replacement from a shop in Williamsport that did custom work, and, before closing time, the car was repaired.

The Packard that was assigned to Lester Hauser for repair was one of Prince's vehicles. It was this garage, River Front Chevrolet in Jersey

Shore, that regularly serviced Prince Farrington's vehicles. Before Hauser was finished servicing the Packard, he also learned that the rear windows couldn't be lowered. Why? Because there were canisters of moonshine inside the rear side panels. It was nice to have such a friendly garage in such a friendly neighborhood. The River Front Chevrolet garage was the property that adjoined the Gamble Farm Inn, the inn once owned by Gladys and George Porter, Prince's daughter and son-in-law.

## THE HOOCH HAULERS

One of this biography's primary goals was to demonstrate Prince David Farrington's great capacity for moonshining. The main evidence sought, month after month, was the growing number of still sites that local people could identify. This effort was rewarded with far more than one could hope to find. The number of sites identified also suggested that dozens of people had to be involved in the many steps of the process: building the sites, gathering raw materials, cooking the moonshine, converting the liquor to a smaller proof number, bottling, and delivering the product to the local and distant markets.

Prince David Farrington sat in the catbird seat within his moonshining and bootlegging business. Farrington had to balance his business interests, of course. He also had to work with a large number of individuals, who might fall into six categories: Suppliers, still operators, haulers, uninvolved neighbors, customers and authorities. On one end of the operation were the men who cleaned and operated the stills, tended the vats and bottled the finished product. On the opposite end of the operation were those vital individuals who delivered Prince Farrington's booze to those who eagerly sought and bought. The haulers were as vital as any group with whom Prince Farrington dealt.

Some drivers will remain anonymous. They would include local people who might haul Prince's moonshine as a way to feed their families. Harry Lytle, mentioned elsewhere, tells of an effective technique used by some haulers, who were distributing a few pint bottles locally. A husband and wife might climb into their car or their horse-drawn wagon. Their children would be accompanying them. With the baby among the passengers, they needed to take a galvanized bucket for the bountiful accumulation of soiled diapers. Suspicious revenuers might stop the car or wagon and look for contraband. They would conscientiously check in boxes, under blankets and so on. However, the haulers knew that a revenuer's sense of duty did not override his sense of smell. The pint bottles of hooch remained hidden, covered by some authentic, used diapers, a form of balance in the Prohibition-created universe.

Here, we list together—likely for the first time anywhere—about 20 of Prince's drivers, individuals who dared to drive into the night with the incriminating intoxicants as their primary traveling companions.

**Emily Packer** (mentioned earlier in this chapter) lives in Lamar, Pennsylvania, the hometown—for most of his life—of Charles Archibald Farrington. Emily was Charles Farrington's daughter-in-law. Unlike her father-in-law, Emily's husband, Tom, was no drinker until well into manhood, when he joined an electricians' union. The union members ended their workday by stopping at a bar. A different member of the group paid for the drinks each day. Tom finally became an alcoholic, a condition which his family thinks helped to kill him a few years later. While most of Prince's whiskey haulers were men, an exception was his brother's daughter-in-law, Emily. As a young married woman, Emily delivered bootleg liquor for Prince. According to her account, Emily was surprisingly active for someone on the distaff side. She and her daughter, Debbie, provided the following destinations: "Beech Creek, over Seven Mountains, Loganton, Lock Haven, Nittany. Yeah, up to Nittany. I favored the short runs. My dad would have killed me if he'd ever known! My dad was George Mateer from Tylersville. He had the store and post office over there."

Once, while delivering to a private home in Laurel Run, Emily saw a police car following her. She was terrified but kept driving, with the car still following. Coming to a fork in the road, she turned away from her intended route. The police car, going toward a different objective, swept past on the other road in the fork. Too upset to drive further, she quickly turned and drove home.

How many others drove for Prince Farrington? Despite the passing of the decades, a number of Farrington drivers are well remembered. Although we'll never know any total number, we can specifically mention several more names to accompany the name of Emily Mateer Farrington (now Packer). If one is willing to imagine the amount of driving by each law-breaking driver, the magnitude of Prince Farrington's moonshine-hauling operation begins to permeate the brain.

It seems that, within the passing of a few decades, the aging drivers were often willing to identify themselves as Farrington drivers. Following is a very shoddy list of some of the drivers. Several are known by personal conversations with the former haulers, but most came from relatives. Their willingness to share this information has really improved the worth of this biography.

Who else drove?

**Melvin Button** of Jersey Mills drove for Prince, when he wasn't tending Prince's remote still in Stradley Hollow, opposite the village of Jersey Mills, as described in Chapter 11.

Jane Bubb Miller (mentioned elsewhere) told us, "I was told that my dad, **John Bruner Bubb**, helped Prince deliver booze. My dad would be the type."

Robert C. ("Bob") Cowfer Jr., of the town of Oval, tells us that his father, **Robert Cowfer Sr.**, was one of the drivers who transported hooch for Prince Farrington. Cowfer also says that his former father-in-law, **Wesley Koch Jr.** and Wesley's father, **Wesley Koch Sr.**, both 'ran' moonshine, with Wesley Sr. having been arrested more than once. All three delivered moonshine that had been stored in the old Paint Mill near Antes Fort.

Priscilla McCloskey Runk revealed that her grandfather, **Blair Rainey**, left the town of Gipsy, in the coal fields of Indiana County, in western Pennsylvania, to come to the Clinton/Lycoming counties area. Once in "Farrington Country," Rainey settled in the town of Antes Fort. Rainey loved poker and would get into all-night poker sessions, earning himself the nickname "Poker" Rainey. Blair "Poker" Rainey was also remembered for a failed attempt to kill another player in a heated poker confrontation. When Rainey wasn't cutting flagstone, timbering pulpwood, or trying to fill an inside straight, he was driving moonshine liquor for Prince Farrington.

Another pair of men from Jersey Shore who were remembered as being drivers for Prince Farrington were **John Eckel** and **Sam Brown**. Brown's most memorable run was the one he took with Julia, his pregnant wife, by his side. They left Jersey Shore and drove toward their destinations of Altoona and Pittsburgh, but authorities stopped them en route. They were jailed but were released in time for Julia to deliver their baby.

**Russell Duck** was not a Farrington driver; but he did deliver moonshine liquor, according to his son, Roy. Delivering moonshine didn't interfere with his duties as a local constable. Duck, a resident of Loganton, was just one more individual who was a member of the law-enforcement community and was also a member of the law-flouting community when alcohol was involved. Russell Duck once had the good fortune of finding a cask of caramel, from which he sold small amounts to anyone who needed it to color their homemade whiskey. His son, Roy, relates that it was common on Sunday mornings—when most area residents were occupied with church services—to have a horse-drawn wagon, driven by a regular Farrington driver, turn off the main road and onto the lane leading to the farm of Frank and Hazel Kreamer. The wagon was stacked high with wood, beneath which were kegs of moonshine. The whiskey was then hidden in the Kreamer barn. John Harbach, who helped to thrash grain at Frank Kreamer's barn, observes, "I never heard that Frank's barn was used to store prohibited liquor, but it wouldn't surprise me, as Frank's family was very poor."

Eventually, it happened. The revenue agents became aware of the ruse and raided the Kreamer farm. Roy, who lived several hundred yards from the raiding site, remembers hearing the cracking of kegs being smashed. Frank and Hazel Kreamer, along with two kegs of confiscated moonshine liquor, were taken to the courthouse in Lock Haven. By the time the raid was completed and the Kreamers were delivered to the courthouse, Prince Farrington had already arrived with the bail money, allowing Hazel and Frank to return home promptly. The fate of the confiscated liquor was not so clear. Of the two kegs taken as evidence, only one remained when needed for trial. Amazingly, a small *flask* of moonshine, also confiscated from the Kreamers, still exists.

Some real Prince Farrington liquor can still be seen at the Gamble Farm Inn, which Troy Musser owns. Prince's daughter and son-in-law once operated this inn. The inn had changed hands several times before Musser became the owner. Musser also wanted another relic that was tied to Farrington; so he paid a goodly sum to a private owner for a bottle of the Prince's whiskey that had, mysteriously, come from the Lycoming County Courthouse in Williamsport. The attached evidence tag is neatly labeled: Frank and Hazel Kreamer, Loganton R.D. 1, PA. The June 17, 1948, date on the tag helps us to pinpoint at least one date involved in the stashed booze on the Kreamer farm. Also noted on the bottle was the name of the arresting federal agent: Richard Baxter.

Although it belonged to an innocent owner, another of the area's large cars was discreetly used for the run to Washington, D.C. Harold "Dutch" Washburn of Loganton relates that his uncle, **Harry Matter**, delivered whiskey to Washington, D.C. Washburn says that his grandfather owned a big, seven-passenger Chrysler that Harry would borrow. Harold doubts that the car's owner, his grandfather, ever knew about Harry's Washington whiskey run. While the reader might assume that all that one needed to do on the Washington whiskey run would be to appear at the Senate office building, and senators would appear, money in hand, ready to purchase. It isn't known who established this lucrative link with legislators, but it's now known that Prince's drivers hauled Clinton/Lycoming counties' moonshine to Washington, D.C. For those who might have thought that some members of the U.S. Senate were spending like drunken sailors during the 1920s and 1930s, Farrington's illicit hooch might have been a factor. Thanks to Prince's niece, Frances Farrington Gardner, we are privy to important aspects of Prince's bootleg delivery system to the District of Columbia. The drivers had to leave at night and had to avoid the law-enforcement 'hot spots' along the way. This required driving on back roads through selected parts of the route. The delivery also had to arrive in the American capital between midnight and daybreak. The system involved contacting the same trusted individual on each trip. This lone contact was a woman. This female, of unknown identity, accepted the shipment and made the payment. That routine cycle of criminal activity lasted for 12 years.

Another relative of Harry Matter was **"Barefoot Sam" Matter**. "Barefoot Sam" was a local character who was normally barefoot. In fact, it's reported that when his dad died in California, Sam traveled shoeless to California to settle his dad's estate.

There was also **Jonathan Lee Rishel** of Loganton. Known as "Lee," he had a sidekick named **Lee Wagner**, also of the Loganton area. The two men traveled in a coupe with a rumble seat and were remembered for delivering Farrington stock seemingly everywhere.

**William "Sandy" Lowe** was originally from Tennessee and had worked in the Virginia coal mines before coming to Pennsylvania and marrying Vida Moyer. He was never shy about saying that he had been a driver for Prince Farrington, according to his son-in-law, Robert Fillman Jr. and according to Patricia and Charles Ulrich. Lowe often told of driving a delivery car for Farrington, a car with an extra gas tank attached, to be used for smuggling Farrington's liquor.

Elsewhere, we mention the anger that Art Decker felt for Prince Farrington. As stated there, this anger grew from the fact that Art's brother, **Torrence ("Diz") Decker**, delivered moonshine for Prince, was arrested and served some jail time.

**Harry Williams** was born and raised in Antes Fort and was involved in hiding liquor for Prince Farrington. Williams's sequestering of Prince's alcohol is further discussed in Chapter 11. Here, we simply wish to note that Harry Williams also drove his own truck while delivering Prince's contraband liquor.

We must add Prince's youngest son, **Prince David Farrington Jr., or "Whitey" Farrington**. His account of a specific driving chore that he performed for his dad is related in Chapter 6.

Prince's nephew, **Charles Farrington Jr.** of Lamar, not only delivered whiskey for Prince; he occasionally acted as Prince's chauffeur. Before his passing, Charles Farrington Jr. was contacted by the author, but he was very reluctant to discuss any aspect of his work with Prince. A lone phone conversation (June 3rd, 2002) gave us the following, but a planned visit and other phone calls were rebuffed. Charles Farrington Jr. said that his dad and mother, Charl and Virgie, along with him and his siblings, visited Prince's every Sunday. There, at Prince's house near Antes Fort, Prince raised foxes that ran along the fence, keeping pace with his dad's car. He also said that, at one time, Prince kept a few rattlesnakes and pet bears that weren't "very pet." When being with a visitor, Prince relished the moment when he would kick the serpents' box and frighten others with the unmistakable rattling within. Once, someone returned from grocery shopping and left open a car door. A bear crawled into the car, rummaged through the groceries and ate the coffee.

Shortly before Prince died, Charles Jr. drove him to North Carolina to visit relatives. The North Carolina towns that Charles Jr. felt were important in Prince's life were Randleman, Jamestown and High Point. Prince had Charles Jr. return without him. Charles Jr. found the return drive to be saddening. He sensed that he had driven Prince back to the Nubbin Ridge area for the last time. Prince lingered for several more days before returning to Pennsylvania with others.

The Floyd Meixel family lived in an old log house at the western end of Nippenose Valley, not far from Rauchtown and just off Pine Mountain Road. **Floyd Meixel**, the patriarch, was born in 1885 and bought the old house in the 1920s. Behind the house was a tool shed. The shed had a cellar, which was the hiding place for more than a hundred kegs of aging liquor. The Meixels both *stored* and *delivered* moonshine for Prince Farrington. Floyd Meixel and two of his seven sons, **Ernest ("Ern") Meixel** (b. 1907) and **Clyde Meixel** (b. 1909), were among Prince's team of drivers. It would appear that they also *distilled* for Prince, as explained earlier in this chapter.

For the Meixels of rural Crawford Township in Clinton County, going to town always meant going to Jersey Shore. There was an incident when Clyde was a young man that he got "dressed up" and drove into Jersey Shore. While in town, Clyde's car had a tire go flat. Clyde was not ready to ruin his appearance by changing a flat tire. There was a solution. He went to Derk's Ford dealership on Allegheny Avenue and bought a new car. One family member observed that that was when Clyde worked for Prince Farrington.

Years later, Clyde recalled the harrowing, late-night incident when someone rapped on their door. Floyd Meixel called, asking who was outside. "Prince," came the clear voice beyond the door. When Prince was admitted to the house, he asked Floyd if his sons were at home. Floyd didn't know but said that he would check the loft. All were home. Then Prince said that he learned that the Meixel property might be raided later that night and that there "could be gunfire." The raid never materialized, but it was a threat that was nervously recalled, even years later. That Floyd Meixel and his two sons were valuable to Prince was evident since an old photograph exists that shows all three Farrington drivers—Floyd, Ernest and Clyde Meixel—sporting shiny new Ford automobiles! Some of the

Meixels later owned the bar, The Rauchtown Inn (locally pronounced ROCK-town), in nearby Rauchtown.

During the 1930s, Ed Snook, mentioned in other chapters, lived with his grandfather, **Newton Snook**. Newton farmed. Ed remembers his grandfather loading potatoes onto a truck and leaving about midnight for the drive to Baltimore, where the potatoes were sold. Ed also recalls the fact that on market day, his grandfather attended the curb market to sell farm produce. Old Newton Snook also ruined Ed's appetite for chicken eggs by sucking the raw contents from the shells. His grandfather always seemed to carry an impressive wad of money. Ed eventually learned that his grandfather, for the midnight run to Baltimore, visited the Meixel property, where he gathered bottles of moonshine from their hiding places beneath the chicken nests. The bottles were then transferred to containers beneath the load of potatoes for Newton Snook to deliver to a buyer, or buyers, in Baltimore.

**Ralph Lehman Sr.** was an exception. During the depression, Ralph contacted Prince Farrington. He knew that Prince delivered moonshine to Chicago and that the Chicago run paid well. Ralph volunteered to make a delivery to Chicago. Prince rejected his offer. Ralph, with four children, was desperate for work. He pleaded. Still, Prince refused. Why? Because of the large brood. Prince reminded Ralph that he was a father to many children and that the Chicago run was too dangerous. He'd send one of the younger, less attached men to the Windy City (Chicago)—the metropolis where Al Capone controlled much of the city's criminal activity.

While Ralph Lehman Sr. was denied the opportunity to drive for Prince, those drivers who can be counted, ending with Newton Snook, above, give us a total number of known Prince Farrington bootleg drivers of twenty-one! Ah, to know the total . . .

*McElhattan Falls, a secluded spot of natural beauty, rarely seen today; but the site of a Farrington still many decades ago. The falls is near the source of the creek that empties into the Susquehanna River near the town of McElhattan.*

*The Millbrook Playhouse in Mill Hall. This large structure once housed a secret storage compartment for Farrington booze. Trucks pulling into the barn for dairy products, left with the dairy products, and a quantity of moonshine beneath.*

# THE COTERIE OF COHORTS 163

*Pictured here is a personal-sized still, owned by Dick Thompson of Jersey Shore. He purchased it from Gladys Farrington Porter, who offered it as one of her dad's possessions.*

*Jersey Mills on the banks of Pine Creek. Opposite this town in an area known as Stradley Hollow, was a hidden Farrington moonshine operation.*

*Members of the James and Rebecca Gamble family, circa 1890. The stately Stewart/Courtright home was once the site of a major Prince Farrington moonshine operation in Lycoming County, PA. Courtesy of Pat and Phil Courtright.*

**THE COTERIE OF COHORTS** 165

*For contrast, compare an early newspaper photograph of the Stewart/Courtright about the time of the two major raids. The barn shown, along with the home, both played major roles in the manufacture of moonshine under Prince Farrington's direction.*

*An early photograph from the Williamsport SUN GAZETTE was once used as a hidden storage place for Farrington's moonshine. Eventually it was raided and the owner spent several months in prison.*

# · 9 ·

# Other Major Players

**THE FLOUNDERING BARRISTER**
No one can avoid all of life's pitfalls, no matter how 'distinguished' his life. Attorney John Crawford Youngman Sr. underwent one of those humiliating episodes. John Crawford Youngman Sr. had a distinguished career in his legal profession and his community. His community was primarily Lycoming County. He was born in Williamsport on January 23, 1903, a descendant of Colonel John Henry Antes, for whom Antes Fort and Antes Creek are named. One of John Youngman's ancestors was the son-in-law of the pioneer, Colonel Antes. Youngman was, for some years, the county's district attorney. He practiced law into his eighties, but he is best remembered for his opposition to capital punishment, his staunch support of the fluoridation of the city's water supply and his long and successful effort to have a flood dike created to protect the city from the ravages of a sometimes-errant Susquehanna River. Louis E. Hunsinger's tribute to the man, in an early 2000 historical piece characterized Youngman as being a 'visionary.' The article also shows the private man, the one who loved the outdoors, including fly fishing in Antes Creek.[26]

Two of Pennsylvania's most unique geological oddities are in the fertile Nippenose Valley. There one can find a cluster of deep sinkholes and a related mammoth spring that bubbles forth to become the primary source of Antes Creek. Much of the land through which Antes Creek flows has been owned by Youngman family members. Antes Creek has been touted, since the 19th century, as an excellent stream for fly fishing for trout. Although John C. Youngman fished in relatively placid waters, his family history included a horrific tragedy. 1889 saw torrential rains

---

26. Williamsport *Sun-Gazette*, "Lycoming County History Makers."

in the area. The downpour created a flash flood that sent the churning waters of Antes Creek sweeping downstream and ripping away the houses of two Youngman brothers and carrying away the two wives, five children and two other women. Most of the nine people who drowned were ancestors of John Crawford Youngman, who was born about fourteen years after the tragedy.

Attorney Youngman owned a cabin by Antes Creek. He fished alone, sending his line undulating over the waters. One day, he lost his balance and fell. With his boots suddenly full of water and the stream waters pushing at his struggling bulk, he was unable to regain his balance and return to a standing position. Simply stated, the former D.A. of the county was losing a battle with the stream of his ancestors.

*Happenstance* is an informal term first used, it is believed, about 1897. The word signifies something that is a purely chance happening. Happenstance, for Mr. Youngman on that day, was the approach of two boys who realized the lawyer's predicament. They rushed to his aid and helped to steady him and guide him from the stream. They assisted his return to his nearby cabin and got him his dry clothes. They also got him a shot of whiskey from a bottle on a shelf. They probably did what any good Samaritan would have done. Still, when they recounted their help for the floundering Mr. Youngman, their grandmother jokingly chided them, "You should have let him drown! He's the one that put your grandpa in jail!"

## THE SEGRAVES SAGA

These were not fictitious given names. Farrington's first name was actually *Prince* and Segraves given name was actually *Colonel*. Colonel Segraves came to Lycoming County from North Carolina and had a traceable family history going back about 1,000 years to England.

The name of Segraves (might also be spelled as Seagraves) seems to have been associated with the arrival, in England, of William "the Conqueror" of Normandy in 1066. When William, as King William I of England, ordered an accounting of people, livestock, etc. for purposes of taxation and control, the resulting record became known as The Domesday (pronounced DOOMS day) Book (1086). That record listed the name Segraves in the Leicestershire area. Family research suggests that the Segraves, coming from England and Ireland, may have settled in America as early as the 1690s. During the 1700s, Segraves were living in several states, including North Carolina. Within the Tarheel state, Segraves were soon found in several counties, including Wilkes County.

Colonel Segraves line is easily traced back to a Rev. William Segraves and beyond; but is most manageable if begun, here, with the reverend. Rev. William Segraves was an ex-Confederate soldier who was, in civilian life, a farmer-preacher. Although of an uncertain birthdate, he married Louvenia Elizabeth Creekmore in 1847. Their second son was John Green Segraves (b. 1849), a 19th-century distiller of corn whiskey and apple brandy. John Green Segraves was the direct ancestor of Colonel Segraves. Louvenia died at the age of 33 years, leaving a widower and eight children. Within months, Reverend William Segraves had a second wife; a 20-year-old bride, who was already a mother of eight by proxy. The second Mrs. Segraves was Eliza Jane Money (b. 8-8-1839). By the time that she stopped bearing children, at age 41, she had borne another ten children. During her two decades of marriage, then, she was pregnant for approximately 7½ years. The large quantity of kids did not prevent the Revenend and Mrs. Segraves from hosting groups of church members in their modest home, which was situated at the foot of Segraves Mountain in Wilkes County, North Carolina. Colonel Monte Segraves was born September 18, 1909, in Wilkes County, North Carolina. This is the same county that was the birthplace of the celebrated racing driver, Junior Johnson.

Colonel M. Segraves found his bride after moving north into Pennsylvania. His wife was Marie Cathern Engel. They were married in Hagerstown, Maryland. Marie's father, and mother were Anthony and Lucy Eck Engel. The Engels owned a farm above the church and near the town of Bastress. The farm was just off Jack's Hollow Road and had a stream that disappeared into a heavily wooded area, unnoticed by outsiders. The still that Colonel Segraves operated for Prince, was located in an isolated glade on his father-in-law's farm. That still is further identified in Chapter 11. Colonel Segraves, who was also an able electrician, and his wife moved into Jersey Shore. Soon after their son, James, was born, there was an incident that is still a story within the family. Marie Segraves left tiny

James in the care of his father while she attended religious services. The moonshiner and a couple of his friends were the designated baby sitters for the church-going mother. Marie returned to an enlightening scene. Papers were scattered on the table, on which the infant, James, was lying. Fellow moonshiner, Torrence "Diz" Decker was trying to keep the baby steady while the moonshiner father, Colonel Segraves was attempting to pin on a fresh diaper. Revenuers posed a lesser challenge.

Colonel Segraves' wife, Marie Engel Segraves, gives the impression of having been a naturally pleasant woman, quickly seeing humor in unfolding events. She noticed the humor of her grandsons' rescue of the man who put her husband behind bars, and the humor of some tough bootleggers shrinking from a routine diaper change. Also, Marie Engel Segraves could accept, with grace, the illegal nature of her husband's secondary profession.

Despite an almost unblemished arrest record, Colonel Segraves did encounter the law. Although his actual *moonshining* never led to his arrest, Colonel Segraves was apprehended while *peddling* moonshine among some Williamsport customers. For this the Colonel spent six months in the now-obsolete stone prison on Third Street in Williamsport. The prosecuting attorney was John Crawford Youngman Sr. It was to this sentencing that Marie Segraves, years later, was referring when her grandson, James Segraves II and her step-grandson Kelly Segraves, pulled a cold and water-logged attorney from Antes Creek.

Prince Farrington wasn't the only one of his crowd to get involved in defense work during World War II. Prince, as noted, worked at the ordinance works northwest of Allenwood. Colonel Segraves began working on a super-secret defense project in Tennessee.

Today, the Oak Ridge Boys, a country-style vocal group, may be better known; but among the older folks, or among many with a modest sense of history, the name, Oak Ridge, has a chilling ring. That is the name of the place that gave birth to the Nuclear Age; the 'town' within which the world's first atomic bomb was fashioned. Oak Ridge is in the Appalachian Mountains, in eastern Tennessee, about 20 miles due west of Knoxville. Seventy-five thousand people were secretly imported to the small city created almost overnight and without appearing on maps. This totally new metropolis was part of a massive program successfully designed to secretly manufacture the "enriched uranium" required to build the atomic bomb.

Several other similarly clandestine sites were established to do certain steps in the process. For example, a laboratory was working beneath the football stadium of the University of Chicago. That laboratory was also working on a critical step in the atomic process. It was there (12/2/42) that Enrico Fermi initiated the world's first nuclear chain reaction. Of course, the secrecy of that small laboratory was much easier to keep, particularly since no one stills hears about that school, even during the height of the college football season.

As a worker at Oak Ridge, Colonel Segraves, an able electrician, worked as a welder. Because of the nature of this classified project, Segraves lived in one valley and traveled through a tunnel to the work site in a neighboring valley. Since the end of the Second World War, the war-created town of Oak Ridge has remained as a normal, small city of about 27,000 people. When Segraves work in Oak Ridge ended, he returned to Williamsport. Later he remarried and was living in New Stanton, Pennsylvania at the time of his death in 1980.

## "PUD" HILL: THE MAN FROM THE MOUTH OF PINE CREEK

Dewitt Bodine "Pud" Hill would likely have remained unknown and unmentioned in this book, except for the widespread circulation of an old picture of four moonshiners standing in front of their tent at some remote still (*see* p. 122). They were, from left to right: "Pud" Hill, Lemuel Groce, Charl Farrington and Colonel Segraves. While the hooch that they were peddling could cause occasional agony for the drinkers and their families, this foursome was, otherwise, rather harmless.

In the days when milk was delivered in glass jars, to people's doorstep or to the end of their rural lanes, Hill was a milkman. Some suspected that his milk route was a cover for his moonshine sales. A one-time neighbor recalled nothing connecting "Pud" Hill to moonshining; but that neighbor only remembered Hill when the former moonshiner was older and was frequently seen driving a small, gray 1934 pickup truck or sitting in his front lawn, facing the road, tobacco juice dribbling down the creases of his chin, while reading a 'western'. Unless one is offended by the tobacco juice image, there was nothing recalled about the one-time moonshiner that was particularly negative. The dairy farm on which he lived was in the bottomlands near the mouth of Pine Creek. This is Porter Township, Lycoming Township. "Pud" Hill's wife's name was Eva. A local milk customer also remembers something else about farmer Hill. His milk was priced at eight cents a quart.

When, "Pud" Hill died in 1955, he was buried in the cemetery at Jersey Shore. His gravestone revealed a modest fact that "Pud" hadn't bothered to reveal to acquaintances, or friends, for all his years of contact with many members of the community. Virtually everyone knew "Pud" only by his nickname. Friends and neighbors only knew him as "Pud." While Richard Grugan spent his childhood on the neighboring farm, he never learned "Pud" Hill's given name. Grugan clearly recalls the pleasure he had whenever he encountered his farmer-neighbor, because "Pud" would always give him peppermint candy. Grugan also recalled the day when he and his dad stopped to speak with "Pud" and they heard "Pud" suddenly swear and exclaim, "Oh my God, Mr. Grugan, your barn's on fire!" To be sure! The fire consumed the barn and everything within! Yet, despite Richard Grugan's vivid memories, he still never learned his neighbor's given name.

In 2011, over a half-century after Hill's death, Rick Shaffer, and his wife, Chris, delivered Memorial Day floral arrangements to the local cemetery. They also took the time to locate and read "Pud" Hill's tombstone inscription. Thanks to their effort, we now know that "Pud" Hill carried the given name of DeWitt. His name matched that of the 19th century governor of New York state, DeWitt Clinton. DeWitt Clinton is historically significant for pushing the great Erie Canal project that linked Albany to Lake Ontario. It was Governor DeWitt Clinton whose name is believed to have been attached to Clinton County (founded in 1839, just 14 years after the historic Erie Canal was completed). Clinton County sits just a few yards from the late DeWitt "Pud" Hill's farm home near Jersey Shore.

**BOYD "DUKE" GREAK**
Dave Berfield is a resident of Bainbridge Island, near Seattle, Washington. He writes of childhood memories that included having a grandmother

who "was very much against drink, and no alcohol was ever allowed in their house." Dave's mother spoke to him of overhearing her parents (Edgar and Edith Weaver Miller) "talking in whispered tones about a relative that worked for Prince Farrington. I am sure this did not please them." He is now sure that his grandparents were speaking about their nephew, Boyd Greak.

Who was this man, Boyd Greak, who caused relatives to whisper of his exploits? It seems likely that they were discussing Boyd at the time that he was working for Prince and not later when he apparently cut all ties to moonshining and was living a life far different than that of his early years. They were likely discussing the man at the time that he was shot by a revenue agent. As one might express it in today's television phraseology, Boyd Greak took one for Prince. That is, he took a non-fatal bullet in the back while tending one of Prince Farrington's stills on Harbach (Harbaugh) Road, a few yards off Rockey Road, in southern Clinton County.

Boyd "Duke" Greak was born in 1906 in the little crossroads town of Rote, on Route 477, north of Loganton and about ten miles west of the spot where he was wounded. He was a hunter and a fisherman who could get lyrical about nature. He is quoted by an adoring daughter, Barbara (now Clark), as offering this observation on the beauty of a tree: "In the spring when the leaves come out they are beautiful and they give you shade. In the fall the leaves turn beautiful colors and they leave the trees because the sap goes down to the roots. Then winter comes and the tree stand in all its glory, waiting for God to bring the sap up the trees to bring forth their new leaves."

When Boyd Greak was a young man, courting Eleanor Sheela, a woman, five years his junior, the distance was daunting for a young man with no automobile. So, for winter courting, he put on ice skates on the river bank at Lock Haven and skated downstream on that great riverine highway, the West Branch of the Susquehanna. About 25 miles later, he arrived at Newberry, near Williamsport. Once at Eleanor's home, she and her beau were allowed to visit in the formal living room. Boyd had no one at home to wash his clothes, so his future mother-in-law would wash them. Since he could not stay in the house overnight, he was given old newspapers to use for bedding. He then went to Memorial Park and slept on a park bench in order to extend his courting of Eleanor into another day.

Boyd, "Duke" Greak had known the smell of sour mash cooking among the shrubs and trees beside the waters of Gann Run. This was just off Rockey Road, on Harbaugh (Harbach) road. He had once worked a still at that site for Prince Farrington. This employment brought "Duke" into that unfortunate situation (*see* Chapter 7). Prince had numerous stills in operation; but Greak happened to be watching one that was destined to be raided by revenue agents. The sudden attack on this still site sent Greak running into the trees. Then he realized that the pressure building in the heated boiler could cause an explosion. He rushed in, cut the pressure and fled once more; but he couldn't outrun an agent's bullet! He was shot in the back, midway between the heart and spine. Had the bullet's trajectory been an inch or two off to either side, the wound would have been crippling or fatal.

Years passed, Boyd and Eleanor were wed, and Eleanor forbade the mention of any connections that "Duke" ever had with Prince Farrington. The very name, "Duke," that someone had given Boyd Greak years earlier, as a nickname associated with "Prince," was used by all who knew Greak except his wife, Eleanor. His daughter, Barbara, declares, "Daddy and I used to be together a lot." So it was a revelation for Barbara to have an old man ask her, years later at a public event, if she was Boyd Greak's daughter. That stranger proceeded to tell her much that she'd not known. The stranger's belated "news" helped to explain the "hole" that she had seen in her dad's back, from a decades'-old wound left by a government bullet. Despite the injury, and the deep wound that remained, Boyd "Duke" Greak reached the octogenarian plateau before his 1989 demise.

Here is an unrelated quote from a cousin of Boyd Greak, Mr. Dave Berfield of Bainbridge Island, Washington. As a youngster he lived in Jersey Shore, close to the stream that flows just west of the town and intersects with the Susquehanna River. Berfield writes of a phrase that he had heard, "If you dip your feet in Pine Creek, your heart will never leave. I think that is true." He would know.

An afterthought: If one looks closely at the main characters in the Farrington Saga, an interesting conclusion can be drawn. Talking with many people about the likes of Boyd Greak, DeWitt Hill, Charl Farrington, Joe Gardner, George Gardner, Colonel Segraves, Jake Kohberger, Turburt Seyler, Walt Wagner, Charles Klobe, Floyd Klobe, Herman Klobe, and, yes, even Prince Farrington himself, it becomes obvious that these were not the personalities that one encounters in the Prohibition tales of the large American cities. Here, in the Pennsylvania hinterlands, people made their own alcohol without fear of retribution from the bigger players. There was no gangland violence and no gunning to death of rivals. Clinton and Lycoming counties experienced considerable moonshining and bootlegging; but, when it all ended, primarily with the death in 1956, of Prince David Farrington, moonshining had already become an obsolete way of making and marketing alcohol.

## YOUNG COLTRANE

B. W. Coltrane (*see* Chapter 6) was Prince Farrington's nephew, who had come to Pennsylvania from North Carolina with his parents and a brother. He told few people his real name, but one of those was his close friend, Leo "Chip" Taylor, from whom we learned that the B. W. was for Batie Worth. He helped Prince in the moonshining business. Through the voices of Fran Bailey Grugan, Tom Bauman, and the late Leo "Chip" Taylor, we get a picture of a pleasant young man who helped Prince tally his moonshine output, etc. and who helped build Prince's image by being himself, a charming young man. Fran Bailey Grugan was the daughter of Leslie Bailey, who managed the service station in Antes Fort at one time. Fran remembers B. W. Coltrane as a very pleasant boarder in their house when she was a young teen. She also offered a couple of pictures of B. W. that were snapped when he was in the military. A verbal glimpse of Batie Worth Coltrane came from Leo "Chip" Taylor, who spoke of a time when B. W. was an older man returning to the area for a visit. The Taylors went to the Antiques Inn with B. W. and B. W.'s lady friend. B. W. Coltrane, by most accounts, was admired by many who came into his presence as a fine-looking and personable man, but this evening, his lady companion walked out of the tavern, offended by Coltrane's heavy drinking. B. W. Coltrane seemed to have joined the growing number of Prince's relatives who had become overly dependent on their own product.

## A LIKABLE YOUNG MAN

Prince had a nephew named Lobby Anthony, the son of Prince's brother-in-law, Scott Anthony of Greensboro, North Carolina. Lobby, too, travelled north to visit with Prince's family. Tom Bauman, the neighbor of Prince, who visited often, happened to be there on a winter day when Whitey (Prince Jr.) was planning to go out the following morning to check his trap line to see if he had caught any muskrats, skunks, raccoons, or some other varmints. Tom Bauman and Lobby Anthony agreed to help Whitey. As it happened, Lobby had brought a pair of boots; but they were too short, while Tom Bauman's boots, which had been given to him, were too large. They swapped boots and seemed to become friends in the trade. The following day, they began their long upstream walk on the bank of the Susquehanna River. Whitey's traps had garnered four or five muskrats and, Tom recalled, a raccoon. Bauman also recalled that it was very cold, but Lobby seemed comfortable in a wool shirt, a leather jacket, and no hat! Bauman was suffering from cold hands from helping check the animals and traps in the cold river water. Lobby then gave Tom the gloves he had been wearing. They were leather and lined with rabbit fur. Lobby said, "Here, these will keep your hands warm." It was a gesture to be remembered for a lifetime. Bauman explained, "We kidded each other about trading boots, and I got to like him. He was just the sort of guy you could like. There was nothing phony about him."

Bauman had another memory to share. "The following year Whitey and I had been down at the farm and were walking up to the house. Gladys and George (Porter) had been living in the brick house with Prince. While we were walking toward the house, we came to three ox-heart cherry trees. It comes to my mind that they were on Muthler's ground (a neighboring farmer), but we climbed into one of the trees. The cherries weren't quite ripe, but we ate a few. We got down out of the tree and here comes Gladys in a car. When she pulled up where we were, she was crying. Whitey asked, "What's the matter?" and she said, "Lobby was killed in a car wreck last night!"

## "HOP"

He was the youngest of Prince's siblings and the one who took the use of alcohol beyond the outer limits. George Hobson Farrington was known as "Hop." The family says that young George Hobson Farrington had such frightening attacks of delirium tremens that they had a physician summoned. The physician, the family laments, gave him a shot to stop the attack, but it killed the patient. There is no evidence that "Hop" Farrington's tragic death had any impact on other family members regarding abandoning their pursuit of alcohol. However, one family friend may have been shocked out of any interest in "demon rum," as alcohol was disparagingly described. Tom Bauman tells of visiting Whitey and Gayle at Prince's house. "Hop" was also there. The alcoholic was leaving one room through the parlor doors. He had just opened the doors when he went into a delirious fit! He screamed, "Don't let them get me." He was screaming and thrashing about, totally out of control, because of his delirium tremens. Bauman was totally unnerved. Prince's middle son, Gayle, was a husky young man who was finally able to get "Hop" under control. Aside from "Hop's" severe alcoholic condition, what triggered his delirious outburst? It happened because, as he opened the parlor doors, he was suddenly confronted by a stranger! The stranger was actually the newel post of the stair railing, topped with Prince's coat and his hat!

Bauman's reflection: "To this day I think seeing "Hop" like that, when I was just a kid, kind of made me ask, 'What in the hell does somebody use that stuff for?' You know, they don't make you drink it. I never had trouble with booze." In 1951 Tom Bauman, the non-drinker, also quit smoking. Six decades later, he remains free of both habits.

## RAY WYNN

Ray Wynn was typical of some of the local people who worked for Prince Farrington. Wynn was a farmer who did some moonlighting by making moonshine. His farming was done with a 1938 Farmall F14, which was modified to hold rims and ties. Ray Wynn did many other things, all legal, to increase his income and decrease his food bill, as mentioned in Chapter 5. The one illegal thing that he did was to work stills at night for Prince. He got caught and put into the Clinton County jail for 30 days, but not for 30 nights! His stay was made somewhat less difficult by Sheriff George Hickoff, who would allow Wynn to go home at night, with the sheriff even delivering Wynn to his family. Ray Wynn also stored liquor for Prince. Prince especially liked Ray because none of the stored liquor was ever missing. Ray was married to a Welshans, linking the Wynn family to one of the historic families of Nippenose Valley. Ray's son, Art Wynn, worked for Jake Kohberger.

## "FUZZ"
Another local man, Harry "Fuzz" Shaffer, worked for Prince until, after his divorce, he moved to New York State and got a job with the Ingersoll-Rand Corporation. Eventually, the locals say, he became the head of Ingersoll-Rands security department.

## TURBERT SEYLER
Turbert Seyler worked for Prince Farrington. They lived as neighbors in the early days of Prince's work in Pennsylvania. Liquor agents tried to catch Seyler with alcohol. One effort they made was to stop Seyler just north of Loganton, near the sulfur spring that sits beside the highway outside of town. The children's presence in the car didn't deter the authorities. They stopped Seyler and had his children climb from the car. Then they pulled out the seats. There was no alcohol to be found.

Seyler's son-in-law was Walt Wagner. He and the family lived in an old log house. Today the house where they lived no longer exists. It was removed when the reservoir was built for the collecting of water for Lock Haven's municipal water supply. Did Walt Wagner work for Prince? No, says his son, John. Walt made his own. The Wagners lived in one side only. The other side housed Walt's special guests: a still and the large mash boxes. John Wagner reminds the listener that a number of people in the area were making their own moonshine. In their case, John tells us, it was a vital part of the family income.

## · 10 ·

# "Moon Shine Farm": The Klobe Clan

### A ROBUST FAMILY NEAR CARROLL

The title of this chapter is borrowed from the painted inscription on a stone at one of the early Klobe farmhouses (note the accompanying photograph). That inscription, however, was said to have been painted by the *current* owner of the house and was not painted by a Klobe family member.

The late Thelma Matthews (*see* Chapter 6) recalled standing with her husband at their house near Carroll and gazing on the wooded flatlands to the south. There the couple would count columns of smoke; the early-morning evidence of a cluster of hidden, illegal stills on the neighbors' property. Those neighbors were members of the Klobe family. The Klobes, too, knew how to manufacture moonshine.

The patriarch of this family was Herman Henry Klobe, the son of a German immigrant. In 1927, Herman, now partially incapacitated by a stroke, was living with a son, Charles. A second son, Floyd Klobe, lived nearby. The Klobe farms were in Sugar Valley, at the town of Carroll and just about a dozen miles from Prince Farrington's first Pennsylvania home, *the Florida Fruit Farm*.

Regarding the relationship between the moonshiner Farrington and the moonshining Klobe family, George Mayes of Antes Fort (*see* Chapter 7) was quoted as observing that it was a Klobe who would set up stills for Prince Farrington. However, one family member insists that Charles "was never affiliated with Prince." Farrington's ties to the Klobes seem to have been with Herman and his younger son, Floyd. Still, another relative says that both Klobes, "Floyd, and brother Charles, made whiskey on their own." There is convincing evidence of that.

Herman also employed a couple of hands, Louis Huntingdon and Earl Knepp to help him with his work, part of which included the making of moonshine whiskey. The tranquility of the eastern end of Sugar Valley was shattered on Tuesday night, August 16th of 1927. On that summer evening, alcohol and a heated argument between Floyd Klobe and Louis Huntingdon led to a violent confrontation between the two. Young Floyd received an ax-related gash that left his cheek scarred for life. The elderly (72-years-old) Herman Klobe, who hadn't been directly involved in the quarrel, wandered onto the scene and, somehow, had his head split by an ax. He died a couple of days later, and the ensuing investigation and trial (see Chapter 7) left no clear perpetrator for the grisly crime.

Herman Klobe's two sons, Charles and Floyd, had their own careers in moonshining over the years, even though, for many years, they didn't speak to one another. The 1927 trial of Louis B. Huntingdon, for the murder of Herman Klobe, openly indicated that Herman and both his sons, Charles and Floyd, were involved, at that time, with making illicit whiskey. The trial resulted in the acquittal of Huntingdon. Further, years after the death of Herman Henry Klobe (see Chapter 7), his older son, Charles, told a friend, Ed Pickett, that his father's death was truly accidental. The presence of a sharp, double-bitted ax, firmly implanted into the chopping block was a poor place to be having a drunken quarrel. While the fight was believed to be over money or moonshine, it was primarily between Floyd Klobe and Louis B. Huntingdon. Herman Klobe, also soused, got involved and, Charles insisted, fell onto the ax, with fatal results. Contradicting that, in part, another family member claimed that, away from the courtroom, Huntingdon had admitted his culpability in the heinous act. Apparently, the true story of Herman Klobe's death will remain forever unresolved.

## A MAN OF MANY PARTS

If one bases his or her evaluation of Herman Henry Klobe entirely on the sensational newspaper accounts of the trial resulting from his bloody demise, the result would be very warped. One would get the impression of an elderly farmer who spent his entire life tilling the soil and dabbling in moonshine, until the night when he met his doom as the result of a back-country brawl. How distorted a portrait!

Herman Klobe's father was a German immigrant who was married to a member of the Martz family of Eastville, in Sugar Valley. Although the family has few written documents, family tradition is strong. Herman's father was a wealthy industrialist in Philadelphia which was, at the time, one of America's largest, most vibrant cities. Here is where young Herman lived. His mother died when he was a young boy and, when he was still a lad approaching his teen years, his father was murdered and his body dumped into the one of the city's rivers. The crime, the family understands, was done on orders from Klobe's business partner, as a way to gain full ownership of the company. At the age of 12, Herman Henry Klobe was an orphan.

At the time of his death, in 1831, Philadelphia's Stephen Girard was possibly the wealthiest man in America. Girard's will endowed a school, Girard College, that would care for and educate white males who were orphans or whose father was dead. Although Girard College can find no record for Klobe, he appears to have been put in the custody and care of Girard College by the court. His descendants were also aware that Herman Klobe had some natural artistic ability and worked for some time at painting scenes for Philadelphia theaters. There was a negative side to his artistry. The paints of the time caused Klobe to experience respiratory problems. He needed to change his environment.

While still a young man, Herman Klobe returned from the great metropolitan center to the home of his maternal grandparents, the Martz family of Sugar Valley. Although Sugar Valley had a number of sawmills, Klobe found work in a large sawmill in Pine Creek Hollow, near the village of Woodward (Centre County). To get to work—weekly, or whenever—he walked many miles southward and across a couple of mountains. While working at Woodward, Herman Klobe met and courted Margaret Louise Miller. A grandchild still has the bundle of love letters that Klobe wrote to his Penn Valley ladylove. On March 21st of 1889, Herman and Margaret were married. They went to housekeeping in a mountainside house in the eastern end of Sugar Valley.

There is something special about those love letters, aside from the passionate prose. They were adorned with sketches, examples of Herman Henry Klobe's artistic skills. He also painted or did charcoal portraits of local individuals, works several of which are still in existence. Equally fascinating: Herman Klobe would go to the general store in Carroll to sit and sketch customers. Lastly, Klobe's granddaughter, Thelma Bierly, owns what she considers to be a prized art work. It is a charcoal work showing a curly-haired little girl and a similarly curly-haired dog.

A look at one of his letters is valuable in showing the letter-writing style of the times, the stage of their relationship, Herman Klobe's superb penmanship and his artistically self-adorned stationery. The message, given here in full and unmodified, says:

*Pine Creek Hollow, Feb. the 9th, 1889*

*Dearest and best*

*Yours of the 5th instand at hand, I feel very lonesome since you have left, time (?) seems long to me, for instance when Saturday night comes I had bin out on Wednesday evening But you had gone of(f) so I felt dispointed. So I stayed at your folks until 9 Oclock Clody told me that you had told hir that I was to go over to see that woman that told you that I had been married I had a notion to do so being you were gone. I had bin over home last Sunday and brought my close over and now Im ready if (the word "if" has a line of cancellation through it.) to get married now at anytime if it suits you, and as you say in your letter you trouble yourself Dear you nead not for I'll never dispoint you for I'll be a Man, and your's only Clody had bin telling Me, that you were troubling yourself about something so your Mother said wether I had told you something which you did not like so I told Clody I wouldent know what it could be. But I'll be up if the wheather is nice next Saturday evinning this is all for this time My dearest hoping to have an early reply from you*

*From Your's forever,*
*H.H. Klobe*
*Please and address to*
*Woodward*
*PA*

Herman and Margaret had three children. The oldest was Bertha, who became Mrs. Bertha Farmer of New York City. She, too, was an artist and did some painting in that metropolis. She rarely returned to her country roots. Their second child was Charles and the third was Floyd, both of whom are discussed below.

Herman's beloved Margaret died in 1924, so she was no longer in his life on that fateful night of August 16, 1927.

## CHARLES LEE KLOBE Sr.

Charles Lee Klobe was the older of the two Klobe boys, having been born August 10th of 1890. He was a native of Sugar Valley, having been born near the town of Carroll. In 1912 he married Margaret ("Maggie") Yarrison. Although his younger brother, Floyd, would father just one child, Charles and Maggie were more prolific. They had eleven offspring. Of their eleven-member brood, only one son, Lindy Herman Klobe, collected a few arrest citations, including shooting at game from an automobile and hunting while his license was suspended.[27]

Those charges were handled when Lindy paid a fine of $90.00 in what was known as a 'field settlement'. Another newspaper report says that Lindy was involved in the theft of sawmill fittings.[28] Lindy may have inherited a genetic defect from his grandfather, since he suffered a stroke, as had his grandfather, Herman. Lindy, more incapacitated than his grandfather, spent years in a wheelchair.

One family member felt strongly that the younger Klobe brother, Floyd, both delivered and stored whiskey for Prince. That person also felt that Charles and Floyd, together, began moonshining when Prince, once again, was sent to prison. Although Floyd was never arrested, Charles Klobe Sr. was. An undated newspaper clipping from the author's file indicates that Charles Klobe Sr. was arrested, along with his wife, Margaret, and one son, Willard, when officers raided the still that they were operating at the Tea Spring. The location of the Tea Spring, a natural area, is about five miles east of their home. Officers came prepared. They had the red pepper needed to subdue Klobe's watchdogs. The size of the operation was impressive, according to the newspaper account. Authorities gave the still size as being 750 gallons. They also confiscated 37 gallons of moonshine and more than a thousand gallons of mash. Ed Pickett tells of a conversation he had with Charles Klobe Sr. in the

---

27. *The Wellsboro Agitator*, 8/16/56.
28. *The Williamsport Gazette and Bulletin*, 1/28/48.

1970s, during which Klobe told Pickett of aging his product by burying it in small caves and that he had an old white mule that was used for carrying his moonshining supplies. Despite those confessions, Pickett fondly remembers Charles Klobe Sr., not so much for his moonshining but for giving Pickett good advice for catching 'brookies' (brook trout).

Despite the fanfare that seemed to surround the arrest of Charles, Margaret and son Willard, no convictions occurred, so both of Herman Klobe's sons kept an unblemished record as far as convictions were concerned.

Although Charles Lee Klobe Sr. did some moonshining in his earlier years, he was obviously highly regarded within his community. He was, at the time of his registration for the military draft for World War I, listed as a lineman for the old Western Union Telegraph Company. At another time, he was an engineer for the Bell Telephone Company. Prince Farrington wasn't the only moonshiner who found employment at the Ordinance Depot that swallowed the town of Alvira. Charles Lee Klobe Sr., also worked at the U.S. government's World War II Ordinance Depot, northwest of Allenwood.

Charles was a member of the Sugar Valley Church of the Brethren, in Eastville. He also farmed, hunted and fished. He was a member of the local branch of the Carpenters Union. In 1957 he also opened a hobby shop and began making apple and potato crates. Maggie and Charles Klobe were chosen as the Loganton's Bicentennial Couple. Then, in 1977, Maggie and Charles were honored as the longest-married couple in Sugar Valley. A few years later, in 1982, when both were ninety years old, Maggie and Charles celebrated their 70th wedding anniversary. She died three years later.

In 1990, Charles Klobe Sr. was featured in a newspaper (The Lock Haven *Express*) while observing his 100th birthday, celebrated in a Lock Haven nursing facility and surrounded by five of his great-great-grandchildren. His one great-granddaughter had been coming to visit him on his birthday for several years, a real tribute to Klobe since they lived in Ecuador. Charles Lee Klobe died later that year. Maggie and Charles are buried in the churchyard in Eastville.

Six of Charles and Maggie's children are still living. Willard, 95, lives in Milton. Dorothy Meixel, 91, also lives in Milton, as does Mildred, who is 88. Another daughter, Thelma Bierly, lives in Tylersville and Charles Jr., lives in Mill Hall where he takes an occasional meal at Aungst's restaurant, where he can chat with the restaurant's manager, Tammy Farrington, who is Prince Farrington's grand-niece. The youngest, Harold Klobe, lives in California. Now retired from a position with United Airlines, he remains on the company's board of directors.

## FLOYD CURTIS KLOBE

Floyd Curtis Klobe was born October 3, 1893. He worked on his father's farm and, presumably, learned the techniques needed for productive farming and for successful distilling. Floyd married a young woman from Rockey Road named Thressa S. Rush. Thressa Rush Klobe, who was born in 1903, was likely the most scandalous figure to come out of Sugar Valley.

Thressa's mother was Ida Mae Confer, daughter of Lincoln and Clara Orndorf Confer. Ida, who was born in Loganton in 1882, appears to have had her first child, Thressa, out of wedlock with a man named David Rush. When Ida bore Thressa, in 1903, she had her baby daughter baptized in Loganton's Albright Evangelical Church. According to some accounts, the infant girl's name was listed as Sarah Teresa Rush. Later, Thressa's mother married Adam Stabley.

Adam Harrison Stabley's ancestors were from York County, where Adam was born. Adam is remembered in Sugar Valley for having his own still (*see* Chapters 3 and 7) and for operating the 101 Ranch. That enterprise, the 101 Ranch was a large house on Rockey Road, close to the farm of Gladys and George Rockey. There was a small, non-bank-type barn on the property. Older residents remember the 101 Ranch as a business that offered alcohol and women to local patrons. It was also described, by one older resident, as having "booze and big parties." A later generation saw the building become the Chester Kulp property. Still later, the house burned. Today, a mobile home occupies the land once occupied by Adam Stabley's rural enterprise. Adam and Ida Confer Stabley had a small brood of children; at least a half-dozen. In their later years, the Stabley's lived on Allegheny Street in Jersey Shore. Adam preceded Ida in death. Ida—Thressa Rush Klobe's mother—suffered for years from diabetes before her death in 1959.

As a young woman, Thressa left Sugar Valley to become a chorus girl in New York City. When the body of an unidentified, and unidentifiable, young woman was found near Rauchtown (*see* Chapter 7), in 1925, some people quickly assumed that it was Thressa. They were wrong. Thressa, in good health, reappeared locally many months later.

When Thressa Rush married Floyd Klobe, they moved to the Jersey Shore area. Floyd worked for the railroad. They became parents of a daughter (April 14, 1919), whom they named Ethel. One day Floyd returned from work to find that Thressa had gone back to the city and the chorus line, abandoning him as well as their baby. Thressa had left tiny Ethel reclining in a dresser drawer.

Floyd, although still married, was suddenly a single parent. He quit his railroad job to care for his infant daughter. His brother, Charles, and sister-in-law, Margaret, also helped care for Thressa's abandoned child. Floyd obtained a divorce from Thressa through the Lycoming County court on May 26, 1924.

About the time that his daughter, Ethel, was approaching school age, Floyd began a relationship with Etta Long Raudabaugh, a widow whose husband had been killed in the First World War. Although they never married, Etta and Floyd lived together for about a half-century, until Floyd's death in January of 1979. Just as critical, Floyd's mate, Etta, and his daughter, Ethel, considered themselves to be in a true mother/daughter relationship, just as, years later, Ethel's children would also consider Etta to have been their true grandmother. Daughter Ethel was a childhood friend of her cousins, Charles Klobe's children, as well as those of the Carroll storekeeper and moonshiner, Jake Kohberger (*see* Chapter 8). Years later, Ethel told her own children that it was Etta Raudabaugh's widow's pension that provided their main revenue for years. There was, of course, whatever Floyd Klobe was earning from his distilling of illegal liquor. He also bought the Gottlieb Derr farm on Winter Road (the road that stretches through the south side of Sugar Valley). It was on this farm that Floyd Klobe's main still was the one hidden beneath a shed floor; one that could only be accessed through a concealed trapdoor. The rough locations of several of Floyd's stills are identified in Chapter 11.

As a small child, Ethel was sometimes visited by her mother. Thressa would arrive in a fancy automobile and with expensive dresses for Ethel.

Ethel, identified, in the terminology of the time as a 'tomboy,' was unimpressed with the clothing and was fearful that her mother would take her away. Sometimes when Thressa would return, Ethel would crawl under the front porch or rush to the attic. She did relate, years later, that she had talked with her mother on a couple of occasions. But, in 1929, Thressa—then in her mid-twenties—was riding with a friend, J. L. "Joe" Hart, in a roadster over Pine Mountain. That road, connecting tiny Pine Station with Rauchtown, has some treacherous turns even today. With Joe driving, the vehicle careened off the road and collided with a tree! Thressa's skull was fractured as she was thrown through the windshield. Her remains were interred in the Mount Pleasant cemetery in Rosecrans. A coroner's jury later absolved Hart of any responsibility for the "death of Miss Tessie Rush." Her daughter, Ethel, was about ten years old.

Floyd Klobe's granddaughter, Beulah Quiggle Neff, felt that the Klobes came to know Prince Farrington through Floyd's ex-wife, Thressa and Mr. and Mrs. Stabley. Prince had lived close to the Stableys when he lived on the Florida Fruit Farm. He was an occasional visitor with the Klobes at their home near Carroll and later at their farm. Prince apparently won the admiration of Ethel, the young daughter of Floyd. She told of his visits and of her awareness of his beautiful teeth and his use of a stick to keep them clean. Here, again, numerous people commented on the brightness of Prince Farrington's teeth. Tom Bauman, a friend and neighbor of the Farringtons, observed, "And when Prince picked his teeth, I don't know. I've had different guys tell me it was a pine stick or birch or something. It wasn't until the last time he was in prison that he started to have some tooth problems. Up until that time, to the best of my knowledge, he never had any fillings or anything." Another observation by Ethel Klobe was similar to that of several other individuals. She, too, told of noticing that Prince Farrington's complexion was darker than others in Sugar Valley.

A specific incident involving Prince and Ethel occurred on a hot summer day. Ethel, wearing gumboots, (high rubber footwear) was working with her dad in the fields when Prince arrived. Ethel's daughter, Beulah, relates how "Prince said something to her about the fact that her Pap was so cheap that he wouldn't buy her a decent pair of shoes; but made her run in hot gumboots in the middle of the summer, and that Pap 'takes care of the horses' feet better than he does yours'". Her daughter tells how young Ethel "took it as a sort-of joke; but, several days later, she had a new pair of shoes. She never knew where they came from—whether Pap was embarrassed or what—but she got a new pair of shoes!"

Not surprisingly, Prince Farrington was a frequent visitor with Floyd Klobe. Floyd, too, combined experience with skill to create another income to supplement his farm earnings. His friendship with Farrington was obviously one of mutual regard. It isn't known, today, whether there was a financial interest behind their friendship. As a young man, Floyd Klobe also worked as a moonshiner in New York City, a job discussed in Chapter 14.

Storing moonshine was another story entirely for Floyd Klobe. When he got company, he'd grab a gun as though he might be doing a little small-game hunting. With his gun, he'd walk to a stone pile in the middle of a field. There, he apparently had a hidden stash of liquor. He'd retrieve a bottle of whiskey and return to his guests. Family members were sure that Floyd Klobe had a second hiding place beneath a massive straw pile behind the barn, a place forbidden to children.

Ethel Klobe's marriage to Earl Quiggle involved another irony. Ethel's moonshiner father, Floyd, used liquor; but was not an alcoholic. Her husband was. She and her toper spouse were the parents of three children, including Beulah Quiggle Neff, who now lives in Howard, Pennsylvania where she helps preserve the history of one of Sugar Valley's most colorful families. As explained in Chapter 14, Beulah is also the individual responsible for the preservation of two stills that once belonged to the Klobe clan.

Prince Farrington clung to his moonshining ways until his health and legal woes forced him to quit. Floyd Curtis Klobe, on the other hand, stopped making moonshine while a young man. It happened, the family believes, when he and his teenage daughter, Ethel, were cooking a fresh batch in the still beneath the shed. She had been taught the process. The father and daughter were surprised to see some revenue agents entering the farm lane. Floyd left Ethel to cap the still while he hurried to meet the revenuers. While Floyd kept the revenuers occupied, his teenage daughter worked to cap the still so that it would stop cooking. The still might have exploded. Floyd recognized the danger. He later confessed, "I might have killed my daughter!" The family thinks that that was the last moonshine that Floyd ever made.

## STALKED BY TRAGEDY

Beulah Quiggle Neff has observed, "I know that my grandfather (Floyd Klobe) did illegal things; but he was a good person. He was very, very good to us. Unfortunately, Floyd Curtis Klobe expressed a fear that he was to become a victim of senseless tragedy. He had solid reasons. His grandfather had been murdered in Philadelphia. Then, his father, Herman Klobe, was killed during the brawl between Floyd Klobe and Louis B. Huntingdon. His fear was palpably reinforced when he was sitting on a bar stool in a tavern near Jersey Shore. A man suddenly came from behind and stabbed Floyd in the back!" The attack was nearly successful; Floyd was severely injured, but he survived. However, his fear of being murdered was reinforced, and he was convinced that the stabbing had been done under orders from a man in Lock Haven. There was also the 1929 automobile accident that took the life of his ex-wife, Thressa. Despite his fears, Floyd Curtis Klobe actually died a natural death. Sadly, there was one more senseless killing of a family member that Floyd would know before his passing.

Forty-year-old Leo Held lived in Loganton and worked at the Hammermill Paper Company plant in Lock Haven. At one time or another, he had been a volunteer fireman, school board director and scout leader. On the morning of October 23, 1967, Leo Held went on a rampage, seemingly resulting from annoyances and grievances magnified. He strode into the Hammermill plant armed with a 45-calibre automatic pistol and a 38-calibre magnum revolver. There, he shot and killed five of his superiors. He also wounded four others. Then he went to the nearby Piper Aircraft factory and shot and injured a woman who was a member of his carpool. Carpool members were said to have criticized Held's reckless driving. He then returned, via a back road, to his hometown, Loganton.

In Loganton, he drove around the school where three of his children were in attendance. He saw no one outside and drove away. The tale of terror had preceded him. The children were all locked within the school. The man who lived across the street from Leo Held was a 28-year-old man named Quiggle. Held had complained to Quiggle about smoke from Quiggle's burning leaves. Quiggle also had a collection of guns. On that fateful day, his wife, Donna, had already taken their son to school and returned. One relative told of Held bursting into the Quiggle home and rushing upstairs to where Quiggle was still in bed. When his wife saw Held, she grabbed the telephone and shoved her daughter under the bed. Leo Held shot the phone out of her hand. As Quiggle started to rise, Held shot and killed him. As Donna Quiggle leaned over her husband, Held shot her in the back. She survived for another ten years but spent that decade as a paralyzed cripple. With the terrified Quiggle child left unshot, Held hurried downstairs and smashed the locked door of Quiggle's gun cabinet. He wrapped an armful of rifles in some bedding and returned to his own house. Held sat weapons at each window in an apparent plan to face authorities from his own barricaded house. Held next emerged from his house, intent on killing an elderly woman who lived in a nearby mobile home. He never got to the mobile home. As lawmen closed in, Held was defiant, shouting: "Come and get me. I'm not taking any more of their bull!" Held's lawn was the scene of the firefight. Despite the pleading of a brother-in-law and having been hit by several officers' bullets, Held continued to return fire until he collapsed from his multiple wounds. He died in the hospital a couple of days later without ever fully regaining consciousness.

Four observations regarding the 1967 Leo Held rampage in Clinton County:

- The local people showed the same concern for Leo Held's family members as they did for the family members of his shooting victims.
- It was the worst such shooting spree in Clinton County history.
- The killing spree occurred less than 15 months after the Texas Tower shooting rampage of Charles Whitman, a killing spree that left 16 people dead and 32 others wounded at the University of Texas in Austin.
- The innocent 28-year-old man from Loganton, who was senselessly shot to death because his leaf-burning smoke drifted or because he had some coveted guns, was Floyd Quiggle, son of Ethel Klobe Quiggle and grandson of the man for whom he

was named, Floyd Klobe. The Quiggles had also named *their* son—the one who was safely in school—for their ancestor, Floyd Curtis Klobe.

Floyd Curtis Klobe, who had been born 85 years earlier at Carroll, died on January 12, 1979. Floyd's daughter, Ethel Klobe Quiggle, died on March 24, 1991. Etta Raudabaugh, the widow who lived with Floyd Klobe for the last half century of his life—and who was recognized as 'mother' by Thressa Klobe's daughter, Ethel—outlived her unofficial stepdaughter, dying November 30, 1991. All three, Floyd, Etta and Ethel, rest side-by-side in the Fairview Cemetery at Loganton, where Ethel shares a grave and a headstone with her husband, Earl Quiggle. The tombstone of Ethel and Earl is decorated with two sketches: Earl's Mack truck and Ethel, in hunting garb and holding a rifle, eyeing a handsome buck deer.

An inexplicable oddity was revealed with Floyd Klobe's death: In his will, he had bypassed both his common-law wife of a half-century, Etta, and his lone child, Ethel. Etta's life-long contribution to the family finances was forgotten. Both women were saddened. Floyd's heirs were his three grandchildren! His legal heirs, however, agreed to re-divide the Floyd Klobe estate to give both Etta and Ethel their proper shares. Beulah Quiggle Neff remains philosophical about the turn of events. She jokes, "Why didn't Floyd Klobe start a *legal* distillery? Then, we wouldn't be worried about money."

Today most, including Steve Neff, think of their families' past not as being shameful; but as being colorful. So it was.

*The gravestone of Zenadah "Nade" Farrington Coltrane, 1896-1934, beloved sister of Prince Farrington.*

**WHITEY'S CARS**
WHOLESALE OUTLET NO. 1
NEW and USED CARS

601 W. CHURCH ST.                    ORLANDO, FLA.

*The business card of Prince David Farrington, Jr. ("Whitey") for his new/used car business, one of his several enterprises.*

*An old photograph showing a Civilian Conservation Corps (CCC) camp near Renovo, Clinton County, PA. Courtesy of former CCC member, Leonard Parucha.*

*A Klobe family relic. A still that once steamed near Carroll as property of Floyd Klobe.*

*The home of Gladys and George Porter and their family, near Torbert, Lycoming County. Prince Farrington was said to have had a still in the basement here at one time.*

The tombstone for Ethel Klobe Quiggle and her husband, Earl, whose Mack truck appears, opposite Ethel's depiction as a huntress. Mountain View Cemetery in Loganton, Clinton County, PA.

Juxtaposed: Trucks used in the Marcellus shale gas extraction process, loading water from the Susquehanna River. In the background, on the top of the cliff is the mansion of the late Prince David Farrington.

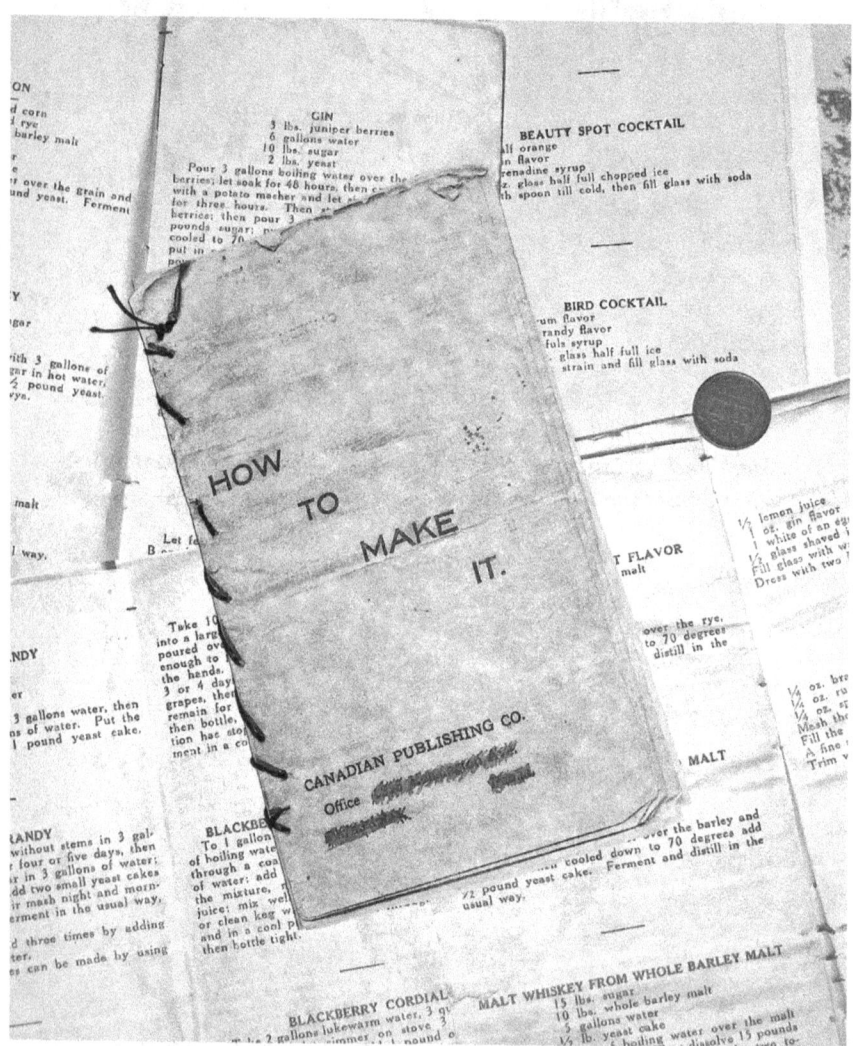

*A 'recipe' book for making a variety of alcoholic concoctions. Apparently printed in Philadelphia and once owned by one or more of the Klobe family members. A Klobe family heirloom.*

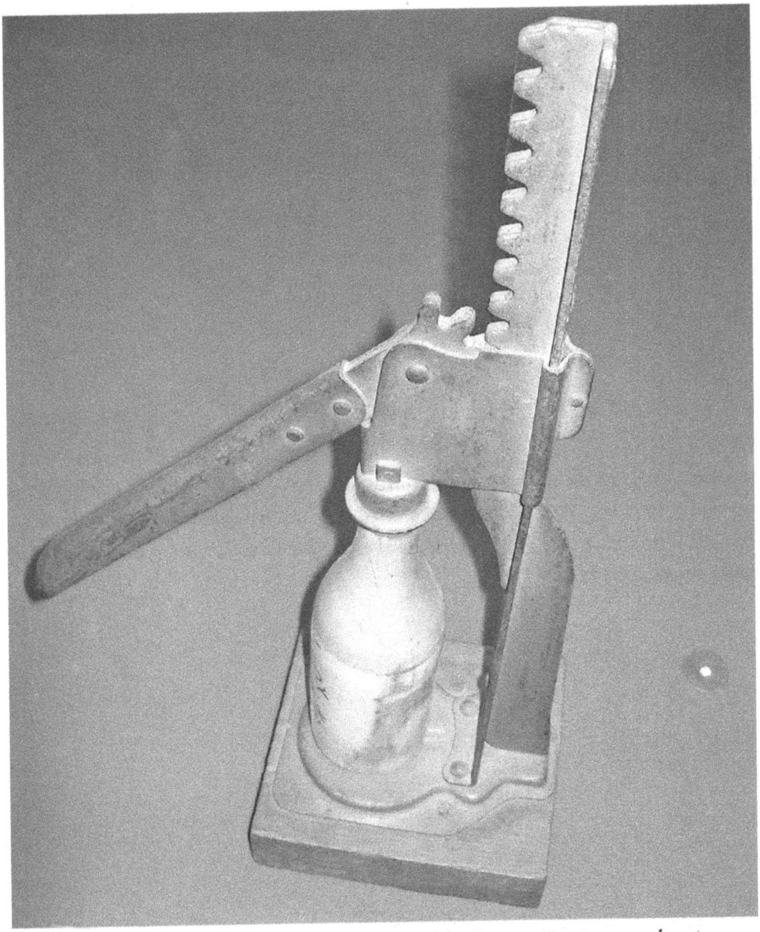

# "Moon Shine Farm"; The Klobe Clan 195

*A bottle-capping device that was once owned by Prince Farrington; but is now one of the moonshining collectibles at the Gamble Farm Inn in Jersey Shore.*

*A metal panel that once marked an upstairs apartment as being named for Prince Farrington. Second floor doorway at the Gamble Farm Inn.*

*Three moonshiners at an unknown location. Note the complexity of the operation, with the wooden containers, the still, a lean-to, a couple of tents and a large number of kegs and barrels. This print was once owned by the late Joe Gardner, who had it hanging in his living room Lock Haven.*

*Self-explanatory poster. Several decades after Prince Farrington died, he name graced the posters of a fundraising event. This event was held for ten or eleven years before interest waned.*

*A 19th century drawing of the Gamble Farm, on the edge of what is now Jersey Shore. The house was converted into an inn many decades later. Courtesy of Wayne Welshans*

*Bunny Wright and her brother, Tony Hyatt, flanking the Farrington stone in the Burnett's Chapel graveyard, near Greensboro, North Carolina.*

*A 'recipe' book for making a variety of alcoholic concoctions. Apparently printed in Philadelphia and once owned by one or more of the Klobe family members. A Klobe family heirloom*

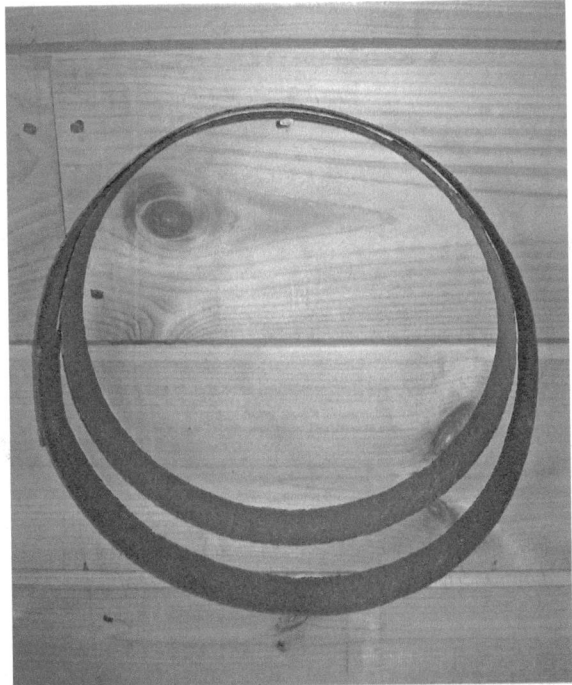

Keg hoops found at a Prince Farrington still site on the lands that were once part of the Florida Fruit Farm. Photo by the author.

A helicopter involved in the geological survey of Clinton County as part of the Marcellus shale gas boom. When not surveying the area's geological features deep beneath the surrounding hills, it rests near the Restless Oaks restaurant at McElhattan.

*The Rauchtown Inn, in the heart of Farrington country, between Antes Fort and Carroll. The road on the left leads to Carroll and to the exit of Interstate 80.*

*Treasurers of local lore, John Wagner, Dave Frankenberger and Harold "Dutch" Washburn at the Twilight Diner, just outside of Loganton. All are Sugar Valley residents.*

*Three of Prince Farrington's workers, relaxing on steps of his old house at the Florida Fruit Farm.*

*James Segraves III, by a woodland stream just off Jack's Hollow Road, near the town of Bastress. The stream and the fog-shrouded path both lead to a long abandoned still site once used by James' great grandfather, the moonshiner friend of Prince Farrington, Colonel Monte Segraves.*

*A ceramic tile silo on the farm once occupied by Prince Farrington's friend, DeWitt Hill and located just south of Jersey Shore, Lycoming County.*

*The grand entrance to the Victoria Theater in Jersey Shore, P.A., where the young Farringtons and their friends saw the current fare out of the Hollywood movie studios. Courtesy of Wayne Welshans.*

*Thressa Klobe's grave stone, near Loganton.*

*Prince Farrington (right), with his close associate, Joe Gardner, and Joe's son, Neese.*

*Thressa Klobe, one of the several unique women in Prince and the Paupers. A metropolitan chorus girl, an absentee mother, whose life was abruptly shortened by a tragic automobile accident.*

*A trio of Farrington workers burying or disinterring some illegal alcohol.*

*A pair of vintage autos; once prizes of the wealthy. The rear one belonged to Prince Farrington.*

*Colonel Monte Segraves, one of Prince Farrington's close friends, with his first wife, the former Marie Engel. He was from North Carolina; she from the Bastress area of Lycoming County.*

*Gladys Farrington Porter as a young woman.*

*Gladys Farrington Porter, Prince's lone daughter, with her first two offspring.*

*Early American family life is captured in this picture of Bernard Wynn's grandmother, Maggie Duck Bower, his aunt Ruth and the family cow, on their homestead on Rockey Road, near Loganton.*

*Prince Farrington, Jr. "Whitey" on a family tractor.*

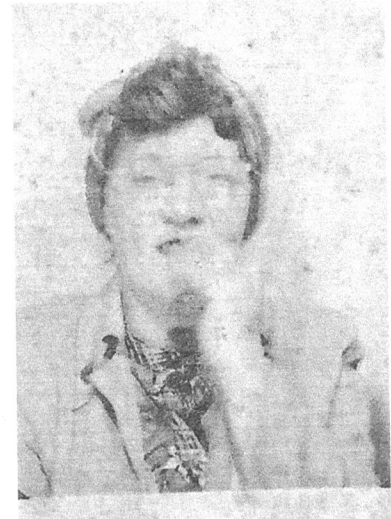

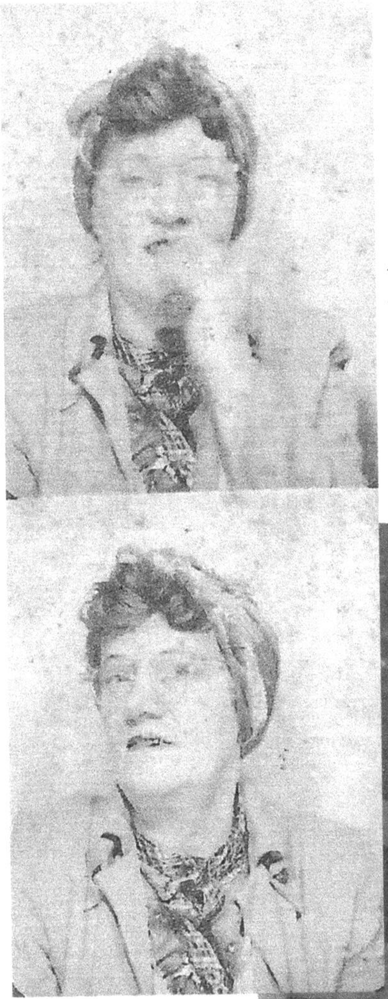

The moonshiner's troubled wife, Martha (Mrs. Prince) White Farrington.

Prince Farrington's friend, Joe Gardner, telling two of his nephews about the grand still he remembered working near Greensboro, North Carolina

*Boyd "Duke" Greak, with his children, Barbara (now Clark) and Lee.*

*B. W. Coltrane, a popular member of the Farrington relation, in military attire.*

"Moon Shine Farm"; The Klobe Clan   211

*B. W. Coltrane with a native during B. W.'s overseas service.*

*Mr. and Mrs. Boyd "Duke" Greak. He successfully transformed from a Farrington worker to a married man who loved hunting, fishing, and nature in general.*

*The gravestone of Margaret and Herman Klobe, in Eastville.*

*Prince Farrington, Jr. ("Whitey") and his uncle, Scott Anthony, who was married to his mother's sister.*

*A memorial brick, near Newport, Virginia, placed in Prince Farrington's memory by his grandson, Dr. Robert Porter.*

*Two of Charl Farrington's children, Frances (later Mrs. George Gardner) and her brother, Robert.*

*A long-time friend of Prince Farrington, Earl W. "Skinny" Ritter, proud of his '29 Nash.*

*A common portrait of Prince Farrington in his more mature years.*

## "MOON SHINE FARM"; THE KLOBE CLAN 215

*"Girty's Notch," a landmark along Routes 11 and 15 north of Harrisburg, said to represent the colonial renegade, Simon Girty.*

*Popular portrait of Pennsylvania-born western outlaw, Harry Longabaugh ("The Sundance Kid") and his mistress, Etta Place.*

*A monument to the man from Mont Clare, Pennsylvania, Harry Longabaugh, erected in Sundance, Wyoming.*

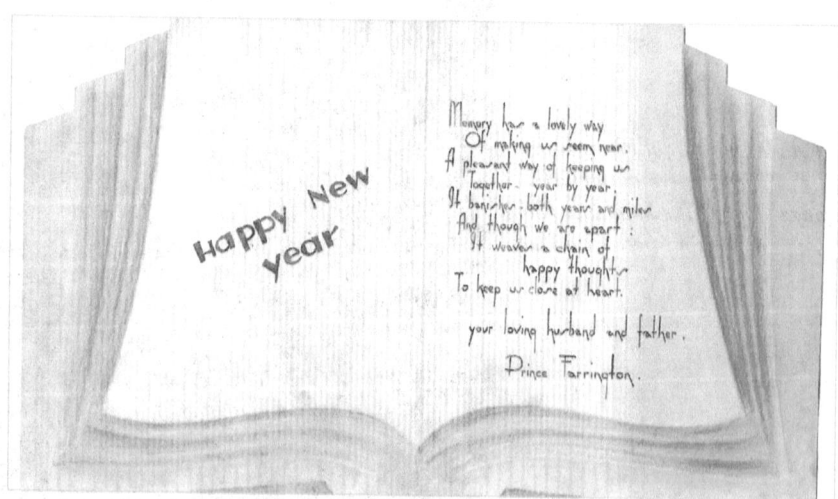

*An early seasonal greeting card from Prince Farrington to his family.*

A 19th century love letter, self-adorned by the artistic swain, Herman Henry Klobe.

> Pine Creek Hollow,
> Feb. the 9th/88
>
> Dearest and best
> yours of the 5th inst and
> at hand, I feel very lonesome
> since you have left, time
> seems long to me, for instance
> when saturday night comes
> I had bin out on Wednesday
> evening But you had gone
> of so I felt dishearted.

> so I stayed at your folks
> until 9 Oclock Clvdy told
> me that you had told
> her that I was to go over
> to see that women that
> told you that I had
> bin married I had a
> notion to do so being you
> was gone. I had bin
> over home last sunday
> and brought my close
> over and now I'm ready
> to get married most anytime
> it suits you, and as you
> say in your letter you trouble
> yourself dear you need not
> for I'll never disapoint you
> for I'll be as man, and
> your's only Clvdy had
> bin telling me, that you
> were troubling yourself about
> something so your Mother
> said wither I had told
> you something which you
> did not like so I told
> Clvdy I couldn't know
> what it could be. But
> I'll be up if the weather
> is nice next saturday
> comming this is all for
> this time My dearest hoping
> to have an early reply from
> you
> from your's forever
> H.H. Klobe
> please and address to
> Woodward
> Pa.

The second page of the letter of Herman Henry Klobe to his then girlfriend, Margaret Louise Miller.

LEO TAYLOR   "Chippy"
Athletic Club 2, 3, 4; Science Nature Club 3, 4; Athletic Association 2; Football 2, 3, 4; Basketball 1.
*Special! Gridiron hero remorseful!*
"Chippy" is quite remorseful these days simply because of graduation. And you know what that will mean — his days on the gridiron will be no more. "Chippy" has been one swell member of our A-1 football gang. Wonder if Miss Edith thinks the same as we do!

GEORGE PORTER   "Greg"
Alumni Treasurer of Class 3; Band 1, 2, 3, 4; Custodian 4; Journalism Club 3, 4; Concert Orchestra 3; Dance Orchestra 2, 3; Orange and Black Staff 4.
*Extra! Buster busts buttons!*
"Little Buster Porter,
Had lost his quarter,
So he looked in his mit,
But upon it he did sit!"
Ahem! That will be the day.

GLADYS FARRINGTON   "Foxey"
Science Nature 2, Secretary 2; Athletic Association 1, 2, 3, 4; Sigma Delta Chi 4; Student Council 3, 4; Alumni Treasurer 2; Secretary of Class 3; Class Play 4.
"Fair to look upon but better yet to know."

*Three yearbook entries from the appropriate Jersey Shore High School yearbooks.*

*An authentic Prince Farrington specimen, now owned by Kim VanCampen, whose father received it as a gift.*

*The old paint mill on Antes Creek, said to have been used for hiding Farrington moonshine.*

*The McElhattan (Clinton County) home of author/fabulist Colonel Henry W. Shoemaker.*

*Bernie Wynn leaning against his dad's 1929 Dodge. Taken at the Bower homestead, on Rockey Road, about three miles from the Florida Fruit Farm of Prince Farrington.*

# · 11 ·
# The Clandestine Network

Once Prince Farrington settled into his new house near Antes Fort, the center of his life would have been that imposing house atop the eastern bank of the Susquehanna River opposite the town of Jersey Shore. From here, Prince David Farrington followed the production of liquor coming from his expanding network of hidden distilleries. From here, he ordered the many supplies needed to turn corn into mash and mash into high-grade, 180-proof whiskey. And, from here, once cut to a drinkable alcoholic content (well under 100 proof), he sent, or carried, his hooch in all directions to grateful buyers.

## A BEVY OF STILLS
### The Cinderella Deception

As mentioned above, Prince Farrington, according to his daughter-in-law, Martha Farrington (Mrs. Tom), had a still in the seemingly inaccessible basement of his house in North Carolina. The only opening to that chamber was beneath the ashes of the fireplace. When the moonshiner was ready to enter or exit the hidden basement, a confederate moved the ashes and opened the trapdoor.

Here are listed many more Farrington stills—all known today to have been part of his secret network of stills in Pennsylvania. The list compiled here, with the input of many individuals, far exceeds the author's expectations. When this book was begun, the author hoped to find the specific sites of two or three of Prince Farrington's stills. Since the entire focus of Farrington's operation involved clandestine activity, it seemed unlikely that we could learn of many of his still locations, hidden, as they were, in wooded glades or disguised buildings. For example, George Porter, the moonshiner's only son-in-law and a man entrusted with critical information, hinted at larger numbers and may have known the sites of most of Prince's stills, but he provided only two or three specific locations. Comments by his daughter, Gladys, suggest that he had an aversion to females, even his devoted daughter, being directly involved with his work. Her evaluation: "I knew about where they were, but he didn't believe in women being around stills because he figured they were bad luck." Luckily, as more people were interviewed, more locations were identified. Although an interviewee might have known of but one still (the one located in his or her immediate area), as each identified a familiar still site, the numbers began to mount. Happily, we can now offer the reader the locations of thirty-two actual, once-hidden stills, an unbelievable bevy of stills that once produced thousands of gallons of illicit liquor daily!

Among his earliest stills would likely have been the ones on or close to his Florida Fruit Farm, his first residence when arriving in Clinton County, Pennsylvania. Others followed until Prince had a large network of clandestine stills. Of course, not all operated at the same time, and no one knows his total number, but, as mentioned above, the interviews yielded enough data to produce the following list of known locations of Farrington stills, as well as some data on how they were designed in order to provide for the most secluded operations. The Pennsylvania still sites are numbered so that the scope of Prince Farrington's operations begins to emerge.

### 1. Beyond the Back Yard
One might suppose that Prince Farrington's first still constructed in Penn's Woods, was the one on the edge of his first homestead in Pennsylvania, a property known as the Florida Fruit Farm. This still was built in Clinton County, on a hilly ridge off a side road, where a small enclosure blocked a spring's overflow to create a pond. There, a couple of years ago, Yvonne and Steve Weaver, both natives of the area of Loganton and Rosecrans, walked to the site with the author. There, we saw the old pond, some bricks, keg hoops, and other detritus of the long idle still.

### 2. Within the Stone Doughnut
Within a field on the Florida Fruit Farm, Clinton County, Harold "Dutch" Washburn tells us, there was, in years past, a huge, innocuous-looking

pile of field stones, similar to stone piles on many farms. These stone piles were created by farmers who piled the stones, which they removed from the field to prepare for plowing. This pile, however, according to Washburn, was only a disguise for a still that was nestled below the line of vision within the doughnut-shaped configuration.

### 3. On the Abandoned Roadway
A few miles to the north of the Florida Fruit Farm, a steep mountain road winds along the side of a ridge. That road was cut through the area by the workers of the Civilian Conservation Corps, a Depression-era federal work program that saw idle city workers clear and improve forest roads and build bridges over forest streams. As the CCC workers built and graded a new mountain road, the abandoned road, off in the old gully, became a convenient—partly cleared and well-secluded—site for a Prince Farrington still.

### 4. On the Road to Salona
On the old road that curves through the mountain gap between Loganton and Salona, there are countless gullies on both sides of State Route 477. Along that winding rural roadway, there is a particular gully, with its accompanying stream that tumbles downward until it joins Long Run about five miles south of Salona. A stream-side path leads upwards toward the ridge's high point. There, Harold Washburn says a rather large illegal Farrington operation was once located.

### 5. A Spring on Spruce Run
Barely a mile south of the still near Salona, mentioned in the preceding passage, and also on State Route 477, a one-lane road crawls along the bank of Spruce Run before that stream flows into Long Run. Several small, spring-fed streams flow through narrow gullies and feed into Spruce Run. Traveling east, a gully on the left marks the place where deeper in the wooded hillside, a Farrington still once percolated and steamed, the second such site to be found by departing to the east off Route 477. This still seems to be among the best-known. At least three local people mentioned the site. Don Cowfer, for example, offered this information: "Hell, there's still moonshining going on today (2009). I

don't know where they're at, but I heard different people say it. I know where one was years ago. Out near the graveyard on Spruce Run Road."

## 6. In the Ghost Town

Many people don't realize that Pennsylvania has a large number of ghost towns. They were born to cater to the logging industry, the tanning industry, the brick-making industry, the oil industry or the coal-mining industry. One ghost town, Eagleton, was a former mining town that had been built on Buckhorn Mountain, about 15 miles northwest of Lock Haven. For Prince Farrington, the appeal of the isolated town was considerable. He established a still in the stillness of Eagleton. Within a year after the ending of Prohibition (December 1933), revenue agents learned of Farrington's Eagleton operation. When the agents visited there—sans invitation—in the late summer of 1934, they found two hastily-abandoned tents with food still on a table. They also found enough vats to hold an incredible 45,000-gallon capacity! The tank that would hold the finished whiskey was of a 2,000-gallon capacity.[29] There were also more than 2,000 feet of pipe and 250 bags of sugar. The operators of the Eagleton-area distillery were able to remove the 40-foot-tall copper column and carry it away. That copper column, alone, was worth a fortune. Since no one was apprehended, there were no arrests in that case; but the authorities had caused a considerable loss for Prince, who quickly built a new still north of Williamsport at the settlement of Powys.

## 7. Bucks Gap

The Carroll (kuh ROLL) area of Clinton County was a popular site for stills, known to have been built by at least two parties, one of whom was Prince Farrington's confederate, Jake Kohberger. In 2009, James Matthews—who lives near Carroll—led the author to the evidence of a long-abandoned still site near his home. This site is in Bucks Gap, east of Carroll and only yards from Interstate 80. Here, one can, as this is written, see a hole (about two feet deep) in the leafy forest floor where a barrel was apparently once submerged. A barrel hoop and a stone base for a firebox are nearby.

---

29. A capacity that was about a thousand times that of a small-time moonshiner.

According to Laura Matthews, more than one moonshiner operated in the wooded bottomland south of Route 880 and slightly west of the small town of Carroll. At least one of the moonshiners who operated there was Prince Farrington. It was this area to which the late Leo "Chip" Taylor referred when, about 2001, he told of having once been fishing with a friend and smelling the unmistakable odor of corn mash being cooked nearby. That aroma caused his companion to observe that the two of them should "get the hell out of here." So they got the hell out of there!

## 8. Obliterated By a Superhighway

In 1959, a shovelful of ground was turned in a symbolic opening of the project to create a complete superhighway, similar to the famed Pennsylvania Turnpike (but toll-less). In 1970, 11 years and 324 million dollars later, a major northeastern highway artery opened. This artery is the Z. H. Confair Memorial Highway (Pennsylvania's section of Interstate 80). That highway, in Clinton County, also bisected what was once recognized by many locals as Farrington country. Interstate 80 snakes across Clinton County less than three miles south of Farrington's first Pennsylvania homestead, the Florida Fruit Farm. That new superhighway left one of Prince Farrington's still sites forever lost beneath the speeding automobiles and rumbling 18-wheelers that travel east and west across the continent. That site, once located in the bottomland to the south of Buck's Gap, was also identified by James Matthews.

## 9. In a Torbert-area Basement

Dave Porter said that one of his grandfather's secret stills had been in the basement of a farmhouse near the area known as Torbert, just north of Jersey Shore and on the lower waters of Pine Creek. The illicit still was about two miles north of Route 220 and about four miles north of Pine Creek's junction with the Susquehanna River. This would be one of at least three Farrington stills known to have been located in the basement of farmhouses.

## 10. The Farm on Ireland Road

If one leaves U.S. Route 15 at the town of Allenwood and turns west on Pennsylvania Route 44, you arrive at the even smaller village of Elimsport.

On a farm near that town, in November of 1927, local and federal officials raided a still. The Williamsport *Sun-Gazette* reported at the time that the farmer was not immediately taken into custody because officials recognized that he had a large family to support. On April 25th of 2009, Margaret and Harold "Bud" Drick, lifelong residents of the Elimsport area, recalled that down Ireland Lane, just west of Elimsport, there was a house that once had huge vats in the basement. This is corroborated by Patricia and Charles Ulrich, also of Elimsport. They note that Prince Farrington had an illegal operation in that old brick house on Ireland Road, just west of town. That house had four or five large concrete vats in the basement, with trapdoors in the floor above each. In Farrington's day, the late 1920s in this case, the house was owned by Russell Brown. The Ulrichs know 'whereof they speak' since they, too, owned the house in more recent years. About five years ago, another party bought the farm, razed the brick structure and built a frame house. The current owners, named Stoltzfus, operate a rural grocery store on the property. Young Isaac Stoltzfus said that he was told that, when the distilling was going on in the basement, the operation was guarded by armed men, day and night, at each end of the property. The Ulrichs added that the distilling operation included the harvesting of about seven acres of grapes from a field across the roadway, a field known locally as "the grapevine field."

### 11. Beneath the Aging Sawdust

Prince's brother, Charles Archibald Farrington, lived on Silver Avenue in Lamar, a small town in Porter Township of Clinton County. There, hidden beneath the floor of an old sawmill, a still was concealed. That still, and its fate is discussed in Chapter 7.

### 12. Where the White Water Flows

Pine Creek is an 87-mile-long ribbon of water that dribbles from the earth in Potter County, Pennsylvania. It then flows east into Tioga County to the village of Ansonia, the site of an old Indian meeting place. There, the creek gathers the waters of Marsh Creek and turns south into nearly fifty miles of a gorgeous gully known as the Pine Creek Gorge. The gorge is up to 1400 feet deep, and it lures nature lovers and white water rafters. Exiting the Pine Creek Gorge, a boater would still have spectacular scenery as

Pine Creek continues its southward journey. It passes between the towns of Avis and Jersey Shore (Lycoming County) before offering its woodland waters to the Susquehanna River's West Branch. But it is far upstream and deep within the gorge that Stradley Hollow successfully concealed a Prince Farrington still.

The Béthune family descended from the French nobility of the Middle Ages. Those who came to rural Clinton County, Pennsylvania, arrived from England, where the name had changed to Button. At the time when Prince Farrington was looking for secluded lands on which to construct and operate illegal stills, Melvin Button owned a tract of land on the west side of Pine Creek, right in the depths of Pine Creek Gorge. There, in Stradley Hollow, Farrington built a still and Melvin Button did some delivery of the finished product. This history is drawn from the memory of Melvin's daughter, Roseltha Lydia Button Miller, a nonagenarian who lives in the settlement of Jersey Mills, directly across Pine Creek from the old still site in Stradley Hollow. "But," Roseltha adds, "it was all undercover." At the time that the still was in operation, there was no paved road through the gorge. Today, some of that wild gorge remains without a roadway along either bank, although State Route 414 goes close to where the still once operated.

### 13. Tobacco and More
In the tobacco barn opposite the Buffalo Inn, along Route 150, in Dunnstown, a still was hidden. Jake Kohberger, a close associate of Prince Farrington, owned both the barn and the inn. Both structures are now gone, with the Buffalo Inn being dismantled early in 2009, just weeks before the author visited that site.

### 14. A Short-lived Enterprise
In 1936, when Farrington had an opportunity to salvage one of his damaged stills, he quickly rebuilt it in a new location. This time, he found a location along old U.S. Route 15 near Powys, a tiny settlement north of Williamsport, in Hepburn Township of Lycoming County. Powys was likely named for a county in central Wales. Locally, it is pronounced to rhyme with 'Howie's.' The still never saw a completed batch of hootch. Federal agents swooped in and raided the Powys still on May 1, 1936, before it was put into operation. Today, U.S. Route 15 offers a beautiful

drive through the mountains, but it bypasses Powys. A tavern, the Powys Watering Hole, is still on the old highway, but the area is even more remote than in Prince's day.

## 15. The Heckman's Gap Operation

The existence and location of both of the next two stills were identified to me by David L. Eck of Jersey Shore. He said that there was a Farrington still at Heckman's Gap. That, too, is a relatively isolated location today. If one leaves Interstate Highway 80 at the Lock Haven exit and drives in the direction due south, opposite the highway into Lock Haven, he or she would be driving right into the maw of Heckman's Gap. The road beyond the gap, through Heckman's hollow, was destroyed by the flood of 1972 and remains impassable today.

A lesser legend, but a legend, nonetheless, tells of a Depression-era hunter named Clair Jones Sr. of Heckman's Gap. He was admired locally for poaching and for providing many of the poor people of the area with meat. One memorable account says that Jones, sometime during the 1940s, walked through Heckman's Hollow with a small caliber rifle, hunting squirrels. He spotted a small Black Bear, estimated to weigh about 150 pounds, walking in the same direction as Clair but some distance in front of him. Clair Jones Sr., with a mere 22-caliber bullet, shot the bear behind the ear for a clean kill.

## 16. Lost in Fortney's Gap

David L. Eck also tells of a Farrington still that operated to the west of Heckman's Gap, in the area of Fortney's Gap. The author was unable to establish a precise location for this site.

## 17. At Springer's Corner

The old Coudersport Pike is a road linking Jersey Shore with the far-off town of Coudersport in Potter County. This 'pike' was a truly isolated roadway and remains so today. However, that is the ideal location for someone wishing to create an illegal distilling operation. Just off that mountain road, Prince Farrington put a still close by what is now designated as Springer's Corner. A gentleman named Springer once had a small store serving this rustic section of Clinton County. Prince approached Mr.

John Springer, who lived nearby and asked him if he would be willing to watch the operation. Mr. Springer's widow, Kathleen, and his son, Charles, still live at that location. Charles said that his dad, John Springer, refused Farrington's offer and wanted nothing to do with Prince's world. Dale Copenhaver, one of the Springers' neighbors, told the author that while working with Woolrich, Incorporated, of Woolrich, Clinton County, Pennsylvania, a co-worker, the late Joe Derr, told Copenhaver that the Farrington still sat "down the hollow from your place."

## 18. Taylor's Surprise

Leo Taylor, in a recorded conversation, mentioned visiting with Prince Farrington's nephew, B. W. Coltrane, and deliberately going into one of Prince Farrington's chicken houses near Antes Fort after Coltrane had ordered him not to do so. There, he found, upstairs, a still cooking, with a man sitting nearby reading a newspaper. The man watching the still seemed unconcerned about the intruder and began telling the youngster how the work was done, but Taylor was too scared to hear the explanation and quietly retreated. The malodorous chicken house, Taylor observed, was likely chosen because its stench would help to mask the illegal operation on the second floor.

## 19. Occupying an Abandoned Shale Pit

Ken Feerrar, whose aunt was the second wife of Joe Gardner, tells of an abandoned shale pit about three miles east of Route 880 on Fourth Gap Road. The shale pit, within two miles of Feerrar's home, likely provided an early businessman of the area with the soft layers of red shale rock unearthed for crushing into dust and forming into bricks. These mud bricks were then heated and became the bricks used for local building projects. During the days of Prince Farrington, the pit became an appealingly isolated place, excellent for hiding a cooker of sour mash whiskey and the product's strong aroma. This moonshine still was one of about a half-dozen located within just a few miles of Prince Farrington's first Pennsylvania home, northeast of Loganton.

## 20. Between the Gulches

Several of the Farrington stills were situated between a pair of gulches. However, the still that Farrington maintained on the mountain road from

Castanea to McElhattan shows a perfect trail going south from Castanea through the gulch of the West Kammerdiner Run, then coursing behind a couple of steep ridges to the east before arriving beside McElhattan Creek to exit from the hills by going downstream (north) along the creek toward the town of McElhattan. It was on that back road that Jacque Groce remembers her father stopping their car, getting out and walking into the woods to a still and returning with a paper bag, presumably containing some 'Princely" potion.

## 21. Within a Splendid Sylvan Setting
If one were to go to the town of McElhattan, midway between Jersey Shore and Lock Haven, and begin to walk upstream along the small McElhattan Creek to its source, he or she would encounter the beauty of McElhattan Falls. The person who trekked those eight or nine miles would have reached the one-time site of another of Prince Farrington's stills.

## 22. On the Banks of Bender Run
There is a small town, Nisbet, on the south side of the Susquehanna River in Susquehanna Township, Lycoming County. The town goes through time unnoticed despite carrying the family name of Admiral Horatio Nelson's abandoned wife, Frances. Nisbet is the starting point if one wishes to visit the site of one of Prince Farrington's stills. This woodland distillery was operating near Bender Run, behind a ridge to the south of Nisbet and slightly east of Route 654.

A few years ago, a visitor to the site, Chris Porter, found little more than a bottle and smaller items, but that was enough for Porter to pinpoint the location of yet another of Prince Farrington's still sites.

## 23. Opposite the Goat Farm
Hard by the Susquehanna River, on Route 120 between Lock Haven and the mouth of the Tangascootack (The "Scootac"), was Nell Burrows' goat farm. "In earlier days," a well-known local historian, Leonard Paruchka, tells us, "people drank goat's milk for upset stomach." The Nell Burrows' goat farm was once the area's only goat farm. The farm was bought by the three spinster sisters of the local Burrows family. On the opposite side of the

highway from the Burrows' property—between Route 120 and the river—lies a narrow stretch of riverbank and several houses. One of those houses, renovated and still standing today, housed a Farrington still. Mr. Paruchka believes that the last time Prince Farrington was arrested was while he was delivering a huge load of sugar to his still at that riverside location. This arrest was made possible because of the large load of sugar. The revenue agents "followed the sugar" and, again, caught the aging moonshiner.

### 24. The Still Behind the Church

Far upstream on the West Branch of the Susquehanna is the village of North Bend. As the name suggests, that little town is on the northernmost bank of the Susquehanna's West Branch. North Bend stands at the mouth of Young Woman Creek and was earlier known as Young Woman Town. Both those names come from the translation of the American Indian word for "Young Woman." At North Bend, there was once a camp for members of the Civilian Conservation Corps. Also, around the year 1890, a church was built in North Bend, the steeple of which can be seen from several miles downstream on the Susquehanna. There at North Bend, behind a small church, was a structure that looked just like a chicken house but was actually a disguised still, the operation of which was overseen by Farrington's friend, Bill Sockman, the owner of a hardware store in nearby Renovo. According to local historian John Paruchka, who worked from that Civilian Conservation Corps camp as a young man, he became aware of the still behind the church. He also suspected that another Farrington still was operating in Renovo.

Renovo is an old railroading town with numerous rail tracks. It was once the largest railroad repair center in Pennsylvania. The author was unable to get a fix on any Farrington still site in Renovo but would hesitate to contradict John Paruchka. If the right citizen of Renovo were approached with just the right questions, the location of such an old still may well be found.

### 25. Meixel's Triple Threat

A trio of Meixels offered a trio of valued services to Prince Farrington's sprawling moonshining and bootlegging operation. As discussed in Chapter 7, Floyd Meixel and his two oldest sons stored a large cache of

Prince's aging booze, and all three were drivers who delivered the finished product. In addition, the brothers, Clyde and Ern, are remembered in the family as having spent most of one winter in the cellar of a chicken house that sat behind their house and shed within a fenced-in apple orchard. That poultry 'dormitory' was two stories above ground, but it also had a finished cement-floor basement. Today, no one recalls precisely who owned the distillery that the brothers operated in that basement, but if one recalls that Prince David Farrington had three of the Meixel's large brood *storing* and *hauling* his hooch, it's reasonable to infer that Prince also paid for the distilling apparatus for the old chicken house. The two boys, in that long-ago winter, rarely left the chicken house beyond getting food and using the old outhouse.

Several years later, some of the Meixels became owners of the Rauchtown Inn in nearby Rauchtown. The inn still serves the thirsts of Nippenose Valley drinkers; but under a changed ownership. It was in that inn that the author found a gentleman from Jersey Shore, Robert Cowfer Jr., whose father, ex-father-in-law, and ex-father-in-law's dad were all drivers for Prince Farrington, as mentioned in Chapter 8.

While Prince Farrington's Pennsylvania career began in Sugar Valley, a very different group of outsiders began an influx into the valley during the 1970s and since. Amish agrarians from Lancaster County, Pennsylvania—also seeking a degree of freedom and solitude, much as Prince Farrington had done a half-century earlier—moved into Sugar Valley and, from there, expanded into neighboring valleys. In 1991, an Amish farmer bought the Meixel farm. Today, there is little evidence of the illegal operations that once kept the farm abuzz with activity. The chicken house, minus its upper tier, is dilapidated but standing. Also today, almost on the very spot where Floyd Meixel's old log house once stood, a small Amish schoolhouse has been erected. Amish youth will be served. The transformation of the old Meixel property is just one of many reminders that the local valleys are losing many of the landmarks long associated with Prince Farrington, although precious memories linger.

## 26. The Nine-Hundred-Acre Wood

The Knight's Huntng Club occupies a 900-acre tract of woodland on the slopes of Short Mountain, about five miles northwest of Jersey Shore.

The size of the tract and its use as a hunting club made it an ideal place for a Farrington still. Prince recognized that feature. He had a barn built within the 900 acre-forest to house all the distilling apparatus. He also had a spring house built to supply his operation with fresh water. When his career ended, the still on Short Mountain was abandoned. Today, the traces of the barn foundation are discernible. The spring house is still standing, giving a bountiful supply of refreshing mountain water to the club members, but there's no bubbling still sweating its potent steam into a lucrative liquid. The property is now owned by the same individual, William McGuire, who owns the rustic Restless Oaks restaurant in McElhatten. The near-empty site can be seen if one stands along Pine Creek, in the area of Poust's taxidermy shop.

As with most of Prince Farrington's stills, the one on the property of the 900-acre hunting club went undiscovered. It was never raided. Unfortunately for Prince, the ones that authorities *did locate* had painful results for the master moonshiner.

### 27. One of the Two Gann Houses
East of Jersey Shore and beyond what is now the airport, a man named Gann built two impressive houses in the 19th century. One was made of brick, and one was made of mountain stone. He wanted the houses to be built for his daughters, and each of his two daughters eventually owned one of the houses. These houses were said to be imposing rural homes set in an isolated area of Nippenose Valley to the east of Antes Fort. Today, the brick house has disappeared, and only part of the lithic wall remains of the other house. Between the days when the houses were fine dwellings and the time when they were abandoned, Prince Farrington used one of the houses to shelter and to hide another still.

### 28. Up Greenburr Hollow
Greenburr was, and remains, a small cluster of houses, where a cross-valley road forms a "T" with the road that runs along the south edge of Sugar Valley. As in similar configurations throughout Clinton County, one can find an unpaved road slithering upward, opposite the bottom of the "T" and winding into a hollow at the base of the mountain, along a mountain stream that terminates at a good, strong spring. Ed Snook of

Antes Fort is familiar with that remote spring upstream from Greenburr. "Every place where there was a good spring, somebody had a still." That location, Snook has related, was the location of one more Prince Farrington still.

## 29. On Whiskey Run

If one crosses the Susquehanna River from Lock Haven, Pennsylvania, to the north side of the river and then proceeds upstream along the Susquehanna, he or she will arrive at the few homes and the imposing old iron furnace that constitute the settlement known as Farrandsville. The iron furnace is believed to be the first hot-blast iron furnace in North America. This modest cluster of houses sits on the banks of Lick Run. As Lick Run is a tributary of the Susquehanna River, Whiskey Run is a tiny tributary of Lick Run. When asked if Prince Farrington had any stills in the Farrandsville area, Theodore Simcox, an elderly, lifelong resident, promptly responded, "Up on Whiskey Run. I never saw it. I was too young." The name Whiskey Run is likely a name that was first applied in the days of Farrington since there is no known origin for the name. Here, again, is an ironic twist. The area was a site for a still operation by a 'prince'—Prince Farrington—while, about 1792, the iron furnace was constructed and associated with a queen, Maria Christina, of Spain, who once owned a large tract of land in that remote area.

## 30. The Shooting Near Rockey Road

The Rockeys lived on Rockey Road. George and Gladys Rishel Rockey were a childless couple who had the same given names as Prince Farrington's daughter and son-in-law. George and Gladys were friends of Prince Farrington and were aware of the still which he operated on their property. George Rockey's dad, Lee Rockey, worked for Prince Farrington while transforming from adolescent to alcoholic. The elder Rockey lived with his son and daughter-in-law for some years, although he and his son, George, were estranged during Lee's later years. George claimed that his dad swindled him when George bought the farm. George said that he was tricked into having to pay about one and one-half the agreed price. He also made it clear that he wanted to be buried in a different cemetery than old Lee. That wish was fulfilled. Both Lee and George—father and son—had reputations for drunkenness, although Lee is the one who got the attention of occasional passers-by while lying, sprawled and drunk, on his lawn.

George Washington Rockey and his wife, Gladys Rishel Rockey, were very successful farmers, having once won a state achievement award for their farming. The area people knew George for his potatoes and Gladys for her flowers. After Lee Rockey and George Rockey had died, Gladys struggled to stay on the farm, although her sight was leaving. Gladys's memory remained clear, and she readily recalled the moonshiner/bootlegger. Prince had been friends with all three Rockeys and had maintained a still on their property. The still was "Right up the hollow," said Gladys. "Right up the hollow" meant that the still was just off Harbaugh Road, an unpaved and even more isolated roadway than Rockey Road. In addition, the still was set in a thick stand of hemlock and along a small stream known as Gann Run. George Rockey was still a teen when he met Prince Farrington, who eventually became a friend of all three, Lee, George and Gladys Rockey.

For years, George and Gladys hosted large numbers of visiting hunters, mostly from the Philadelphia area. Gladys cooked for the many guests, who also spent many hours at the card table and reduced George's supply of homemade liquors. Even today, local rumor says that there is a stash of George's hidden liquor supply, still to be unearthed, on the Rockey farm.

At the time of my visit, Gladys Rockey, an outgoing widow whose health was much diminished, had already sold the farm to Attorney Charles Rosamilia Jr. of Lock Haven. Mr. Rosamilia also shows a genuine appreciation for the five-generation history of the Rockey farm [founded in 1838]. Rosamilia also has an enviable collection of related historical documents.

George Rockey died before Gladys. Shortly before Gladys Rockey died, she could still affirm that "There's a big pile of coal there, yet." In a recent telephone interview, the current owner also confirmed the existence of detritus from the old Farrington still. Such items as coke, ashes, barrel staves and other remains were undisturbed on the site. One other thing that remains intact at this site is the memory of the shooting of Boyd "Duke" Greak, as related in Chapter 7.

## 31. On the "Scootac"

The secluded still site on the Tangascootack Creek is the one discussed at some length in the first pages of this book. It was a major operation, with a fortune in equipment and in the finished product. It was also the object of the last raid on a Farrington still, the one that finally finished Prince Farrington's moonshining career. That raid led to what should have been Prince Farrington's final arrest, but, as related above, it led to Prince Farrington's flight, exile and final apprehension.

Although several of Prince's stills were exceptional in their organization and output—such as the one on the Tangascootack Creek and the one in the sylvan ghost town of Eagleton—there was one that might be thought of as the truly fabled of the Farrington properties. This site remains in a near-pristine state, brazenly displayed in unencumbered solitude on the sloping bank of a grand river. This site begs to be designated as . . .

If one began following a stream in Sugar Valley during the days of Prohibition, what were the odds of locating an illegal whiskey distilling operation? There are no statistics, of course, but the late Dan Schrack once observed (personal conversation, 6/10/04) that, "It seems that where almost all the streams in the area ended, there was a still." Readers of the earlier book (*see* Chapter 12) may recall that the sites of over 30 stills were identified, all of which were believed to have been operated, at one time or another, by Prince Farrington. We now know that one of those sites, the one that disappeared beneath the Lock Haven reservoir, was owned by John Wagner's father, Walt. We can now add the precise locations of another dozen sites, but without certainty regarding which were or were not those of Prince Farrington.

## 1. Beneath the Shed on Winter Road

A couple of roads run from one end of Sugar Valley to the other. Sugar Valley folks refer to the two roads as the Winter Road and the Summer Road. Winter Road runs East-West along the lower ridges on the south side of the valley. On the opposite side of the valley, running roughly parallel with the Winter Road, is the Summer Road. There are about a half-dozen connecting roads that cross the valley between the large farms and small villages. For some years, Floyd Curtis Klobe lived on a farm on the Winter Road. Hidden there was one of several of Floyd's stills.

His granddaughter, Beulah Quiggle Neff, could say, "I know that Pap made whiskey at the farm. He dug the side out of the shed and made an underground basement. The still was under there. On the first floor, he had a trapdoor, as well as a workbench and so on. You know, it looked like a shop, but I don't think he was fooling anyone." However, authorities never found any of Floyd Klobe's stills. In the 1980s, he sold the farm. He then built a shed attached to his daughter's shed. Although there was never any activity involved with that newer shed, it was padlocked, and Floyd warned, "You don't ever get in there!" Shortly after Floyd died, his curious daughter and granddaughter left the door padlocked but unscrewed the hinges and peeked inside. Somehow, unseen by the family, he had sneaked his old still into the shed. That is the one that later found a home in Howard.

### 2. Close by the Beaver Dam

Beulah Quiggle Neff, as a child, spent considerable time with her Pap, Floyd Klobe. Apparently, Floyd was satisfied that Beulah accepted his law-breaking lifestyle. On one occasion, he allowed his daughter, Ethel, and his granddaughter, Beulah, to accompany him on a visit to a still site that is now forever lost beneath Interstate 80. Although Beulah didn't see any still at the site, he identified the area as one of his still sites. She did note the small stream that flowed into the area, apparently from a source in nearby Fourth Gap. This is the same still that was identified (*see* Chapter 11).

### 3. Somewhere Near McCall's Dam

There is a largely unpaved mountain road connecting the town of Eastville in Sugar Valley, Clinton County, with Route 192 in Union County. A tiny park, McCall's Dam State Park, sits roughly midway between the two ends of that road. The road is closed and impassable for several winter months. It may have had just the isolation needed for a clandestine operation. There, a family member reports, the Klobes were believed to have operated an illegal still.

### 4. The Still Near Tea Spring

Although one or both of the Klobe brothers had known still sites in Floyd Klobe's shed, and another was located near a beaver dam, while a third was located beneath what is now the great causeway known as Interstate 80, a fourth Klobe still site was back in the mountains near a natural feature known as the Tea Spring. This is believed to be the same site where three Klobes—Charles Sr., his wife and one of his sons—were arrested, as described in Chapter 10. That spring is still so labeled on topographic maps. That still site is also further identified in the opening paragraphs of Chapter 16.

### 5/6. Pickett's Pair

Ed Pickett is a Sugar Valley resident and a retired military veteran. Several decades ago, Pickett and his sons fished the area's mountain streams. One site visited was down an old wagon road near Fourth Gap Road, southeast of Ravensburg State Park. There, in Wagner's Hollow, Pickett reports, he and his children would fish for 'brookies' (Brook Trout). They had the necessary grease and gear so that they could cook and eat their catch by the stream. They could easily identify areas where people had discarded garbage over the years, but they saw, as well, two clearly discernible areas that had debris that was much more specialized. They saw barrel staves, broken glass and the hoops that came from whiskey kegs. The Picketts saw enough relics to identify two long-abandoned distilling sites. Their location suggests that they might have been important moonshining operations for either one of the Klobes or for Prince Farrington.

### 7. Where Brown's Run Gurgles Forth

Dave Ritter of Trout Run has identified this still site. The operation was located at the very upper end of Brown's Run, which would place it about seven miles west of the run's mouth on Pine Creek. However, it would be much more accessible if one were to drive north, on Route 44, from Haneyville and then walk a few hundred yards to the stream's source, but that route would only make sense to someone who knew what he sought.

## 8/9. Two, Through a Nimrod's Eyes

Warren Gottshall has told us, and given us an annotated topographic map, where two stills had once boiled and distilled near the village of Caldwell. Until the Marcellus shale oil outfits began prospecting in the area, Gottshall and the other residents of the Coudersport Pike corridor knew the beauty of the phrase "splendid isolation." The area was ideal for hunting game or hiding stills.

As a young man, Warren Gottshall had been shown the two nearby stills and their abandoned apparatus. According to his carefully annotated map, one of the stills was in an area known as "Whiskey Hollow," an area visited many times by Mr. Gottshall while hunting deer and bear. That still sat only about two miles from the farm where Gottshall grew up and where he lives today. He often saw the remnants—brick, crockery and rusted metal—of the moonshiner's trade. Gottshall saw the other site less often while hunting ruffed grouse as a teen. Both sites, which sit about a mile apart, are north of Swissdale and within a mile west of Route 664. That places them slightly less than five miles and slightly more than five miles, respectively, northwest of the clothing manufacturing town of Woolrich in Clinton County.

## 10. In the Spring Garden pump house

This one was the Farrington still, northwest of Allenwood that was identified in Chapter 4.

## 11. Rote's Still in Ram Hollow

Ed Rote did some moonshining. His lone still was located at the head of Ram Hollow, near the village of Swissdale. The waters from Ram Hollow form a small stream that flows nearly due west and empties into the Susquehanna River a couple of miles downstream from Queens Run.

Leroy Wenker remembers a time when Rote saw several of the Wenker boys and remarked, "Oh, you Wenker boys! Your great uncle, C. Irvin Wenker, told me when revenuers were coming. He'd let me know, and I'd give him a jug of whiskey." Rote also related an incident when revenue agents came to his place looking for moonshine whiskey. Rote went into his cellar and brought out a jug of cider. They accepted enough cider that Rote had to descend into his cellar again for another jug. Ed

Rote bragged that the lawmen got drunk on cider and left without ever finding his whiskey.

Leroy Wenker's great uncle, C. Irvin Wenker, was in an excellent position to warn a friend when revenue agents were about to pounce. C. Irvin Wenker was the sheriff. Although Wenker might warn a moonshiner of an impending raid, there was a limit to his disregard for the law. When alcohol was confiscated and put away for trial, Sheriff Wenker was offered $1,000 if he would let the key lie where someone might just find it. Wenker refused.

## 12. About Three Miles from Antes Fort

One must go to where the information is. Sam Fuller, Bob Johnson, Ed Carothers and Bob Miller are just a few of the local sages gathered at Ed and Gerrie Snook's Thursday morning flea market crowd in Antes Fort. All have knowledge that they willingly share. Bob Miller, for example, told of seeing an old still of unknown ownership about three miles south of Antes Fort off Route 44. That abandoned still remained in place until the mid-1950s, when the equipment was later sold as junk.

## 13. Incriminating Pipes Off Jack's Hollow Road

Getting along with one's spouse is important, but sometimes it is also helpful to get along with the in-laws, particularly if one needs an isolated place to make a little moonshine. Several of Prince's stills were not listed in this book and remained unknown to the author. Thanks to Carol and James Segraves, one more excellent site can now be identified.

It was here that James's father, Colonel Segraves, had operated a still. He and several other men would arrive at Engels for breakfast for several days running. After breakfast, they would disappear into the woods. One day, James half-sister, Teresa, decided to follow them. She learned what they were doing when they noticed her behind them and sent her away with a sharp rebuke, "Never come down here again. Don't tell *anyone* what you saw here!" What she had seen was a fully operational still beside a spring with a pipe channeling the water. In the spring, there were large pines, around which there was a large turn-around on which a horse-pulled wagon could maneuver easily.

## A REFLECTION

The aging equipment and supplies, once critical parts of someone's moonshining operation, have been idle for decades. No one can go there today and smell the distinctive aroma of grain cooking and pushing steam through the coils in order to feed droplets of pure whiskey into large containers. No one can watch as the liquor is reworked in order to reduce the alcohol content for human consumption. Nor can they observe the casks and kegs holding liquor that is being aged for several years before bottling and shipping to the thirsty imbibers who lived close to the stills or who lived a thousand miles away. With a thirst to slake and their money in hand, they had helped Prince Farrington amass a fortune that flowed through his hands as if he was trying to hold the intoxicating liquid itself.

### 32. *Camelot* on the Susquehanna

This still site must be recognized as the most exceptional of the many places where Prince Farrington chose to defy the law and produce great quantities of illegal liquor. If one permits one's self to think of the millionaire moonshiner, Prince David Farrington, as having been the ruler of a royal domain, covering much of Clinton and Lycoming counties, then the revenue agents were the hated Saxons, Mattie was his Guinevere, while his brother, Charles, along with Henry Sampson, Lemuel Groce, Joe Gardner, Jake Kohberger, Henry Shoemaker, and Clair Thompson were the members of his round table. To advance the analogy, the sprawling 19th-century Stewart-Courtright farm, with its large, brick farmhouse fronting the Susquehanna River in Lycoming County, was Farrington's Camelot. Finally, the perfect mason jar of moonshine was Prince's holy grail. But, no matter the configuration we see for Prince Farrington's moonshining domain, the Stewart-Courtright farm on the riverbank was its centerpiece.

Samuel Stewart, the first sheriff of the fledgling Lycoming County, owned an immense tract of superb bottomland in Nippenose Township in the early 19th century. He had several identical farmhouses constructed on the land, one for each of his children. The farm which survives today was later occupied by Samuel Stewart's son, also Samuel. This is the same house purchased in the 1920s by Prince Farrington. This house, one of the two surviving, original Stewart houses, sits on the river bank across the great stream from the Sechrist Riffles. This magnificent farm acquired other names as other proprietors replaced the Stewarts. Currently, it is the Stewart-Courtright farm, owned by Pat and Phil Courtright.

Nippenose Township played a major role in the career of Prince Farrington. The township includes all the rich bottom land within an oxbow of the Susquehanna River, as well as the ridge, Bald Eagle Mountain, that virtually closes the south side of the land. Eventually, railroad tracks were pressed between the river and the ridge. One highway enters the land by crossing the bridge from Jersey Shore, passing directly in front of what was once Prince Farrington's house and then exiting from the opposite side of the bottom land by passing through the town of Antes Fort and snaking through the narrow pass in Bald Eagle Mountain. All other roads and lanes on this peninsula are dead ends within the isolated confines of the township.

The Stewart-Courtright farm is in that subdivision of Lycoming County known as Nippenose Township (Nippenose is an Indian name, thought to mean 'summer-like'). That fertile soil is believed to have made one of Farrington's predecessors on the land, Bill Gheen, the area's first millionaire. The large house sits among the usual agricultural outbuildings. The view of that structure today makes one wonder if the scene was ever captured by one of those itinerant 19th-century artists or by some Currier-and-Ives-style printers.

The house could also be exited through a tunnel that linked to the river bank. This is believed to have been a pre-Farrington burrowing to be used for the escape of slaves as part of the fabled Underground Railroad. It may have served Farrington, as well, since it would have made an appealing storage area for illegal whiskey. The house stands in Lycoming County, a couple of miles north of Antes Fort and a couple of miles east of Jersey Shore. This house was at the terminus of a long lane, ideally situated so that no one ever passed the house to reach some destination beyond.

Prince Farrington and his family did not live in this farm home. The Farringtons lived at the edge of the bridge that crossed the Susquehanna onto Long Island. The roadway then crossed the river on another bridge, carrying travelers into the town of Jersey Shore. While he was its owner, it had more value to him as a property that was at least *occupied* by others.

Prince had his sister, Zenadah ('Nade') and her husband, Kyle Coltrane, along with their daughter, Hilda, and sons B. W. and Wade, move north from North Carolina and onto the Stewart farm. Kyle and the boys helped Prince in his moonshining operation. The five Coltrane family members lived in one half of the farmhouse. Sister Zenadah ('Nade'), who later succumbed to breast cancer, wrote from Pennsylvania to the North Carolina relatives, complaining of her unhappiness because of the wild parties being held in Prince's social circle.

While the Coltranes lived in one side of the Stewart farmhouse, the other half was reserved for Prince's use. He converted his half into a giant still! The basement had 12-foot ceilings. Whiskey, produced in the basement, was pumped through 4-inch water pipes to other parts of the house for capturing, cutting (reducing the excessive alcoholic content) and bottling. Filled kegs were stored under straw in the barn. Several neighboring farmers also provided large amounts of storage space. Tons of corn, sugar and molasses were shipped to the house at night. Those who worked at this distillery had to accept 24- to 48-hour shifts in order to reduce traffic, just in case federal agents had the place under surveillance. Professionally printed, phony import stamps were used here, as were forged labels announcing "William Penn Dry Whiskey" and "London Dry Gin," All were part of Farrington's program of deception.

When Prince Farrington moved to the Jersey Shore area, he bought two acres that already held an imposing house atop the cliff overlooking the river. This large house became the house where the Farrington family lived. Prince's two acres butted against the farm property of the neighboring Muthler family (MOOT ler is the family pronunciation). The Muthler family had farmed the adjoining land for generations. The earliest Muthler in the family had come from Germany. When he landed in New York City, he walked the entire distance from the great, bustling port city to Reading, Pennsylvania. During his long trek, he slept in corn shocks and dined on the occasional turnip from the roadside fields. Prince Farrington soon learned that the current patriarch of the Muthler *freinshaft* was unimpressed by Prince's lucrative livelihood. The entire family of J. Casper Muthler did not use alcohol. However, although Muthler was not inclined to report Prince's illegal activity, he was opposed to helping him. Prince quickly got Mr. Muthler's kind permission to use one of Muthler's spare sheds. Prince quickly had kegs moved into the building. "No, I can't have that," J. Casper objected. Prince, just as quickly, had the kegs removed. When Christmas time arrived, Prince gave gifts of moonshine to friends and neighbors; except for the hams that he distributed to the Muthlers and other area teetotalers. Prince also understood the value of renting storage space from willing neighbors, hiring some neighbors and buying grain from some. Thus, almost all of Prince's neighbors had a financial stake in perpetuating the Farrington vortex.

For a time, when foxes were prized for their furs, Prince raised silver foxes in pens between his house and the Stewart farm. One local estimate put the number of foxes at 160. He had a small herd of Brown Swiss milking cows. He also kept flocks of geese and guinea hens, as well as dogs, at the Coltrane-occupied farm. The dogs and the fowl all made good sentinels, sending up a loud cacophony of barks, squawks and honks if anyone approached. Despite all of these precautions, on a cold day in January 1931, the 'Saxons' invaded

Where did Farrington fail? He might have admitted to himself that a man who already had a moonshining and bootlegging record in several counties in North Carolina and Pennsylvania and who had spent time in the federal penitentiary in Atlanta should no longer expect to operate without being under the watchful eye of federal agents. The agents also knew that if one followed the sugar, the molasses, the corn, or the jugs and kegs and other resources that a large-volume moonshiner needed in vast quantities, those traveling supplies would lead them to the whiskey man of Antes Fort.

Actually, there were two very fruitful raids on Prince's river-side Camelot during the 1930s. The first was made in 1931 while Prohibition was in full force and when the federal government was ordered to destroy illegal liquor. In the 1931 raid, five agents, under the direction of federal agent Mr. J. O. Loos of Lewisburg, approached the farm in mid-afternoon. That raid seems to be better remembered than the one that occurred there in 1934, likely because of the enthusiasm of local gentlemen who rushed to the site of the 1931 raid with mason jars, tin cups and half-loaves of pound bread to be used as sops. The 1931 raid began on a very cold January 3rd and lasted for days. Agents dug a trench and poured barrel after barrel of the legendary liquor into the trench, by which route it rushed into the Susquehanna River, where the icy waters further cut the whiskey to a near-zero-proof liquor. As they worked, the agents vainly urged the teary-eyed locals to stop scooping liquor from the frozen ground and pouring it into their mason jars.

Prince couldn't possibly have thought of everything, but he anticipated much. Anticipating one of the raids on the Stewart farm, he had some of his regular helpers go to the farm and move the valuable farming equipment across the fence row to rest on a neighboring farm. By doing this, Prince was ensuring that—should the still or the whiskey be found by government agents—the farming equipment wouldn't be confiscated. Years later, Lee Koch, who lived nearby, related the story about how, before an anticipated raid, the equipment was moved. With that done, the loyal Farrington workers stayed in the area to swill some alcohol and watch developments. For this occasion, one of the group had arrived in his shiny new car, with its sporty rag top. While they were relaxing and downing some of the 'hard stuff,' someone glanced up and saw a comical sight: a goat was standing atop the new car and was eating the cloth top! The owner, less amused than the others but equally drunk, grabbed a stone and threw it at the goat, but it hit and shattered the car's windshield instead.

For the next couple of years, Camelot was quiet. Prince Farrington rebuilt the apparatus and the entire operation was humming once again. This time, the moonshining program at the Stewart farm was even more extensive than the earlier one. However, the climate for moonshiners had changed remarkably. The nation had scuttled Prohibition. Prince was no longer simply making an illegal drink. This he was doing. Now, with the close of Prohibition, Farrington's booze would be illegal because it was now being taxed. Prince was holding back tens of thousands of dollars that was due to the government. The legal distillers—the Jack Daniel's types—were paying their taxes. Prince wasn't. Thus, the second raid on the Stewart-Courtright Farm, on Prince's Camelot, was made because agents discovered that Prince was again creating and marketing moonshine surreptitiously and tax-free.

It was after ten o'clock at night, on November 14, 1934, that the second raid occurred. This raid on the Stewart farm came just a few weeks after the raid on Farrington's still at the ghost town of Eagleton (see above). For this raid on the Stewart farm, federal agents had begun to follow a truckload of molasses from the town of Wapwallopen near Wilkes Barre, Pennsylvania. Since this occurred prior to the opening of Interstate 80, the trailing of the molasses would have involved a journey of about 100 miles. The truck led the agents directly to the old Stewart house. The trailing of that truck was the prelude to a hugely successful second raid. An eyewitness to the 1934 raid was Jane Bubb Miller. She told of being about ten years old. She and her father drove to the farm to see what was occurring there. "So, I witnessed the 1934 raid and saw them smash and dump the barrels of liquor into the Susquehanna River." Also witnessed by onlookers was the dumping of molasses barrels. This raised the chaos level somewhat since the white, leghorn chickens were soon struggling to free themselves from the molasses. Meanwhile, inside the house, family members relate; Prince grabbed a stack of his counterfeit stamps and hid them inside the tube that held an old piano roll.

There may be skeptics. There may be those who would still doubt that Prince Farrington was anything more than a common back-country moonshiner. For the true skeptics, we simply say, ponder this: The 1931 raid at the Stewart-Courtright farm netted 2,000 ten-gallon kegs, 16 fifty-gallon barrels, 500 gallons of alcohol and a 500-gallon vat. The value of the liquor found was estimated to be, at its 1931 value, about $750,000. All three floors of the uninhabited half of the Stewart house were filled with containers of liquor, filtering charcoal and empty containers. While the agents took inventory of all equipment and liquor, they neglected to count the as-yet unfilled containers since there were so many.

The agents involved in the 1934 raid at the ghost town of Eagleton found a vat with a capacity of 45,000 gallons, 2,000 feet of pipe, and 250 bags of sugar. For comparison, a back-country hustler might have a vat capacity of a mere 450 gallons!

During the 1934 raid at the Stewart-Courtright farm, federal agents found equipment that could produce 2,000 gallons of 190 to 195-proof alcohol every single day. The daily tax loss to the federal government, if the still had been left to operate, would have been nearly $12,000! The listing on court documents, dated June 8, 1937, mentions all sorts of items that Farrington or his helpers had been using. They mention, among other things, 175 five-gallon cans, all full of alcohol; 53 such cans not yet filled; a 3' x 8' copper vat; 3 empty 50-gallon wooden kegs; 25 pounds of charcoal; a dozen empty glass jugs; a filtering tank, and five shotguns. That impressive listing was only for the first floor of the farmhouse! Similar listings exist for the second and third floors and the basement. Then there is the massive inventory for the barn's first floor and the basement of the barn.

How strange must have been the feelings of Robert Bubb when he revisited the farm in 1992. Bubb, who died in 2007, told the current owners, the Courtrights, that he had worked on that farm for Prince Farrington. He related that it was prior to the great 1934 raid that he also helped to install and operate the boiler in the phony 'kitchen' and to bury the piping that was attached to the apparatus in the barn.

All that Prince David Farrington would have needed was a proper factory and legitimacy and he would have been among the nation's major distillers. After the three major raids on Prince Farrington's enterprises, he might have wanted to take some time to reflect on his career and to ponder the problems of his past and what might lie ahead. The federal government would soon be providing just such time.

In summary, if we consider the known number of Prince Farrington's once-secret still sites, plus their total time in operation, and then factor in the many clandestine storage sites, one conclusion becomes obvious: The record of the revenue agents for raids or arrests was woefully small.

The above still sites are the ones recently identified for this book. While there may have been a few others, the question raised here is this: If the more productive stills were spewing forth hundreds of gallons of sour mash whiskey every single day, how did one keep *secret* the presence of all the booze that the revenue agents *didn't* find? Prince Farrington's ingenuity must be credited.

## THE RAINS CAME

Jersey Shore was a vibrant town during the 1930s; although it had known a series of riverine floods in its couple of centuries of existence. Again, in 1936, three days of rain sent the West Branch of the Susquehanna rising and roaring. Dave Poust remembers it clearly. He and another boy were putting a puzzle together when Dave's father, who owned a hardware store, stopped to tell his family to move all that they could easily carry. He told them to carry everything that they could carry onto the second floor. It seemed almost farcical in recollection. Dave's mother thought that her husband was exaggerating, so.—When Dave's dad returned later, he found that Mrs. Poust had done a lone act of flood preparation: She had taken her sweeper and rested it on the *bottom* step of their stairway. When the uninvited flood waters finally did enter Poust's Jersey Shore home, it didn't stop rising until it had reached the very ceiling of the first floor, with just enough water seeping into the second floor to soak the carpets.

Jersey Shore's Main Street, which runs parallel to the river, soon resembled the river itself as waters swept through the town and drove the occupants to higher ground. Across the river and downstream a short distance, waters quickly inundated the lower fields of Nippenose Valley. With Prince once again in prison, Mattie and daughter Gladys helped to take care of the cattle at the old Stewart farm. The quickly rising waters made Gladys and Mattie retreat into the house and up to the second floor. Two local young men got a canoe and began removing threatened or stranded individuals along the river. The young canoeists went to the Stewart farm and offered their services to Prince's wife and daughter. As the stranded women gingerly crawled from the second-floor balcony into the canoe, their rescuers told the women to sit very still. The women seemed eager to comply. Although the canoe's pilots had to row especially hard to draw away from the river currents, they were able to get Mattie and Gladys away from the flood and up to Prince's house, where they spent the remainder of the flood scare. During the awesome flood of 1936, Prince's house, as well as the Muthlers' house next door, sat "high and dry" above the Susquehanna's devastating deluge. The 1936 flood set a local record for depth, having attained a final crest that exceeded 30 feet.

Not everyone was disappointed to see the heavy rains. Because this moonshiner/bootlegger was also a farmer, Prince Farrington got the warden's permission to leave the prison for a few days in order to take care of any damage that the flood might have done to his farm. Thus, Prince was able to help restore his flooded farm, although he also made some time to check his moonshine business, before returning to 'the big house'.

With so much of Prince Farrington's very being invested in the Stewart farm, one would suspect that it may be the last property he would ever unload, but in 1941, a new deed was executed. That document transferred the land and improvements—as a 79-acre estate—from "Prince David Farrington and Martha J. Farrington, his wife" to "Ivan W. Fritz and Selinda B. Fritz, his wife."

One local individual says that Prince Farrington sold a considerable plot of other Nippenose Township land to a gentleman farmer, Bill Hayes, who had an extensive potato-growing operation. Eventually, a portion of the historic old Stewart estate became the land on which the Jersey Shore airstrip was created. That tiny grass airstrip still serves the Jersey Shore area today and is still known locally as the "Jersey Shore International Airfield."

Today, Pat and Phil Courtright own and occupy the historic Stewart property. They bought the Stewart farm from another owner after the Fritzs moved on. That interim owner was unrelated to Prince Farrington, but he, too, spent some time in prison. That owner, before he resettled in Florida, hosted cockfights on the historic property.

All who have an interest in the story of Prince and this property will be interested in knowing that the Courtrights are adding to the farm's appeal and its value by researching and creating their own history. The Courtrights rightly identify their historic property by combining the name of the first owner with that of the latest owners. It is, in their thinking, the Stewart-Courtright property. Their history has a rich tradition on which to draw, from the early settling of the area, through its great agricultural days, its active role in the Underground Railroad, through a raucous moonshining period, a later history of hosting cockfights and the return to a modern Currier-and-Ives style agrarian estate.

## THE STORY OF THE STORING

During the Prohibition era, every step of Farrington's distilling and bootlegging process was illegal. The building of the hidden stills and the distilling of the liquor, as well as the transporting and the sale of the liquor, were all forms of outlawry, as was the storing of the valuable whiskey. His team of drivers delivered the increasingly desired Farrington whiskey to markets as far south as the Carolinas, as well as north into Canada. One must maintain the thought that Farrington did not grab the kegs, fresh from the stills, and go peddling. Prince

Farrington insisted that his liquor be properly aged in order to ensure its quality. Just as the whiskey was distilled out of public view, so, too, the aging bottles, barrels and kegs needed several years of privacy—lots of privacy. One place used for seclusion in order for the liquor to age was mentioned earlier: the cellar beneath the tool shed of Floyd Meixel of the Rauchtown area. Among others?

In telephone interviews (January 20, 2009 & February 7, 2010), Marjorie Bossert Kamus, of Jersey Shore, said that Harry Williams was born and raised in Antes Fort. He once owned the "old paint mill" and two accompanying buildings along Antes Creek. Harry was not into bootlegging but allowed Prince Farrington to store moonshine in the two buildings located on the eastern bank of the Antes Creek. The larger building was a former woolen mill that morphed into a paint mill, producing both paint and a powdery filler purchased by other paint manufacturers. The office for the mill was in another building directly across the rural highway from the mill. Since the mill itself was then used for storage of feed, Prince had arranged to hide large quantities of whiskey behind the feed. He also stored a quantity of alcohol in the basement of the mill office. When, in the 1920s, the office basement was raided by federal agents, Harry Williams (but not Prince) was arrested and spent about six months in the Lycoming County prison. Marjorie Kamus later bought the infamous office from Harry's son, Louis ("Louie"), and, for more than a decade, operated a craft shop and antique shop from that building. Louie, who became a friend of Marjorie, had some of Prince's liquor. He gave several bottles of the Farrington moonshine to Marjorie, who still possesses two full, sealed bottles and one smaller bottle. Those three bottles of genuine Farrington moonshine remain among Marjorie's prized possessions.

### In the Basement of the Old Paint Mill Office

Just south of the old Paint Mill, by Antes Creek, an old road leads up into the hills to the east (to the left if one is going south), off Route 44. On that road, according to one local individual who hunted deer in that area with family members, was a large stone building that might have been a Farrington still site. This is questionable since the structure being considered may only have been used to collect and channel water. That water, however, appears to have been used in milling, not distilling. However, as mentioned, there were known *storage* sites in the area of the old Paint Mill: the one behind the feed bags in the Paint Mill and another in the basement of the stone office building. A third, not yet mentioned, was in an old, abandoned house in the wooded area to the east in Morgan Valley.

The paint mill, too, was said by many to be another site for a Farrington still; but Marjorie Kamus emphatically disagrees. As mentioned above, Mrs. Kamus was a close friend of Louie Williams and was once the owner of the paint mill office. Mrs. Kamus says that she is certain that no still sat in the paint mill. She argues that no one would have put a still in there because, if it had been discovered, the paint factory would have been put out of business.

From the late Leo "Chip" Taylor, we learn of two more methods used by Prince for storing moonshine.

### The Abandoned House near Antes Creek

Even further east from the paint mill, along the Morgan Valley road, said Leo "Chip" Taylor, he and Prince's nephew, B. W. Coltrane, once tallied a hidden stash of liquor. Taylor recalled, "B. W. called me one day and said, 'Come on, I want to take you for a ride,' and I said, 'Where to?' and he said, 'You'll know when you get there.' We went up the Morgan Valley road about a half-mile, I'd imagine. We got back to where this log house was. We looked around the outside to see whether anybody was there, and we couldn't see that anybody was around. That's when I saw these logs shoring up the second floor, and we went up to check it, and we uncovered these barrels of whiskey and we started to count them. We counted them twice to make sure that we had the same amount. I don't remember how many barrels. I would say about 20 barrels or something like that—and then, later on, we got out of there and went home. B. W. helped Prince keep track of those things. He had B. W. check on things like that and he was getting me into it."

### Burial of the Booze

After Prince Farrington moved from the Florida Fruit Farm to the imposing house between Antes Fort and Jersey Shore, the Florida Fruit Farm was sold to several buyers. In 1965, Bud Webb of Salona bought a parcel of the Florida Fruit Farm. Since then, he has been buying additional parcels of the old Prince Farrington property as it became available. Today, Mr. Webb owns most, if not all, of the original property, with a spread of more than 300 acres. Although Webb never met Prince Farrington, he had one incident to recount. Some years ago, while deer hunting on his farm, he stepped into some kegs that were barely concealed in the floor of the woodland. He found three rotting kegs, all of which had lost their precious contents over the long decades since Prince was the owner of that land.

As Bud Webb's account reveals, the practice of burying the illicit product had begun before Prince left the Florida Fruit Farm. Ed Snook's tale reinforces that belief. Ed, a resident of Antes Fort, told of having once worked at the farm, doing normal farm work. That farm once had more than 40 acres of apple trees of several varieties. When new owners had the farm, they got heavy equipment and pushed some of the apple trees from the earth. Then Ed, with a plow, turned the ground for planting. Suddenly, "bottles came flying out." Ed's plowing activity had unearthed buried bottles of moonshine. His dad told him that they were some of Prince's long-buried cache.

As recently as October of 2010, a Jersey Shore area resident, Louise Brown, told the author that her farm was the object of such "buried booze" rumors. An area gentleman, she confides, often sat on a nearby hill and watched as the Browns plowed their fields, vainly hoping to see them uncovering some long-lost cache of Farrington's finest.

Lester Seiler, quoted several times in this biography, needs to be quoted here regarding buried kegs or barrels of moonshine. Here is a stream of recollections by the late Mr. Seiler related to Prince Farrington's urge to sequester booze beneath the sod. Lester recalls:

> There were some of the barrels. I don't know if they are gone now, but before I was married—I purtin' near broke my neck one evening, huntin' rabbits—my leg went down, and I took a flipper out through! Here, I broke through a barrel that was buried. The hoops stuck up about that far. It was rotted, you know.
>
> Then, there was one I used to run into down there on the other side, down in the woods where the pig pen was—that one

probably stuck out that far. They probably had it covered over with leaves when it was hid—You could see that one—I'd seen it when I was huntin' in there.

And there's one right out there, right now! Right outside that window where I put my coal in. I don't know who buried that barrel right outside the cellar wall—I don't know who opened it up—Lee Rishel or who; but they took some of the wall out to put coal in—I put three wheelbarrow loads of stone in the thing—How they got it or how they operated with it there, I don't know. It's still out there. I didn't take it out. I just took and put stones in it and covered it and left it lay.

Aware of the accounts of Bud Webb, Louise Brown, Ed Snook and Lester Seiler, does one need better proof of Prince's burial of booze? If so, Leo "Chip" Taylor offered it.

## Corn Rows As Cover

The late Leo "Chip" Taylor told of a day, about 1930 or 1931, while he was still in grade school at Antes Fort when he had an invitation from Prince's nephew, B. W. Coltrane.

> B. W. said to me that on Friday we could go horseback riding and that I should be down at their farm at seven in the morning so that I could help feed the horses and milk the cows. The next morning, on my way there, I heard a strange sound as I got closer—like a tractor running. It was B. W. on a bulldozer. I had never seen one before, so I got up on the dozer with him and asked where he was digging. B. W. said that he was digging just over the fence in the pasture next to the backyard. I was told that if I wanted to know what was going on to stay in the barn and look out through the cracks, but be quiet. I went into the barn, fed the animals, got the milk bucket from the house and was milking the first cow when I heard three trucks going around the barn. I went up the ladder to the back of the barn and saw the workers leveling off the bottom of a large pit. Then, they laid down planks to set the barrels of whiskey on. It wasn't long after

that until they had it covered, and corn was planted on top of it. Then, B. W. and I went horseback riding as planned.

Prince's nephew created a lot of misinformed people by rarely revealing his true name. "Chip" Taylor was one of the few who knew, and he kept the secret through many decades. Coltrane told his army buddies that his name was *Bert Williams*, a lie, and he rarely told anyone the correct names. Even his obituary carried only his initials. One lifelong resident of Antes Fort asserted that he was the only one who knew the true meaning of the initials B. W.; they stood for Baytworth Wadsworth. He was wrong! However, Leo "Chip" Taylor, one of B. W.'s lifelong friends, said that B. W.'s true name was Batie Worth Coltrane. B. W. was among his Uncle Prince's most loyal helpers.

### The Barn in Mill Hall

For a century, a large dairy barn served a farm at the northeastern edge of Mill Hall in Clinton County. Later, the barn was converted into a theater, the Millbrook Playhouse. Some years ago, Dan Reinhold, a lifelong resident of Mill Hall, leased a wing of that theater. Shortly after leasing part of the barn, now turned theater, he and two acquaintances toured the building. One of Reinhold's companions was an architectural student at Pennsylvania State University (Penn State). It was the student who, at one point on the tour, observed, "There's another room here!" Upon examining the wall, they found a portion of the wall that was really a secret entrance into a hidden room. Once inside the secluded room, they recognized a small opening in the wall. It was finally learned that this building, during the days of Prince Farrington, was a clandestine storage room for moonshine. Milk trucks once pulled into the barn from one side. It then had jugs of liquor from the hidden stash passed through a small opening to be placed on the truck. In front of the booze, milk was stacked, and, in front of that, butter was loaded. Then, the truck was driven from the far side of the barn, making room for the next Farrington truck to move into the loading zone.

### "Sang like a bird!"

For a variety of reasons, some of Prince's supporters aided authorities. The promise of jail was effective with some. The Porters tell of a friend, the farmer Clarence "Chippy" Dunlap, who farmed in the Jersey Shore area. In later years, Dunlap told of his having hidden Farrington liquor. While this was true, Dunlap neglected to say that he had, when pressed by the federal agents, given a detailed account of his pro-Farrington activity. As Gladys Porter later observed, "He sang like a bird!" The family noted that Prince understood such a response from people who had farms and families to protect.

### Right Neighborly Folk
In January of 1931, the month that the Stewart/Gheen farm was raided, those same revenue agents made a series of raids on other places in the Antes Fort area of Lycoming County, in the area where Prince David Farrington lived. The raids were meant to uncover some of the hidden stores of Farrington whiskey. On January 3, Spong's house was raided. On January 9th they raided the Bauman's. The house of Wesley Koch, (KŌKE) Sr., was raided as well. The Koch family, with more than a dozen family members, was extremely poor. The family head was Wesley Koch Sr., who secured some income by working for Prince Farrington. Still, daughter Grace Koch told a neighbor that the family had almost no furniture. When the family gathered at the table to eat, some had to sit on whiskey kegs. After the Koch family endured the trauma of a raid on their house, Charles Dorwart's mother, Ruth, stood her children in a line and emphasized that they shouldn't mention a word about the raid to the Koch children.

As mentioned above, Wesley Koch Sr. hauled bootleg whiskey for Prince Farrington. Among his other Farrington roles was that of the main boiler operator at the Stewart property. As a boiler operator, he was the only worker who escaped during one raid. He sneaked through a tunnel to safety. Eventually, he worked for Mr. Bill Hayes, the potato farmer who bought much of Prince's property. It was while working for Mr. Hayes that Wesley Koch Sr. lost a leg in a farming accident. The amputation resulted from his working with an early potato-picking machine. Still, the ties between the Kochs and the Farringtons eventually resulted in Betty Koch marrying one of Prince's nephews, Wade Coltrane. Betty Koch Coltrane and Wade Coltrane had one daughter, Margaret. They lived in Jersey Shore. Wade died in 1999, and his widow died in 2007.

## A COUPLE OF RAIDS ON THE SEILER FARM

Lester Seiler remembered a half-dozen raids at the farm where he lived with his father and other family members. Two, in particular, brought his memory to life.

> We was raided a couple of times there at Dad's. One time—the revenue guys come there to our place in the spring of the year. We had the window open, you know. They came in on the porch. Came in like that. Anyway, Dad met 'em outside. They showed up with badges—they were revenue men and searchers. Well, my sister, Edna, was in there, and she was washing dishes. There was a pint bottle [of booze] on the sink, right next to the drain sink. She grabbed that pint bottle and smashed it on the cast iron drain sink, and turned the water on! They woulda took her for destroying evidence, only she wasn't of age, so it didn't matter. They couldn't do nothing about it. Boy, did they ever search, though! They hunted every place, high and low, but never found no more. They did take the cork and the [broken] bottle—but that's all they had. We never heard no more about it.
>
> One time Lester Fidler (He lived over at Bull Run)[30] was on the tower. Anyways, we put our still out in the field, after haymaking that was. We had two stone piles in the field out from there. We had laid the still up against the stone piles in the field, so it didn't show.

Lester Fidler saw the smoke through his binoculars but couldn't figure out its location when nearer the site but on the ground. That was a major break for the moonshiners.

## PREPPING FOR A REVENUERS' VISIT

One might ponder how the career of Prince David Farrington would have fared if he had not had prior warning of many of the raids of the revenuers. Among the more elaborate of his responses was the one in which Lester Seiler participated and recalled for a 1983 interview:

---

30. Lester Fidler was a state employee who manned the fire tower in the area, from which he was supposed to get an early spotting of any smoke that came from the state forest lands.

But, when they was gonna have a raid, he told Dad (see, we used to get our sugar from him)—He always called Dad, "Turban" [His real name was Turbit Seiler] He says, "Turban, you'll have to clean up. They're gonna raid us. We can't buy 'em off any longer." He [Prince] said, "On such and such a day, they're going to be here." We didn't think too much of it. We cleaned it up right away. That was about a week or ten days before the time that they were gonna raid. Finally, he come to our place one afternoon. He said, "Turban, how about a couple of you and the boys helping me tonight?" Dad said, "Well, what do you want to do?"

"Oh," he said, "I want to haul them barrels away." [Seiler pronounced the word barrel as BARR ul] Here, when we went out there—brother Raymond and I and Dad—we worked purtin' near all night; about 3:30, something like that, when we got done, Lee Snook and his milk truck and who's the other truck was, I don't know.

I was out of school. About 16, something like that. Maybe 15. I don't know. When we went out there, just before dark, here was 84 barrels on that side of the hill, there, fulla whiskey. Charl [Charles Farrington], from Lamar, was there and the one they called "Hop" [Farrington] at that time. He was about that big around and purtin' near to the ceiling, about six-six or six-eight, and another fellow or two. Hep [?] Berry was there? He's dead now, too. Anyways, me and Hep [?] Berry, we rolled 'em down the hill. Charl was up on the truck. We rolled 'em up on the truck. Frank was standing up there on that truck, and he'd get a hold of those barrels on the end, like this, and, somehow, with his knee, he'd put that barrel up on top of the first one, two barrels height. Prince helped some. Where they took it, I don't know. But, I did hear Lee say—he told Dad (he used to haul our milk, Lee used to), and he told Dad, "Half the barns in Sugar Valley's got moonshine in them!"

I don't know where they put it, but, you know—about three o'clock or a little after we got them all loaded up—and at seven o'clock, the revenue men were there!

What made Prince the maddest: They put a stick of dynamite in the boiler—in the firebox and blowed her up, and that there busted his flues, you know. He said they wouldn't have needed to do that. That made old Prince pretty mad . . .

# THE CLANDESTINE NETWORK 259

*Legendary FBI director, who outlasted all presidents, ran the Federal Bureay of Investigation from 1924 until his death in 1972. Hoover seems to have taken a personal interest in the FBI's apprehension of Prince Farrington.*

*The old Clinton County jail, in Lock Haven. Another Prince Farrington alma mater. A newer facility now sits near McElhattan.*

*Another jail where Prince Farrington was incarcerated. Reidsville (Rockingham County), North Carolina.*

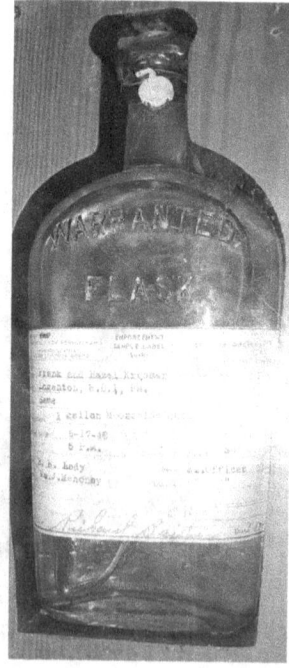

*This bottle has survived many decades; having once been evidence in a case; but somehow going from court evidence back into the community.*

# THE CLANDESTINE NETWORK 261

*Government agents ready to dump contents of many bottles of moonshine. From an old GRIT newspaper account.*

*Gamble Farm Inn of Gladys and George Porter: Where Prince lived following his last release from prison.*

## · 12 ·

# The Long Arm

The *legendary* Prince Farrington outwitted and eluded authorities and spent little time incarcerated. The *real* Prince Farrington had nearly five decades of criminal activity, during which he had numerous encounters with the law and for which he garnered an ample share of the trials, verdicts and sentences proffered by our American judicial system. He also understood the economics of that judicial aberration that peddled favors for money or moonshine.

Prince Farrington's criminal record didn't reach as far into his youth as the myth makers would have us believe. Several speakers and writers have repeated the tale of the 12-year-old Prince being arrested. Let the actual records clear the matter. In May of 1905, as Prince was closing his 15th year, he appeared before judges in Guilford County, North Carolina. This was the case discussed in Chapter 2, the arson offense against a neighbor.

We list, here, some of Prince Farrington's encounters with the law. This is not meant to be a comprehensive listing. With this admittedly selective listing, the reader will also find Prince Farrington's age at the time of each brush with the law. We post here, again, his birth date: June 3, 1889.

- 1905, May (16 years old at the time of trial's conclusion)— Prince appeared before four judges and the case concluded in June of 1906. This case was discussed in Chapter 2. It resulted in Prince serving prison time and being assigned to an inmate county road crew.
- 1913, June 20 (24 years old)—Prince appeared before judges Lane and Devin (2).

- 1914, August 27 (25 years old)—1914—Prince's father, Tom Beverly Farrington, co-signs a bail document with Prince, who is charged with "Ill dist. (Illegal distribution).
- 1915, June 10. (26 years old)—Based on four counts of law-breaking,
- 1924, March (34 years old)—Guilford County, N.C., appearing before Judge Lane. This action occurred several years after Prince had moved to the *Florida Fruit Farm* in Clinton County, Pennsylvania.
- 1924—This year was also the year that the government raided the old paint mill on Route 44, south of Jersey Shore and Antes Fort. The *GRIT* newspaper reported that "Farrington pleaded guilty but said the whiskey had been made on orders from Washington" for use in an official celebration. The *GRIT* reporter who wrote the 1950 account informed readers that "The charge was not pressed." Really? Such a statement by Prince would have amounted to a confession. This may leave the readers feeling skeptical about those court proceedings. Did no one ask Prince Farrington just *who* in Washington gave such 'orders'? Did the court really approve a function in the national government that violated the 18th Amendment and its supporting laws?
- 1934, August (46 years old)—Federal agents raided the still at the old mining town of Eagleton, northwest of Lock Haven.
- 1936, May 31 (47 years old)—A newly built still near Powys, north of Williamsport, in Clinton County, was raided.
- 1936, November (48 years old)—Charges brought against Prince for possession of illegal and untaxed alcohol, with bail set at $2,500. The evidence included 855 gallons of alcohol and 2,072 gallons of whiskey and brandy.
- 1944, June (54 years old)—Prince and Henry Sampson were fined by Judge Henry C. Hipple and his two associate judges, James Bridgens and Charles Dunn of the Clinton County court. The sentence was for the illegal manufacture of alcohol. Prince's fine was set at $250, and Samson's was $75. While no alcohol was found, the mash and the equipment were sufficiently damning evidence. It was noted that Henry Sampson, who had

never been before the court before, was placed on probation. Prince Farrington might have received a stiffer sentence, but he pleaded for leniency based on the fact that he had a 200-acre farm to cultivate and two of his sons were serving in the military. [Samson's conviction is also mentioned in Chapter 8.]

- 1946, August 26, 1946 (55 years old)—One of the milestone raids on a secluded Prince Farrington distilling operation was the one on the Tangascootac Creek. This was the raid that saw Prince and two of his helpers, Harry McGonigal, 45, and William P. Lynch, 50, jailed. This was featured in Chapter 1.
- October 1946 (55 years old)—Pennsylvania Liquor Control Board agents arrested Prince D. Farrington on a water pollution charge, because of the still he was operating on Tangascootack Creek. His sentence: 115 days in the Clinton County prison.
- 1946, November 3 (55 years old)—Following a plea of "guilty" to a charge of illegal possession, Prince was sentenced to "pay the costs of prosecution and a fine of $100 and stand committed until the sentence is complied with."
- 1946, December 15, 1946 (56 years old)—"Lying low for a while" was not a concept in Prince Farrington's thinking. Before the sawdust and the legal dust had settled from the raid on his Tangascootac operation, Prince loaded a three-quarter ton Chevrolet truck, with no license tags, piled on nearly 200 gallons (198, officially) of whiskey, on which he had paid no tax, and drove it into Reidsville (Rockingham County), North Carolina. There, H.H. Gillie and Constable J.M. Pettigrew arrested him for violating liquor laws. Prince posted the $500 bond and skipped the trial.
- Not only did he skip his trial in Rockingham County, North Carolina, but he skipped the trial and the state when it was time to appear for the federal trial in Williamsport, Pennsylvania. As discussed in Chapter 1, that was when Prince David Farrington became a fugitive.
- 1947, October, (57 years old)—(Clinton County)—Prince was to "pay a fine of $100 and the costs of prosecution and stand committed until this sentence is complied with."

- 1948, January, (57 years old)—Prince and Harry McGonigal were indicted on four counts of violation of the Internal Revenue Code.
- 1951, March 20 (61 years old)—Copies of the indictment, transfer consent order and all other papers in the case were sent to the Southern District of Florida (Tampa, Florida).
- 1951, April 16 (61 years old)—Prince David Farrington arrived at the federal penitentiary in Springfield, Missouri.
- The long-running ordeal involving Prince Farrington and the several courts of the American judicial system was coming to a close.
- 1952, June 14 (62 years old)—Prince David Farrington walked from the federal penitentiary in Springfield, Missouri. He had seen his last jail cell. However, ahead lay a different form of incarceration; the dual-walled prison of crippling health and economic impoverishment. Still, he knew that his last years would be brightened by his being near to his children and his grandchildren.

## PRINCE AS A HEADLINER

The career of Prince Farrington has left us with dozens of lurid headlines worthy of the likes of a film star or a sports celebrity. Here are some random headlines culled from several Prohibition-era newspapers. One can judge the community thoughts that must have been created by Prince Farrington's lawbreaking and by the headlines spawned by his crimes.

- Liquor Worth Quarter Million Dollars Seized Near Jersey Shore.
- DRY AGENTS MAKE RAID: Find Thousands of Kegs and Barrels of Whiskey and Alcohol and Moonshine Manufacturing Plant.
- NO ARRESTS ARE REPORTED: Officers Discover Farm House Empty When They Make Surprise Visit—Booze Tests Ninety Percent Proof–Investigation Expected To Reveal Identity Of Owners of Place–Farmer and Family Living in One Side of House Not Held.
- Dry Agents Seize More Than $1,000,000 Worth of Liquor [headline over 4 columns].

- STORAGE PLACE RAIDED: Officers Under J. O. Loos Find 32,350 Gallons of Whiskey.
- BIGGEST SEIZURE MADE: Liquor Estimated to Be Worth $750,000 Destroyed At Former Barrett Farm, Near Jersey Shore, Yesterday.
- More than $1,000,000 worth of intoxicating liquor has been seized and destroyed by prohibition administration forces of the middle district, operating under the direction of Deputy Administrator J. O. Loos of Lewisburg, during the last three weeks.
- The largest seizure was made Friday afternoon, when agents raided the Raymond Bauman farm near Jersey Shore and found in storage of the cellar of the house and in the barn whiskey valued at $750,000, the destruction of which was completed yesterday afternoon.

## "COURTHOUSE WHISKEY"

When Lester Seiler was interviewed in 1983, the phrase "courthouse whiskey" was mentioned. It was identified as "whiskey that disappears." In other words, "courthouse whiskey" was used to identify whiskey that had been confiscated by legal authorities and placed in the courthouse to be used as evidence in a future trial. However, there were times when the evidence disappeared before a trial commenced. Seiler was asked if that happened more than once. His terse reply: "Oh, every time, about."

In March of 1933, the Williamsport Sun-Gazette commented on the destruction of some recently confiscated liquor by an officer, Fred Seitler. Seitler said the old clipping "mixed a gigantic cocktail of all the confiscated liquors—about 50 gallons—and then poured the entire great 'cocktail' into a drain outside the courthouse doors."

## OUT WITH A WHIMPER?

The late attorney, John C. Youngman of Williamsport, observed (January 27, 1980, interview with O. M. Ostlund Jr. of the staff of the *GRIT* newspaper) that Prohibition was "a rank failure." Prohibition "made crooks out of otherwise honest people. Also, "alcohol was so easy to make, it was impossible to stamp it out."

Within the Keystone State, the sages of the senate quietly voted (December 5th, 1933) to ratify the 21st Amendment and to negate the 18th Amendment. Pennsylvania became the 34th state to vote for repeal. The rejoicing over repeal by the pro-alcohol crowd promptly smothered the whimpering lamentations of the members of the crumbling temperance movement. Neither their voices nor the echoes of their voices have been heard since. The 18th Amendment became the only constitutional amendment ever to be jettisoned. The bunghole of the national keg was ripped open.

That repeal of Prohibition was disheartening for all those who opposed a heavily-liquored American populace. Of course, the repeal was also disheartening for individuals like Prince David Farrington, whose income would suddenly nosedive in the face of poorer quality but cheaper, legal—and more easily obtainable—liquor.

## THE STEADFAST ONE

Criminal charges made during the latter days of Prohibition were pursued even as the repeal process was grinding to a halt. Ten federal agents were summoned to the court in Scranton (March 1933) and charged with having accepted bribes in return for protecting local liquor law violators. How ironic: among the witnesses was a man who understood bribery as well as anyone: Prince David Farrington. He was there to testify against any of the ten that he may have encountered. Sadly, the available account says nothing about the outcome.

On November 14th of 1934, *less than a year after Prohibition's wildly celebrated end*—December 5, 1933—Prince Farrington gave convincing evidence that he was not changing his behavior. On that date, he was apprehended with bootleg liquor. That supply was listed in the Lycoming County court documents as being "855 gallons of alcohol 146.2 proof and 2,072 gallons of whiskey and brandy less than 100 proof," all of which he had failed to declare to the state, in violation of the Beverage Tax Laws. This was followed by a petition to that same court in September of 1936 to void the charges because "This defendant, Prince D. Farrington, has just completed the serving of a sentence in the United States Penitentiary at Lewisburg upon the sentence imposed upon him by the Federal authorities involving the same set of circumstances upon which the above-entitled charge is based."

## THE RETURN TO THE FEDERAL PRISON SYSTEM

On July 12, 1937, Prince David Farrington returned to be hosted by the Federal Prison System. Charged with conspiracy to engage in the business of distilling, he had received his sentence at proceedings in the federal courthouse in Scranton, Pennsylvania. As inmate number 5784-NE, he began serving his 20-month sentence in the new (1934 opening) facility in Lewisburg. Here, he appears to have developed an amicable relationship with Warden Henry Hill. Prince became a trusty for Warden Hill.[31] The family told of Farrington being allowed to roam the prison grounds. Once, using some of the skills of his youth, he set a trap that snared a wild pheasant. The bird was cooked, and, so the family says, Farrington hosted a meal of pheasant with Warden Hill as his guest. The warden complimented his charge on the excellence of the meal and remarked that Farrington ate better fare than he, the warden, did. The warden, however, was not the complete moocher. Warden Henry Hill provided the liquor for the occasion from his private stock. Prince observed to his family, "I'm living well; I'm just not going anywhere!"

Farrington was released from this period of incarceration in the Autumn of 1939 (September 27). Upon his release, he gave his daughter Gladys the cigar box with his few prison mementos. Within the cigar box, Prince had been keeping, among other things, his release papers, his watch and a cigarette holder. He told Gladys that he had started a bad habit while in prison: Cigarette smoking. (While cigarette holders were not widely used, President Franklin Roosevelt was among the few who used one.).

As discussed above, Prince Farrington had already been incarcerated in a federal prison facility when he served time in Atlanta. Lewisburg's federal pen had become just one more prison for Farrington to add to his growing criminal resume. Prince remained undeterred by repeated arrests and incarcerations, nor was he deterred by swelling competition from the heavily financed and organized legal brewers and distillers. A count of the criminal cases indexed in the Clinton County courthouse from 1940 to 1948 shows 34 indictments listed under the F's, with 10 of those indictments going to Prince or Charl or Virgie Farrington!

---

31. A *trusty* is not the same as a *trustee*. A trustee is either a person who helps manage a college, church, etc., or who handles someone's finances. A trusty, as used here, is a convict who is trusted to have a few liberties while in prison.

## THE CALL OF THE RILED: THE FBI'S 12-MONTH MANHUNT

The above record is most impressive, whether or not one appreciates the criminal life that spawned such a resume. However, at the age of 57, Farrington may have lacked the will to face another term in prison. So, he had climbed into his green pickup truck, with a coupe automobile on the back and his ex-wife, Martha, beside him, and headed south over Fourth Gap Mountain Road.

For a fugitive in flight, the world is his hiding place. When Prince David Farrington went flouncing across Fourth Gap Mountain in order to avoid the start of his 1946 trial in Lewisburg, people speculated on his eventual destination. Rumors had the fugitive hiding somewhere close to home or close to his childhood home in North Carolina. Rumors also mentioned Mexico—or, perhaps, Texas. In reality, Farrington eventually reached exile in Orange County, Florida, near the town of Apopka, on the northwest outskirts of Orlando. Here he lived for the next several years. In Orange County, Farrington did some farming and fishing, along with the making of wine from oranges. He was bold enough to take some of his farm produce to a local market for sale. Here, in Orange County, seemingly forgotten by the Federal Bureau of Investigation, he had rare visits from family members.

Lycoming County, Pennsylvania, was created in 1795 and was named for one of its principal streams. That stream, Lycoming Creek, carries a Delaware Indian name, meaning 'sandy' or 'gravelly stream'. Some local political maneuvering brought the county seat designation to an unappealing and unpopulated area already known as William's Port. The population of Williamsport, Pennsylvania, today is about 30,000. This small American city sits on the northern bank of the Susquehanna River's West Branch, about 20 miles downstream from Prince Farrington's home at Jersey Shore. The city bustles today as the cultural and commercial center of north-central Pennsylvania. Williamsport became a thriving town known through the years as having three unique features. Firstly, during the late 19th century, Williamsport, Pennsylvania, was America's principal logging center. Secondly, the town is now famous as the 1939 birthplace of, and today the world's capital for, Little League Baseball. Thirdly, and most critical to the life of Prince Farrington, from 1882 until 1983, Williamsport had the publishing offices for a nationwide weekly newspaper, *GRIT*.[32]

For decades, the *GRIT* newspaper had been reporting on the criminal career of Prince D. Farrington, but it was in April of 1950 that Williamsport's *GRIT* ran a serialized, two-article feature about the missing moonshiner. The journalist Richard B. Stone, as mentioned at the close of Chapter 1, concluded his coverage of Prince David Farrington and his flight from the law with the phrase, "He may be riding still . . ."

If *GRIT* had been a local newspaper, its two-part feature on Farrington would likely have gone unnoticed elsewhere. However, at that time, the *GRIT* targeted rural America. Thus, it was being mailed or hand-delivered to many thousands of homes across the nation. The Federal Bureau of Investigation, apparently aware of the impending *GRIT* coverage, suddenly had a strong renewed interest in the apprehension of Prince David Farrington, the moonshiner fugitive of Jersey Shore. The Farrington family blamed the *GRIT* reporting for spurring the bureau's interest in locating and apprehending Prince Farrington. From that point in time, the Bureau's investigation was relentless.

An order dated March 29, 1950, initiated the Farrington chase. In that memo, the Special Agent in the Philadelphia office notified long-time (1924 - 1972) bureau director J. Edgar Hoover of a 1948 warrant having been issued for the arrest of Farrington (still listed as having no aliases) by the Federal Court of Scranton, Pennsylvania. The order cited violations of four separate sections of the Internal Revenue Laws (2810, 2831, 2833 and 2834) and described Farrington as a 48-year-old, white American male who was also a ruddy, gray and balding, heavy, American farmer with a mole on his left cheek and with multiple scars on his scalp. That document also listed, directly below the 48-year age, the birth date of 1889, creating an insurmountable discrepancy of about 13 years! This order also listed Farrington's current FBI file number as being 1089550. That number would now be common to many documents in the bureau's year-long investigation and pursuit.

The forfeiture of the $1500 bond that cohort Lemuel Groce had posted was noted in a memorandum of August 7, 1950.

---

32. *GRIT*, www.Grit.com, still publishes; but it has become a monthly magazine, now published in Topeka, Kansas. It's current circulation exceeds 100,000.

An April 25th document from Director J. Edgar Hoover to the Philadelphia office offered photographs to the Philadelphia office. They are shown here in substandard reproductions.

A few weeks later (July 5, 1950), a memorandum went from Miami, Florida, to Bureau headquarters. It reported the accidental arrest of Randall Farrington of 1730 North Mill Street in Orlando, Florida, under the notion that he was Prince Farrington Sr. Actually, Randall Farrington would have been Prince's middle son, Gayle Randall Farrington. Once Gayle Randall Farrington proved his identity, the federal agents took the opportunity to interview the moonshiner's son before releasing him. Gayle told them he hadn't seen his father in the past half-year and had no awareness of his father's whereabouts. He also mentioned the extended (two months') visit, in late 1949, of Prince D. Farrington Sr., at the Duke University Hospital for foot surgery due to the crippling effects of gangrene. Had the Bureau but known. While they had arrested the wrong Farrington, they had inadvertently arrested—and released—Prince's fugitive son and they had been in the right state!

That first FBI document identified four sections of the Internal Revenue Laws as being those of the original indictment, under which he fled.

An April 25, 1950 memorandum from Director Hoover to the special agent in Philadelphia included the newly prepared memorandum from the FBI's Identification Division along with two photographs of Prince Farrington. It also described their quarry: Prince Farrington, it was noted, was a 57-year-old white, born on one of two possible dates (both in 1889) and in one of two possible locations, both in North Carolina. His weight range could be from 187 pounds to 225 pounds, carried on a frame ranging from 5 feet 7¾ inches to 5 feet 10 inches; with a ruddy complexion, bald head, a mole on his left cheek and a scar on the bridge of his nose. Prince's occupation was listed as farmer. He is listed as having four accomplices: Joe Gardner, Harry McGonigal, William P. Lynch and Nunery King. A list of other friends or acquaintances was also offered, but not as real cohorts of their quarry. It appears that the first three of the above were gleaned from a 1946 arrest incident in Pennsylvania, while the fourth can be found on the criminal records of a 1915 arrest in North Carolina.

Over the next year, the manhunt generated somewhat more than 100 pages of memorandums and reports. During this investigation, the FBI contacted the Pennsylvania State Police in Wyoming (Luzerne County, near Wilkes Barre), Pennsylvania, who notified the FBI that they had no information on Farrington since his arrest in 1935, except for a picture taken in 1936.

Was Prince David Farrington *really* lost? Hardly.

## A NITPICKER'S PICNIC?

The professional skills one expects from the much-vaunted Federal Bureau of Investigation seem to be lacking in Prince Farrington's pursuit. If one wishes to denigrate the early Bureau, there is material here.

A. Two documents list two possible birthdays for Farrington: One is June 3, 1889. The other, also appearing on two documents, gives the same year, but the date is June 31!

B. As noted above, the March 1950 document lists both his age (48) and his year of birth (1889), which creates irreconcilable differences!

C. A document dated April 20, 1950, lists "Places of Birth: Randolph County, North Carolina as well as Pleasant Garden, North Carolina. There are two towns named Pleasant Garden in North Carolina, but neither one is in Randolph County.

D. The agents also seem to have been particularly naive when they express the complaint that "the subject's relatives have been most uncooperative." Should we assume that the relatives of other criminals would never have failed to cooperate with the G-men?

E. Lastly, they mention having accidentally arrested Prince's son, Randall, whom they released as quickly as he convinced them that he was not his father. However, in a later document (August 7, 1950), agents report from the Philadelphia office: "Another son, GAYLE or GAIL FARRINGTON, is a fugitive from a state court indictment since GAYLE FARRINGTON has been accused of swindling between $30,000 and $40,000 in connection with the operation of a secondhand auto lot which he operated at Lock Haven, Pennsylvania. His present whereabouts are unknown, but information recently received by the ATU at Wilkes-Barre indicates that GAYLE FARRINGTON was last known to be somewhere in the state of Texas; however, no information was received indicating the location where he was residing in Texas, and no action to date had been taken by the ATU to locate him."

Let's review the report of July 5, 1950. That report, out of Miami, Florida, revealed that a U.S. Deputy Marshal and two Alcohol Tax Agents from the Treasury Department had "arrested by mistake" the wrong Farrington, having arrested "RANDALL FARRINGTON, son of Subject."

That bureaucratic snafu concluded with the quick release of Randall Farrington "when he proved to the United States Deputy Marshal that he was not PRINCE FARRINGTON Sr." Apparently, no one realized that GAYLE FARRINGTON, the fugitive from a Pennsylvania swindling indictment, was none other than Gayle Randall Farrington, the man whom agents arrested by mistake, but quickly released. Had the agents realized their error while Gayle Randall Farrington was in their custody in Florida, they would not have needed to speculate on his being in Texas.

## 'PHILIP HARRINGTON' AT DUKE UNIVERSITY HOSPITAL

Because of the mistaken arrest of "Randall," the federal agents were able to learn, by quickly interviewing [Gayle] Randall Farrington before releasing him, that his father, Prince, had secretly visited the Duke University Hospital in 1949, more than a year before they got that information.

Still, the FBI sent an agent to Duke University Hospital in Durham, North Carolina. There, the agent learned that Prince Farrington had been admitted to that facility for surgery to remove the gangrenous toes of his left foot. (Family members attribute the amputation to frostbite, from his having suffered through intense cold while tending one of his stills. Of course, diabetes was inhibiting recovery.) The official who shared her file with the agent let the Bureau see that Prince entered the hospital on September 30, 1949, and was discharged on November 23 of that year. He used a simple letter substitution to create an alias: Prince Farrington became Philip Harrington, whose wife was Martha White Harrington, born in Orange County, North Carolina. For his parents, Betty Williams Farrington became Beth Williams Harrington, and Tom Farrington became Tim Harrington. The agent also learned that "All toes on left foot amputated . . ." and that Farrington, as Harrington, left behind his five digits as well as a bill for $600.

When Prince was sentenced to the federal penitentiary in Lewisburg (April 22, 1936), he had 13 co-defendants listed, all of whom were either acquitted, fined or fugitive.

The FBI got the pursuit underway with orders to their offices in Charlotte, Miami, Richmond, Boston, Philadelphia, and Pittsburgh.

Agents from the Miami office learned that, in late 1949, Prince had been living with a niece, Louise Stubefield (also known as Mrs. Bohumil Dolezel) and that she was still getting the bills from Duke University Hospital for Prince's surgery. Stubefield told the agents that she had not heard from him; but that someone said that he was in Texas. She also suggested that agents might contact Prince's children, "as subject is known to be without any funds whatsoever and would contact the children if he contacts anyone."

On October 28, 1950, a letter left the desk of Director J. Edgar Hoover and reminded the Miami office that their report showed no progress in the investigation of the fugitive Prince Farrington despite the passage of a full half-year. The Miami office was scorched by Hoover for "a deplorable condition that must be corrected forthwith. The Bureau will not tolerate excessive delay in handling investigative matters."

Their investigative work encountered officials in Orange County, North Carolina, who admitted knowing Prince Farrington by reputation as a former bootlegger in their county more than 25 years previously.

The FBI learned that Scott Anthony was related to Prince through marriage and that Scott, too, had once been in the bootlegging business but had not been so occupied for more than eight years. Anthony (whose relationship with Prince was through Anthony's being married to Martha White Farrington's sister.) also expressed reluctance about helping the FBI find Prince but that he would be willing to try contacting him and urging his surrender.

Similarly, Prince's brother (*see* Chapter 2), John Alexander, said that he wouldn't want to tell the FBI where his brother was, even if he knew, but that he'd be glad to encourage Prince to surrender. Naturally, brother John Alexander emphasized, Prince "would be in much better condition in custody."

John Alexander also volunteered the name of Lee Cannell, an ex-attorney from Pleasant Garden, North Carolina. Why an ex-attorney? Cannell, John Alexander explained, had been disbarred because of his connections with Prince. John Alexander, Prince's brother, also identified a section of neighboring Randolph County as the Black Ankle Section, notorious for its bootlegging history.

In October of 1950, agents reported to Washington that they found the name of a Prince Farrington in Delray Beach, Florida, but that it couldn't be the moonshiner since the woman visited was a negro and that "the address is in the negro section of Delray Beach, Florida. Inasmuch as the subject in this case is a white man, [this] Prince Farrington, who is a negro—is eliminated."

On the 5th of January, 1951, Miami notified Washington that someone (a redacted name) "advises [that] subject may be presently residing at 311 South Orange Avenue, Orlando, Florida." It was another false lead.

The FBI also hoped to catch Farrington in a lapse of judgment. Perhaps he tried to keep his driver's license and his registration tags active. They contacted the Pennsylvania Department of Revenue, only to find that his Pennsylvania Driver's License had been allowed to lapse. Prince had no driver's license or registration tags for the years of 1948, 1949 and 1950.

Agents also got no help from interviews with the Porters, George and Gladys (*see* Chapter 13).

One man, Edward F. Swartwood, told of seeing Prince in 1950 in Salona. This sighting, if true, would have Prince visiting the area, at least, since his flight. Swartwood said that he exchanged greetings with Prince, with whom he was long acquainted and that Prince was dressed like a tramp and had about three-inch whiskers. He had no other information except to tell the agent that Prince Farrington was driving a 1949, two-door, black Chevrolet of unknown registration.

Lemuel Groce, the man who lost $1500 when the justice system lost Prince, told an agent that Prince, back in 1948, left the Jersey Shore area with some trucks and cars. The agent who spoke with Joe Gardner, Prince's long-time associate, confirmed that Prince loaded several cars on trucks and drove them to North Carolina. Agents found that a man named Robert Riley, of Greensboro, North Carolina was one of the drivers. The cars were apparently sold to Riley's brother, owner of the Riley Motor Company of Greensboro.

Among the dozens of people interviewed was Prince's only older sibling, Badie Farrington. Badie was in the military during World War

I. After the war, rather than returning to Guilford County and Nubbin Ridge and the moonshining world, he lived for a time in Coatesville, Pennsylvania (west of Philadelphia) and settled in Rehoboth Beach, Delaware. There, he worked for one construction company and then joined another, the Sussex Construction Company of Rehoboth Beach. He did underwater salvage work. Badie was, according to the FBI witness, living "alone in a shack by the Rehoboth Canal." When contacted, Badie told the FBI of his lack of contact with Prince and others in his family. He told of a visit by one relative, nephew John Rayle of Asheboro, North Carolina, who did not mention Prince. His only other information was a letter, which he produced, that he had received from his niece, Cindy Toomes, who, likewise, did not mention Prince.

## PAYDIRT

In the pursuit of a fugitive, a limitless number of interviews might be conducted, with all data gleaned leading nowhere. A conspiracy of silence, both planned and unplanned, might protect the fugitive. However, if just one knowledgeable interviewee cooperates with authorities, all the silence will be shattered by the truth. After many months and many miles of investigation, one such appeared in the Prince Farrington case. Family members never doubted that one of the family's disgruntled in-laws was the 'snitch.' That unknown informant will likely live forever as a redacted name on the FBI reports, a name forever lost to curious eyes because it is hidden beneath a thick, bureaucratic scribble. The information provided led Director Hoover's agents directly to Florida and Farrington.

Finally, this telegram arrived in Washington, D.C:

FBI, MIAMI 3-13-51 3-29 PM EST
E C E DIRECTOR, FBI AND SAC, PHILADELPHIA
..URGENT..

PRINCE DAVID FARRINGTON Sr., WAS., FUG, BD. SUBJECT APPREHENDED TODAY NEAR APOPKA, FLORIDA, BY AGENTS. LODGED ORANGE COUNTY JAIL, ORLANDO. [etc.]
MASON

### The Criminal Chronology Generated by Just One Lone Case:
- ARREST: August 28, 1946—At his still site on the Tangascootac Creek, Clinton Co., PA.
- INDICTMENT: January 31, 1948—Middle District of Pennsylvania, Scranton, PA.
- FLIGHT: June 4 or 5, 1948—As the trial in Williamsport, PA was approaching.
- BOND FORTEITURE: October 11, 1948. Farrington's friend, Lemuel Groce, lost $1500.
- FEDERAL BUREAU OF INVESTIGATION LAUNCHES SEARCH: March 29, 1950.
- APPREHENSION: March 13, 1951. Near Apopka (Orange County), Florida, by FBI.

### AGAIN, WITH THE SPARK PLUGS

What might Prince Farrington have decided was his net gain or loss from having skipped his trial in Williamsport? He had delayed his imprisonment by about 33 months, although Prince's self-imposed confinement and isolation greatly tempered that delay. By being three years older when his prison term finally began, Prince's changed physical condition might have made his stay a bit more difficult when it finally transpired.

In March of 1951, Bureau agents learned that Prince Farrington's son, Prince Farrington Jr., was living near Apopka, outside Orlando, Florida, where his daughter (the fugitive's granddaughter) was attending the Apopka Public School system. Working through the school and the post office, an agent learned that Prince, the long-time fugitive, was living in a tent near a fishing camp, about one-half mile from Prince Jr. On March 13, 1951, two agents went to find the fugitive.

His time as a runaway from justice had been spent living in a tent, doing some farming, some fishing and some distilling of orange brandy. His self-imposed exile had been enlivened somewhat by visits from his family. For a while, his daughter, Gladys, and her family lived in Orlando, where Prince visited them.

Farrington's second creation of an alias seems to have been used but once, on a document in which Farrington, perhaps more from whimsy than from scheming, gave his given name as Ponce. That fanciful name likely was inspired by Prince Farrington's stay in Florida, where the fountain-of-youth legend and the story of the Spanish explorer Ponce de Leon remains current. His last brief use of an alias appears in the FBI report of his capture. That report tells of his being confronted, while fishing, by two federal agents at his tent near Apopka, in Orange County, Florida, a few miles northwest of Orlando.

They had already taken the precaution of removing the spark plug wires on his truck. They also confiscated the oranges that he had been using to make his own citric brandy.

One of the officers asked, "Are you Prince Farrington?" Their report tells us that "The subject, upon being confronted, stated his name was 'STEWART.' However, he immediately admitted being identical with the fugitive." Farrington confirmed his identity, and the FBI agents finally had their quarry. Arthur Cornelius Jr., the special agent in charge of Philadelphia's FBI office, made the announcement.

The FBI's capture of the aging fugitive was covered by the local newspapers in Pennsylvania; but it was also covered by the *Associated Press* and by the old news agency, the *United Press*. The U.P. article appeared on page 8 of the Washington *News* [April 4th, 1951], telling the world that Prince David Farrington had 13 prior convictions. The Williamsport *Sun-Gazette* reported the apprehension, with Prince Farrington sharing the front page of that edition with a Pittsburgh steel strike and the U.S. Senate hearings for "rackets overlord," Frank Costello.

Prince was promptly hauled before the U.S. commissioner, Walter A. Daley, in Orlando, Florida. Daley set his bond at $3,000 and, with Farrington unable to pay, ordered him jailed. The Williamsport *Sun-Gazette* stated that Farrington, "notorious in this part of Pennsylvania," was promptly committed to Florida's Orange County prison.

His apprehension in Florida led to his appearing in the federal courthouse in Tampa, the court serving the Southern District of Florida. Prince was charged with violation of the Internal Revenue Liquor Laws. He was registered as prisoner #71183-A and was handed a fine as well as a sentence of one year and one day of imprisonment.

In order to serve his sentence, Prince Farrington was sent back to one of his early penal alma maters, Atlanta. Farrington entered the federal facility in Atlanta on the 16th of April, 1951. However, he left Atlanta's federal penitentiary within a few months.

## PRISONER EMERITUS

Prince might have been the poster boy for a national organization for recidivism. According to the tally by the Jersey Shore Herald (April 3rd, 1951), he now had a record of "at least 14 convictions."

The man who might have been one of the nation's leading legitimate whiskey distillers had to face one last incarceration, this one in a far-off facility in the state of Missouri. Because of his gangrene and serious diabetic condition, his last, of many terms in prison, was served in the federal penitentiary for invalid or sickly federal prisoners in Springfield. Prince David Farrington arrived at the Springfield, Missouri, prison on the 27th of September, 1951. Once again, Prince became a cipher among ciphers. The prison photographer shot the obligatory two portraits of the aging criminal. Beneath the direct frontal view, the prison recorded the date, 6-10-51, and MCFP [Medical Center for Federal Prisoners], SPRINGFIELD, MO. Beneath those inscriptions was Farrington's newest government-assigned number. After many years in many prisons with many inmate numbers, this one, 8141-H, was to be his last.

Prince Farrington's jailhouse resume would include such 'alma maters' as Guilford, Rockingham, Lycoming, Clinton, Atlanta, Orange Co. FL, Lewisburg, and Springfield. The Springfield, Missouri, federal facility would be his last prison home. He had another five years of life, but the first of those five years would be as an inmate in the Springfield penitentiary, from June 10, 1951, until June 14, 1952. That date (June 14, 1952) is a key date in the Prince Farrington saga. It was the last date in which this perennial prisoner was within a local or federal prison. After that date, anyone who might admire the jailhouse lifestyle could justifiably think of the 62-year-old Farrington as a prisoner emeritus with an enviable collection of prison records. While he languished in prison in Missouri, his most loyal supporter was working feverishly to have him freed once again. Thanks to Gladys's endless effort (*see* Chapter 13), her father's time in Springfield was reduced by several months.

*One of the Farrington brothers, Tom, with his wife, Martha (who bears the same given name as her mother in law, Martha ("Mattie") Farrington*

*George and Gladys Porter as the gracefully-aging couple.*

*Upper Left: A pensive George Porter, Prince's son-in-law. Upper Right: Gladys and one of the boys. Lower Left: Gladys Farrington's high school graduation picture. Lower Right: Prince David Farrington, Jr. or "Whitey" with his niece, Gladys' daughter, Lisa and her baby.*

*A sketch from George Porter's notebook.*

*George Porter's renowned grandfather, Dr. George Tibbins of Beech Creek, with family members and a friend on a turn-of-the-century (1900) vacation. This picture was from an undated clipping from the Lock Haven Express.*

# · 13 ·

# The Bootlegger's Daughter

Prince and Martha Farrington were the parents of four children. There was no molding of offspring here. The four had vastly different personalities. In the order of their births, they were Thomas "Huss," born about 1913; Gladys, born September 22, 1918; Gayle Randall, born about 1921; and Prince David Farrington Jr. "Whitey" born about 1925. The elder three were natives of North Carolina. Prince D. Farrington Jr. was born in Clinton County, Pennsylvania.

## THE BOYS

**Thomas Farrington**, Prince's eldest child, was—according to Charles Dorwart of Antes Fort—an unruly character. Tom, who always carried the nickname "Huss" within the family, was the oldest and, for a time, it seemed, the wildest. One evening, Tom had his pony kick out all the basement windows on one side of the Granville School in Antes Fort. Then he and his friends entered the school and stole things from inside. One thing that disappeared was a fountain pen that an aunt had given Charles Dorwart. The expensive pen had Charles' name in gold lettering, but he never saw it again. Tom's dad, Prince, took care of the window-replacement costs.

Tom was also the one involved in an incident recalled by Leo Taylor (*see* Chapter 7) involving Tom's hobnail shoes marring a classroom floor. He was also the son who was said to have asked a brother to stop at a restaurant while they were traveling. The other argued that they had no time. Tom bet that he could be in and out of the restaurant within just a few minutes. The brother, sure that he could win the bet, stopped at a restaurant. Tom hurried into the eatery, waited for someone else's order to come from the kitchen, quickly claimed it as his own, paid it—and rushed from the restaurant in time to win the bet! It is also Tom's name that appears on a Clinton County court record in 1936, with a charge of "Drunken Driving."

Tom did a lot of driving for his moonshiner father, including one unusual trip to Philadelphia. Tom drove his dad's Brockway truck. He may have been hauling booze to the city. He certainly was there to get a huge load of sugar. Tips regarding potential arrests were common, and when he got to the great port city, he was told that revenue agents were looking for him and his Brockway. Tom made a quick phone call to Prince for instructions. Prince's quick decision: "Trade the damned truck!" So Tom quickly got rid of his dad's Brockway and arrived home with a big load of sugar and a new Reo.

So, Tom Farrington's reputation wasn't expected to change with his pending marriage. After all, one is reminded that maturation and matrimony aren't always synonymous. Still, for Tom "Huss" Farrington, there seems to have been a substantial change. While his three siblings spent much of their lives struggling with employment and finances, Tom, once married, was transformed. He married a local contractor's daughter, Martha Williams. She sold cosmetics, with Tom sometimes acting as her driver.

While his father was a fugitive in Florida, Tom and his wife moved to Pittsburgh, where he worked for about six months as a carpenter before being discharged for shoddy workmanship. Then Tom and his wife left Pittsburgh and an unpaid landlord (June 1950).

But, Tom also found steady employment at the Piper Aircraft Company factory in Lock Haven. His work with Piper likely kept him out of military service since Piper was building large numbers of light aircraft that were useful to the military. Tom was the brother who, once an adult, never had trouble with the law. Tom, or "Huss" Farrington, worked for the Piper Company until he retired, several years before the plant closed and some years before he died in 1986.

The Piper Aircraft Company was a fixture of Lock Haven industry for many years. Having begun in Rochester, New York, in 1927 as the Taylor Brothers Aircraft Manufacturing Company, they later moved—for a few short years—to Bradford, Pennsylvania. In 1937, the company moved to an abandoned silk mill in Lock Haven. That's where it became the Piper Aircraft Corporation and where it built its solid reputation. That facility was practically destroyed by the flood waters of Hurricane Agnes in 1972. Before the 1972 flood, the company had already begun moving its operation to Florida. The Lock Haven plant was totally closed in 1981. In recent decades, the company has had a checkered history of ownership and production.

Meanwhile, the old Lock Haven plant has been converted once again. It is now the Piper Aviation Museum, with Russ Nelson as its principal researcher. It stands as a memorial to a company that once thrived by producing single-engine, then twin-engine, and, finally, jet-engine planes for general aviation purposes. One early goal of the company was to create 'simple-to-pilot' aircraft. Thus, there is little wonder that nearly two-thirds of the Piper aircraft ever produced are still being flown!

In 1974, Tom Farrington's wife, Martha—who carried the same given name as Tom's mother—addressed the Clinton County Historical Society. In that program, which was mainly about her criminal father-in-law, Mrs. Tom Farrington suggested that—of Prince Farrington's children—her husband, Tom, was most like his dad. The son who was most like Prince died in 1986.

**Gayle Randall Farrington.** His nephew, Dave Porter, says that Gayle Farrington "was great to be around." Porter also remembers that Gayle gave him and his bride a very nice wedding gift. Although Dave also tells of his dad complaining that if it were easier to do something legal, Gayle would still do it the wrong way! Gayle is also fondly remembered by Tom Bauman. "Once they picked up Gayle down in Florida. He had scammed a couple of guys who had a shoe repair business. They were sleazy bastards!"

And now, whether or not the shoe repair owners were sleazy, Gayle had swindled them out of some money. So, there was a warrant for his arrest. In April of 1950, while Gayle was living in Florida, he was arrested by mistake when the FBI was tracking Prince. Unknown to the agents who arrested, then released, Gayle Randall Farrington, he, too, was a wanted man, a fugitive like his dad. He was wanted under a Pennsylvania state indictment for the alleged theft of $30,000 to $40,000 related to the used car sales lot he had been running in Lock Haven. This fugitive, Prince's middle son, was the person who took Prince to the Duke

University Hospital (1949) for the repair of his feet. In 1956, when Prince died, Gayle was living in Barberton, Ohio.

Thanks to Tom Bauman's description, readers can sense the atmosphere of a relaxed, rural county jail. As Bauman recounts the scene: "They had always been my lifelong friends, you might say. I knew Sheriff George Hickoff, so I told my wife, 'I'm going to go over and see if I can see Gayle. So I went over. Hickoff could have been sheriff until he was a hundred and five years old. He was a heck of a nice guy. It got so that they couldn't even get someone to run against him for sheriff. Anyhow, I went over and went into the office. The sheriff was talking with someone. He asked, 'Can I help you?' and I said, 'I just wondered if I could see Gayle Farrington. I hear he's in here.' 'Yeah,' Hickoff said, 'He's back there. Go on back.' I went back. The cell door was open. Robert Farrington (Charl Farrington's oldest son) and Huss (Prince Farrington's oldest son) were already there visiting. All three were sitting on the jail cot, talking.

"I walked in, and we shook hands all around. I hadn't seen Robert for quite a while. Robert was married to a good friend of my wife and I used to see him pretty often. Gayle was always likable. We sat there talking. I asked them where their dad was. I wasn't absolutely sure that the authorities had picked him up; but they had got him soon after they got Gayle.

"Then these two brothers who had the shoe business came in. They had recently talked to Tom ("Huss") on the telephone. One of them said to Huss, 'Well, I see they picked up the old man. It's too bad the old bastard didn't die,' or something like that. Well! You didn't say something like that to Huss! They had said this on the phone. Boy, when they walked in the cell, Huss was up off that cot, and I thought he was going to clobber those guys! If it hadn't been for Robert and Gayle grabbing him, he would have clobbered them. And he was capable of cleaning them up. He was a pretty wiry guy. I thought, 'What the hell is going on?' but Gayle said, 'Let me talk to them.' Gayle (the brother that they said had swindled them) stepped out into the hall with those two. I don't know what he said. Anyway, the two brothers left.

"It wasn't too long after that that those two brothers (who operated the shoe business) were put in jail. They were making girlie movies in their store, and one of the girls turned them into the police, and the police raided them. They had all these movies that they had made—and there were three or four girls involved—and so they ended up in jail.

"That was the last time that I saw Gayle, but, as I said, I worked at Piper with Huss.

"Gayle had moved out and was living near Dayton, Ohio. He was still a little shaky in business. One day (at Piper), a co-worker (name omitted) came over to me. He said, 'We were just out and visited Gayle. He's up to his old tricks. He's selling real estate.' One day, this same person came in, and he saw me. I was on a test flight (a job Bauman did at Piper Aircraft Company for several years), and I was going up to the office for some reason. I passed the department he was in. 'Hey! Hey Tom!' He says, 'Your friend, Gayle, sold non-existent real estate, and now he's in jail.'" Gayle had to face charges a number of times in both state and federal cases. While spending some time in jail, Gayle was viciously attacked, with his skull being visibly damaged. Gayle Randall Farrington died several years later of a brain tumor.

**Prince David Farrington Jr.** known to the family as "Whitey," was also familiar with the law and with incarceration as a lawbreaker. The youngest child of Prince and Mattie was rarely addressed as 'Prince.' He went through life simply as 'Whitey,' from his school days until he died. He was remembered (*see* Chapter 4) for the time he innocently washed some of his dad's illicit paper money because he heard his mother complain about the 'dirty money' that his father obtained. He was also remembered by his poorer Southern cousins for having an actual mechanical toy automobile, a rare toy reserved only for the wealthiest youngsters of the time. More recently, a former neighbor recalled hearing young Whitey saying, "Daddy, I need some change."

"Whitey was a wild one," observed Sam Fuller. Gigging fish or frogs involves spearing them with a long, metal rod with illegally attached fishhooks. Gigging was done from a rowboat or canoe, and it was done at night with a flashlight when the frogs weren't so easily disturbed. Gigging was, and remains, illegal. Fuller accompanied Whitey on gigging trips. Fuller held the flashlight while Whitey gigged frogs to obtain their hind legs for cooking and eating. Sam Fuller also tells of a group of teens going 'out on the town' with Whitey, in his 1941 *Lincoln Zephyr*. "He was crazy. He'd get half-whacked. Prince gave him hell for speeding!"

Whitey speeding? Tom Bauman has similar memories.

While living in State College, Prince David Farrington Jr. ran off with someone else's wife, fathered a child with her and, apparently still unmarried, left her to go to Florida. Years later, now in his sixties, his sister, Gladys, reportedly struck him with her purse and her sailor's tongue, calling him a "son of a bitch!" for considering marriage to a woman in her twenties. Yet, his nephew, Dave, remembers that Whitey had given him a $100.00 wedding gift, a substantial sum in that place and time.

In early 1943, he and his brother Gayle were arrested for having rifled the summer cottage of Charles Steppe in Lycoming County. Their loot, according to the Lycoming County court document, included dishes and cooking utensils, a clock, a flashlight, a pair of goggles, a lamp and a canvas belt containing several shotgun shells. As evidence of the price levels of that era, the total value of the stolen items was listed at $30.00. In April, Prince D. Farrington Jr. was sentenced to three months in the Lycoming County prison and was required to restore the stolen property to its owner. The court record regarding Gayle's fate in this crime was unavailable.

Bauman is blunt: "Whitey always drove like hell! He was a good driver, but he always drove fast." Bauman then goes on to tell of a time that he and his wife were visiting his mother on the farm to which they had moved, near Lock Haven. At the time, Whitey's brother, Gayle, had a used car lot on Bellefonte Avenue in Lock Haven. The night that Tom and Geneva were visiting his mother, Whitey was apparently speeding again. He was driving up Church Street with cops chasing him. He led them on a high-speed chase. He knew he could turn on Park Street and zip down to the river, cross the railroad and race down around the creek road and over to the home of Tom Bauman's mother. There was one small catch . . .

Whitey turned on the wrong street. He was racing toward the canal that provided water for the paper mill. Knowing that the police would soon be coming down that same street, he couldn't turn around. He must either stop or drive into the canal. So he slammed the brakes, stopped his car and jumped out. Since he had a small head start, he ran unseen, along the canal and across the railroad. Then he plunged into Bauman's cornfield!

Tom Bauman, his wife, and his mother were sitting and chatting in his mother's living room. His mother said, "Somebody's in the kitchen." Tom went to investigate. There was Prince David Farrington Jr., 'Whitey' to all the Baumans who were present. He was soaking wet from the neck down from running through the cornfield.

Bauman asked, "What'n the Hell happened?" Whitey's response: "Oh, Jesus! Can you take me over to the Sons of Italy?" Bauman repeated, "What in the Hell happened?"

Then Whitey explained the chase. His solution, which Tom helped him to achieve: Tom drove the Bauman's old V-tag truck that they used on the farm and for hauling coal on occasion. He took Whitey to the Lock Haven lodge of the Sons of Italy. Whitey went into the lodge and found his brother, Gayle, the auto dealer. Gayle, the businessman that he was, joined various social clubs. Whitey told Gayle about the chase and all. Then he asked Gayle to: "Call the police like you are leaving, and tell them that your damned car has been stolen!" Gayle certainly didn't want anyone to know that Whitey was in the Sons of Italy with him and that Whitey had taken that car. The ruse worked. No one ever found out. The paper reported that a car was stolen from Gayle's parking lot.

Then, there were the trips that Tom Bauman and Whitey Farrington took to Altoona. Prince had been raising sweet corn on the farm of Wesley Koch. Prince had recently bought a new Ford pickup truck. Tom Bauman and Whitey were given the job of filling the new truck with sweet corn and hauling it to Altoona to sell door-to-door. They loaded about 200 dozen ears onto their truck and drove it to Lock Haven to Johnny Ripley's ice plant. There, they scattered several kegs of ice onto the corn to keep it fresh before setting off, in the wee hours, for Altoona. Once in Altoona, they'd have breakfast, then drive into a neighborhood and make just one stop. Word quickly spread through the streets, neighborhood to neighborhood. Within about four hours, their couple thousand ears of corn were sold, and they could return home.

Sam Fuller wasn't the only one impressed by Whitey's lead foot. It was while leaving Altoona on one visit that Bauman saw his best evidence of Whitey's passion for speed. He came to a rise in the road. Bauman glanced at the speedometer. The needle was at 100! Whitey had to quickly slow because of the road conditions, which put his speed down to where the state policeman they passed didn't even stir.

Despite Whitey's somewhat more advanced age, he and Tom Bauman worked and socialized together. Even after the Baumans moved to the Castanea area, outside Lock Haven, Tom, who was just entering his teens, would break down a shotgun, wrap it in a burlap bag and peddle his bicycle all the way to Prince's home outside Jersey Shore. Then Bauman and Whitey would go hunting together.

Still, Whitey worked as hard as he played. He is often seen working on the farm. In support of a smoother operation, Whitey taught young Bauman how to drive a 1938 Ford one-half-ton pick-up truck. He also sold his dad's sweet corn to the produce-starved people of Altoona. He also ran a trap line as a young man. Briefly, Whitey was also in the used-car business and, at one period of his life, he worked for the Tennessee Valley Authority. And Whitey was the only one of Prince Farrington's sons who was in the military service. He got his basic training in Texas, before going to Nebraska for schooling as a gunner on a 4-engine, propeller-driven B29 Superfortress bomber. He was still in training when the war ended, so Whitey never left the States.

Tom Bauman's memories of his last two encounters with a lifelong friend: "The last couple of times I saw Whitey . . . he had that used car lot up on Hogan Boulevard (outside Lock Haven). He introduced a woman to me as his wife. And she had two kids. I don't think that they were Whitey's. They were too old. Then, I didn't see him again until I was up at the Pine Creek Inn one night. I was going in there, and he was coming out. He was by himself. I guess he was in there having a few drinks. I saw him there and talked with him for a few minutes before he got into the car and left. That was the last time I saw Whitey."

There is a story out of Lycoming County that harks back to the waning days of Prince Farrington's career. It has been said that Prince Farrington gave one of his last stills to his sons. However, the boys neglected to dismantle and hide the still before hunting season. Hunters saw and reported the still. Revenue agents then went to the still and blew it up.

When the FBI began tracking the fugitive, Prince Farrington Sr., a couple of people provided grist for the rumor mill. As the rumor mill had churned the story, Prince's son and namesake, Prince Jr., had been working in State College, Pennsylvania, when he met and ran off with another man's wife. The rumor also added a bit of substance to the story by saying that Prince Jr. and the woman (a beautician named Arlene) were now living as man and wife. One witness told FBI agents that Prince Jr. and his wife, Arlene Ebert Farrington—if she really was his wife—had a baby, born in the Lock Haven Hospital. Prince Jr. then left for Florida, and his mate, Arlene, returned to her home in Allentown, Pennsylvania. Before that particular report ended, an agent was announcing plans to visit Allentown in order to interview "Arlyne (Arleine) Farrington, nee Ebert," whom the agent now identified as Prince Farrington Jr.'s "paramour." At this point, one might ask whether the FBI investigation of a dynamic moonshiner/bootlegger had morphed into an afternoon soap opera.

Eventually, Prince Farrington Jr. relocated to Florida, where he worked in car sales. His business card lists his business as "WHITEY'S CARS," which was located on West Church Street in Orlando. Returning to his home area, he and Gladys enjoyed a close sibling relationship. However, Gladys was angered shortly after "Whitey" entered his sixties. He announced to his sister that he was interested in marrying a woman in her early 20s. Gladys attacked him with her purse while loudly condemning him, "You're sick, you son-of-a-bitch." Despite years of living in Pennsylvania and Florida, Prince David Farrington Jr. was living in Atoka, Tennessee, at the time of his death.

## GLADYS FARRINGTON PORTER

Prince David Farrington's only daughter, Gladys Julia Farrington (Mrs. George Porter after their marriage in 1939), gave fresh meaning to the phrase "dutiful daughter." Much of Gladys's life, as a child, as an adult prior to her father's death, and, again, as an adult after her father's passing, was lived within the vortex of Prince Farrington. Partly because of her nearness to her popular, outlaw father and partly because of her effervescence, Gladys is easily the most remarkable of the offspring of Prince and Martha Farrington.

Gladys was born in North Carolina. She was about two years old at the time of the family's move to Sugar Valley, Clinton County, Pennsylvania. The mountain-top estate where she and her siblings once lived is relatively isolated. Once she attained school age, Gladys attended the one-room Brungard Elementary School near the small cluster of homes that is Rosecrans. From her school desk, she could look to the west and see a cemetery and the church beyond. Lester Seiler, her farmer-boy neighbor, remembered, "I had a pony and, for a couple of years, I carried milk over there to Prince. A gallon or two gallons, whatever he wanted—almost every day—Well, when she [Gladys] was over there—now she's big and heavy . . . a big woman that way—But—you could wrap her around your little finger—is all the bigger she was then when I used to carry the milk and went to school. A lot of times, in bad weather, I'd take her books along with. I'd take my pony and go to the schoolhouse and step off onto the porch. I'd take my pony and tie the reins up—and the pony'd go home . . . and she'd go home in a hurry, too."

From her earliest days, Gladys was exposed to her Dad's show of farming as well as the several raids and arrests. Separations from her incarcerated father often followed the arrests. Gladys chided Prince after his release from the federal penitentiary in Lewisburg, Pennsylvania (the town that is also home to Bucknell University).

"I told him he used to talk about it like he went to college at Bucknell."

His response was, "Well, I'll bet I learned a lot more than those college kids ever did."

"He was a good father. He was good to us, and he loved children." His children wanted to please him, claimed Gladys. She also said that Prince was "possibly not stern enough," but he also bragged about his children.

The Prince Farrington that she saw was the one who responded to her sad lament about having fresh bananas to eat in school while her schoolmates had none. Prince later brought bananas to the rural school for distribution to all the students.

Regarding his reputation as a moonshiner/bootlegger, Gladys confessed, "I was a little embarrassed about it, particularly when I was going to a Methodist church and would get temperance talks." She verified the rumor that Farrington's whiskey got into the halls of the national government. "I was with him one time when we were heading to North Carolina. He dropped the stuff off in Washington, in the Senate building."

Gladys's dental work was done in Williamsport, not for lack of a capable dentist in Jersey Shore, but because "Daddy" had moonshine business to conduct in Williamsport.

Marjorie Kamus of Jersey Shore knew Gladys Farrington Porter, whom she says was "kind of a character." She also recalled that when

Prince Farrington was destitute in later years, he was able to move in with Gladys and George. Also, when Prince was a fugitive in Florida, his ex-wife, Martha, lived some of the time with their daughter, Gladys, and the Porter family. Gladys had a line: "It's like the 'George Washington Slept Here,' claims since so many places claimed ties to Prince."

Life within the Prince Farrington sphere becomes far more believable when one realizes that the nation once had hard economic times unlike anything imaginable for current generations. Charles Dorwart, of Antes Fort, recalls a childhood of poverty similar to that of many of the area families. He recalls the times when his mother fed the family of nine—Charles had three brothers and three sister siblings—and (since there simply wasn't enough food) would say that she wasn't hungry enough to join them for supper. As a maturing child, Charles earned pennies by spending the night visiting and caring for an elder individual. He also earned 15 or 20 cents by hand-mowing someone's large lawn. Occasionally, Charles would have saved a full dollar that he could use for entertainment. A typical result: Walk from Antes Fort, the two miles to Jersey Shore; attend a Saturday matinee (that was usually a Western film) at the Victoria Theater, walk up the street to Fred Miller's hot dog shop, return for a refreshing treat from The Villa ice cream parlor that sat beside the theater, and then walk home again, with a few cents remaining.

Charles Dorwart's sister also had similar poverty-driven memories. Dorothy (Dorwart) Knarr of Antes Fort has fond recollections of the moonshiner's daughter. Dorothy traveled with Gladys Farrington. Gladys would come by with a few dollars and invite Dorothy and several other high school girls to go to Jersey Shore to see a movie and get refreshments. They would go to the Victoria, a spacious movie house that had opened in 1917 and could seat more than 550 patrons. Following the movies, the girls would adjourn to the ice cream parlor. The movie tickets and the refreshments were Gladys's treat. Dorothy Knarr has memorialized a specific evening when she was one of a party of four teen girls who were invited to join Gladys Farrington for a visit to the Jersey Shore movie house. (For Dorothy, this was a two-mile jaunt). As they were ready to leave the Farrington mansion, Gladys's mother asked her to change the sheets on her bed before they left. Gladys consented and pulled clean sheets from a bureau drawer. Then she told her friends that she wanted *new* sheets. So, she went to another room and returned with a new set of linens. The four friends were impressed. Dorothy, writing many decades later, observed that the other girls barely had *spare* sheets, much less a supply of new ones. Anyway, once they had helped Gladys prepare her bed, the five girls walked across the bridges and island and proceeded up Allegheny Avenue to the theater. When the film ended, Gladys announced, "I'm going to treat you to ice cream!" They exited the Victoria and walked next door to a small ice cream shop, The Villa. Dorothy remembered Gladys starting such an evening with $20. If she happened to run short of cash while still entertaining her friends, she'd simply end the dilemma by declaring, "Charge it to Pop!" "She paid for all of the entertainment," Dorothy Knarr wrote in her concluding comments about an evening with Gladys Farrington: "We thanked her, and we all walked home. She was a wonderful friend in all ways. She was also an 'A' student."

The film they had viewed that evening was a recently released film based on the 19th-century best-selling novel by T.S. Arthur: *Ten Nights in a Barroom*. What was Gladys's reaction to the film, which was among the most famous anti-alcohol films ever put to celluloid? Dorothy remembers no comments from Gladys. It was also Gladys who, while a student, won an essay contest that the Women's Christian Temperance Union sponsored.

Several times, she was absent from school because she would get another girl and drive to Williamsport. The late Sara Good left a story with her grandchildren. Sara and Gladys Farrington were friends. There was a time when Gladys and Sara planned to go to the movies. However, they found that Gladys's brothers had taken the car. The annoyed teen declared: "To hell with them boys!"

Gladys knew how to drive one of her dad's old pickup trucks. She borrowed the pickup truck without asking, and the girls went to the movies. However, when they exited the theater, there was a small, chattering crowd gathered. A local lawman, Mr. George Slifer, approached Gladys and (Gladys wrote later) told her, very emphatically, "My Gawd! Go home!" She left immediately. When she arrived home, Prince was seen to be wringing his hands and acting very nervous. As it turned out, his daughter had driven into town with a pickup truck that had considerable moonshining equipment stashed openly on the truck bed. While the incident must have been unsettling to Gladys, as well as to Prince, it gave her something to laugh about while retelling the story in later years.

That same Sara Good had a wedding surprise for her grandson, Dave Ulmer and his bride. She shared some Farrington whiskey with the bride and groom. Her source? Her friend, Gladys, had given several bottles to Sara years before. The memory of that event and the presence of authentic Farrington whiskey remains clear for Dave Ulmer after the passing of many decades. Equally clear in Ulmer's memory was the excellence of the whiskey involved.

As a teen, Gladys visited the home of the neighboring Muthler family. Charlie Muthler remembers the time that Gladys expressed an interest in making some potatoes on the hot lids of the iron wood stove. Although that method of cooking was unconventional, Mrs. Muthler consented and allowed Gladys to create her stove-top snacks.

Gladys doesn't appear to have been directly involved in Prince's work. She would burnish his reputation at every opportunity throughout her life. Among the lesser support she gave was in allowing a vehicle's registration plates to be registered in her name, as was the case with the three-quarter-ton truck that was involved in the moonshining operation when Revenue agents raided the still on the Tangascootack Creek.

None who met her ever forgot her. Gladys Julia Farrington Porter was described as a 'character' whose speech was both plain and profane. She was the bootlegger's daughter who married her childhood sweetheart, George Porter, and bore him four children: Dave, Robert, Craig and Lisa.

From the standpoint of this biography, Gladys Julia is most significant as being a sometimes-effective and loyal supporter of her father, Prince. At one time or another, she and George managed a barroom in Mill Hall (for George's father); another at the mouth of the Tangascootac Creek, at another time, as well at the Broadway Hotel in Jersey Shore. Their memory, however, is best associated with the Gamble Farm Inn in Jersey Shore. That inn has prospects for continued use and expansion with the ownership of Troy Musser.

Tom Bauman's opinion of George Porter: "George was a likable guy, but he wasn't that energetic. I got a vehicle from him one time. George told me, 'Look, I'm gonna tell you something. Not all my vehicles are A-L, but I bought that one from a farmer and he used it to haul produce to markets. "It was a Dodge panel truck. I had it for about five years, and it worked fine. It was kind of interesting to be around him." The author spent several hours in the company of Mr. Porter, and he must concur with Bauman's opinion. George Porter was a very interesting individual.

Tom Bauman had been friends with all of Prince's children. When Tom and Geneva Bauman visited Geneva's mother in the Manor Care nursing facility in Lock Haven, Tom saw Gladys Porter in a wheelchair. She, too, had suffered some memory loss. Tom relates, "I walked over to her, and I said, 'I bet you don't know who I am.' Gladys kind of sat back in the wheelchair . . . looked at me a little bit. Then she kind of got a grin on her face, and she said, 'Tommy!' It wasn't too long after that that Gladys passed away. George hasn't been dead all that long. They're buried in the Jersey Shore cemetery."

## A NEIGHBOR'S RECOLLECTION

In a telephone interview (April 27, 2009), Jane Bubb Miller related the following, beginning with her recollection of seeing Prince Farrington "and his little Indian cohort walking up the road to our house. Prince was wearing bib overalls."

"I was about ten. My dad, John Bruner Bubb, and I walked down to the farmhouse by the river to see what was going on. So, I witnessed the [1934] raid and saw them dump the booze into the [Susquehanna] river.

"We later lived in that same house, so we were in the flood of 1950. My dad had a green '29 Ford coupe. We called it 'The Green Hornet.' During the flood, he'd wade out to check his car. We were worried that he'd be swept away. Finally, the water stopped rising right at the top of our basement steps, so we didn't have to move furniture.

"I loved George and Gladys. I just thought that they were wonderful. They were true blue. They had four children. Dave and Robert, both of whom were close to their grandfather, Prince; then Craig, who was killed in an automobile accident; and lastly Lisa. Gladys was flamboyant. She was the leader of the pack.

## "DUSTY"

If the Farringtons were among the new, and the new rich, people of Clinton and Lycoming counties, the Tibbins were among the area's gentry. Dr. George H. Tibbins practiced medicine in Beech Creek, Pennsylvania, a town on the very southwestern edge of Clinton County, about 25 miles north of State College. The doctor and his family were among Clinton County's financial and social upper crust. A photograph from the early days of the 20th Century, within an old newspaper clipping, shows Dr. Tibbins and his three daughters and an unidentified gentleman in the physician's early Cameron automobile. Here, we learn that Dr. Tibbins and his companions were vacationing at Harvey's Lake, a prominent Victorian-era resort near Wilkes-Barre.

Dr. George H. Tibbins again broke into the newspaper in 1917 while the First World War was raging in Europe. Shortly after Dr. Tibbins—who was of French lineage—volunteered for military service in France, he visited the local barber shop. While seated and in the middle of being shaved, the doctor was irked by the remarks of a German sympathizer. The offending individual had the temerity to declare that the Germans would defeat the United States army and navy, as it had already battered the British and French. The lathered doctor leaped from the barber's chair and attacked the sympathizer, leaving the man bloodied from a sudden Tibbins' punch to the face.

There are Porter townships in both Clinton and Lycoming counties, but this did not indicate a well-to-do family. Stanford Porter, who married Florence Tibbins, one of Dr. George Tibbins' daughters, was once described as a 'black-shirted Irishman'. This meant that he was from the working class. Stanford and Florence Porter gave Dr. Tibbins three grandchildren, one of whom was George "Dusty" Porter. Since George was an excellent student, his family expected him to bring additional renown to the family name by studying and becoming a doctor. Unfortunately, for the aspirations of Florence and Stanford, their scholarly son, George, attended high school in Jersey Shore.

Prince Farrington's daughter, Gladys, was a year ahead of George Porter at the Jersey Shore High School. Her yearbook entry (*The Orange and Black*, 1936) gives her a nickname that she didn't carry beyond high school, "Foxey." It also describes her thusly: "Fair to look upon but better yet to know." George Porter's high school yearbook entry (1937) shows the young scholar whose most consistent school activity involved four years of band membership.

His parents never could have imagined their son, George, falling in love with a young woman whom his family thought of as "the bootlegger's daughter" as George recalled years later. The Porter/Tibbins reaction to the romantic relationship ranged from disappointment to dismay to anger. Their disapproval of the relationship caused George's father, Stanford, to declare his son's options: Either go to college or marry the bootlegger's daughter. College was no longer in George's equation. The condemnation went beyond the verbal. George admitted to his children, many years later, that his father, Stanford Porter, had actually struck him and knocked him to the floor, so angered by the romantic union that was sidetracking their son.

Whose prior sphere will be the more widely occupied by a newly-married couple? The Porters' 1939 wedding may have offered clues. The newlyweds took their vows in Burnett's Chapel in North Carolina. That was, and remains, the primary church of the Farringtons of Nubbin Ridge.

Excerpts from a letter written by George's mother, Florence Tibbins Porter, after George and Gladys's first two sons were born suggest that the mismatched couple's marriage did not result in lasting alienation on Florence's part . . .

> *Dear George, Gladys and Boys –*
> *Those were certainly beautiful corsages you people sent, and we enjoyed them very much—we certainly had a lot of pleasure from them—Thank you so much."*

After a chatty four handwritten pages, Florence closed with:

> *Love to all. Write soon.*
> *Mother, x x x x x Your Dad is sending fruit.*

## A BROAD-BRUSH PORTRAIT

Gladys seized every opportunity—every chance—to swipe her brush and create another aspect of her father's positive image. Consider the quotes as reliable as the reporters' who recorded them.

"He (Dad) came here particularly to make whiskey because he heard the mountains in the area had good water and he heard that the people here liked good sour mash whiskey."

"He was not the gangster type. He was soft-spoken and very outgoing, quite a charming personality."

"He couldn't see anybody going without, and we were taught to share."

"I personally know of his paying for dozens of operations" for needy individuals.

She was also quoted as saying that Prince purchased clothing for needy families.

And, "He helped people buy a lot of homes. He had mortgages on them, but I can remember the day he tore all his mortgages up when the Depression came.

In summary, "He really was good-hearted. He was a country gentleman."

"If there was sickness in a family, a jug of whiskey would be found on the doorstep in the early dawn."

"Any kids from anywhere around were always welcome at our place. There might be 24 or 30 kids around there at one time."

"If he saw some kid who looked pitiful, he'd go buy him some clothes."

"He really was good to people. That's why they'd call him Robin Hood."

"I have no idea, and he didn't either, how much money he had. He seemed to go through it pretty quickly, so he had to go make some more whiskey."

Regarding her father's failure to attend church, Gladys informed listeners that Prince was a friend to preachers and priests. He summarized his religious situation thusly, "I do believe in a Supreme Being, and if you live by the Golden Rule, you don't have anything to worry about."

## HARDLY PRINCE'S FAULT?

The side of Prince Farrington that his daughter adored was the side described earlier that radiated humor and compassion. During her interviews, she worked to dispel his unseemlier side. Unlike Prince, careless moonshine makers cooked and sold whiskey that wasn't properly mixed or aged. Their hooch might even sicken or kill the users. This information worked itself into the interview reports that Gladys Porter offered to readers of several area newspapers during the 1980s. However, if a reader reflected on the reasoning behind her arguments, he or she might conclude that Gladys offered excuses, and not reasons, for his outlawry. Over the years, she described her father as not being a gangster but a soft-spoken and charming individual, a good man who happened to make whiskey at a time when it was illegal to do so. Gladys also claimed that she knew of no one who would say anything bad about her father. She was quoted as observing that "nobody today says one word against him. Even the ones who wronged him must figure they were wrong." Gladys also suggested that "This area must have needed a celebrity in the dark days of the Depression." "I have no idea, and he didn't either, how much money he had made. He seemed to go through it pretty quickly, so he had to go make some more whiskey." One of her lines reflected on the dangers of inferior moonshine. "I asked him, 'Why do you make this whiskey, Daddy?'" She quoted his response, "I feel I'm really doing people a favor."

## A CONTRARY VIEW

One can list the number of supporters and detractors among an individual's friends and neighbors. Can we look to an editor to be more dispassionate than most? This biography opened with an account of Prince Farrington's capture at his secluded still site on the Tangascootack Creek in late August of 1946. Here, from the *Williamsport Sun-Gazette*, are editorial comments that were inspired by that arrest. They appeared in the paper's August 29, 1946 edition and were reprinted in the edition of September 9, 2001. Other than a paragraph that questioned his failure to become a legitimate distiller, the full text is offered here:

> Seizure of another still and the arrest again of Prince D. Farrington is becoming familiar news in this area and certainly should point up the declaration "crime does not pay."
>
> The local office of the Pennsylvania Liquor Control Board is to be commended on its action. It has never been charged that

Farrington, in any of his operations, produced inferior liquor, but the fact that he has persisted in seeking to evade laws has made him a menace to society.

The successful growth of our nation has resulted from observance of laws and regulations set up in the best interests of all. If many followed the path beaten by such men as Farrington, our entire system of government would crumble.

Eventually, Gladys learned of her fugitive father's whereabouts in Florida. Then, says her son, Robert, "we all piled into a World War II navy surplus Ford 'woodie' station wagon and joined Prince" in Florida for a first visit.

George and Gladys struggled financially. For a time, they were living in a cabin on Antes Creek, a short distance from Prince's home. Prince had actually been living in that cabin with the Porters at the time of his flight from the law. That was where he had modified his truck before speeding south over Fourth Gap Mountain road and into temporary obscurity.

As money problems increased for the Porters, Gladys sold some of her dad's objects.

George and Gladys ran a Jersey Shore car dealership from about 1959 into the 1970s. They also owned an inn in Jersey Shore, which was in the mansion of the old Gamble Farm. For some time after the Porters owned it, the inn was known as the Antique Inn. Gladys also dealt in antiques for several years. When their money problems worsened, Gladys sold several of her presumably authentic Prince Farrington objects.

The Antique Inn was located almost directly across the Susquehanna River from the home where Gladys and her three siblings spent their teen years. Gladys's staunch and lively support of her father may have aided in the development of a close relationship between her husband, George, and her dad. Prince confided in young George and had his son-in-law accompany him on a couple of escapades. Still, George was ever aware of his having abandoned an academic path for love. Notebook scribbles and sketches from the car dealership days suggest considerable idleness of body and thought.

In later years, George Porter would tell interviewing reporters, "People said I married her for her money. Hell, the monkey was dead, and the show was over by the time I got on the scene."[33] He lamented further, "He spent all the money before I got a chance to spend any." In that same interview, George said this about any booze that might still exist, "I drank it all."

Jane Bubb Miller's impression of George Porter was that he was bright but without drive. She recalled, "At one time, I used to fix my own 1940 Plymouth. One day, I wanted a part. I went to George's car dealership and asked for the part. George handed me a wrench and sent me to get my own part—which I did—from a car no longer in service.

"My husband and I were administrators at the Manor Care nursing home in Jersey Shore. In his last years, George was a client there. George was brilliant and both the boys were brilliant.

"Martha[34] was in the background, and you rarely saw her. In her later years, she became very peculiar in the way she dressed."

The children (grandchildren of the bootlegger) of Gladys and George Porter were David, Robert, Craig and Lisa. A family friend who admired Gladys also noted that Gladys would have little patience with boisterous children in the back seat of her car. She was described as a lioness who would roundly cuff her cubs into obedience. The older sons and daughter went on to careers of their own. Craig died young, killed in an alcohol-related automobile accident.

Once the FBI returned to the chase, their agents appeared in Lycoming County. Gladys, however, taught her sons how to respond. Gladys instructed her son, Dave, that when agents asked about his grandfather, Dave was to tell them that he didn't know anything, and then he was to begin crying. Dave says that he was able to do the crying part very convincingly. For Gladys herself, the response was somewhat different. When agents asked her a question, she had an effective and abrupt response, "Why don't you kiss my ass!"

Gladys Farrington Porter might ponder, for the remainder of her days, just who it was who tipped the Federal Bureau of Investigation as to her dad's whereabouts, but no matter who had exposed his hiding place, Gladys continued her unwavering support.

---

33. *Centre Daily Times*, October 15, 1985.

34. Prince's wife, prior to their divorce, and his occasional companion throughout his remaining years.

## LAST YEAR'S SUMMER

When the FBI apprehended Prince at his tent hideout near Apopka, Florida, he was ordered to stand trial in Tampa, Florida. Before his trial reached the sentencing phase, Gladys Farrington Porter had petitions ready to present to the court. Her petitions were beseeching the court to parole Prince Farrington for health reasons. Prince's medical problems were surely more legitimate than some of the signatures gathered. A family member estimated that perhaps 10 to 20 percent of the signatures were bogus.

There were petitions with many signatories from Pennsylvania and petitions with many signatories from North Carolina. There were also a few individual petitions. Some of the Pennsylvania petitions stated the following: "We, the undersigned, have known Prince D. Farrington as a good family man and a responsible parent; a citizen of personal integrity; an individual with deep human sympathies; and one who was always generous to the poor of this area. Therefore, we request the Court to show leniency toward him."

Other Pennsylvania petitioners made this plea: "We, the undersigned, with due respect for the court and legal justice, request that such justice be tempered with mercy and compassion in the case of Prince D. Farrington. His many generous and charitable deeds in this area are common knowledge, to such an extent that he is a living legend as a Jersey Shore and Lycoming County 'Robinhood.' He is admittedly broken in health, as well as finance. For these reasons, we respectfully plea for lenience from the court."

Some North Carolina petitions were rather different, offering the following: "We the undersigned wish to say, to whom it may concern, that we have known Prince D. Farrington for many, many years, some of us for his entire life and wish to state that he has absolutely no criminal tendencies. He was over-ambitious in making money perhaps, but he was very generous and had many friends in any part of the country in which he lived."

Among the individual petitions of clemency is that of Lee Thompson, at whose store Prince purchased huge quantities of sugar plus other groceries and meats. The two were close friends. Another individual petition came from Ernest W. Meixel, son of Floyd Meixel and brother of Clyde Meixel. The three Meixels had helped Prince make, store and deliver his moonshine whiskey.

Signatories included many farmers, laborers, businessmen and professional men and women. Signers included newspapermen, including Mr. George Lamade of the *GRIT* newspaper in Williamsport. Mr. Lamade was the man for whom the Little League field in Williamsport, Lamade Stadium, is named. Although a few signatures were illegible, a tally of the legible signatures: Pennsylvania—294, North Carolina—57, Other—3.

The principal town for signers in Pennsylvania was Jersey Shore with 153, followed by Mill Hall with 33, Lock Haven with 27 and Loganton with 16. Almost all of the signers (51) in North Carolina listed a Greensboro address.

Prince Farrington was awaiting sentencing in Florida when Gladys circulated the petitions on his behalf. Her petitions asked for Farrington's release for health reasons. This could be a convincing argument in her dad's favor since he was in terrible shape. He was admitted to the penitentiary in Springfield on June 10, 1951. Prince's medical problems were surely more legitimate than some of the signatures gathered.

To gather signers, Gladys went to where her father was best known. Most of the signatories were from two addresses: Greensboro, North Carolina and Jersey Shore, Pennsylvania. Several people wrote single letters of petition. One such came from the pen [typewriter?] of A.R. Tate. Tate's letter, beneath a Victoria Theater (Jersey Shore) letterhead and dated on "3/31/51," declared—on Farrington's behalf—"This man's offense compares with last year's summer." Several other individuals also submitted letters of support. Her total number of petitioners—fraudulent ones and all—seems to have eclipsed the three-hundred-and-fifty mark. That total falls a bit short of the 5,000 signatures claimed in the Rombach paper (p. 10).

The great petition effort was wasted. The judge, W. S. Barker, hearing Prince Farrington's case in Tampa, admitted that he'd never seen anything quite like the petition avalanche. He took several hours to review the petitions; but then followed the prosecution's plea and denied clemency and parole. Instead, Prince D. Farrington, a man with a criminal record approaching a half-century, was sentenced to three years in prison and a fine of $1300.

Gladys's effort also involved the beseeching of aid from U.S. Congressman Al Bush of the Hughesville area. That effort netted some positive results. Prince Farrington recounted his last days in prison to his son-in-law, George Porter. He told of knowing that he was to be denied parole at an upcoming parole board meeting. Prince claimed that he was rejected for parole one day, but the very next day, he was released from prison. That, he said, made him realize that someone was "pulling strings." The string pullers were U.S. Congressman Al Bush, Mr. Lamade of the *GRIT* newspaper and, naturally, Gladys Farrington Porter.

A copy of a 1952 Associated Press telegram resides among the Gladys Farrington Porter collection of documents. It reads as follows:

> JERSEY SHORE, PA, JUNE 6—(AP)- MRS. GLADYS PORTER WAS NOTIFIED TODAY HER BROTHER [It should say, FATHER], PRINCE FARRINGTON, WOULD BE PAROLED ON JUNE 16 FROM THE MEDICAL CENTER FOR FEDERAL PRISONERS AT SPRINGFIELD, MO.
>
> FARRINGTO0N WAS SENTENCED IN APRIL 1951, IN FEDERAL COURT, FLORIDA, TO THREE YEARS IN PRISON ON CHARGES OF VIOLATION OF LAWS.
>
> CONGRESS. ALVIN L. BUSH WROTE MRS. PORTER THAT FEDERAL OFFICIALS HAVE AGREED TO FARRINGTON'S PAROLE FOR HEALTH REASONS.

### THE BAWDY BEDROCK

A neighbor who knew Gladys Farrington Porter and knew Gladys's local reputation observed that: "She had a little bit of a drinking problem." Said the same neighbor, "You should have talked to Gladys when she was sober."

Gladys might have been described as having good dis-organizational skills. She might also be described as a bawd, so far as employing obscenities was involved. George identified her in one of his notebook jottings as Gladys Julia Farrington Porter, "Queen Bee." However, Gladys also emerged as the bedrock of a dysfunctional family. When others had crises, they turned to Gladys.

During the 1950s, Gladys was drawn to Florida to help her dad, a fugitive and, briefly, a federal prison inmate in that state, before he was transferred to the federal prison in Springfield, Missouri.

It was Gladys who pulled the family together after son Craig's death and who worked "anyplace anybody needed me," including the Piper Aircraft Company of Lock Haven, the car lot that she and George ran for many years, and the Antique Inn that she and George operated in Jersey Shore.

More than a decade after her dad's death, Gladys had a brother, Gayle, in a Florida prison.

In a letter written in 1970, Gayle wrote to his sister. He lamented, "I was hoping and praying to receive a letter from you and this month is about past with no word from you." Six lines later, he made his pitch:

> *Gladys, will you please write more often as it helps me a lot and if you can send a few dollars once in a while, I would sure appreciate it. Several months have gone by since I have received any financial assistance, and it gets to where you are glad for anything to help with personal needs like shaving cream & razor blades. A few dollars would sure help. I know things must be rough for you, but <u>please</u> write me. I am sending you a magazine that is published by the correctional institution. They have a poem I wrote for them in it. I know you will enjoy reading it. This magazine is for the purpose of helping others and expresses the experiences and hopes of the Sponsors and members of our A.A. group here.*
>
> *Love to all, your brother, Gayle.*
>
> *P.S. Tell Mother to take care of herself and George and the boys the same. Give little Lisa a big hug for me. Let me know how you are doing.*

Clearly, Gayle Farrington needed help. His father was gone, and his mother had her own physical and emotional problems. Gayle turned to Gladys.

When Prince was released from the federal penitentiary in Springfield, Missouri, he moved into a room provided by Gladys. Lester Seiler observed, "Then, at the last place, he came up here, you might say, to die when Gladys had him there . . ." When Prince died (June 14, 1956), it was his daughter, Gladys, who signed the dreadful document that proclaimed the passing of what Gladys noted to be a 'farmer.' Thus, she was able, with a single flourish of the pen, to remove the bane of her life, her dad's criminal occupation.

When Prince's widow, Martha, died in 1972, her grandson, Bob Porter, and his family were living in Michigan. At the time, no one told Bob of her passing. Two weeks passed before Bob and his family learned of the death of his "Gram."

Grace Sheddy of Jersey Shore made some of the more recent observations regarding Gladys Farrington Porter. Having been a patron of the Inn and a friend of the Porters, she proclaimed, "I never heard her fuss at anybody. She was a very likable person. She did a lot of the cooking, and she served awfully good food!"

## THE PRINCE FARRINGTON GREAT RACE

Gladys supported and aided in the annual Prince Farrington Great Race (1979 to 1989), which was a fund-raising event held in the area of Williamsport, Pennsylvania. There was a Prince Farrington Great Race Revival in 2003, sponsored by the American Red Cross organization. This commemorative event is properly identified in Chapter 16.

## GLADYS'S VISION

Gladys was determined to immortalize her father through a biography. She, herself, flirted with the notion that she would pen such a book. She made brief notes and labeled some photographs. She collected old news clippings. She spoke with a few contemporaries, and she wrote a letter to the Williamsport Hospital (April 30, 1984) and obtained his medical records. She collected the materials she had and put them into a small suitcase. It was red, decorated with white hearts. She also summoned the press and told them of her plans. Even if the reporters doubted that she would complete the project, Prince Farrington's name always made good copy.

As Gladys found the book project to be more and more daunting, she turned to one of her sons and then the other to consider the project.

Prince's grandsons, both of whom had the necessary academic skills, were aware that much that needed to be said in a serious biography would be the very material that their mother did not want to be written. They hedged, and she looked elsewhere.

Gladys's brother, Prince David Farrington Jr. ("Whitey"), "always wanted to make a fortune to help the entire family and make everybody rich . . ." says Gladys's son, Dave. Once, while "Whitey" was staying with his sister and her family, he decided to write his dad's biography. He grabbed the red suitcase and ran up the street with Gladys in pursuit. They squabbled over the collection, but Gladys retrieved the suitcase. With the project languishing, "Whitey" found a girl in a college writing class whom he felt could write the book. She did enough writing for "Whitey"'s nephew, Dave Porter, to evaluate. When Dave criticized her work, she cried and ended her effort. In the 1990s, Gladys was interviewed by several area newspapers regarding the book she said she was writing about her father. However, one acquaintance noted that the Lock Haven *Express* newspaper once contacted her and offered her their own related newspaper files before they were discarded, but she never went to get them.

Regarding any book writing, that same person added, "I don't think she did a blessed thing." She did, however, approach Wayne Welshans, a highly-regarded local historian. She asked him to write her father's biography, but Welshans, still working full-time, declined her offer.

Another false start occurred in the writing of a Prince Farrington biography with the effort of Prince's son, Tom and Tom's wife, Martha. They made some effort and spoke about the subject at a meeting of the Clinton County Historical Society, but the project may have died with Tom's death.

Dave and Bob Porter sincerely wanted their grandfather's story to be written. Eventually, when this author approached the Porter brothers, they were ready to surrender the red suitcase, with the hope of having a serious effort develop. At that time, Bob was living in Virginia, and he agreed to meet the author near King-of-Prussia, Pennsylvania and surrender the suitcase until all documents could be copied.

While Gladys doesn't appear to have written a single page of biographical narrative, she left some fascinating notes in several notebooks. Her jottings are notable for their arbitrary use of capitalization and punctuation, as well as her unique short forms of words.

One 3" x 5" notebook,[35] with a top spiral binding, had these words on the cover:

> The True Story
> of
> Prince David
> Farrington by
> his only daughter
> Gladys Porter[36]

Within, Gladys had this writing:

> INSIDE FRONT COVER: Ins. (and telephone number)[37]

1. 1 ST SALES Price? Desc. of farm. Heck and Bros Dad at home School Move to Town
2. Bridge Mansion Prosperity Dad drove Fords Trades Booze for Fords Farmers hauld grain 3.00 Brother Whity—Reo Tr & molasses from south Sorghum
3. [Description of mother, Martha?] Dishes unwashed Curtins Down Brkfast—Biscuits Sausage Tomatoes Clean Bed No Noise Couldn't Sing loved co. music (Country music?)
4. Mom played co. [Country music?] [Gladys appears to switch here, to describing her father] Loved To farm Garden—Stuff not all at once Bought fine cattle Soy Beans—Clover Horse kicked [apparent reference to Prince's having been kicked as a child]
5. Only a 919 telephone prefix number [North Carolina's Durham-Raleigh area]
6. (telephone number and illegible single name) Antlers—Barbed [?] Wine—draged home Brake loss—Nash Fox Pens Gargles with Carbolic Suits washed (??) burned Proud of patch I made

---

35. Returned to Dave Porter in State College, June 15, 2009.
36. This is followed by some illegible writing.
37. Pages are numbered by author, for own reference. No evidence of torn or removed pages.

7. Giant Raid at Farm Frozen holes Men Dipping Whiskey in cups–great party–cust list? Tunnel to River Big still—R.R. Boiler
8. 22 mo. Lewisburg liked Ital. wine Dick Wynon cabin 2 wk parties Fish at Zx Factory Dam Lee Thomson Cabin Bro Hopp—Spoiled
9. You win WCTU Award Can't start w out [Trial humor] late for trial Got Jury laughing Hard to keep Easy to make Prob. Back [Back problems?]—make honest living again
10. Lewisburg life Warden garden Snares Turkey Beer in N. Car. Bbls—at Rock Md Trip to California Will Rogers
11. The Great Tomato fiasco Celery Crates of Eggs Decline in health Fla—Trial in Tampa Gladys—Petition Release from Spring [Springfield, MO federal pen]
12. Rufus S. banjo 6 ft. of earth—twice in life doesn't matter whose neighbor and when youre in hospital nursery
13. Helped kids with Soap Box Race Last trip to N.C. Passing in Wm hos [Prince's death in Williamsport Hospital] Body shipped to N.C.—Boyhood Home Ballads 4 Dollar Whiskey``
14. Doc's & Hospitals used whiskey as medicine pure not shine Thermometers in aged booze Darker color He warned-never drink shine Bob Porter at H.S. Hus wanted radio-Dad said get cow catcher first
15. People say they saw him in P Up in mountains on moonlit nights Men still talk of his whiskey at Bars–nothing like it since
16. Hunters stumble on Still Prince meets in woods Hit at Wheel Club [Prince mentioned this club—in Canton PA- and its owner, in one of his last letters.] [Several illegible notations end this page.]
17. Old Crow Story Bbl of Prince J??? Bananas–Log School Court house–Water in bbls. Mowing at White Deer—Pipe fitting
18. Red Pick-up no brakes. Hauled milk Hauled coal Most careful Must have been right or would have been mangled
19. Girl on dads lap-pony incident He liked kids we could have many at home if we wanted to Pine Creek still, etc. Tunnel to Creek

**THE BOOTLEGGER'S DAUGHTER** 311

20. Stop at Prince's and get some medicine. Drs all bought Dr. Angle– <u>out of rasp juice</u> On trip in Ford handed Dad a candy he shared it with fellow W W. [?]
21. [Only listings are of two telephone numbers.]
22. Bridge falling Bought Red Brick Dad bought yellow brick Helped him count $ to buy red brick from Jas Gheen Took kids to Sunset park–cars Took load of kids to circus in truck. [From previous line]: He liked circus also
23. [A lone telephone number]
24. [Man's name and telephone number] Loaned $800 to a man who needed it Bob [got] pepper in eyes, [Prince] grabbed olive oil pured in eyes then washed out–eyes not red
25. Race track bet on Snipe Hunt ["Snipe Hunt" sounds like a horse's name] Sleigh tracks on farm on mt. Taking things to people at Xmas Dad broke one Xmas, so he butchered 18 pigs had meat cut up and we gave it away Goat at Mt farm at [ate?] money [???] dropped $
26. Trip to Cal! Broadway WW2 Leo's Dress Shop
27. Soy Bean Crop Hunters from city ruined at least 8 acres out of ten No more tramping said Dad. Guys from Penn State came down to study the Crop Great farming. [from previous line] Showed them weeds. What are these? Marijauna. We'll plow these under said Dad. I'm in
28. enough trouble without any more. Why make whiskey? People want it. Doctors buy it and recommend it to patients as medicine.
29. [After many empty pages there is but one page, the last within the notebook. It simply gives an apparent grocery list.] milk, Bread, O juice bananas tomatoes, green peppers[38]

Another set of notes that she made was found in a spiral-bound notebook that was used in the auto sales business of Gladys and her husband, George Porter. Most of the notes in that notebook refer to their used car business. However, Gladys also left some clipped, handwritten notes that reveal an effort to write a fictional sort of biography. The following is

---

38. There is no longer a back cover on the notebook.

taken from a five-page composition, given exactly as it appears, with the exception being that the original was handwritten. The question marks indicate undecipherable bits of the handwriting.

Time 1920—
Volstead Act in full force
Men of Susq Valley loved good drink of smoo(?) whiskey unable to buy anything but home brew
????? no good sour mash whiskey being made in
Pa mts of Pa
[four words in left-hand margin here] ? brand of moon
500 miles south near Gsboro NC a man noted for his ability to make good sour mash whiskey learned of this cond. (condition?) His name was Prince David Farrington. He d long considered to come to the Susq. Valley and investigate. He heard about good moun spring water in Sugar Valley near Loganton Pa good
The scene now shifts to a small Town along the Susque with the innocuous name of Jersey settled by people from New Jersey

[Second page]
Eddie Elder coowner of Eld Bros rest is wiping pocalin top of restaurant when he notices a model T ford coverd with splatters with red clay mud of N.C. The door opens & all chatter stopped when door open & tall well built stranger ? planters hat– smiled showing most beaut set of teeth from a ruddy complexion They had ever seen. Every man was Spellbound & seemed to sense that this was a most unusual man entering their rest. Thus he P—had arrived in the valley. He quietly ordered meals for family 3 child a bottle for the baby. Asking if anyone knew where he could purchase a small (?) farm with good mt spg water. Someone said he heard Fla Fruit Farm near Loganton was for Sale

[Third page]
After finishing the meals he got directions as how to get to the farm. Met owner in person & concluded the agreement paid cash for the farm & ???? [immediately?] took up residence

Though he was a farmer, his # 1 ability was the brewing of sour mash whiskey. In a few days he had trucked in all equip he needed to set up a large still in the woods near a spring near the farm. Purchases were made from Dickey's Hdware. Batchlet [Batschelet] Bros in J.S.
Setting up of it by Dutchmen in Sugar Valley. Pinella [Pinelli?] in Lock Haven. Mash ???? built with wood from Myers' nearby sawmill the Prince was in business.
In a few months Farmers hauled good grain for which he paid trice

[Fourth page]
3 times normal price. They were happy to be part of the enterprize because the economy and seemed to enjoy helping him in in any way. Soon the word flashed out in a mysterious way that a smooth grade of sour mash Bourbon was available. Kaplan in Wmspt [Williamsport] got a carload of charred oak kegs and bbles [barrels] for him in which he could age the whiskey.
People were amazed to see caravans of this going down road loads conceled with tarps. Good whiskey was seen at most the hotels & sev. prominent clubs in the areas. He was busy supplying Doctors & Druggists so they could prescribe this medicine for their patients. No usual small still were [where] we [we're] talking

[Fifth or last page]
To age whiskey at that time they buried it in the ground
Confair Bltg—Hauled Syrup from So [South?] during war & sugar shortage

Gladys was interviewed—in the 1970s—by a college student who was writing a paper (Rombach, p. 11) about Prince Farrington, as part of his master's program. Gladys informed the scholar that her father had died of diabetes. Such a response might remove some of the stigma associated with the heavy use of alcohol. The death certificate which Gladys signed, tells a very different story; the story of a man brought low by a cirrhotic liver.

## THE GAY DECEIVER

Minor damage to a new car can seem to be catastrophic to the owner. That's why a quick decision to deceive was required when Gladys fell asleep while driving her mother-in-law's 1939 Lincoln Coupe to Florida to its waiting owner. The travel was delayed for several days while bodywork returned the Lincoln to its original splendor. Gladys had no intention of revealing the mishap to Grandma Porter. A tense situation had been avoided at the hands of some skilled bodyworkers en route to Florida. The elder Mrs. Porter's contentment was quickly dispelled, however, when her bright young grandson, David, chimed in, "You can't even tell where it was bent."

## A SINGULAR TRIBUTE

Several pages of Gladys's notes show impatience and increasingly more illegible notes, the momentary inspiration of alcohol. Even when writing while sober, much that Gladys Farrington Porter wrote about her father rambles as though she was rushing to get notes onto paper. These, she must have assured herself, would grow into a beautiful biography when she found the time to expand and to rhapsodize. However, on one occasion she seems to have written with a measured and reasoned style. That result appears to be her best writing. Those few sentences suggest that—with the right atmosphere and level of sobriety—she might have had the ability that she envisioned for the penning of her opus. That evidence comes from thoughts that she left on the outside of a manila envelope. Here, in its entirety, is the result of her very brief burst of literary flair.

> Will The Real Prince David Farrington Please Stand Up?
>
> By his only Daughter, Julia Gladys Farrington
>
> To the residents of Clinton and Lycoming counties, he was a mysterious character who quietly moved in from N. Carolina and bought an old farm near Loganton, oddly called the Florida Fruit Farm. The fruit he raised was sour mash whiskey, made as only a true Southerner could make it.
>
> To me, he was a kind and loving father who spoiled me and my three bros deliciously.

We had everything—riding horses, expensive bicycles, ponies, small electric cars, and spending money.

To our mother, he was a problem in dress [dressing?] as he loved to pull on boots and wander over his farm in the fine suit she has pressed for him."

To the poor, he was the Robin Hood of Susquehanna Valley.

To the Alcohol Tax Bureau of Philadelphia, he was not the Prince but the King of Bootleggers.

To the hotels and clubs, he was the source of fine whiskey in the dry years from the '20s to '33.

## GLADYS, MOTHER TO MANY

Gladys Porter, the bootlegger's daughter, was recognized by many as an authentic 'character.' When asked if he knew Gladys Farrington Porter, Bob Cowfer of Oval snapped, "Who didn't know Gladys and the old man [meaning husband, George]? I spent a lot of time in their inn."

Dr. Robert Byington (*Two Penny Ballads and Four Dollar Whiskey*) emphasizes that "Almost invariably, the legend is most vibrantly alive among those who are at least one *and usually two or three* removes from the Prince himself." [Emphasis added] The grand exception to the 'usual,' of course, is that Farrington's daughter, Gladys, established herself as her father's staunchest legend builder.

Dr. Robert Porter, Gladys and George Porter's second son, and another grandson of Prince, wrote a poem about his grandmother, Mrs. Martha Farrington. When Gladys died, Robert also wrote something in memory of his mother. Dr. Porter's cousin, Tammy Farrington, recalled that she had never laughed so hard at a funeral. Why? Dr. Porter again put his fingers on the computer keyboard and created the following eulogy:

Gladys Farrington Porter: A Son's Eulogy.
Robert Porter
April 28, 2000

Generosity of spirit. It's hard to summarize the essence of anyone's life, especially your own mother's, in just three words, but this phrase has been rattling in my head for some time now, and today, I want to share with you why I think it's the best way to remember Gladys Porter. Generosity of spirit.

This may seem a little odd to some of you because when speaking of my mother over the years, most relatives and acquaintances have remarked on her colorful personality. To say Gladys Porter had a colorful personality is to say that there is a little bit of coffee in Brazil. From her decision to go blond back when Lady Clairol came in a plain brown wrapper, to the big floppy hats, to a taste for martinis and brightly colored sports cars, to a large handbag that could become a lethal weapon at any provocation, to the big grin and full belly laugh, to a voice that could peel wallpaper when it came time to straighten out a sassy kid or cuss out an uppity cop, my mother had color.

"Age cannot wither her, nor custom stale her infinite variety." Shakespeare has one of his characters speak of Cleopatra in this way, and it seems apt to think of Gladys's memory in this way. Like Will Rogers, she never met a straightforward, honest person she didn't like. Likewise, she never met a snooty, arrogant, conniving snob that she didn't hate. And no one who ever knew her had any trouble figuring out right away who she put in which category.

She loved being with people who liked other people and having a good time, especially if an improvised get together featured lots of good old stories, lubricated of course with the right beverages, legal or illegal.

When it came to child discipline, Mom was of the grizzly bear swat school, where a single swipe with a fast backhand could catch all the kids in a row sitting in the back seat, making for peaceful car rides and saving a lot of time and wasted words.

Sell? Man, could she sell. During the days of Porter Auto Sales, she might not have known a coupe from a four door, or a six cylinder from a V-8, but if the car had a spiffy color and looked even a little sporty, she liked it, she bought it and could talk almost anybody else into liking and buying it too. Who knows how many happy customers in Jersey Shore drove off our lot, only to wake the next morning wondering who on earth owned that turquoise Hudson convertible sitting in our driveway? (It also has something to do with why George Porter is sporting around town even today in a red Pontiac Trans Am.)

Temper? Well, hell yes she had a temper. Yes, she did break a china plate over my brother Dave's head, and yes she did break his door damn near off the hinges with her shoulder when he ran to his room after sassing her, but in my humble and objective opinion as the younger brother, he had it coming. Oh yeah, when we were teenagers, she'd find a novel way to wake us both rather abruptly in the middle of the night, with a good old fashioned leather belt strapping, but in that case, then I guess we both had it coming.

Shortcomings? Well, housekeeping wasn't exactly her forte. In fact, Mom was to housekeeping as Bill Clinton is to telling the truth. She knew it was there and that some people considered it important, but most of the time she managed to skirt the issue entirely. Her idea of household order seemed to range along the lines of theme piles. There was a pile of clean laundry in one corner, many piles of old shoes in many corners, stacks of old magazines and newspapers throughout the house, old clothes bulging out of every closet, and whenever a particular room got a little too full or too chaotic, she simply closed the door, and shifted the family living quarters to rooms with a little more open space. As we lived in the huge rambling structure now called Gamble Farm Inn, this was a very practical tactic. Talk about a mansion with many rooms. The problem was, sooner or later, most of the rooms, even in that big place, would fill, which was okay for the private viewing of just the family, but inevitably she would bring a housekeeping crisis upon herself by opening the place to the prying eyes of people with more conventional habits.

One such crisis occurred when she invited the Presbyterian women's group for evening tea. For days and weeks, she mentioned the coming event, promising that the Big Cleanup was coming. But still, the piles remained in all the usable areas, filling every corner and smothering every horizontal space. This was Mom's surefire way to work up the energy required for her traditional last-minute cleaning frenzy. Meanwhile, the men in the family, which included Dad, Uncle Frank, Dave, me and our younger brother Craig, had strict orders under pain of death not to disturb any of the piles unless directly supervised by her, and for God's sake, don't throw anything out! We laid low and awaited disaster. But on this occasion, Mom surprised us with a contingency plan. On D-Day, she brought in Betty Brower, a trusted friend who had already seen most of the mess anyway and was apparently beyond shock. Like men ordered out of a birthing room, we were shooed away while the women went to it. Time ticked by. Boxes and bags were filled, and some piles shrank a little bit, but as the clock ticked toward the witching hour, disaster loomed. Then, as always, Gladys found inspiration under fire. Rather than trying to remove all the stuff, she found that by simply shaping a pile of clutter into a rounded, symmetrical form, she could cover it with a bedspread and create something that looked a little like, well, bean bag furniture, covered in chenille. Anyway, the Presbyterian ladies arrived on time; of course, tea went smoothly, and amazingly, the occasion was deemed a success. Some even commented on the unusual lamp hanging over the dining room table, not seeming to realize they were admiring a floor lamp hung upside down and nailed to the ceiling. For months afterward, anyone who accidentally opened the wrong door or cupboard was hit with an avalanche that made Fibber McGee's closet look like kid stuff.

Dylan Thomas, in that great poem to his dying father, wrote:

Do not go gently into that good night;
Rage, rage against the dying of the light.

As her light gradually dimmed, Gladys Porter didn't rage. Ironically, as the disease took hold, much of her famous volatility mellowed into a nearly constant good humor, even as she struggled to stay alert and connected with people and everyday reality. Even then, some of the old caginess would shine through at odd moments, and real humor came out, just like the old times. One day I visited the nursing home, and as

I walked into her room, she immediately brightened, recognizing someone, but she wasn't quite sure who it was.

"Well," she accused. "Haven't seen you in a while." (Best defense is a good offense.)

"Okay," I said, rising to the challenge. "Do you know who I am?"

"Of course!" she shot back, offended.

"All right," I said, thinking I had her. "What's my name?"

"Why?" she demanded. "Don't you know?"

The nurse sitting behind her nearly fell out of the chair laughing.

Generosity of spirit. Many of you know, and may have personally experienced the generosity of her father, Prince Farrington, a bootlegger and an outlaw, but a great spirit with an enlarged heart, a very large heart, who, when the times were good shared himself and his money with anyone who needed a helping hand, whether they were poor kids during the depression who needed food at Christmas or a church that needed a new roof. He rarely expected to be repaid, and, it must be said, he was rarely disappointed in that regard.

His only daughter carried on that spirit in fine fashion, and her children are immensely proud of that fact. Just two simple examples. Twenty-four years ago, in 1976, I was working on a hotshot Bicentennial project that involved a grant application to a major national foundation. My associates and I had worked up what we thought was an awesome concept that certainly deserved funding from the foundation, and we wrote it up into many pages of handwritten material. Over the holidays in Jersey Shore, I searched for someone who could type this magnum opus into a presentable manuscript. The name of Eleanor Myers popped up, as she had recently retired as secretary to the high school principal. I remembered her immediately as the shy but very efficient guardian to Ira Grugan's inner sanctum during my high school days. I found her, she accepted the lengthy stack of notes, and called me later that day with the first draft. It was immaculate, but even with a few small corrections, in those days of typewriters and ribbons of permanent ink, the whole thing had to be done again, which she did, perfectly this time. Grateful and relieved that we could get the thing in on time and in such good shape, I took out my checkbook, and asked how much I owed. Ms. Myers folded the checkbook back in my hand, saying that she had been looking for a way to repay Gladys Porter for an act of kindness she had shown to her mother many years before. It seems Eleanor's elderly mother had a fainting spell in Beach's Restaurant, and was near collapse. Eleanor told me that of everyone in that busy restaurant, Gladys Porter was the one who offered help, took her to the hospital and saw to it she got the proper care until the family could arrive. Now years later, Eleanor was glad I had showed up out of nowhere and she made it quite plain that my money was no good in her house.

A second story, shorter but also involving Jersey Shore Hospital, where three of Gladys's four children were born, and one has died. Mom had one of her first serious Alzheimer's attacks when she attended my son Christopher's wedding in that hot summer of 1995. Not long after, we knew she needed special care, and admitted her to Manor Care's Arcadia unit. Now, the people who work there are very special, very professional and very caring, but still, the first months were hard as the family had more difficulty adjusting to the new situation than she did. One day, after failing to get a conversation going, I wandered from the nursing home into the hospital corridor, feeling frustrated and impatient with her. When I turned into the hospital lobby, and noticed some plaques on the wall placed there to honor people in the community who have given extraordinary service to Jersey Shore Hospital. One of them honors Dr. Robert Lauler, who helped found the hospital and who delivered Dave Porter and me. Another lists people who made outstanding contributions to the hospital's various fund drives in the 1950s and 1960s. There, listed among the major contributors is the name Gladys Porter. She is among the lifetime honorees, and it is not a long list. Now, most of you here today know that her financial fortunes were not always rosy, especially in recent years. But, the lesson that hit me that day is this: When she had, she gave and gave more than her share.

(I'd like to pause now and ask if anyone here has a memory or experience with Gladys to share with us. Come on now, you know she'd love to hear you tell it!)

So, Dr. Robert Porter concluded his funerary tribute to his mother, Gladys Julia Farrington Porter.

```
In the Court of Common Pleas of     Lycoming                      County

Mattie Jane Farrington          Of 188    December    Term, 1929.
also known as Martha J.
Farrington                      No. 188
        VERSUS
Prince D. Farrington                      DIVORCE
```

And now *May 5* 1930 The Court having heard this case, and having fully considered and proceeded to determine the same as to law and justice appertain, do sentence and decree, that Mattie Jane Farrington also known as Martha J. Farrington divorced and separated from the nuptial ties and bonds of matrimony heretofore contracted between her, the said Mattie Jane Farrington, also known as Martha J. Farrington alsohe libelant, and the said Prince D. Farrington respondent; and that thereupon all and every the duties, rights and claims accruing to either the said Mattie Jane Farrington, also known as Martha J. Farrington or the said Prince D. Farrington at any time heretofore in pursuance of said marriage, shall cease and determine, and the said Mattie Jane Farrington, also known as Martha J. Farrington and Prince D. Farrington shall severally be at liberty to marry again in like manner, as if they had never been married,

By the Court,
H. W. Whitehead
P.J.

Attest:
Theodore Beck
618                              Prothonotary.

*The divorce decree of May 5, 1930, Lycoming County, PA.*

*Prince and one of his oldest grandchildren, David Porter.*

*Prince in an informal shot, with his two oldest grandsons, David, standing, and Robert.*

*A hangdog demeanor of an oft-convicted and oft-jailed master moonshiner. Other pictures from his later years still show a very upbeat individual, despite the weight of justice and his badly-diminished health.*

*Friends and family party at the Gamble Farm Inn of George and Gladys Porter. Gladys is standing, third from right.*

# · 14 ·

# Days of Destitution

**FAILURE TO GO 'LEGIT'**

To become a legitimate, legally approved distiller, Prince Farrington would have had to create and offer bonded whiskey. That means that it was stored in a warehouse, where government agents watched it age for at least four years before being bottled. Needing such an arrangement in order to use his skills and to garner some income, a desperate Prince Farrington tried to 'go legit.'

Lock Haven was another major town in Prince Farrington's life. North of Lock Haven is the settlement (It hardly qualifies as a village.) of Farrandsville, clinging to the eastern bank of the Susquehanna River. Transportation-wise, the place is virtually at the end of the road. That is, the highway from Lock Haven northward ends at Farrandsville, with no improved road stretching beyond Farrandsville, in any direction. The visitor must normally turn about and drive south, again. The principal structure in Farrandsville is a picturesque, early iron furnace [color shot here]. However, on the road to Farrandsville; across the river from Lock Haven there was, in Farrington's day, the Lockport Brewery. The structure still stands, a silent monument to the day when many small breweries dotted the landscape.

Prince Farrington considered buying the Lockport Brewery in his later years. Family members say that the government required Farrington to submit his whiskey-distilling 'recipe,' which he refused to divulge to anyone, not even a government agency that seemed to hold all the cards. He is said to have made a move toward getting a New England brewery as well; but that, too, failed to materialize.

## CINCO DE MAYO

The marriage of Prince and Martha White Farrington was shaky from its earliest days. Still, no one seemed to anticipate its conclusion. In fact, and truly bizarre, years passed before many in the immediate family learned of the huge step that Mattie took way back in 1929. In December of that year, Martha filed for divorce in Williamsport, the county seat of Lycoming County, Pennsylvania. Prince was not present to contest the procedure. Mattie stated that Prince was often drunk and that he beat her roughly weekly. On May 5, 1930, the divorce was granted. The empowering document, number 188 of December 1929, gave her name as Mattie Jane Farrington, also known as Martha J. Farrington. The marriage of the philandering moonshiner and his southern belle was terminated.

Their divorce was more bizarre than their marriage had been. Their relationship, prior to 1929, suggested that the two warring partners weren't married; but they were. Their relationship after divorce suggested that they weren't divorced; but they were. Many in the family didn't realize, for years, that a legal break had occurred. The full split in their relationship never followed. After their divorce, most of their deeds, and other legal documents still listed them as husband and wife. While one document (a deed dated at 1931) exists that identifies Prince as being "single," most (if not all) later documents, including deeds and FBI records, still listed them as being married. Even the FBI, with its great investigative resources was, during its last pursuit of Prince, listing them as being married. Their relationship, ever strained and stormy, continued for the rest of Prince's life. The divorce was so universally *unnoticed* that Dave Porter, the oldest grandson of Prince and Mattie, was unaware that his grandparents were divorced..until he was a college student. Even their obituaries and gravestones didn't recognize the divorce. When, fourteen years after Prince's death, Mattie died, the family had no qualms about placing her remains beside that of the man from whom she asked the court to separate her way back in the winter of '29.

## DAYS OF DESTITUTION

Although there is no data to support the claim, Gladys identified the number of Prince's fortunes (made and lost) as being four. But, his daughter admitted he died broke. His pathetic efforts to try to gather a few outstanding dollars support this. The once-rich moonshiner found his declining years to be mired in poverty. Prince would write letters to people whom he hoped, usually in vain, would return something on his earlier investment of generosity. The old days of making whiskey for 50 cents a gallon and selling it for $10 a gallon were gone. That was during the heady days when he could make liquor in huge quantities and sell it in bulk quantities as well. Now, his grandson, Dave, remembers traveling with Prince in a truck to deliver small quantities of the once-popular Farrington whiskey to customers in Lock Haven. The once gushing stream of currency had become a mere trickle.

While still in Florida, he, too, wrote to Gladys for financial support. Here, with a few question marks for uncertain words or passages, are three letters, all of which seem to have come from Florida, while he was incarcerated there; prior to his being transferred to the federal medical facility in Springfield, Missouri.

The reader will be able to make several observations by reading these letters. Among them:

- Prince Farrington bordered on illiteracy, yet without these letters, we'd be denied a significant and touching part of the man's life.
- Prince's warmth and humor manifested themselves in his letters.
- He was a doting grandfather.
- He was a loving brother who joked with his nearest sibling, brother Charles.
- Prince had been badly damaged by years of alcohol abuse, but he expressed satisfaction that two of his sons may have stopped using it.
- In all three letters, he suggested ways that Gladys could collect some money on his behalf, and he expressed some anxiety about getting some money.
- A specific need was addressed when he wrote of getting his teeth fixed when money became available. The reader may recall, from Chapter 6, that Prince Farrington's unorthodox program of oral hygiene was praised by others. Different parties recalled the beauty of his teeth in his earlier years. As alcohol had taken its toll on Prince's once-husky physique, *time* had taken a toll on his teeth.

From a 1951 letter:

*April 6th*

*My dearest Daughter*

*I am O K and hoping all is well in Pa I hope you and Hazel got home O K I hope George and the Boys were O K when you got home. Kis the boys for me ??? ??? to. You seemed to be worrying about them letters and papers you and Hazel brought down*[39] *after I look them over I relized it sure took some work to get them I didn't think they was that many People that knew me from what I can hear they must have saved me about 2 years. I don t know just when I will leave here not before next week. if you see Charlie tell him I am O.K. Not to worry about me. for when I get out I will worry him enough. There was a man In Wilimsp. by the name of Frank Hammer [t]hey called him Mo Hammer he had a marble yard at Pen st between third St and the river*[40] *I am ritind Hazel a line or to*

*(Over)*

*I don t think it is there now He had a little Printin ofice there. he owes me $120 Some time when you are down there look him up if he is still living he will pay you. You can see if you can get up the money to pay my fine other people that owes me an will that will help will be graitly apricated Gayle told me what you had for me You cant imagine how much I aprechate that and what you have done. about the fine it don t have to be paid untill I get out but I think it would be a good ida to work on this now. Gayle and Whity was here yesterday They are coming back Sunday I will [write?] when I get settled down. I don't think I will be able to write while I am in quartine. 30 days I hope you cnd [can?] make a success in your business You know how hard it is to get a start once you are down and out*

---

39. This passage identifies Hazel, who was Gladys's aunt on her mother's side. It also refers to the petitions and testimonials that Gladys circulated and collected. As mentioned, elsewhere, they did not sway the judge into releasing Prince Farrington; but his letter suggests that it may have resulted in a shorter sentence.

40. The next eight words are written upwards along the margin of the first page.

The preceding is Prince's letter in its entirety unless there is a lost page or two. There is no signature. The following week, he was again writing and, again, repeating a request for money. That letter follows:

April 15, 51 Sunday

*Dear daughter and Famley*

*I got your letter sure was glad to hear from you and George and the boys Tell Dave and boby i am glad they are so good to little Cragie Gayle and Merim and Jake was her Just left Whity did not come He had to work today I think I will go to a Hospital before long*

   *You ask me if I was glad I had the trial moved down here and pleaded Guilty I know I could have done better up there I plead Guilty to a lot I was not guilty of they mis led me in to pleading Guilty If I had it to do over I wouldn't plead Guilty if I knowed they would hang me if the Jury found me Guilty when I get able to think clear I am going to find out If there cant be something done. Say Colonel Segraves owes me some money He has owed me since and and ??? Did business togather you said something about sending me money I will need some about getting teeth fixed but Gayle is going to sell my car and (over and some other little things I have and Whiey owes me some I going to try to get enought out of that to spend for what I want. Say why did you and Hazel leave Scotte at home when you come down I bet he put some cussing in it. I got a letter from Hazel Yesterday She said that her and Scotte took you home. I have to ans. her letter She didnt have much news. I don t have any news I will write again before I leave here. if I Know when I am going to leave. I don t Just when.*

   *tell the boys to be good I know they will I allways said they were the best boys. I ever seen. I still say so I sure would like to see them and be with them*

   *Closing with Love*
   *to all*
   *ans. soon*
   *Dad*

*Dear daughter and famley*
*I am still at Orlando dont know when I will get away from here. Gayle and Mom and Whity and their ??? were to see me yesterday Gayle bought me a pair of ??? socks I was glad to get them. I sure would like to see them boys Robin shur did give me a good huging and kisses he sure is a cute little fellow. The first time you go to Lock Haven go to see Joe Gardner and tell him if I could get some money I could get out in a few months he owes me $400 tell him to get me $500. If you could get to Rube Bressler he would get us some for me he was running the Wheel Club at Canton Pa the last time I seen him M??? could tell you where he is now. Don t make any special trip but if you ever get up there stop and see him. See ????? i think he would help me. They had a boy in here from ??? falls Pa they called him Whitey. he looked like my Whitey and acted like him they give him one year on the Chane gang he must not have liked it he didn't stay with them but one day. He turned the ??? ??? tell George and Davie and baby and Cragie to be good boys*

*(over)*

*and I will [give] them candy when I come to Pa. I dont have much news as I dont go out much to gather any news I will rite you again in a few days if I dont leave here. If I do will rite you as soon as I can. I dont want any of you kids to worry about I sure am glad Gayle and Whitey has cut out their drinking You can rite Gayle and he can give it to me if I am still here I may be here for a week yet and I may go away anytime have you herd any thing from Hazel Since you got home I rote her a letter but I thought I was going a way be for now*

*You see Charlie Not to worry a bout me that I am living the life of Riley dont have any body to [get] mad at me Still I get something to eat Ask him how much antie freeze it took to keep him from freezing last winter tell Robert if he could send me what he owes me I need it to get my teeth fixed. if I can get my teeth and feet fixed up. I will be a young man a gain I am not going to get old while I down here I am going to grow young I cant afored to grow old yet. I will close with Love to all*

*Dad*

## HE, OF THE ALABASTER TEETH

Should one's teeth become the stuff of legends? Should the beauty of his teeth become part of the mythology of Prince Farrington? We see the subject discussed in Parker's article, which seems to have been nourished by discussions with Prince's daughter, Gladys Porter. Others added different facets to the gem.

Without exaggeration, one can claim that Prince Farrington was a man with a regal smile. One can read the claims of others or simply look at the portraits of the smiling moonshiner. Also, sometime between the age of dinosaurs and the present, there was apparently an age where men proclaimed their admiration for other men's pretty teeth. As Parker relates, there was a time when a very portly neighbor fellow admired Prince's radiant teeth. Reportedly, Prince replied, "You fat son-of-a-bitch, if you'd missed as many meals as I have, you'd have beautiful teeth, too."

Prince's grandson, Dave Porter, remarked, "I think that he only had one cavity in his whole life. He died with a beautiful set of teeth. But, they didn't have candy back then."

Some writers and speakers have had much to say about Farrington's unusual approach to his own dental hygiene. As with many aspects of his life, the care he gave to his teeth was unconventional. Actually, different sources suggest that Prince had different approaches to dental hygiene. Grandson, Bob Porter related that his grandfather, Prince, used a pocket knife and Ajax cleanser for cleaning his teeth. Another source (Parker), tells of Farrington carrying a small pine stick, whittled into a blade-like shape. This self-made tool was used for scraping tartar from teeth that Parker speaks of as being "perfect in formation and white as alabaster."

Now, the reader can draw his/her conclusions regarding the moonshiner's teeth by revisiting the two quotes from his writings. In the first of the two letters quoted directly above, Prince Farrington lamented, "Say Colonel Segraves owes me some money—I will need some about getting teeth fixed." In the second letter, Prince again lamented: "Tell Robert if he could send me what he owes me. I need it to get my teeth fixed. If I can get my teeth and feet fixed up. I will be a young man again."

There was another quote from that last letter that we can use to introduce one of the two health problems that were slowly consuming Prince Farrington. Alcoholism and diabetes were the two circling vultures that were now waiting for his carcass. He was obviously aware of the toll taken by his long years of dependence on strong drink. Thus, the concern he expressed for his sons. "I sure am glad Gayle and Whitey has cut out their drinking."

## SEIGE

René Theophilé Hyacinthe Laënnec (1781–1826) was a celebrated French physician. He invented the stethoscope, and his name has been attached to Laënnec's pearls (a specific type of sputum), Laënnec's catarrh, and the illness that applied to the aging Prince Farrington: Laënnec's disease. Laennec's disease identifies the type liver pathology connected to alcoholism.

When Prince Farrington had been apprehended in Florida in 1951, he was already suffering from most of the ailments that would accompany him through the last half-dozen years of his life. At that time, he was crippled by diabetes and arthritis. Both feet were being eaten by gangrene and some toes had been amputated. He was barely able to walk. George Mayes, a long-time acquaintance from Antes Fort, was working as a butcher in Thompson's Meat Market in Jersey Shore, when Prince made one of his last visits to the store. Mayes said that the employees heard a car horn tooting. Mayes was among those who walked outside to see who was summoning them. It was Prince Farrington, who was ordering from his car. Prince's feet were so gangrenous that, says Mayes, "they really stunk. It's a wonder the buzzards didn't fly around them!"

His ailments in early 1956 would have included gangrene, plus diabetes, heart disease and—almost as a given—the malfunctioning, alcohol-damaged liver: Laennec's disease. The symptoms of cirrhosis are the hardening of the liver, with accompanying pain and abdominal bulging, and the jaundice that gives the entire pathology its name, cirrhosis (yellow-orange). Despite that lengthy list of ailments, he still faced one more demon: A ruptured esophagus.

When he was admitted to Williamsport Hospital on June 2, 1956, his condition was already beyond help. The attending physician, Dr. A. M. Cook, noted that Prince's social history indicated that he "Drinks heavily." Still, when grandson, David Porter, then a teenager, visited him, Prince asked David how his Studebaker automobile was working. David, the eldest grandson, and the one who is considered to have most strongly resembled his grandfather, was proud of his two-door, black, six-cylinder—with overdrive. He told his grandfather that his car was operating nicely. Prince then mused, "Then, when I'm out of here, you can take me to see some of my old friends." David readily agreed to do "Paw Paw" that favor. However, within days, Prince David Farrington, too ill for release, died in the medical facility where, years before, his moonshine had sometimes been tested for quality.

Just how wracked with disease can a body become in six and one-half decades, most of which were spent in hard drinking? As his grandson, Dave Porter, remembers, Prince had truly curbed his thirst for whiskey in his enfeebled last years. While Prince David Farrington's moonshine was regarded as being of superior quality, one must remember: The quality of whiskey is not judged by its therapeutic effect on the drinker's body.

The cumulative result of all the drinking that Prince Farrington did with brother Charl, with friendly lawmen, and with untold acquaintances can be recognized by looking at a few of the most serious results listed above the signature of Dr. Merl Colvin, the pathologist who signed the autopsy report (6/14/56). Which system wasn't damaged by decades of decadence? For the heart: *myocardial hypertrophy*. Respiratory system: *Bilateral pulmonary edema*; Gastro-intestinal system: *Esophageal varices, marked*. Genito-urinary system: *Adenocarcinoma of the prostate, grade II*. Endocrine system: *Hyperplasia of the adrenal cortex*. Spleen: *Marked long-standing passive congestion of spleen*. Pancreas: *Diffuse pancreatic fibrosis*. Liver: *Advanced portal cirrhosis and malignant hepatoma*.

His death certificate, signed by his daughter Gladys, listed the cause of death as "Primary Carcinoma of Liver" due to "Portal cirrhosis" and "Malnutrition." In this document, Gladys informed the world of her father's livelihood. She listed his occupation as *farmer*.

*Grave stones of Martha and Prince Farrington.*

*Miller Stamm, Loganton centenarian, remembers much.*

*Burnett's Chapel and graveyard, south of Greensboro, NC.*

*Hoop and sunken spot in wooded area around Buck's Gap, near Carroll (Clinton County) indicate location of a one-buried barrel of moonshine.*

*A Prince Farrington personal still, now owned and displayed by the Clinton County Historical Society in Lock Haven, PA.*

## · 15 ·

# A Roadshow of Relics

**THE HOME ON SILVER AVENUE**
Those who appreciate local lore must be especially grateful to those owners of history-rich houses or estates who dedicate the time and finances to the restoration of their properties. This was mentioned in Chapters 6 and 7 regarding the Stewart-Courtright property that sits along the Susquehanna River near Antes Fort. That majestic home was once the centerpiece of a 19th-century estate, where it served as a farmhouse and a refuge for runaway slaves. Under the ownership of Prince Farrington, the building shared family quarters with distilling equipment and, at one time, a speakeasy. That historic homestead is now being restored to an earlier majesty by its present owners, Pat and Phil Courtright.

Similarly, a magnificent property sits on Silver Avenue in the village of Lamar, near the interchange of mile 173 on Interstate 80. This stately three-story home was built in 1895 by James A. Wolfenden, a native of England. Wolfenden was an engineer who was employed in Pittsburgh. He hobnobbed with Henry Ford and contributed to the design of Ford's first automobile. Wolfenden also flew the American Flag; although on one day each year, the queen's birthday, he flew the British "Union Jack." Several decades after its construction, the grand home on Silver Avenue was considered as a possible Pennsylvania governors' mansion. Wolfenden pushed that proposal; but his political influence couldn't outweigh the distance from Harrisburg. When Prince Farrington lived near Loganton, he lived about 12 miles due east of Lamar. When Prince wanted his brother, Charles's, support in his moonshining/bootlegging enterprises, the house was a convincing part of the package. The home's four previous owners couldn't have envisioned the wildly new role that the house would play.

Charles (Charl) and his wife, Virginia (Virgie) lived in the three-story home for the remainder of their lives. The Silver Avenue mansion saw distilling in the basement and beneath the foundation of the nearby chicken house. It saw Charles and his brother, Prince Farrington, sitting on the back stoop and downing whiskey together. It saw black-suited agents raiding and moving through the house like ants through a cupboard. It saw arrests of its patriarch as well as its matriarch. It saw children, grandchildren and other relatives and friends celebrating life with music and moonshine. Then, within one year, 1971, it saw the passing of Virgie and Charl and the passing of the colorful role it had experienced for several decades. Silver Avenue returned to its former tree-shaded solitude.

The fact that the home was part of Prince and Charl Farrington's life, made everyone suspect that the mansion had hidden passages or false storage spaces for concealing booze. There were small closets; but they didn't conceal anything. The Victorian house on Silver Avenue was without any mysterious spaces. Even after the present owners, Nell and Tom Muir, moved into the property, no such hiding place was found. The Muirs did see a suspicious area in their house. Beneath one first-floor stairwell, was a closed space; but neither the steps, nor the wall opposite the steps, showed any way whatever to access the space beneath the stairs. However, after several years, the Muirs had some work done in the basement. The contractor noticed a small latch among the beams of the ceiling of the cellar. There it was! Unnoticed by everyone before, the contractor had found a well-disguised trapdoor that opened into the *bottom* of the space beneath the first-floor stairs. There, undiscovered for many years, was an authentic, secret storage area.

The bustling nature of Charl Farrington's Silver Avenue home was related before (*see* Chapter 8). However, one gentleman who was a teen in Charl's heyday, Walter Overdorf, experienced his own Lamar episode. It was about 1943, just a year or two before Walt entered military service. It seems that Walt was sitting on the front steps of Cora Overdorf, his grandmother's house. This was in Booneville, in Sugar Valley, on a late Saturday afternoon. Bill Schrack and his cousin, Glenn Smith, drove up, stopped and asked Walt if he wanted to go along. He did. They didn't tell him of any particular destination. Glenn Bierly happened to be walking along the road at Booneville, so they stopped and picked up Bierly, too.

Walt still had no idea where they were going; but it was Saturday evening in rural Clinton County and he was riding with friends. That was all one needed to know.

The four teens drove west through Tylersville, out of Sugar Valley and into the Fishing Creek Narrows. Just beyond the "Narrows" they entered the town of Lamar. The driver knew his destination. They were going down Silver Avenue to a Saturday night gathering at Charl Farrington's place. When they arrived, there were cars parked "all around the place."

As they walked onto the porch, Walt could see a huge juke box sitting inside and "blaring loudly." Suddenly, as Walt and his friends were trying to enter the house, everyone inside began shoving and pushing to get out! Police were rushing to join the party through the back door! Some escaping carouser grabbed Walt by the pants seat and his neck and tossed him over the porch bannister and into the bushes. Walt hid there momentarily before he and his three companions were able to leave without being stopped. That was Walt Overdorf's first, and last, visit to the house on Silver Avenue.

Several years later, after Walt was out of the military service, he and Nelson Wolfe were riding Wolfe's new, large, black 74 Harley-Davidson motorcycle with overhead valves. The cycle was supposed to be able to reach a speed of 120 mph; but Walt says he only ever saw it hovering around 110 when he peeked over Wolfe's shoulder! They stopped at the Nittany Inn near Lamar. There was only a bartender and one other patron. They asked for drinks; but the bartender refused. When they asked again, the lone customer growled, "Give the boys a goddam drink!" So they were served. Their patron? A customer who was so faithful that he had his own bottle opener at the Nittany Inn: Charl Farrington.

## ANOTHER FLASK

*Distinguished.* That is the most appropriate word for one whose life had accomplishments piled one upon another. If you want to be convinced that the word is properly used here, look at the record of a Lycoming County native and lifelong resident, Dean R. Fisher (1924-2000). Fisher graduated from Jersey Shore High School and was in college when World War II erupted. He abandoned his studies in order to enlist in the U.S. Navy. He left service as an Ensign and later resigned his commission with the rank of Lieutenant, j.g. Fisher returned to school, enrolling at Muhlenberg College. He then got a law degree from the University of Pennsylvania. He was associated with many area fraternal and professional organizations for the coming decades, always demonstrating leadership and innovative skills. Dean R. Fisher's intellect, energy and humanity were shared with his wife and two children as well as the community.

One of Dean Fisher's public roles was as a member of the Pennsylvania Liquor Control Board. It was in that position that he received a gift of one of the few surviving bottles of Prince Farrington liquor. That relic was passed to his daughter, Kim, who provided pictures of that rare bottle of Farrington moonshine, for this biography of the king of moonshiners. A close look at the label indicates that one is reading the confiscation data for a bottle taken in 1948. The label also indicates that the bottle contains one pint of "moonshine" and it bears the name of Prince Farrington, apparently written on the label by a policing agent. Another bit of data: his flask is now a prized memento of Fisher's daughter, Kim VanCampen of Williamsport.

**MEMORABLE GLASSES**
In the early 1940s, Prince urged Earl Ritter to buy the Brown's Run flats, a property that was priced at $2,000. This land, coveted by Prince Farrington if someone else held title to it, was located in the remote Pine Creek valley, just south of Jersey Mills and close to where Route 44 and Route 414 split. Why would the moonshiner encourage a friend to buy this somewhat isolated real estate? Because Prince already had a still operating there and, if the property was owned by someone other than Prince, himself, it might avoid government scrutiny. However, Earl Ritter made an independent decision, since he wanted to own a different property, a farm owned by the Campbell brothers. The farm that Ritter actually acquired was located in the same general area, between Jersey Mills and Cammal. Also, although the farm had 546 acres, the asking price was a more modest $750. The still identified here by David Ritter will be more precisely pinpointed in Chapter 11.

While still a pre-teen, David Ritter would accompany his father on visits to the *Gamble Farm Inn* or *Antiques Inn*. This was while Prince Farrington was staying there. Later, David Ritter graduated in the same

Jersey Shore high school class as Prince's grandson, Craig Porter. Shortly after their graduation, Craig was killed in an auto accident (*see* Chapter 14). Ritter notes that Gladys tried to restore an antique atmosphere at the Inn, but, he observes, as time passed, things got broken or stolen. Gladys, who remembered the friendship of Earl Ritter and her dad, called Earl's son, David, and asked him to visit. That's when she gave him some of the remaining glasses used at the inn, the very glasses that once held drinks that were consumed in friendship by Earl and Prince.

## EARL'S PRIDE AND JOY

Another relic worth showing is the 1929 Nash that belonged to Earl W. "Skinny" Ritter, another close friend of Prince Farrington. Ritter, mentioned in the previous article, eventually spent about four decades working for the Pennsylvania Power and Light Company. Ritter was a foreman at the P.P. & L. Jersey Shore substation and had supervisory duties over an area from the eastern edge of Lock Haven southeast to the area around Oriole. Ritter also declared that his '29 Nash automobile was the first car *ever* to climb up and over the Elimsport mountain in high gear!

## A GENTLEMAN'S WALKING STICK.

The ancient Greeks had a riddle. What walks on four legs, then on two legs and, finally, on three legs? The nice thing about ancient riddles: Countless individuals have learned the answer. Who is unaware of the answer to this one? The answer is: *a human*. He, or she, crawls on all four limbs during infancy; walks upright and on two legs throughout childhood and most of adulthood; and finally, with debilitating age, walks with the support of a cane. At some point in his life, Prince Farrington carried a man's walking stick. The *walking stick* of the time was *not* meant to support the weight of an invalid; but was a fancy, *straight* stick to be used as part of a dapper wardrobe. This would have been before his worsening gangrene and the loss of several toes would have made a more substantial support vital to Prince's painful mobility. Also, among Farrington's several chauffeurs was one named Leroy Ruch of Duboistown. Ruch, was the eventual recipient of a gift from Prince: a walking stick. Ruch later worked until his retirement, for the Pennsylvania Power and Light Company. For years, Leroy Ruch and his wife, Mae, were close friends of another area couple, Dorothy and Howard Thomas. Ruch later gave the walking stick to Howard. Recently, Howard's widow, the lively-96-year old Dorothy Thomas, donated Prince Farrington's fancy walking stick to a local institution. Thus, through a nonagenarian's generosity, the walking stick that was once Prince Farrington's, is now a part of the museum treasures of the Thomas T. Tabor Museum in Williamsport, Pennsylvania.

## A RESET GEM AND AN EMPTY RING

As a young man, Floyd Klobe, the moonshiner from rural Greene Township in Clinton County, Pennsylvania, worked for a New York City jeweler. A token of the jeweler's appreciation was the gift of a man's diamond ring, with a sizable stone. That 1927 night that Floyd Klobe was fighting with Louis Huntingdon, Klobe wore the ring. The condition of Huntingdon's face suggested that Klobe had made serious contact several times. He never wore the ring after that fateful night.

After Floyd's death, his daughter, Ethel, had the stone removed and reset into another diamond ring, resting between two smaller stones. This Ethel had done for herself. After her own death, both the diamond ring and the gem-less original became prized possessions of Floyd's granddaughter, Beulah.

## KEG HOOPS FROM A FARRINGTON STILL SITE

Likely, the most common Prince Farrington artifact that one might find today is the metal hoop from the long-abandoned barrels or kegs. About the year 2001, the author was introduced to one of the many Farrington still sites by Yvonne and Steve Weaver of Loganton. The site is on the Florida Fruit Farm and was visited by leaving the rural road on the farm and following a small stream upwards through a wooded slope. There, at the rivulet's source, was a small collecting pond, apparently constructed in Prince's early years in Pennsylvania, to create a more reliable water supply. One could see, nearby, some broken bricks, hoops and other detritus from a nearly century-old still. The author retrieved a pair of small rusting hoops 10½ and 12½ inches in diameter, the continued ownership of which was cleared through the courtesy of Bud Webb, the present owner of the legendary farm.

## A BOTTLE-CAPPING DEVICE

As mentioned in Chapter 16, the Gamble Farm Inn, in Jersey Shore, possesses an authentic bottle-capping device once owned by Prince Farringon.

## KLOBE'S RECIPE BOOKLET

There is a small booklet that is a mere twenty pages (ten folded sheets) and that measures about 3½ by 6 inches. A granddaughter absolutely identifies it as having belonged to Floyd Klobe. It was valuable enough to some in the Klobe family that it was passed through several generations and, when it began to fall apart, some concerned member of the family took what appears to have been black upholstery thread and crudely, but effectively, sewed the pages together. This booklet is a machine-printed document, filled with the recipes needed to create many types of liquor. The front cover is plain and sports a title, all in caps: HOW TO MAKE IT. Also on the cover, in smaller letters but still upper case: CANADIAN PUBLISHING CO. Adding to the mystery are the words of the very bottom two lines. They say: Office 2356 Washington Ave., Philadelphia Penna. The four-digit street number is not quite clear; and is assumed to be the number given.

Why was the Canadian Publishing Co. publishing a booklet in Philadelphia? We have no answer. One guess is that this was printed either just before Prohibition or shortly thereafter, since it openly identifies itself and its address. However, this may not be true. The entire cover could have been a fraud. All we know, with certainty, is that the interior pages are crammed with some precautionary advice for using the recipes and with the recipes themselves. The list, with original spellings: Whiskey Egg Nogg; Wine Lemonade; Auto Cocktail; Bourbon; Corn Whiskey; Scotch; Cognac Brandy; Raisin Brandy; Slivovitz (a prune and brown sugar concoction); Rye Whiskey with Malt Flavor; Malt Whiskey from Ground Malt; Malt Whiskey from Whole Barley Malt; Home Made Lager; Wild Cherry Wine; Elderberry Wine; Raisin Wine; Plain Alcohol; Dandelion Wine; Kimmel; Whole Rye Whiskey; Whiskey from Ground Rye; Sprouted Rye Whiskey; Fruit Mashes; Apricot Brandy; Apple Jack; Red Beet Wine; California Port Wine from Grape Juice; Apricot Wine;

Dream (lemon juice with gin flavor, etc.); Brandy Julep; Elks' Delight; Grape Wine; Blackberry and Huckleberry Wine; Blackberry Cordial; Gin; Gordon Gin; Rum; Beauty Cocktail; Beauty Spot Cocktail and Bird Cocktail. The back cover helpfully explains how one can convert many of these recipes into barrel lots. At the right time and the right place, such a booklet could have given someone a lucrative vocation.

One drink listed in that old booklet was a puzzler. What is *kimmel?* Dictionaries were consulted, including *The Oxford Universal Dictionary*—a word authority that lists hundreds of obsolete words. Internet searches were similarly fruitless. Finally, some sleuthing by staff members of the Bloomsburg (PA) Field Office of the Penn State Extension program yielded an answer: *Kimmel* is a Yiddish term, based on a German word. It indicates that the drink had a caraway source.

## THE MILLHEIM STEAM BOILER

Two of the Klobe stills, a large one and a miniature model, remain as treasured family relics. The larger of the two has been moved twice since Floyd Klobe's death. That still was once used by the Klobe family patriarch, Herman, and his son, Floyd. While it was still making moonshine for him, Floyd moved the still from place to place near his Sugar Valley home. When Floyd Klobe died, his granddaughter, Beulah Quiggle Neff (widow of the late Robert Neff) and her son, Steve Neff, removed the still from its last Sugar Valley hiding place, beneath the floor of a shed. Beulah and Steve loaded the copper boiler and its several attachments onto the back of an old Ford pickup truck and took it to the Neff property in the town of Howard (Centre County). Since Beulah was always nervous about having the still nearby and fearful that the years might not stop revenuers from appearing, the still was kept hidden, even in Howard. Today, Steve, great grandson and great-great grandson of moonshiners, operates a funeral home in Howard and in Millheim and he has moved the still to a garage near his business in Millheim (also Centre County). Today, the many descendants of the moonshiners/bootleggers of Clinton and Lycoming counties can enjoy discussing the ghosts that still linger in their family closets. We all benefit from their willingness to share that colorful past.

## · 16 ·

# The Legend Aborning

The Ballad of Prince Farrington
~ 1889—1956 ~

Old Carolina's native son:
Prince Farrington, Prince Farrington.
A lad of sixteen tender years,
When taken from his youthful peers
And placed within a Dixie cell.
Crime gripped him in its lifelong spell.
Soon, Pennsylvania's wooded hills
Were hiding his illegal stills.

From Loganton to Antes Fort
And on the Pike to Coudersport;
On hilltop or in swampy sink,
Prince cooked a very potent drink.
For grain, he paid inflated rates
And helped all those in troubled straits.
He bought protection from the law,
So raids were few—the ones he saw.

Prince spent his years at moonshine's pail,
Ignoring whiskey's deadly trail.
Drink killed one brother, very young,
Whose ode to life was never sung.
Another brother, daily drunk.
Spouse Martha, often in a funk.

> His world left many folks with scars;
> His world . . . of barrels, kegs and jars.
>
> Bizarre's the tale I'm telling you;
> Yet, all I've told you here is true.
> His ling'ring legend has begun.
> Prince Farrington, Prince Farrington!

More than a half-century after Prince Farrington's death, his legend is vibrant. This might be attributed to two principal factors. The first is Prince's very colorful life, which is easy to discuss repeatedly and pleasantly. The second is America's seemingly irrational love of alcohol, as demonstrated by songs, television shows and the many negative alcohol-related statistics with which we are confronted. An article in the *Centre Daily Times* (May 23, 2002) told of the newly discovered still in a Philadelphia garage. Similar news items elsewhere remind us that even moonshining is not a lost art.

What are the dynamics that demonstrate the legendary status of Prince David Farrington? They are numerous, with many matching a common pattern, leaving little doubt that Prince Farrington is an authentic legend. The proper question might be: With Time's falling sands, will the legend of Prince Farrington whither or expand?

## A KEGFUL OF QUOTES

Any legend will benefit from someone like Parson Weems. Mason Locke Weems, you may recall, was the early (1800) biographer of George Washington. The later editions of Weems's work carried the charming story of a youthful George, taking his ax to one of his father's prized plantings, a cherry tree. When Washington was confronted by his angry father, wrote Weems, George admitted, "I can't tell a lie, pa—I did cut it with my hatchet." Parson Weems, however, did know how to tell a lie! His cherry tree story—the tale that launched a flotilla of annual February ad campaigns—was fabricated. Similarly, Ned Buntline's pen created the wildly exaggerated adventures of William Cody. Although the adventures occurred only within the Buntline imagination, Cody was able to build on the fabricated feats in order to become the fabled showman, "Buffalo Bill."

Thanks to a handful of speakers and writers, there are now exaggerations that may forever be attached to Prince David Farrington. We find quotes relating to Farrington that lacerate logic and skew the historical record. Such claims tell us that Prince Farrington:

- "is said to have employed nearly every farmer within a fifty-mile radius of Williamsport." [from Connor].
- "told Al Capone to 'Go to Hell!'" (Parker, p. 82)[41]
- had, "in all probability, the best whiskey in the world." [Byington. See the bibliography.]
- had a delivery system that put his moonshine "all over the eastern half of this country." (mongopawn44@hotmail.com)
- had a distilled product that "rips the top off your skull and burns stars into your eyeballs." [Ibid.]
- had a product so superb that it "leaves the Devil himself begging to let go of your soul." [Ibid.]
- "Spent the remaining eight years with his daughter . . ."[42] Actually, Prince was released from the federal prison in Springfield, Missouri, in June of 1952, and he died just four years later, in June of 1956.
- "Moonshining was the only way he knew how to make a living." [Teeples, storytrax, op. cit.] There is ample refutation for that claim. It seems quite likely that, if Prince had devoted the time to farming that he had invested in moonshining, he would have been occupationally and financially successful. Prince was raised on a farm and surely learned the dynamics of agriculture. Douglas Clyde Parker stated flatly that "this man knew his farming." William Rombach (p. 9) adds his own observation, "He knew a good deal about farming and was moderately successful." Also, the members of several classes from Penn State University ("The Nittany Lions") visited Farrington's farm to study his exemplary farming methods. Lastly, remember that Bill Gheen—Farrington's predecessor on the same old farm as the one that was twice raided—was thought to have been the area's first millionaire.

---

41. The background and full quote by Gladys Farrington Porter, is given below, under the heading of Rubbing Elbows with the Eminent.
42. Teeples, www.storytrax.com/node/186, "Moonshine," 11/10/06.

- Prince was "almost always a few steps ahead of the feds." [Douglas Clyde Parker] Prince showed no magic formula for avoiding raids and arrests by federal agents or local authorities. As suggested elsewhere, more of Prince Farrington's success came from the proliferation of hidden stills and stores than from any craftiness or bribery efforts. We might remind ourselves that he even had overlapping legal problems in both North Carolina and Pennsylvania during the early 1920s. One cannot be "almost always a few steps ahead . . ." and still garner more than a dozen arrest warrants.
- "The Prince himself, of course, didn't drink." [Paul B. Beers]

This legend-building claim was absurd! In fact, several incidents of a tipsy Prince have already been cited in these pages. We also have these examples:

- Byron Brooks told of his father, Ernest Brooks, being summoned to help a driver who got his truck stuck in a ditch near the cemetery at the top of the hill in Jersey Shore. Ernest Brooks, who worked for decades in the River Front Chevrolet garage on Main Street, got behind the wheel and maneuvered the truck back onto solid ground. Why couldn't that experienced driver have avoided the problem or maneuvered his own truck to freedom from the ditch? Because he was too intoxicated. Who was this besotted driver? Prince Farrington.
- Leo "Chip" Taylor, Tammy Farrington and Emily Farrington Packer are among the many who are on record as having seen Prince Farrington enjoying his own product.
- Lester Seidel, whose family lived near the Florida Fruit Farm of Prince Farrington, had a somewhat limited time in which to observe Prince before Prince moved away from that farm and north to the area of Jersey Shore and Antes Fort. Seidel's recollection, recorded in 1983, was as follows: "If he wanted a drink of whiskey—he wouldn't very often drink whiskey just so. He'd most generally—well, I didn't check there at the house, so I didn't see it, but when he was out there at the still or out here at the barn, we always had a little creek running down

through. That's spring water, you know. There'd be a jug that had buttermilk in there. And Prince would take a big dried-beef glass. They'd hold about a pint and a half. You used to get them that way. And he'd fill that about half full of whiskey and fill it up with buttermilk. Like I say, I never seen him drink just plain whiskey. I never seen Prince that you could say that you thought he was even drunk or drinking." (Seidel interview)

- Other examples: Different family members recounted the story of Prince and his brother, both intoxicated, taking each other home because each considered the other to be too plastered to drive. His son, Whitey, as mentioned elsewhere, told of Prince returning from hunting and having his hunting buddies join him for a drink. And again, we are reminded that shortly after Prohibition ended, Prince was charged with drunken driving. We also have his wife's uncontested divorce suit, which declared that Prince was often drunk.

Hyperbole is not history. The historical aspects of one's life shouldn't be expanded beyond reason by hyperbole and exaggeration. This is as silly as it is dishonest. Yet, can one doubt that such exaggerated observations—although intemperate and untenable—will become steel threads in the fabric of the Prince Farrington myth?

## A REFRESHING NATIONAL CONVENTION?

Some of the grossly exaggerated claims about the fabled moonshiner, such as those just discussed, can be countered with factual data. Some cannot be so easily refuted. Such an unprovable claim is the one that says that the conclusion of the Democratic National Convention of 1924 in New York City was delayed by several days because Farrington booze was arriving on a daily basis. The inference, of course, is that the selection of a party candidate was postponed so that conventioneers could stay where their enjoyment of Farrington moonshine could be prolonged.

## HOOCH FOR HOOVER?

Among the more fascinating of the Prince Farrington stories is the one claiming that some of Prince's confiscated liquor was sent to the inaugural celebration of President Herbert Hoover. Among the many versions encountered by the author is the one related by Leonard Parucha of Lock Haven. In Parucha's words: "He furnished all the booze for President Hoover's inauguration of 1928." Leo "Chip" Taylor said that he learned from a local fellow, "Miley" Reich, that one of the government men at one of the two raids on the Stewart (Gheen) farm admitted to Reich, "Hey, Miley, I'll tell you what they're doing with that whiskey. They're taking it down to Washington. The president's having an inauguration. They're having a party for him, and they're taking that whiskey down for the party." In Taylor's account, as in Parucha's account, the man being so honored was Herbert Hoover. Even Prince's daughter, Gladys, nurtured the claim. For William Rombach's thesis, Gladys told (p. 15) of remembering "the night that she accompanied her father to the nation's capital in the back seat of a car loaded with moonshine, to be delivered to Hoover's inauguration."

That oft-repeated claim is doubtful. Why Hoover? It was the confiscated booze from one of the raids on the Stewart (Gheen) farm that was said to have provided the inaugural refreshment. But, both of those raids occurred in the 1930s, while Herbert Hoover's lone inaugural celebration would have been held in 1929, following his 1928 election. A shipment of confiscated whiskey from the 1931 raid would have been two years premature for the Franklin D. Roosevelt inauguration of 1933, while the moonshine taken during the 1934 raid would have been tardy by a year. The only conclusion that one can comfortably reach is that whiskey may well have reached the halls of Congress or the white house through the help of the McElhattan folklorist, Col. Henry Shoemaker, as mentioned above, but its shipment to the District of Columbia for the Herbert Hoover presidential inauguration is likely a myth.

Also, Spencer Howard, the Archives Technician at the Herbert Hoover Presidential Library in West Branch, Iowa, would remind us that Herbert Hoover's wife gave away their California wine cellar and did not allow alcohol in their house. Howard is convinced that Hoover—who was admired worldwide for his humanitarian work and who referred to Prohibition as a "noble" experiment—would not have set a bad moral example by flouting the law, either publicly or privately.

One local barrister may have known the truth of the 'Hoover inauguration' legend. The late John C. Youngman was once (1932-1935) the district attorney of Lycoming County. He prosecuted dozens of bootleggers and remembered the raid at the paint factory. That raid resulted in the arrest of the foreman there. The paint factory raid yielded 900 kegs of whiskey. A writer for the *GRIT* newspaper, O. M. Ostlund Jr., quoted Youngman (January 27, 1980) as declaring, "The funny thing was [this]: that whiskey was sent to Washington to be used in celebrating the inauguration of Calvin Coolidge in 1925. At least that's what was generally believed at the time."

That same article relates that when Prince Farrington was arrested in 1924, the charges were left unpressed after Prince told the court that "the whiskey had been made on orders from Washington and was to be used in an official celebration. Note the date. Poor Herbert Hoover, one of America's finest citizens but also among America's most maligned presidents (because the Great Depression began while he was in office), had his name repeatedly linked to this flawed Prince Farrington fable.

## THE LOCAL PRESS

If Prince Farrington ever entertained thoughts of a legacy, he should have appreciated the local press. The newspapers—including some now defunct—of Jersey Shore, Renovo, Lock Haven, Williamsport, State College and Harrisburg found that Farrington's career filled lots of column inches with fascinating reading. Then there was Williamsport's weekly newspaper, *GRIT*. The *GRIT* reporters, too, were eager to tell their readers of Prince's exploits. More importantly, the *GRIT* was distributed nationally.

The *GRIT* newspaper, however, had a two-pronged result. Whenever it published articles on Prince Farrington, the local readers could enjoy reading about his adventures, but, as noted earlier, *GRIT*'s national distribution also shook the federal hornets' nest. A later feature in *GRIT* appeared in 1980 (January 27th) when they offered an article by O. M. Ostlund Jr., which summarized the career of Prince Farrington as it appeared in various editions of their newspaper.

In addition to *GRIT*, the United Press began reporting the later news generated by Farrington. That, too, had an impact far beyond the dual counties of his primary activity. Thanks to the United Press dispatches, an article headlined "Prince of Bootleggers Has 1500 Pals" appeared in the April 4, 1951, edition of the old *Washington Daily News* and managed a reference to Prince's local reputation as "the Robin Hood of Lycoming County."

The post-obituary newspaper coverage of Prince Farrington was limited to commemorative pieces. If a legend were to be perpetrated and perpetuated, Farrington lore would have to shift to books and magazines. It did.

In 1966, ten years after Prince's death, a book of area folk tales appeared. Kenneth S. Goldstein and Robert B. Byington edited that book *Two Penny Ballads and Four Dollar Whiskey*. The book contained a full chapter of anecdotal material (pages 81–94) written by Professor Byington, then a faculty member at Lycoming College in Williamsport. A quarter-century later (1991), a second Farrington-related book was published. In that work, *Snakebite*, the late author, James York Glimm, related about 90 rural stories from the North Central Pennsylvania hinterland. Three of Glimm's tales (pages 78–83) involved Prince Farrington. It was James York Glimm who observed (p. 50) that "people who become legends, like Prince Farrington, often are truly extraordinary." Both books make fascinating reading, and both add a splash of color to the Farrington legend.

## THE MAGAZINES

Several Pennsylvania magazines carried feature articles on Prince Farrington. Among the best, although still presenting a few erroneous and exaggerated claims, was *Town and Gown* magazine, out of State College, Pennsylvania. Their article, entitled "The Prince Who Died A Pauper" (November 1979), was reprinted for the publication *The Best of Town and Gown: 20 Years* in October 1986.

## RHYME OR REASON

Folk heroes have been celebrated in poetic verse for the past millennium or longer. These traditional verses are identified as ballads. The finest ballads are moving stories, simply told. Unaccompanied by music but melodic in their recitation, the early ballads stirred the listeners just as they first stirred their illiterate versifiers. Identifying them as *ballads* separates them from other forms of poetry and from 'loftier' themes. Exaggeration is often part of the ballad's charm.

Since Prince David Farrington has been compared, frequently and favorably, with Robin Hood, it's worth noting that one of the earliest ballads, "The Vision of Piers Plowman" (about 1375), offers the earliest known mention of Robin Hood. While another legendary figure, King Arthur, was thought to be the ideal example of leadership for the privileged noble classes, Robin Hood came to represent the ideal sort of common person. Robin Hood opposed government oppression, radiated cunning and humor, and displayed a concern for the poor. That characterization of Robin Hood was easily applied, over five centuries later, to the moonshiner of Antes Fort.

Although the writing of a single ballad—whether about such heroes as Robin Hood or Jesse James (1847–82)—can be enough to fuel the legend, Prince David Farrington has been the subject of three ballads, all set to music. Thanks to the kindness of those who own the rights, we are here able to offer the reader the lyrics of all three, so that the total impact can be sensed and so that comparisons can be made.

It appears that the first 'ballad' to recognize Prince Farrington's life came from the pen of Lawrence Lebin, who lives near Mill Hall, in the very heart of what might be labeled "Farrington Country." Lebin is a retired professor of English at Lock Haven University.

Lawrence Lebin's ballad was written to be part of a projected musical play. His late wife, Shirley, had written the music for the ballad. They also had considerable encouragement from Gladys Farrington Porter. Sadly, the play was incomplete at the time of Shirley's death, and the endeavor remains unfinished. The lyrics to that ballad follow:

> ODE TO PRINCE FARRINGTON
> There is this bar in Jersey Shore
> Known as the Antique Tavern
> But the legend started long before
> The bar at the Antique Tavern
>
> It was in the 1920s
> Prohibition everywhere
> They were makin' bootleg whiskey
> No one seemed to care.

And the whiskey's made for sippin'
And making you feel whole
When you're drinkin' Prince Farrington's whiskey
It reaches and touches your soul.

Prince Farrington stilled his whiskey
In the Pennsylvania hills
Every mountain has its hollow
Every hollow has its still.

Prince Farrington stilled his whiskey
As smooth as smooth could be
You could ask anyone for miles around
Every one would agree.

And the whiskey's made for sippin'
And makin' you feel whole
When you're drinking Prince Farrington's whiskey
It reaches and touches your soul.

Revenuers chased Prince Farrington
As the sheriff chased Robin Hood
But Prince Farrington would outsmart them all
As only Prince Farrington could.

They say he was a hero
And he always took care of his friends
And he made the best damned whiskey
It's a pity it all had to end.

At the bar at the Antique Tavern
Drinkin' whiskey from dusk till dawn
Let's drink a toast to Prince Farrington
His legend goes on and on

And the whiskey's made for sippin'
And makin' you feel whole

> When your drinkin' Prince Farrington's whiskey
> It reaches and touches your soul
>
> It's the spirit of freedom
> It's the essence of this song
> Prince Farrington stilled his whiskey
> The days and the whiskey are gone.

These lyrics appear here with the kind permission of Lawrence Lebin, who offers them as a tribute to Shirley's memory.

The lyrics and music to another song, "Prince Farrington," were written by Steve Hulslander of Williamsport while he was a member of a local musical group offering a ragtime/funk program. That group, The Morgan Valley Road Boys, was together for more than a decade and used Hulslander's Farrington ballad as a staple for their programs. It is no coincidence that Morgan Valley, as Chapter 11 mentioned, was the location of one of Prince's stills. Our thanks are gratefully expressed to Mr. Hulslander for permission to reprint his lyrics here.

## PRINCE FARRINGTON

### I
Prince Farrington was a fine one, a real winnin' soul
Came from Carolina makin' corn into alcohol.
Had been an old tradition passed from father down to son
So the Prince came here to the north lands to pass it on to everyone.

### CHORUS
Prince David Farrington where have you gone?
We need a man of your ambition, we need him here and now.
Your business sense and elegance both came shining through
But the thing we all miss the most is that fine ol' Farrington brew!

### II
He made great bootleg whiskey, he made an excellent brew
He said it cured pneumonia, he said it cured the flu.

They said it sure was potent about 100 proof
And if they weren't lying, I suppose it was the truth.

III
His mind was the best in business
His heart went out to all
He gave to all the charities
He gave out from his soul.
When times were the hardest
The Prince always seemed to care.
He was a regular hero who
Seemed to be always there.

IV
He shipped his wares all over.
He shipped them near and far, from here to California
He helped equip the bars.
When the policemen were having their annual policeman's ball,
It was Prince David Farrington who provided the alcohol.

V
When feds came in to bust him
Oh, how the beer did flow
But the Prince just stood steady
And said, "I guess it's time to go."
Soon, the busts and booms were over, and the Prince's fate was sealed
People voted in Washington, and Prohibition was repealed!

Our third ballad was not born in Farrington country and the balladeer freely admitted that he used Prince Farrington's already celebrated name and applied it to an incident that involved someone else from someplace else. The song "Smile" was written by Shaun Wolf Wortis, a native of Bucks County, Pennsylvania. He explained that the incident mentioned in "Smile" "is a fictionalized account of a true event that may not have involved Prince Farrington at all, but did involve whiskey runners in Pennsylvania and a murder." Here, then, is a third lyrical mention of

Prince David Farrington. While it adds nothing to the *historical* Prince, it further promotes the *legendary* Prince. Again, the permission of Mr. Wortis is gratefully recognized.

SMILE—Shawn Wolf Wortis

Smile on me, ladies, fill your tin cups with rye
Smile on me, ladies, wish me well when I die.

The chaser's the killer, the killer's the king
The fool is the money, and the money's the thing
The numbness is queasy, the queasy turns sick
For the sickness is whiskey, and the whiskey is quick.

Some men are cutters, lay down the pines
Some men here work the drills in the mines
I am a plain man, and I would do anything
and around these hills that means I run whiskey for Prince Farrington.
They came one morning and took me in chains
and told me I'd pay for the man I had slain
A priest and a bullet-riddled Hudson was pulled out of the mud
They said I left him face down in his blood.

If the truth be told, and rare it is
I did take his life, but it was mine or his
The priest had stolen two barrels of our grain
I swear I watched them wash away in that driving rain.

He pulled a knife and his face turned red
And he shouted some bible verse about the dead
He moved like a bear with one foot in a trap
And so I dropped him there and he died like a rat.

I stand before you as I stand accused
and you'll bury me cold but forever amused
As Prince Farrington knows behind these thick walls
You can take a man down when he's got no where else to fall.

Smile on me, ladies, fill your tin cups with rye
Smile on me, ladies, wish me well when I die.

While these three ballads are not based on authentic historical material, all are authentic legend builders.

## THE UNRELIABLE COPYCAT DISTILLERS

Douglas Clyde Parker's article (see bibliography) of 1979 identifies another dynamic of a legend, the claims of the imitators. He says that there were distillers in the area of Snow Shoe, a town to the west of Farrington Country, along what is now Interstate 80. Those distillers were known for taking shortcuts with the coloring of their liquor and even shorter cuts with the aging process. Years of aging were reduced, in their backwoods' operations, to weeks. Yet, despite the utterly different standards, or lack of them, used by these imitators, they were quick to tell customers that they were buying the genuine article: Farrington sour mash whiskey.

## AN ACQUAINTANCE OF MARSHALL "CARBINE" WILLIAMS?

In 1952, Warner Brothers released a motion picture, *Carbine Williams*, starring Jimmy Stewart. The movie was 'adapted' from the life of a real moonshiner, David Marshall Williams, who was convicted of murder in the shooting of a revenue agent. He spent years in prison. While in prison, Williams was allowed to work in the prison shop, where he invented an improved firing mechanism for the carbine rifle. He was eventually pardoned and worked with the Remington Firearms Company and garnered dozens of patents. Partly because of the film, Williams became known as "Carbine" Williams.

When *Carbine Williams* was playing at the Victoria Theater in Jersey Shore, Prince Farrington, who rarely attended movies, attended this one with his grandson, Dave Porter. "That was the only time I ever saw him dressed up. In my memory, Prince always had khaki-like work clothes on. I was surprised to see pictures of him in his heyday. He was always dressed up. Like a clothes horse, almost. But, I knew him as an older man." According to Porter, his grandfather complained that the film was not authentic. Prince also said that he knew the film's real-life protagonist, Marshall "Carbine" Williams. Porter was skeptical but consider Prince's claim.

Some comparisons:

|  | D. Marshall Williams | Prince D. Farrington |
|---|---|---|
| **Life span** | 1900–1975 | 1889–1956 |
| **Home town** | Godwin, NC | Near High Point, NC[43] |
| **Marriage** | 1918 | 1912 |
| **Criminal Activity** | Moonshiner | Moonshiner |
| **Arrest(s)** | 1921 | Multiple, 1905 - 1951 |
| **Trial Court Location** | Cumberland | Guilford |

If two men live about 90 miles apart, one a plumber and one a physician, it is unlikely that they have met. However, if the two are both plumbers or if the two are both physicians, there is an increased possibility. Also, if the two men are involved in the same criminal activity, the *possible* may become the *probable*. There is another parallel in the parallel lives of David Marshall Williams and Prince David Farrington. Although they did not appear in the same courts, someone else did.

In the film *Carbine Williams*, Williams' family laments the change in judges for the sentencing hearing in Cumberland County. The bailiff identifies this replacement as Judge Henry P. Lane. A glance at trial documents for Guilford County for trials in January of 1914, March of 1914, and March of 1924—all attended by defendant Prince David Farrington—were assigned to Judge Henry P. Lane. Judge Lane (1857-1932) was a judge in the state's 11th district from 1911 until 1925, according to the North Carolina Manual.

Two additional facts intertwine with the story of David Marshall ("Carbine") Williams and Prince Farrington.
- During one court session involving Prince (as so many did), another defendant, in an unrelated case, was a man named Luther Williams. A connection cannot be found or dispelled.

---
43. The towns are about 90 miles apart.

- As mentioned elsewhere, Prince Farrington's mother was a member of the Williams family but without an established link to "Carbine's" family. One must conclude: While nothing given here *proves* that the two Carolina moonshiners—Farrington and Williams—ever met, there is enough coincidental information to at least *suggest* that Prince Farrington spoke the truth.

The old motion picture indicates that David Marshall Williams had a wife who did not approve of his criminal activity; he operated several secluded illegal stills at one time; he produced a quality whiskey; he sprinted away from a raid and outran his pursuers; he spent time in prison and, while in prison, he became a friend of the warden. Prince Farrington had to have realized that he was concluding a life that was parallel to that of the one he saw unfolding in front of him on the so-called 'silver screen' of the *Victoria Theater* in Jersey Shore, Pennsylvania. What thoughts must have been stirred in the ever-active Farrington mind?

## A MISCELLANEOUS MEMORIAL
There's a brick in Virginia that sits among the other fund-raising bricks to be found at the Clover Hollow Covered Bridge. The covered bridge spans a country stream along the unpaved Clover Hollow Road near the village of Newport (Postal Zip 24128), a few miles southwest of Luray Caverns. The commemorative brick is imbedded among the others about midway between the land of his birth in North Carolina and his haunts in Pennsylvania's Susquehanna River valley. The rustic setting and the splendid isolation would likely have appealed to Prince. Thanks to a contribution by one of his grandsons, visitors can read the brick memorial's plain message, "In Memory of Prince D. Farrington."

## LOST IN COUDERSPORT
Ironically, Prince David Farrington wasn't the only prominent figure of the time to experience a dismal decline in the quality of his life during the post-war years. A gentleman who lived about 50 miles to the north of Jersey Shore and Lock Haven had once been a national figure. He was so prominent, in fact, that two television series and a movie would

eventually be made about his life. But in post-war America, that man, Eliot Ness (1903–1957), saw his celebrated name losing its charm. He had resigned from his high-profile federal position in 1942 following an automobile accident where Ness, who had been drinking, smashed into another car and promptly left the collision site. He later worked in Washington, D.C. and Cleveland, Ohio, in the 1940s but left government employment in order to become chairman of an Ohio company. In 1947, he failed in his bid to become the mayor of Cleveland. He was out as company chairman in early 1951 and accepted a job in the small town of Coudersport, Pennsylvania, in the heart of northern Pennsylvania's famed hunting country.[44] Eliot Ness was 54 years old and still living in Coudersport, Pennsylvania, in 1957 when he had a fatal heart attack. His ashes were scattered in a cemetery pond in Cleveland, Ohio.

How strange the whims of Fate that Eliot Ness, the most noted Federal agent in the years of the turmoil surrounding Prohibition, spent his declining years at the opposite end of a lengthy mountain road from Prince Farrington, the man who must be recognized as the nation's master moonshiner. That connecting road stretches through some of the Keystone State's most rugged mountain country. Farrington, while living at his house near Antes Fort, on the banks of the Susquehanna, was living just about 75 miles southeast of Eliot Ness, each near opposite ends of an old back-mountain road known as the Coudersport Pike. Also, as mentioned elsewhere, Prince Farrington had at least one of his stills in an isolated hollow near Springer's Corner on the Coudersport Pike. Prince Farrington died in 1956, less than a year before Ness.

## LOOMING LARGE

The legend lingers, thanks to a series of articles and public talks by a number of different people. Of course, there are countless private conversations within the area families and business places. The bibliography reveals some of the ongoing interest in the Prince Farrington story. Casual conversations with local individuals also show that many younger people who never saw the man, will embellish the Prince Farrington legend and carry it far into the future.

---

44. Heavily-forested Potter County, where Coudersport is the county seat, immodestly refers to itself as "God's Country" on tourism materials.

Prince David Farrington's legend is embellished by a wealth of incidents and names that are associated with him. Dr. Robert Byington, for example, wrote of Prince Farrington as "the old master moonshiner from the faraway hills" and as the "Robin Hood of the Farmers." His legend is also reinforced by the presence of his properties and the known still sites. There are also the many words that have been written for magazines or books and many retellings of the already-churned accounts of individuals who had direct contact with Prince Farrington and of the offspring of those individuals. There was, in years past, a Farrington Room at a motel along Interstate 80 at Lamar. For some years now, that motel has been one of the Comfort Inn motel chain and it no longer has a Farrington Room. Still keeping the torch glowing, however, is the Farrington Room and several authentic Prince Farrington objects now displayed at Troy Musser's riverside Gamble Farm Inn in Jersey Shore (once Gladys and George Porter's Antiques Inn). There is also a Farrington photographic display at the Restless Oaks Restaurant at McElhattan, situated between Lock Haven and Jersey Shore.

Further, in the nearby town of Muncy, there was once an inn built in the early 19th century. Known as the Moran Hotel in the 1950s, the underground bar had murals done by a local artist depicting scenes from the Prohibition era, including one painting that had kegs of liquor and the name "Prince Farrington" displayed. Today, the building houses a government agency, and the underground bar is closed so that this subterranean tribute to Farrington is no longer visible to the public.

Patrick Reynolds, an illustrator living in the town of Willow Street (Lancaster County), Pennsylvania, created a feature "Pennsylvania Profiles." that ran in twenty state newspapers for several years prior to 1991. The illustrated feature dealt with quirky, offbeat stories from the state's history. One such segment, in 1980, featured the story of Prince Farrington, whom Reynolds identified as "America's Finest Moonshiner."

## SLOW TO GAIN MENTION IN LOCAL BOOKS

Despite growing discussion about the presence of Prince Farrington in the Sugar Valley area, writings coming from the valley have been slow to acknowledge his historic presence there. A case in point: The new (2011) book, *Images of Sugar Valley* (see the bibliography), has more than

125 pages, of captioned pictures, with a total of about 225 appealing old photographs of the Loganton/Sugar Valley area. Yet, it is only in the book's introduction that the reader will find one mention, and a fleeting one at that, of the valley's (and the county's) best known historical figure. The full quote, from page 10, states, "Two other well-known Rosecrans residents were Samuel Motter and Prince Farrington. In the second half of the 1800s, Motter gained a reputation as a trapper, fisherman and eccentric adventurer. Farrington was a legendary bootlegger during Prohibition. He purchased a farm at Rosecrans as a cover-up for his stills."

## A TOUCHING LEGEND

A story out of rural Lycoming County informs us that Prince Farrington was said to have given one of his last stills to his sons and that they neglected to tear down the still before hunting season opened. The still was spotted by hunters, and authorities were notified. Agents then went to the site and blew up that relic.

## GAMBLE FARM INN: A HISTORIC 'WAYSIDE INN'

This particular 'wayside inn' is on U.S. Route 220, a bustling highway stretching from the Pennsylvania/New York border, at Waverly, New York, across the entire stretch of Pennsylvania to disappear into Dixie. In Lycoming County, Pennsylvania, it passes just a few hundred yards from the *last domicile* of Prince David Farrington, the Antiques Inn (Now known as The Gamble Farm Inn.) Ironically, this same U.S. route also passes Prince Farrington's *childhood* home, Nubbin Ridge, by a mere three miles before reaching its terminus at the town of Rockingham, North Carolina.

As the writing of this book was entering its last days, a local entrepreneur, named Troy Musser, opened the restored Gamble Farm Inn in historic Jersey Shore. This means that what was once the residence of the aging and ailing Prince Farrington has been handed a vibrant new life. Not only did Musser revitalize the old Inn; but he erected a new motel on the premises. As noted above, the inn-motel complex is very close to an exit on busy U.S. 220. Musser already owns several authentic Farrington relics, including an unopened bottle of Prince's moonshine and one of his bottle-capping machines. The gift shop will feature Prince Farrington items, just as the dining room will carry a Farrington-themed cuisine. Musser's enterprises are bound to enhance the legend of the once-flamboyant moonshiner.

## AGING STOCK

For a more reliable evaluation of the Farrington legend, one must also mention the several individuals who still own, as prized possessions, bottles believed to be authentic Farrington moonshine. One of these images would be the privately owned pair of bottles belonging to an individual just south of Jersey Shore, while the other would be the attractively displayed flask that still carries the markings of court evidence from Lycoming County court in Williamsport. There are, as well, the two small Farrington distilleries (stills); one owned privately, by Dick Thompson, and one owned by the Heisey Museum in Lock Haven. There are many lesser objects, such as the keg hoops, the bricks, etc. These last named have little monetary value, but they remain the prized possessions of several individuals. Lastly, the largest collection of Prince Farrington-related documents remains in the possession of Prince's descendants. All these objects are relics that are tied to the story of the ambitious farm boy from Guilford County, North Carolina, who became the king of the American moonshiners. There will be no successors.

Another typical aspect of a legend is conflicting accounts. The author once checked the birth data for Harry Longbaugh, remembered today through the Robert Redford film portrayal of Longbaugh, who became legendary as the "Sundance Kid." Internet data had the infamous outlaw being born in New Jersey, in Wyoming, and in Conshohocken, Pennsylvania! The last-named place was Longbaugh's true birthplace. Similarly, Prince David Farrington's age at his first arrest varies—from a youthful 12 to a mid-teen—from account to account. He was 16. Also erroneous was the date of the moonshiner's birth (erroneously appearing as 1890, one year too late), depending on the source consulted. Several obituaries mention Prince and Martha as being man and wife, despite the existence of a document that records their divorce in Pennsylvania's Lycoming County Court dated May 5, 1930, 26 years before Prince's death. Beyond contradiction, apparently, is the obituary of Martha Farrington that appeared in the Greensboro (North Carolina) *Daily News*. There, one learns that Martha Farrington "died Tuesday at the Williamsport Hospital, Lycoming County, Pennsylvania." That means that the reclusive and disturbed mother of Prince Farrington's four children outlived their outlaw father by nearly sixteen years and died on February 15, 1972.

## RECOGNITION BY A NATIONAL CARTOGRAPHER

If the late Prince David Farrington's name had not yet gained entry into the privileged few who get national recognition, it did gain such recognition in 1985. In the March issue of *National Geographic* magazine, an article appeared that featured the Susquehanna River. The article was introduced by a photograph of the magnificent giant oxbow on the river's North Branch near Towanda, Pennsylvania. An accompanying map offers about a half-dozen inscriptions, including this one: "The Florida Fruit Farm in the hills near Loganton was the headquarters of Prince Farrington, one of the most successful bootleggers in the East during Prohibition. Known for his generosity, he was famous as a local Robin Hood." The reporter, researching that feature, happened to stop by the Antique Inn, and when Gladys learned the purpose of his mission, she spun the tale that reached the editorial offices of the *National Geographic* headquarters in Washington. That accomplishment was matched by the recognition of her father's memory that she helped to generate with her support of the decade-long Prince Farrington Great Race in Williamsport.

## THE PRINCE FARRINGTON GREAT RACE

In Williamsport, beginning in 1979, a fund-raising competition was held. Sponsored by several organizations, including the Williamsport Recreation Commission, the event featured a triathlon: canoeing, running and biking. The event was named the Prince Farrington Great Race. For several years, the event gained in participants (up to more than 500) and was held annually for more than a decade.

Much of the organizing of the Prince Farrington Great Race was done by Phil Landers of Williamsport. Also working closely with Phil was Gladys Farrington Porter. She helped with the promotion of the annual event, and she would help hand out awards and hug the winning team members. For more than a decade, The Prince Farrington Great

Race thrived. The memory of the great moonshiner was kept before the citizens of Lycoming County. With the promotion of the first of these commemorative races, the local Williamsport paper, *The Sun Gazette,* editorialized (July 31, 1979) on this inappropriate honoring of Farrington. That paper's editorial stated that some individuals were "incensed over the naming of the great race activity after such a person." The editorial concluded, thusly: "Farrington was notorious but hardly illustrious." Despite the editorial writer's criticism, the racing event was held annually for more than a decade. After some sponsorship was lost, the event was discontinued. Gladys, who had not been involved with the race in its last couple of years, had returned to her dream of a biography of her father.

In 2003, the Williamsport Chapter of the American Red Cross scheduled a repeat of the Prince Farrington Great Race, but that one failed to generate the interest of the earlier races and was, again, discontinued. Somewhere today, there are hundreds of closets and bureau drawers still holding T-shirts, silk-screened and colorful, with their images of the "notorious" outlaw, Prince David Farrington.

### INDEPENDENT SPEAKERS

At least three individuals have been known to accept speaking engagements in order to speak on the life of Prince David Farrington. One speaker was Martha (Mrs. Tom) Farrington, the daughter-in-law of Prince. A second is Bruce Teeples of Aaronsburg, who has had a web site devoted to the collection of Prince Farrington data and remembrances. The third is Bill Tyson of Beech Creek, a few miles west of Charl's home in Lamar.

### RUBBING ELBOWS WITH THE EMINENT

As mentioned earlier, Prince Farrington was on very friendly terms with businessmen, civic and political leaders and a few lawmen. His family mentions his attending a party in Williamsport at one of the fine homes on Grampian Boulevard, the street once known as Millionaire's Row. In all likelihood, the quality of Farrington's whiskey helped to lubricate many friendships.

Among his most eminent local friends was the folklorist Col. Henry Shoemaker, who broke into the pages of this biography in Chapter Six.

As noted in that chapter, Shoemaker was, at one time, the state folklorist, the U.S. minister to Bulgaria, the owner of several newspapers, and much more. Although his stories were as unreliable as Prince's whiskey was reliable, Henry Shoemaker appreciated Farrington's whiskey and, so Farrington members claim, Shoemaker got Farrington's whiskey into the halls of government in Harrisburg and Washington.

If name-dropping is a becoming human trait, one can readily see why local newspapers enjoyed visiting with Gladys Farrington Porter. She had a stock of names of prominent individuals that could be forever attached to her father's name. For example, Gladys was quoted as saying that the famed heavyweight boxer Jack Dempsey "always had a keg [of Farrington whiskey] at his restaurant in New York."

Family members suspected American Indian lineage for Prince David Farrington and his siblings. Thus, it seems strangely ironic that Prince had a long-term friend, Henry Sampson, who was a full-blooded Chippawa Indian and that, of all the thirsty celebrities in Hollywood, Prince became acquainted with Will Rogers (1879-1935), who was part Cherokee Indian. Prince Farrington and Will Rogers seemed to agree on whiskey's role in life. It was Will Rogers who once compared (perhaps facetiously) bootleggers with motion-picture stars by observing that "bootlegging is an honor. There is something to it. It means something. You are selling a staple article, something that is good today—The movies is something that is made for children while bootlegging is made for men..." (P. J. O'Brien, p. 187-8). While in California, Prince contacted his brother, Charles ("Charl") and told him to ship some Farrington whiskey (labeled "molasses") to California by rail. Charl went to the train station in Lock Haven and shipped several barrels of "molasses" to The Golden State, where it was delivered to the nation's top humorist of the day, Will Rogers. Prince Farrington's daughter was pleased to inform listeners that while Prince had been in Hollywood, her dad stayed at the Will Rogers Ranch.

It appears as a cryptic note in a spiral-bound notebook of Gladys. The entry says simply:

> Bucknell—Warden Hill
> Walter Annenberg (Mose)
> Annenberg

Apparently, Gladys was aware that Moses Annenberg had been an inmate at Lewisburg and she wondered if her dad's period of incarceration overlapped with Annenberg's. Why the interest on Martha's part? Who was Moses Annenberg? Moses Annenberg bought the *Philadelphia Inquirer* in 1936 and was later sentenced to the federal penitentiary in Lewisburg for income tax evasion. His son, Walter, (1908-2002) became far more celebrated, as newspaper owner, philanthropist, ambassador, and founder/publisher of *T.V. Guide* magazine. If the federal terms of Prince David Farrngton and Moses Annenberg overlapped, Gladys would have the name of one more noted person to link with her father's name. Here are the stats needed to see if Gladys's father and Walter's father might have been cellmates or even prison mates: Prince served in Lewisburg from July 12, 1937, until September 27, 1939. Moses Annenberg, however, wasn't sentenced until July 1, 1940, and became an inmate a few weeks later (July 23rd). In the case of Moses Annenberg, then, Gladys's hope of 'dropping' a prominent name was thwarted by a discrepancy of less than ten months in their incarceration times.

Prince Farrington, the skilled moonshiner and bootlegger from the North Carolina/Pennsylvania countryside once met with Alphonso Caponi (Al Capone, 1899-1947). Capone, the alumnus of a New York City criminal gang, became the crime boss of Prohibition-era Chicago. Capone is easily the best known criminal in American history and—unless the status of politicians changes—he will likely remain so. Capone, from his hotel headquarters in the Cicero, Illinois, suburb, ran a huge criminal enterprise that led to a lengthy prison term and the agony of a syphilitic body and an early death. But what occurred when Prince Farrington met the king of organized crime? Dave Porter says they had a confab in northeastern Pennsylvania that seemed to have resulted in a verbal agreement regarding territorial imperatives. Gladys's account was a bit more colorful. She told one writer (Parker, p. 83) about her moonshiner father's meeting with the Chicago mobster who was credited with countless murders, including the gruesome St. Valentine's Day slaughter (February 14, 1929), "Dad wouldn't deal with Capone, because Capone was a gangster. When Capone found my father's whiskey in Chicago, he warned him to keep it out of his territory. My dad told Capone to go to hell, and that was that!"

## FARRINGTON'S FUTURE?

Beyond the realm of sports, the Keystone State has been limited in statewide folk heroes, much less in folk heroes known beyond the borders of the Commonwealth. The strongest candidate for a real folk hero out of Pennsylvania would have to be John Chapman (1774-1845), known throughout the nation as "Johnny Appleseed." Now, however, the memory of Prince David Farrington has the potential to change that situation. As Professor Byington observed in his essay on Prince Farrington (p. 93ff), future developments may allow Pennsylvanians to "be able to boast of a folk hero—in prominence with Jesse James himself." The reader may or may not wish to agree.

## THE TANTALIZING TALES

Legends of lost treasures aren't confined to the mountains of the southwest. Lost treasure tales have been told in 'Farrington Country,' as well. Charles Dorwart and George Mayes, long-time residents of Antes Fort, expressed their certainty that there is still buried Farrington whiskey in the Antes Fort area—sort of a "Prince's Lost Whiskey Stash." Equally tantalizing: More than a decade after Prince had died, Clyde Meixel, a former Farrington driver, encountered Prince's brother, Charl, in the Lamar area. Clyde related that Charl expressed a particular desire: He wished that he had a secure location to construct a still. Charl still had, he told Meixel, the Prince Farrington recipe for top-grade moonshine. Did brother Charl hold a written recipe, or had he simply learned it from repeated application? Did the recipe die with Charl in 1971? One is free to speculate.

## THE RETURN TO GUILFORD COUNTY

When Prince David Farrington died, June 14, 1956, his devoted daughter, Gladys, wanted his burial to be in Jersey Shore, Pennsylvania. Her brothers were joined by their mother, Martha, however, in insisting that Prince be buried in North Carolina. Outvoted and, perhaps, out–muscled by her brothers, Gladys Farrington Porter and her son, Dave, represented the Pennsylvania faction of the relation in far-off Guilford County.

If Prince were to return today, he'd not recognize the old Carolina homestead on Nubbin Ridge. A comfortable and attractive house has replaced the original. To the east, a lake now sits, fed and emptied by the stream of his childhood, Deep River. To the west, some of the acres that once belonged to Thomas Beverly Farrington are becoming a housing development. Along with a homestead of reduced acreage, another reminder of 'the old days' for the current generations, is Burnett's Chapel, several miles away.

Burnett's is a church of the United Methodist faith. It sits along the old Randleman Road, south of Greensboro, North Carolina. It was built, in part, through the organizing efforts of Hilda White Anthony, Martha Farrington's sister. It was also built, in part, with funds contributed by Prince Farrington. For decades, Burnett's has been the house of worship for many in the family. The body of Prince David Farrington was placed in the earth in the country cemetery beside Burnett's chapel.

Martha White Farrington, Prince's troubled mate through marriage and for decades after their divorce, eventually left Gladys's home to reside in the Lycoming County nursing facility at Warrensville. Her last five days were spent in the nearby Williamsport hospital, where she died early in the morning of February 15, 1972. The three sons and one daughter of Mattie and Prince were all surviving. Her burial, too, was set for the Burnett's Chapel graveyard. A small contingent from Pennsylvania again drove south to join their Dixie relatives in paying respects to the moonshiner's former wife.

The mortal remains of Martha and Prince are buried side-by-side beneath separate headstones. The two graves are linked by a much larger headstone to the rear, set close to the cemetery's edge. A wall of rhododendrons forms a flowery backdrop. The lone name, in upper-case lettering, on this polished marble headstone is FARRINGTON. A smaller inscription offers the stone's only other words: A FRIEND TO ALL.

The early English poet laureate John Dryden (1631-1700) offered a few lines that suggest that a truly worthy person doesn't require fictitious embellishment.

> Draw him strictly, so
> That all who view the piece may know
> He needs no trappings of fictitious fame.

The testimonials of many, many individuals remove the need for imaginary tales of Prince Farrington. No matter what the reader's opinion of the man might be, the legitimate praise heaped on Prince Farrington's memory is enough to sustain the opinion that he was a unique member of his community. Before he died in 1956, he was already becoming legendary. The legend remains and grows.

While this biography has concentrated on Prince's two-county area of activity, Clinton and Lycoming counties, Dave Porter, Prince's grandson, says that Prince was also well-known in Penns Valley, another rich agricultural belt in Centre County.

Jim Phoenix is a coach of girls' softball at Central Mountain Middle School. During the 1980s, he worked at Reading Meats in Flemington. There was, he recalls, a strange individual who walked the streets of Flemington (the town that links Lock Haven and Mill Hall). This man had crutches and a wagon. This man would enter the meat shop and talk of making moonshine. He would ask to buy sugar but never wanted to buy a full five pounds. He also offered, in return for the granular sweetener, a 'pint' of excellent whiskey. Reading Meats never accepted his offer and never learned the true identity of this stranger, who may or may not have been related to Prince Farrington Sr. It was simply that those who encountered him assumed that there must be a connection.

Just as the unidentified stranger who once moved through the streets of Lock Haven on crutches has become part of the legend, the claim attributed to Art Decker fits that description. Decker, of Antes Fort, was a lineman for a utility company. But, Art had also claimed to have driven for Prince Farrington, and he also claimed, in later years, that there were still caves in which Prince's booze was hidden.

When one learns of the many ways in which Prince Farrington kept secrets from authorities and others, the unproven claim of hidden storage caves or similar caches becomes more convincing. Perhaps that's why Lawrence Lebin, a retired educator from the Mill Hall area, has expressed suspicions that Prince Farrington may not have been 'penniless' as some suggested.

More evidence of a Farrington legend involved a mention in National Geographic Magazine, several ballads with musical support, many newspaper and magazine articles and, for a decade or so, an annual charity event, The Prince Farrington Great Race, in Williamsport.

Admittedly, a neighbor boy, Tom Bauman, was almost like a son to Prince Farrington. Several incidents showed this trait. Here's one. Bauman relates:

> We were still living down there on the farm, and there was a guy over in Antes Fort who had something like a little hardware store. He sold seeds, tools, shovels, picks and so on. His name was Newt Thompson. Prince had come down to the house for something. Dad came in and told Mom, "I'm gonna go with Prince. He wants to go over to Antes Fort to the store." I said, "Can I go along?" "Yeah, come on." So, I went out and got in the middle of the front seat. Prince drove us over there. We went into this guy's place. I don't know if you remember: The Case company used to have this display card with all different kinds of pocket knives. Boy! I looked, and I really wanted a knife. So, I asked my dad. It wasn't near Christmas or anything like that. It was summertime. "No," he said, "You'll only cut yourself with that . . . or you'll lose it."
>
> I went out and sat on the porch 'cause they were still inside shooting the bull. I saw them coming out, so I went and got into the car. They got in the car, and Prince backed the car and headed over toward the farm. I felt Prince fiddling at my pocket and reaching down, but Prince just took my hand away. Anyhow, we got home, and he took us down to the house, and we all got out. They had to go to the barn or something. I couldn't wait until they were out of sight. There was that pearl-handled pocket knife! Boy! I didn't say anything to Dad. I had it for quite a long time before Dad ever found out. (Anyhow, if I had that knife today and we carried them the way we did, then we'd get expelled from school!) But I carried that knife through school and through high school. (In high school, his knife was loaned and lost.)

Prince Farrington's charm has been reported in newspapers, as well as in the endless conversations that are still occurring. Mary Lee Troup, of Beaver Springs, in Snyder County, was a native of the Williamsport area.

She tells of her mother, as a young woman, being employed, at one time or another, in the offices of two Williamsport area companies: The U.S. Rubber Company and the C.A. Reed Company. This was in the 1920s, within the early years of Prince Farrington's residency in Pennsylvania. He was, at that time, aside from his moonshine-making, delivering soft drinks. Ms. Troup's mother related the impression Farrington had on the women when he stepped into an office, removed his hat and bowed deeply while saying, in his finest Southern accent, "Good morning, Ladies!" As Mary Lee Troup relates, all the office girls thought Prince to be "quite handsome." Ms. Troup also tells of her parents, as a young couple, knowing the location of a Farrington still site along the old Coudersport Pike. The young couple would walk from the highway into the woods, where they directly bought from the operators, a quantity of Farrington whiskey.

Prohibition, mentioned in Chapter 1, gave rise to secret still sites, but it also gave rise to countless secret places where the thirsty could purchase the outlawed alcoholic drinks. The illegal barroom was just one cultural phenomenon born of the Prohibition era. Operating outside the law made barroom owners very careful not to allow strangers to patronize since the strangers might be law officers preparing to raid the illicit business. Thus, a potential patron would whisper, or *speak easy*, to the doorman to gain admission. That precaution led all such secret barrooms to become known as "*speakeasies*." The term, '*speakeasy*,' went out of style in 1933, with the end of Prohibition.

At one time, Prince Farrington operated a *speakeasy* on the old Gheen (now Courtright) farm. With the passing of Prince's sister, Nade Coltrane, Kyle Coltrane, the widower, and his three children moved in with Prince for a while. B. W., who helped Prince tally his inventory, etc., was especially popular locally, but it was B. W.'s brother, Wade, who married a local girl, Betty Koch.

After the Coltranes vacated the Gheen farmhouse, Prince welcomed the Spong family to be his tenants in the former Gheen house. He engaged the woman, Minnie Spong, an experienced bartender, to manage his speakeasy. Minnie was said to have managed a hotel somewhere, before working for Prince. Also, years later, one of Minnie's daughters was running the Venture Inn a couple of miles north of Jersey Shore on Pine Creek. Prince's personal speakeasy on the Gheen farm offered patrons the opportunity to buy alcoholic drinks, play four or five nickel slot machines and, sometimes, listen to live music. When they departed for the night, customers often took along a supply of liquor for later- perhaps a quart bottle; maybe a gallon jug. Bauman says, "They always had some kind of entertainment." Minnie Spong once hired a regional band to provide some music at the speakeasy. That band had four members and offered customers the sounds of an accordion, a banjo, a guitar and a washboard, the last of which was played by a fellow wearing thimbles.

Tom Bauman's mother, Meda Leah Bauman, wanted to hear the music, so she drove the family's 1929 Chrysler automobile down the lengthy country lane to the Gheen farm. Meda Leah and young Tom enjoyed the musical program. Tom tells us that, at one point, the band's accordion player told the patrons that he was going to sing a song that was a favorite of Prince's. With the small band accompanying, the accordion player then sang (except for the occasional humming of some forgotten lyrics) the country hit, "Have You Ever Been Lonely?" That song, composed by Peter De Rose and with lyrics by Billy Hill, was published in 1932 and was first recorded in 1933. The song was especially popular, with recordings by nearly two dozen artists. Such noted singers as Teresa Brewer, Jim Reeves, Jim Ed Brown and Patsy Cline gave voice to the lyrics of apology and regret. However, the recordings of those four singers were all made *after* Prince Farringon's death. The most likely versions to have been heard by Prince Farrington would have been the first one recorded (in 1933, by Ted Mack, a now-nearly forgotten singer) and the 1947 rendering by country star Ernest Tubb. It would be silly to speculate on whether or not Farrington applied the lyrics to his broken marriage with Martha White Farrington. Still, the words excerpted here fascinate:

> Oh, be a little forgiving.
> Take me back in your heart.
> How can I go on living,
> Now that we're apart?
> If you knew what I'd been through,
> You'd know why I ask you:
> Have you ever been lonely?
> Have you ever been blue?

Tom Bauman of Castanea has other marvelous recollections of Prince Farrington. Tom's father, Raymond Bauman, another non-drinker who moved among the moonshiners, remained a friend of Prince Farrington throughout his lifetime. The '29 Chrysler that Mrs. Bauman drove to the Gheen Farm speakeasy was part of a pair that was purchased at the same time. The 6-cylinder Chrysler that Tom's father owned was similar in color to the 8-cylinder 1929 Chrysler that Prince got. Tom says that Prince's fine, new machine was purchased with a proper mix of cash and liquor.

Few living people have more than a memory or two of having encountered Prince David Farrington. For the boy, Tom Bauman, encountering his neighbor, Prince Farrington, was almost commonplace and certainly wasn't limited to the time that Prince bought him a pearl-handled pocket knife.

Positive opinions of Prince were also commonplace. For example, Tom Bauman's wife, Geneva Goodman Bauman, a lifelong resident of Castanea, states emphatically that Prince Farrington "was a good man." And, she adds that his family members were also good people. Her husband gained a similar opinion from regular contact with Prince and his family members, as mentioned in the Chapter 1. However, Tom Bauman had several additional encounters to recall.

Young Bauman was with Prince and Whitey on a trip to Jersey Shore. There, Prince and Tom Bauman waited in the car for Whitey to get his hair cut. While the bootlegger and the farmer's son were waiting, Prince asked, "How is your dad? I haven't seen him for a while." Then, "Your Mom?" When Tom Bauman acknowledged that they were alright, Prince followed with, "I want to tell you something. Your dad is the only person that ever worked for me, that never tried to take me. He's as honest as the day is long."

The raid, about 1932 of Prince's place was a chaotic time for the Baumans (two parents and three children). Tom remembers the raid as being like a circus. It lasted through two days and a night. Local people were rushing to see and, if possible, to sop (gathering as much of the spilled liquor as they could get before it sank into the ground or flowed into the river). Since the authorities made little effort to keep spectators away, they accumulated to enjoy the spectacle. After all, how many people are lucky enough to witness a genuine revenue agents' raid? Bauman muses about the crowd. "Every drunk in Lycoming County, I think, was down there."

At Prince's neighbors' farm, the Baumans saw their cellar steps removed so that the officials could create a makeshift setup for getting whiskey kegs up from the cellar. They were then rolled downhill while an agent stood on each side and tried to smash open the two ends with sledgehammers. Not every barrel end broke; but some that did still held some of the valuable moonshine.

Even then, when the raid finally ended, the Baumans found a barrel in the cellar that hadn't been removed or smashed. Their maternal uncle, Floyd Shaffer, salvaged that last full barrel and sold it to Joe Gardner. It was worth, by the gallon, nearly $500. All the moonshine that had been on the Bauman farm had been aging for about five years, which made the loss even more painful. Agents had checked the tractor shed, silo and just about everywhere imaginable; but had found no more booze. Then, when it seemed that their portion of the raid was completed, one of the agents decided to drive a 3/8-inch piece of metal pipe into the haw mow. "Thump." The hay had been covering a huge and valuable stash, now destined to flow into the Susquehanna, from which no revenue would ever flow back in return. Yet, despite the agents likely finding over a hundred kegs and barrels of moonshine in their several hiding places, the Baumans were only questioned but not arrested.

When Floyd Shaffer and Prince Farrington were in Lewisburg, Floyd's sisters, including Tom's mother, took Tom and drove to the penitentiary. Although Tom was not allowed to any inmate, his mother and aunts got to speak with Floyd but were denied visiting privileges with Prince.

Another time, authorities came to Prince's house. While searching, they ran across a bill that was lying on Prince's desk. A local individual had submitted the invoice to Prince for payment. The bill showed that Prince had hired the man to set up a still. That bill incriminated Prince, who was saddled with an eleven-month prison sentence in the Lewisburg penitentiary. Tom's uncle, Floyd Shaffer, who had set up the still and who had submitted the bill, earned a nine-month stay in the same walled facility as his employer.

## A CLUSTER OF POSITIVE TRAITS

Prince David Farrington had so little formal education that he barely got through the first eight grades. Yet, he was a skilled welder, a knowledgeable farmer, an impressive dresser, a natural diplomat, an astute businessman and an expert distiller. Farrington possessed considerable common sense and a coolness under pressure. To observe Prince Farrington's best traits, one need only review his many encounters with his neighbor, Tom Bauman. Bauman didn't simply observe numerous positive traits of the master moonshiner. He was the beneficiary of several.

Another major incident involving Bauman and Prince Farrington reveals several of Prince's personal qualities at once. Tom narrates a very different and very personal story. He tells of working with Prince and Prince's youngest son, Whitey. "There was a field," Bauman relates, "out there, right below the (Antes Fort—Jersey Shore) airport. Prince and Whitey had taught me how to drive their Ford tractor. So they were at the barn on the Gheen farm, getting ready to plant soybeans while I was plowing. If it (an incident) had happened at any other time, I might have lost a leg or something.

"Anyhow, I'd just started down along the old fence row, trying to plow all the land that I could. I was driving the Ford tractor, which had a hydraulic lift. Just as I picked up the plows, the left front wheel caught a fence post that was hanging out on its wire! It jerked the steering wheel out of my hand. As I reached to grab the wheel, my foot slipped down and right under the right tire! Luckily, I had the throttle (speed control) back, and it stalled the tractor, but it stalled it right on my leg! There I was. I started screaming like a wild Indian!

"There was an old, one-room schoolhouse down at the end of that field, and earlier, I had seen these guys at the old schoolhouse, fiddling around with furniture or something. I started hollering like hell! Anyhow, I didn't know this; but Whitey and Prince had come out the road in their pickup truck. They stopped to wait for me; then decided that I must be plowing another round. They sat there for a little bit, waiting. Then Prince asked, 'Whitey, isn't that Tom hollering?' Whitey said, 'Yeah!' so they came tearing down over that unplowed ground in the Ford truck. I thought they were flying! When they pulled out onto the plowed ground, the truck stalled!

"They bailed out of the truck and ran over to me. Whitey jumped on the tractor and was going to try backing it off of me, but Prince said, 'Don't! You might spin the wheel on his leg!' They, too, had seen the guys at that building, so Whitey ran down through that field . . . it must have been two or three hundred yards down there, and he was out of breath when he got there. Those guys asked Whitey, 'What's the matter?' Whitey said, 'My buddy's under the tractor up there!'

"Meanwhile, Prince got under that wheel . . . and he was strong! Nobody will ever tell me that he wasn't extra strong! Prince pulled up, and he held as much of that weight off my leg as he could. Then he slipped, you know, and he'd have to let it down again . . . and I'd moan a little bit more.

Finally, here comes Whitey and those guys in that old Chevy car, and they all jumped out and jumped over the fence. They all got hold and pushed the tractor off of me.

"Prince reached down and picked me up just like I was a baby. When he picked me up, I said, 'I'm alright, Prince. I'm alright. Just let me down.' Prince let me down, but he held on to me till I walked around a little bit.

"The wheel on my leg had shut the blood flow in my leg, and I also had the tire track bruise right down that leg, you know. Also, the tractor had wooden pegs where you rested your feet. When I slipped off the side, those pegs tore my pant leg and bruised the *inside* of my leg. I often thought about that. If that tractor hadn't stalled and would have kept going, with those plows up in the air, they probably would have slammed right into me!"

Tom Bauman stayed at the Gheen house until the circulation returned and he could walk comfortably. When Raymond Bauman arrived to take his son home, Prince told him what had happened. "It wasn't Tom's fault," Prince declared. "That damned fencepost, hanging out on that wire, just jerked the steering wheel out of his hand," Tom assures us that his dad still liked the Ford brand of tractor. He says that just a year after that accident, Raymond Bauman bought his first Ford tractor from "Doc" Derk in Jersey Shore ("Doc" was a car dealer, but he was also a veterinarian). Over the years, Raymond Bauman had a total of four Ford tractors.

Amid people's negative and positive recollections of Prince Farrington, a few stand out. Another couple of Tom Bauman's positive remembrances must be offered here so that this, the second half of Farrington's biography, can end on a positive, yes, on a *very* positive note.

Tom relates that when he was about five years old, his mother ordered a shepherd dog for him. It was ordered from a place in Wisconsin. He had that dog for 16 years until it died when he was a senior in high school. The shepherd dog was purchased because Tom had already been given a police dog, but his mother had read about a police dog maiming a boy, so she asked the gift giver to take it back. The man who graciously accepted the police dog's return was the Bauman's generous neighbor, Prince David Farrington Sr.

Another interaction between Tom Bauman and his moonshiner neighbor, in Tom's own words:

> Prince was like a favorite uncle to me. He gave me the first gun I ever owned. Dad and I were visiting down there one time. Whitey Farrington had this Benjamin air rifle. You pumped it up, and it shot .22-caliber pellets. Well, Whitey had shot some windows out of the garage or something. So, when Dad and I were going out to get in the car, Prince reached in the corner and said, 'Here,'" and handed me the rifle.
>
> With that air rifle, I shot a good many rats and pigeons in our barn. The damned pigeons would shit on our equipment. My dad would try to keep the barn closed, but those pigeons would always find a way in, you know. My dad was a stickler for putting equipment inside when you're done with it, not so much the harrows, but we had binders, corn planters, and a mower. They had to be inside. He didn't want them rusting. That's where my gun helped. I could shoot my Benjamin air rifle in the barn. My brother had a single-shot 22-gauge rifle. I wouldn't dare shoot that in the barn because it would blow holes out through the roof!
>
> After I'd come home from military service, I was working for my uncle. This was about 1946 or 1947, about the time that Prince had a still up on the Scootac. (Tangascootac Creek). We were doing work up near the Jersey Shore High School. As I was going up on Church Street, I passed a garage and saw Prince putting gas in his one-half-ton pick-up truck. I parked my truck and got out. We shook hands, and I said, 'I haven't seen you . . .' We exchanged greetings. It was the last time I ever saw Prince.

Tom Bauman, who used no alcohol, expressed only positive thoughts about America's top moonshiner. Let's conclude the Bauman praise with one clear quote: "You know, in all the time that I knew Prince, I never heard anybody say anything bad about him."

As was stated before (*see* Chapter 6), Prince Farrington made sure that local children attending the Lycoming County Fair had some money available. He also sent barefoot children to a Jersey Shore shoe store where he kept an open account. He was also remembered for having first graders start their educational journey with a new pair of jeans, a new shirt and a new pair of shoes.

## VOICES IN THE WILDERNESS

The evidence is clear: Prince David Farrington was highly regarded among his friends and neighbors. The positive remarks made about the man far outnumbered the negative statements. However, we would be remiss if we neglected to present the thoughts expressed by people who did not appreciate whatever it was that Farrington was doing for the community.

In Chapter 13, we quoted at least one individual critic as well as a forceful statement in a newspaper regarding respect for the law and the sort of society we would have if everyone took the attitude of Prince Farrington. Individuals did complain. They may have been in the minority in the area, but let's hear their voices.

David Doerr's family moved into Sugar Valley in 1870. They lived in the area east of Loganton, near the Price Cemetery. That cemetery once was attached to the Price Evangelical Church; but the church had a small congregation and eventually offered only monthly services. The Doerr family tale tells us that there was only a crawl space beneath the church, but Prince Farrington hid whiskey in the crawl space. As a teen, Robert Doerr was given $5 by Prince Farrington to watch the stash and let Prince know if it was disturbed. Some felt that Prince increased his acceptance in the community by giving money for some exaggerated or imaginary needs. In any case, young Robert Doerr used his money to buy a bicycle. He could now ride his bike the three-and-one-half miles to school. Sadly, he soon had a cycling accident that broke his arm.

Later, Robert Doerr became a binge drinker, and his aunt was quick to let the community know that Prince Farrington gave her sottish nephew his first drink.

As an aside, we might mention Charles Womeldorf, who also lived east of Loganton, was said to have made his own booze in the 1950s and sold some of it. In fact, Robert Doerr's spinster sister, Eleanor, later converted Womeldorf's mash tubs into handy planters and used them for growing flowers.

Marjorie Kamus (*see* Chapter 11), of Jersey Shore, is unsparing in her criticism of Prince Farrington. Regarding his fame, she now observes: "It wasn't a good famous. It was an 'Al Capone' famous, except that Prince didn't carry a gun. He was good to people because he needed drivers and other people to run the stills and so on." In more recent years, Marjorie herself, has owned the store across the highway from the old paint mill on Antes Creek. She also recalls accompanying her dad on a visit to Colonel Henry Shoemaker's home in order to see the author's antiques. Why? Because, she tells us, "people did things that didn't cost a lot of money."

Another individual who heard some unvarnished criticism of Prince Farrington was Phil Ferrar. Phil's grandfather, Edward (Joseph Edward Ferrar), worked for Prince. 'Edward' Feerrar told Phil that he had been a runner for Prince and recalled taking Farrington alcohol to Washington, D.C., for delivery to several people, including the U.S. president. However, Phil expresses some doubt about the claims of his grandfather since Edward "had a huge drinking problem in his middle years." Phil Feerar notes that his "siblings blamed his relationship with Prince as leading to the destruction of his marriage and to his losing his faculties." Phil Feerrar concludes, "Growing up, I was taught Prince was a felon, not someone to admire."

## MORE PLAUDITS FOR PRINCE

Another neighbor, John Muthler, lived on the neighboring farm when Prince Farrington lived near Antes Fort. Muthler, whose own family did not use alcohol, says that he never saw Prince drunk and that he was "Always dressed in a suit." That was before Prince's stay in the Federal penitentiary in Lewisburg. After his release, however, Muthler says that Prince was normally dressed as a dirt farmer.

Bernard Wynn, whose grandfather worked for Prince, suggests that his great aunt would have considered Prince Farrington to be "a common crook," but Wynn declares, "In my (immediate) family, you really didn't say anything bad about him."

Harold Adams is a retired educator who was born and raised in Sugar Valley. He offered this summary of Prince's reputation in Sugar Valley: "When Prince Farrington had the Florida Fruit Farm if farmers had trouble selling their crops, they could sell them to Prince. Prince always kind of looked out for the people over there. And to this day, you can't say anything bad about Prince Farrington in Sugar Valley. If you do, you're going to get into an argument. That's the way it was. He was well-liked."

## THE TIME FACTOR

If we want to learn of the reaction to Prince David Farrington in the two primary counties involved in his wildly colorful career, we must align events of his life with the calendar.

When Prince first arrived in Pennsylvania, the reception would have been mixed. Those who wanted a source of alcohol would have been pleased to make his acquaintance. Still, a large number, likely more than half, might have said, "The last thing we need around here is another person pushing alcohol!" The longer he was here, the smaller that chorus would have become. As his supply of moonshine increased, his appreciative customers would have grown in quantity. Finally, even though the institution of prohibition was ending, larger numbers of local people would have been impressed with the wealth he continued to generate and share. The sentiment would likely have been something like, "The main thing that we need around here is someone with money to spend!" Prince Farrington's influence may have increased steadily until his last arrest. Once Farrington's presence was lacking, his importance waned.

## SIX TO STAY IN SHANGRI-LA

James Hilton (1900–1954) was an English novelist. His one book, *Lost Horizon* (1933), told of a fabulous land lost in a mountain range, where most residents barely aged. The name of that fictitious land gave us a name for any place that borders on the idyllic: *Shangri-La*. For Prince and his Tarheel friends, that might have been Clinton/Lycoming counties in Pennsylvania. Perhaps it's the friendly people. Possibly, it's the air. Or maybe it's the magnificent scenery. We can't know. What we do know is that Prince, his brother Charl, Colonel Segraves, Joe Gardner, George Gardner and Lemuel Groce all came from rural North Carolina to make a little liquor in Pennsylvania, and all six remained for the rest of their lives in the Keystone State. So far as we can determine, all but Prince are buried here, as well. Clearly, this sextet of moonshiners and neighbors became forever attached to the land and the people of Pennsylvania.

## FULLER'S FRANK EVALUATION

Despite a sometimes reluctant welcome from his relatives around Nubbin Ridge, Prince Farrington did return home for visits. One never knew if he was drawn south by real family ties or by something related to his moonshining occupation. However, one visit seems to have been clearly motivated by family ties. Sam Fuller, who did considerable driving for Prince, including that of chauffeur, remembered the trip during which he drove one of several trucks that Prince was delivering to Oklahoma City, Oklahoma. On the return trip, Sam and Prince came through North Carolina, where they spent three weeks visiting Prince's old homestead. Fuller, now in his 80s and filled with rich memories, remains active and gets to South Williamsport to attend weekly dances. Sam Fuller also offered this very succinct observation about Prince Farrington: "He was a helluva nice guy!"

The principal characters who graced the pages of this book have left many, many descendants to carry their names or their bloodlines into future generations. One example: When Ida Stabley died in 1959, a local newspaper noted that she had 65 descendants. That number should exceed 100 in 2011. A second example: Herman Henry and Margaret Miller Klobe had two sons and a daughter, Charles, Floyd and Mildred. Those three had, respectively, eleven children, one child and one child. That baker's dozen of grandchildren of Herman and Margaret Klobe has now swelled to more than a hundred descendants!

Similarly, Wesley Koch and his wife, Emma, had 11 children, a number that generated many dozens of descendants. Lastly, Prince sired four children with Mattie, while his brother, Charl and his sister-in-law, Virgie, had seven children. Although an accurate count of offspring might not be possible, a tally of descendants for Pennsylvania's two Farrington brothers, numbering in the dozens, is surely valid.

The Farrington legend is daily nourished by the presence of many area residents through whose arteries the diluted blood of a moonshiner pulses. A widening pool of descendants inhabits what was once "Farrington Country." Today, countless area citizens can trace their lineage back to the local moonshiners. They cling to a growing cluster of legends about the colorful days of Coltrane, Farrington, Gardner, Groce, Klobe, Koch, Kohberger, Rockey, Segraves, Seyler and Yarrison, plus the dozens of lesser players. The moonshiners' local offspring, as well as many other enthusiastic local citizens, will ensure that the legends thrive and that they are lovingly carried into countless tomorrows.

# BIBLIOGRAPHY

**BOOKS:**

Allen, Frederick Lewis, *Only Yesterday*, 1964 edition.
Bailey, Thomas A., *The American Pageant*, 1956.
Dabney, Joseph Earl, *Mountain Spirits*, 1974.
Day, Savannah Segraves, *The Reverend William Segraves and His Descendants*, Pocohantas Press, 1989.
Donehoo, Dr. George P., *Indian Villages and Place Names in Pennsylvania*, 1928 (Reissued in 1977).
Glimm, James York, *Snakebite: Lives and Legends of Central Pennsylvania*, 1991.
Goldstein, Kenneth S. and Robert H. Byington, *Two Penny Ballads and Four Dollar Whiskey*, 1966.
Graybill, Guy, *Keystone*, 2004.
Gross, Rebecca F., 1983 *Lock Haven Sesquicentennial Yearbook*, p. 23.
Holy Bible, Scofield, C. I., D.D., editor, 1967 edition.
*How To Make It.* Canadian Publishing Company of Washington Avenue, Philadelphia, Penna.
Huddy, Stephen C., and Paul C. Metzger, *Alvira and the Ordnance*, Montgomery Area Historical Society (Montgomery, PA), 2009.
Kagan, David Ira and John W. Harbach Sr., *Images of America: Sugar Valley Villages*, 2011.
Meginness, John, *The Early History of Lycoming County*, 1892 (reprinted, 2005).
Nevins, Allan, *The Gateway to History*, Revised Anchor Books edition, 1962.
O'Brien, P. J. *Will Rogers*, 1935.
*The Oxford Universal Dictionary*, 3rd edition, 1955.
Parucha, Leonard F., *Retire-miniscing*, c. 1982.
*Pennsylvania Atlas and Gazetteer*, 2000, DeLorme.
*Pictorial Atlas of the Greater United States and the World, 1902.* (publishing data lost).
Utley, Robert M., *The Indian Frontier of The American West: 1846-1890*, 1984.
Welshans, Wayne O., *Images of America: Jersey Shore*, 2006.
Welshans, Wayne O., *Images of America: Nippenose Valley*, 2008.

**PERIODICALS/MANUSCRIPTS/SPEECHES**

Beers, Paul B., article in the *Evening News*, Harrisburg, PA (presumed to be a 1966 issue).
Bernard, Lou, several scholarly papers.
Briggs, Norma Jean Smith, *"Memories of My Grandfather: John Alexander Farrington,"* privately printed, February 5, 1977.
*Centre Daily Times*, State College, Pennsylvania, 5/23/02, 10/13/85.
*Clinton County Democrat*, July 14, 1922 issue.
*Express*, Lock Haven, Pennsylvania, numerous issues.
*Express*, Lock Haven, "A Peek At The Past," Matt Connor, 5/3/08.
Farrington, Prince David, Three letters, 1951.
*Greensboro* (North Carolina) *News and Record*, issues of April 24, 2005, May 15, 2005.
*GRIT, Issues of April 9, 1950, April 6, 1950, etc.*
Hunsinger Jr., Lou, *Prince Farrington: The Robin Hood Bootlegger*, Williamsport *Sun-Gazette*, Date unavailable.

*Lock Haven Express*, LockHaven, PA, several issues.
*Loganton and Sugar Valley—1965*, Photocopied production for 125th Anniversary.
*Loganton and Sugar Valley Sesquicentennial—1840—1990*. Photocopied production.
Mattern, Billy N., *Local Buffalo—Fact or Fiction*, undated.
Macneal, Douglas, *Centre County Heritage*, Vol. 24; Number 2, Fall, 1987.
Myers, Harold D., *The Tangascootac, Beech Creek and Bald Eagle Valleys of Clinton County, PA*, 2005.
National Geographic, "Susquehanna: America's Small-Town River," Peter Miller, March 1985.
*Newsweek*, 11/6/67.
*Now and Then*, Muncy (Pennsylvania) Historical Society, Volume XXI, Number 11, April 1986.
Osborne, Elsie, undated, from Clayville, Virginia.
Parker, Douglas Clyde, "*The Prince Who Died a Pauper*," *Town and Gown* magazine, Barash Advertising, State College, PA, November 1979, and reprinted, issue of October 1986.
*Renovo Record*, Renovo, PA, Selected editions, 1927 and 1928.
Reynolds, Patrick, *History and Mystery of Pennsylvania*, (historical comic book edition).
Rombach, William, *Prince Farrington: Life and Legend*, masters thesis, Shippensburg, PA, 1973.
Seidel, Lester, interview on cassette tape, recorded June 1, 1983, by Richard Brown. That tape, never published or used for any speaking engagement, is owned by Dan Hills of Mill Hall. Dan Hills loaned it to the author (May 2010) for use with this book. Hills retains the original, and I own a copy.
*The Snyder County Historical Society Bulletin*, 1996.
*Standard*, Milton, PA, edition of March 10, 1962.
*Sun-Gazette*, Williamsport, Pennsylvania, numerous issues.
Ternent, Mark, mternent@state.pa.us.
*Time*, 11/3/67.
*Wellsboro Agitator*, Wellsboro, PA, 8/18/1956.
*Williamsport Gazette and Bulletin*, 1/28/1948.

## PRIVATE CORRESPONDENCE
Howard, Spencer (Archives Technician at the Herbert Hoover Presidential Library, West Branch, Iowa, e-mail dated 6/24/09.

## INTERNET DOCUMENTS/WEBSITES
Teeples, Bruce, http://www.storytrax.com/node/186
Teeples, Bruce, mongopawn44@hotmail.com
Wilson, Ellen, A Passion for the Past
http://www.carnegiemuseums.org/cmag/bk_issue/1996/julaug/dept5.htm 9/3/11
http://genforum.genealogy.com/shoemaker/messages/747.html 9/3/11
http://phmc.state.pa.us/bah/dam/mg/mg114.htm 9/3/11
http://www.psu.edu/ur/about/myths.html, 9/4/11
http://www.psupress.org/books/titles/0-271-01486-5.html 9/3/11
https://mail.google.com/mail/h/lqzx04qdsvied/?&v=c&smi=13293622295c14e1#m_1329...
http://thepennsylvaniarambler.blogspot.com/search/label/Henry%20Shoemaker, 9/4/11

# INDEX OF PEOPLE AND PLACES

## A

Aaronsburg, PA, 365
Alamance Co., NC, 18
Albany, NY, 115, 171
Allentown, PA, 291
Allenwood, PA, 3–4, 56, 169, 183, 229, 239
Altoona, PA, 157, 289–90
Andrews, Evan, 111
Annenberg, Moses, 366–67
Antes, Col. John Henry, 49, 166
Antes Creek, 8, 166–67, 169, 219, 250–51, 301, 380
Antes Fort, PA, 35, 38, 49, 64, 68–70, 89–90, 94–95, 97–98, 104, 116, 126, 145, 148, 152, 156, 159, 166, 174, 178, 200, 221, 229, 233–34, 240, 242, 244, 250–55, 263, 283, 293, 331, 336, 345, 347, 352, 360, 368, 370–71, 376, 380
Anthony, Hilda White, 369
Anthony, Scott, 61, 175, 212, 274
Apopka, FL, 269, 276–78, 303
Arthur, T. S., 294
Asheboro, NC, 276
Atoka, TN, 291
Auburn, NY, 118–19
Avis, PA, 148, 227

## B

Bald Eagle Mountain, 242
Barbee, Algernon, 18
Barberton, OH, 286
Barker, Judge W. S., 304
Bauman, Raymond and family, 58–61, 174–76, 186, 255, 266, 285–90, 296, 371, 373–79
Baxter, Emma Cross, 3
Baxter, Reverend T. G., 3
Baxter, Richard, 3–9, 54, 158
Bay City, MI, 142–43
Bear Swamp, 2, 48

Beech Creek, 155, 282, 297, 365
Beers, Paul B., 347
Bellefonte, PA, 88, 110, 128, 288
Bender Run, 230
Bitner, Stanley, 131
Bixel, Mildred ("Millie"), 112, 114
Black Ankle region, NC, 16, 275
Bloomsburg, PA, 92, 142–43, 343
Booneville, PA, 39, 80, 337
Boston, MA, 40, 274
Bowes, Lee Marshall, 120
Bowes, Lynn, 89, 120
Bradford County, PA, 147
Brennan, Walter, 47
Bridgens, J.F., 144, 263
Briggs, Norma Jean Smith, 26–27
Brooks, Byron, 347
Brooks, Ernest, 347
Brookside, PA, 69, 98
Brown, Hazel, 95
Brown, Jim Ed, 373
Brown, Louise, 252–53
Brown, Richard, 143
Brown, Russell, 226
Brown, Sam and Julia, 156
Bubb, J.B., 156, 296
Bubb, Robert, 247
Buck's Gap, 225, 335
Buckhorn Mountain, 224
Bucks County, PA, 355
Buckley, Tom, 81
Bulgaria, 149, 366
Bull, Mr., 104–105
Burrows, Nell, 230–31
Bush, Alvin, 305
Button, Melvin, 156, 227
Byington, Dr. Robert, 315, 346, 351, 361, 368

## C

California, 158, 184, 310, 342, 349, 355, 366

## INDEX OF PEOPLE AND PLACES 387

Cambria Co., PA, 145
Campbell, S. R., 41–42, 339
Canada, 7, 56, 249
Cannell, Lee, 274
Capone, Al, 62, 161, 346, 367, 380
Carlisle, PA, 141–45
Carroll, PA, 39, 106, 116–17, 147–48, 178, 181–82, 185–86, 190, 192, 200, 224–25, 335
Castanea, PA, 8, 89, 110, 126, 137, 139–40, 230, 290, 374
Caudle, Artis, 34
Caudle, Bob, 25–26
Chapel Hill, NC, 18, 21, 23
Chapman, John, 368
Charlotte, NC, 151, 274
Chicago, IL, 4, 153, 161, 170, 367
Chippewa Indians, 15, 142–44
Clayville, VA, 28, 33
Clinton County, PA, viii, vxi, 1–3, 6–9, 18, 24, 39, 43–44, 49, 66, 69, 71, 77, 90, 95, 102–103, 107, 109, 113, 115, 118, 120, 133–34, 139, 145, 150, 153, 156, 158, 160, 171–72, 174, 176, 189, 191, 193, 199, 220, 222, 224–29, 233, 237, 239, 241, 254, 259, 263–64, 268, 277, 279, 282, 284–85, 291, 297, 308, 314, 317, 335, 338, 341, 343, 370, 381
Coatesville, PA, 276
Coira, Charles and family, 152–53
Coltrane family, 16, 244, 383
Coltrane, B. W., 38, 90, 92, 104, 174, 210–11, 229, 251, 253–54
Coltrane, Hilda, 28, 243
Coltrane, Kyle, 59, 90, 243, 372
Coltrane, Margaret, 255
Coltrane, Wade (and Betty Koch Coltrane), 243, 255
Coltrane, Zenadah Farrington, 59, 90, 191
Colvin, Dr. Merl, 332
Connor, Matt, 346
Cook, Dr. A. M., 331
Cooper, Ernest, 108
Cooper Hollow, 107–108
Copenhaver, Dale, 229
Cornelius, Arthur Jr., 278
Coudersport, PA, 228, 359–60
Coudersport Pike, 228, 239, 344, 360, 372
Courtright, Pat and Phil, 372
Cowfer, Don, 96, 120, 223
Cowfer, Robert Jr., 156, 232, 315

Cowfer, Robert, 156
Crocker, W. D., 44
Cumberland County, NC, 358
Currin, Scott, 109–11
Custer, Lt. Col. George A., 141

## D

Daley, Walter A. 278
Dawes, Henry L., 141–42
Decker, Art, 98, 159, 370
Decker, Torrence "Diz," 98, 159, 169
Deep River (NC), 13, 369
Derr, Joe, 229
Devin, Judge, 262
Dix, Ed, viii, 39
Dorwart family, 89
Dorwart, Charles, 64, 66, 70, 89, 96–97, 282, 293, 368
Dorwart, Ruth, 96
Douty, Russell, 114
Drick, Margaret and Harold, 226
Duboistown, PA, 147, 340
Duck, Russell and Roy, 157, 208
Dunlap, Clarence "Chippy," 255
Dunn, Charles, 144, 263
Dunnstown, PA, 227
Durham, NC, 273, 309

## E

Eagleton, PA, 2, 224, 236, 245–46, 263
Eastville, PA, 39, 180, 183, 212, 237
Eck, David L., 139, 228
Eckel, John, 156
Elimsport, PA, 110, 225–26, 340
Embick, Leonard, 131
Erie, PA, 5, 171
Ernst, John B., 41–43, 107
Espy, PA, 93

## F

Fannettsburg, PA, 3
Farrandsville, PA, 58, 234, 324
Farrington, Arlene Ebert, 291
Farrington, Batie, 11–12, 14, 16–18
Farrington, Betty E. Williams, 11, 13–15, 273
Farrington, Charles ("Charl"), 11, 24–26, 73, 122–23, 126–36, 159, 170, 174, 213, 257, 268, 286, 332, 337–38, 366, 368, 382

Farrington, Cora Grace McCandless, 26–28, 128, 151
Farrington, Debbie, 31, 123, 134, 155
Farrington, Gayle Randall, 18, 60, 141, 176, 271–73, 283, 285–89, 306, 327–29, 331
Farrington, George Hobson "Hob", 11, 26, 33, 99, 175–76
Farrington Gurney (England), 13
Farrington, John A. (Prince's grandfather), 13
Farrington, John Alexander (Prince's brother), 26–28, 33–34, 128, 151, 274–75
Farrington, Juanita, 128, 132–33
Farrington, Martha (Mattie), 9, 30–31, 33–34, 52, 60–61, 107, 131–33, 241, 248, 280, 287, 325, 369, 382
Farrington, Martha (Prince's daughter-in-law), 18, 30–31, 33, 80, 231, 283, 291, 315, 363–64
Farrington, Mary Alice Tinsebloom, 15
FARRINGTON, PRINCE—The subject of this biography.
Farrington, P. D. Jr., ("Whitey)," 18, 60, 79, 81, 88, 92–93, 159, 175–76, 191, 208, 212, 281, 283, 287–91, 308, 329, 331, 348, 374, 376–78
Farrington, Sarah March Dillon, 11, 15
Farrington, Tammy, 60, 128, 130, 132, 134–35, 184, 315, 347
Farrington, Tom (Prince's son), 13, 17, 59, 273, 285, 365
Farrington, Thomas B., 11, 13, 15, 17, 20, 127, 369
Farrington, Thomas M. (Charl's son; Prince's nephew), 128–29
Farrington, Virginia ("Virgie") Tinsebloom, 123, 127–29, 132–36, 159, 268, 337, 382
FBI (Federal Bureau of Investigation), 9, 28, 30, 140, 151, 259, 269–78, 285, 290–91, 302–303, 325
Feerrar, Ken, 229, 380
Fidler, Lester, 256
Fillman, Robert Jr., 159
Fiorini, Georgiano, 30
Florida, 249, 265, 269, 271, 273, 275–78, 284–85, 288, 291, 293, 301, 303–306, 314, 326, 331
Florida Fruit Farm, 178, 186, 199, 201, 220, 222–23, 225, 251–52, 263, 341, 347, 364, 381
Fourth Gap Road, 9, 229, 238

Fritz, Ivan and Selinda, 95, 249
Fuller, Sam, 58, 98, 151–52, 240, 287, 289, 382

# G

Gann Run, 173, 235
Gardner, Frances Farrington, 88, 94, 158, 213
Gardner, George, 126, 128, 137, 174, 213, 382
Gardner, Joe, 25, 42–43, 47, 79, 126, 130, 136–38, 144–45, 148, 174, 196, 204, 209, 229, 241, 271, 275, 329, 375, 382–83
Gardner, June (Mrs. Joe), 138
Gardner, Thomasina, 137
Geronimo, 141
Geyer, Stewart, 114
Gheen, Bill, 59, 89, 242, 255, 311, 346, 349, 372–74, 376–77
Gibbons, James, 41
Gillie, H. H., 264
Gilson, S. L., 118
Gipsy, PA, 156
Glenn, Joe, 15
Glenn, Samuel, viii, 10, 15
Glenn, Nannie Herbin, 10, 15
Glimm, James York, 90, 351
Glossner, Susan, 147
Godtchall Road, 94
Godwin, NC, 358
Gold, Eli, 150
Goldstein, Kenneth S., 351
Good, Sara, 294–95
Grampian Boulevard, 103, 365
Granville School, 35, 97, 283
Greak, Boyd, "Duke," 78, 119–20, 171–74, 210–11, 235
Greasy Grass or Little Bighorn (MT), 141
Greenburr, PA, 39, 131, 138, 233–34
Greensboro, NC, viii, 10, 15–18, 20–21, 24, 61, 175, 197, 209, 275, 304, 334, 363, 369
Groce, Herbert and Ollie Jenkins, 139
Groce, Jacque, 139–40, 230
Groce, Mary Thompson, 139–40
Groce, Venetta, 139
Groce, Lemuel, 8, 25, 120, 122, 126, 138–40, 148, 170, 241, 270, 275, 277, 382–83

# Index of People and Places

Guilford County, (NC), 3, 13, 16–18, 20–21, 23, 25–26, 30, 34, 61, 149, 262–63, 276, 358, 363, 368

## H

Harbach, Gloria, 110, 137
Harbach, John, 110, 112, 157
Harbaugh Road, 172–73
Harrisburg, PA, 1, 88, 98, 142, 149, 215, 336, 350, 366
Harvey, John Jr., 89
Harvey's Lake, PA, 297
Hauser, Clara, 102
Hauser, Rev. Dean, 88, 102
Hauser, Harry, 102–103
Hauser, Lester, 153–54
Hayes, Bill, 249, 255
Heckman's Gap, 228
Heimer, Jake, 76
Helsman, Elizabeth Jamison, 3
High Point, NC, 13, 18, 138, 160, 358
Highfill, Dorothy Lee, viii, 27, 30, 128
Highfill, Ray, viii, 30
Hill, Henry, 268
Hills, Dan, 45, 79
Hills, O. B., 79
Hipple, Henry, 119, 144, 263
Holden Beach, NC, 151
Hollis, William, 115, 118
Hoover, Herbert, 62, 350
Hoover, J. Edgar, 259, 270–71, 274, 348–49
Hopple Hollow, 112
Howard, Spencer, 349
Hughesville, PA, 97, 305
Hulslander, Steve, 354
Huntingdon, Louis B., 116–19, 179, 188, 341
Hyatt, Joe, 28
Hyatt, Tony, viii, 27, 197

## I

Indiana County (PA), 156
Ireland, xii, 13, 120, 168, 225–26

## J

Jamestown, NC, 160
Jersey Mills, PA, 156, 227, 339
Jersey Shore, PA, viii, xii, xv, 30–31, 41, 49, 54, 58, 60, 64, 68–70, 79, 81, 89–90, 92, 94–98, 104, 120–21, 126, 139–41, 144–47, 151–53, 156, 160, 163, 168, 171, 173, 184–85, 188, 195, 197, 203, 218, 221, 225, 227–28, 230, 232–33, 242–43, 247–52, 255, 263, 265–66, 269–70, 275, 279, 290, 292–93, 295–97, 301–307, 312, 316, 319–20, 331, 338, 340, 342, 347, 350, 352, 357, 359, 361–63, 368, 372, 374, 376–80
Johnson, R. G. Jr., 68, 149–51, 168
Jones, Clair Jr., 228

## K

Kamus, Marjorie, 98, 250–51, 292, 380
Kentucky, xiii, 44, 149
King, Nunery, 12, 19–23, 271
Kline, John, 103
Klobe, Charles, 116–17, 174, 178–20, 238
Klobe, Floyd, 115–17, 119, 174, 178–20, 237–38, 341–43
Klobe, Herman, 116–19, 174, 178–20, 382
Klobe, Maggie, 116, 178–20, 382
Knarr family, 113
Knarr, Dorothy Dorwart, 293–94
Knarr, Harry, 114
Knepp, Earl, 117, 119, 179
Koch, Grace, 255
Koch, Lee, 245
Koch, Wesley and Wesley Jr., 156, 255, 289, 382
Kohberger, Geraldine and John, 147
Kohberger, Jake, 83, 126, 131, 146–48, 174, 177, 185, 224, 227, 241
Kohberger, Mary Jane, 147
Kreamer, Frank and Hazel, 5, 138, 157–58
Kulp family, 113, 184

## L

Laennec, Dr. R. T. H., 331
Lamade, George, 304–305
Lamar, PA, ix, 73, 91, 123, 126–31, 134, 136, 155, 159, 226, 257, 336–38, 361, 365, 368
Lancaster, PA, 232, 361
Landers, Phil, 364
Lane, Judge Henry P., 25, 262–63, 358

Latimer, Robert, 105
Laurel Run, 155
Lebin, Lawrence, 352, 354, 370
Lebin, Shirley, 352, 354
Lehman, Ralph Sr., 161
Level Cross, NC, 25–26
Lewisburg, PA, 6, 8, 31, 87, 136, 244, 266–69, 274, 279, 292, 310, 367, 375, 380
Lick Run, 234
Linden, PA, 103
Little River, NC, 16
Little, Tom, 81
Lock Haven, PA, 1–2, 7, 24, 40–41, 43–44, 46, 49, 57–58, 65–66, 71, 76, 79, 88, 110, 114–18, 120, 124, 126, 130–31, 136–41, 155, 157, 172, 183, 188, 196, 224, 228, 230, 234–36, 259, 263, 272, 283–85, 288–91, 296, 304, 306, 308, 313, 324, 326, 329, 335, 340, 349–50, 352, 359, 361, 363, 366, 370
Lockard, W. R., 41, 44
Loganton, PA, 37, 39, 43–44, 66, 78–79, 81, 90, 106, 109, 111–13, 126, 137, 145–47, 155, 157–58, 172, 177, 184, 188–90, 193, 200, 204, 208, 222–23, 229, 304, 312, 314, 334, 336, 341, 344, 362, 364, 379–80
Long Run, 24, 223
Longbaugh, Harry, 363
Loos, J. O., 244, 266
Lowe, William and Vida, 159
Lower Pine Run Road, 102
Luray Caverns (VA), 359
Luzerne County, PA, 272
Lycoming College, xiii, 351
Lycoming County, PA, viii, xii–xiii, 1, 3, 5–6, 8–9, 39, 43–44, 61, 66, 69–71, 90, 95, 103, 113, 156, 158, 164, 166–67, 171, 174, 185, 192, 203, 206, 227, 230, 241–42, 255, 267, 269, 279, 288, 290, 297, 302–303, 314, 321, 325, 338, 343, 350–51, 362–65, 369–70, 374, 381
Lycoming County Fair, 97, 379
Lycoming County Jail, 44–45, 250, 288
Lycoming Creek, 269
Lycoming Creek Road, 103
Lynch, William, 264, 271
Lytle, Harry, 98, 109–11, 154

## M

McElhattan, PA, 68, 104, 140, 148, 162, 199, 220, 230, 258, 349, 361
McElhattan Creek/Falls, 162, 230
McGonigal, Harry, 6, 8, 264–65, 271
McGuire, William, 233
Mackeyville, PA, 143
Maguire, Arthur A., 7, 94
Maria Christina, Queen of Spain, 234
Marsh Creek, 226
Martin, Vincent, 41
Martz, Grace & Harry, 115, 180
Mateer, George, 155
Matter, Harry, 158
Matter, Sam, 158
Matthews, James, 224–25
Matthews, Laura, 81, 225
Matthews, Thelma, 77, 81–83, 95, 99, 116, 178
Matthews, Milburn, 66, 83
Mayes, George, 116, 178, 331, 368
Meixel family, 160–61, 232
Meixel, Clyde, 160, 304, 368
Meixel, Dorothy, 183
Meixel, Ernest, 160, 303
Meixel, Floyd, 160, 231, 250, 303
Messner, William J., 30
Miami, FL, 271, 273–76
Mildred, PA, 30
Mill Hall, PA, 79, 97, 162, 184, 254, 295, 304, 352, 370
Miller, Andrew, 45
Miller, Bob, 240
Miller, Catherine, 45
Miller, Edgar & Edith Weaver, 172
Miller, Jane Bubb, 156, 246, 296
Miller, Margaret Louise, 180, 217, 382
Miller, Roseltha, 227
Millheim, PA, 40, 343
Milton, PA, 3, 90, 183
Morgan Valley, 251, 354
Morris, Bill, 90
Motlow, Lemuel, 139
Moyer, Earl, 108
Moyer, Vida, 159
Muncy, PA, xii, 105–106, 361
Musser, Troy, 5, 157, 295, 362
Muthler family, 69, 243, 295, 380
Muthler, J.C., 243

## INDEX OF PEOPLE AND PLACES 391

**N**

Narrows, The, 95, 338
Ness, Eliot, 360
New Jersey, 115–16, 312, 363
New York, 115, 118–19, 171, 177, 284, 362
New York City, 24, 145, 181, 185, 187, 243, 341, 348, 366–67
Newark, NJ, 115
Newberry, PA, 152, 172
Newport, VA, 213, 359
Nippenose Valley, 160, 166, 177, 232–33, 241–42, 248–49
Nisbet, PA, 230
Nittany, PA, 155
Nittany Inn, 130, 338
Nittany Lions, 346
Nittany, Mount, 138
North Bend, PA, 231
Northumberland County (PA), 117
Nubbin Ridge (NC), 10, 13, 15–16, 18, 26–28, 33, 139, 160, 276, 298, 362, 368, 382

**O**

Oakdale, NC, 137
Oklahoma City, OK, 151, 382
Oldham family, 16
Orange County, FL, 269, 276–78
Orange County, NC, 18, 273–74
Orlando, FL, 269, 271, 275–78, 291, 329
Osborne, Elsie Farrington, 16, 33
Osborne, James Carl, 33
Ostlund, O. M. Jr., 266, 350
Oval, PA, 156, 315
Owens, Leonard, 5–6
Ozmont, Fred, 17–18

**P**

Packer, Emily Mateer Farrington, 123, 129–30, 133, 155, 347
Parker, Douglas C., 83–84, 330, 346–47
Parucha, Leonard, 79, 96, 191, 349
Peacock I and II (mining towns), 2
Penn's Creek, PA, 150
Pennsylvania Liquor Control Board (PLCB), 4–5, 134, 264, 300, 339
Pennsylvania State Police, 88, 272

Pettigrew, J. M., 264
Petty, Richard (and family), 151
Philadelphia, xiii, 4, 24, 41, 72, 140, 180, 188, 194, 198, 235, 270–72, 274, 276, 284, 315, 342, 345, 367
Pine Creek, xiii, 95–96, 146, 163, 170–71, 173, 180–81, 225–27, 233, 238, 290, 310, 339, 372
Pine Mountain Road, 160
Pittsburgh, 5, 24, 72, 157, 274, 278, 284, 336
Pleasant Garden, NC, 272, 274
Plymouth, PA, 117
Porter, Chris, 230
Porter, Craig, 92, 295, 340
Porter, David, ix, xii, 9, 14–15, 104, 121, 133, 143, 225, 285, 295, 308–309, 320, 322, 325, 330–32, 357–58, 367–68, 370
Porter, George, viii, 2, 14, 18, 90, 92, 104, 140–41, 143, 149, 152, 154, 175, 192, 221, 261, 280–81, 295–98, 301–302, 305, 311, 315, 317, 323
Porter, Gladys Farrington, viii, 92, 128, 163, 175, 192, 207, 255, 261, 280–81, 291–93, 295–96, 300, 302–303, 305, 307, 311, 314–16, 318, 320, 323, 330, 346, 352, 364, 366, 368
Porter, Dr. Robert, ix, 31, 134, 149, 213, 295, 307–308, 310, 315, 320, 322, 330
Porter, Stanford and Florence (Tibbins), 297–98
Porter Township, 171, 226, 297
Potter County (PA), 226, 228, 360
Poust, Dave, 97, 247–48
Powys, PA, 224, 227–28, 263
Pratt, General R. H., 142
Prince, Dr., 14
Punxsutawney, PA, 5
Purman, William, 40

**R**

Rainey, Blair, 156
Randleman, NC, 20, 22, 85, 139, 151, 160, 369
Randolph County (NC), 139, 272, 275
Rauchtown, PA, 9, 66, 115, 160–61, 185–86, 200, 232, 250
Rauchtown Creek, 114, 116
Ravensburg State Park, 9, 238

Rayle, Alonzo, 11, 19, 29
Rayle, John, 276
Rayle, Phoebe Farrington, 11, 14, 19, 26, 29–30
Reeser, Morton B., 41
Rehoboth Beach, DE, 16, 276
Reich, "Miley," 349
Reidsville, NC, 260, 264
Reinhold, Dan, 97, 254
Renovo, PA, 118, 131, 191, 231, 350
Revelton, PA, 2
Reynolds, Patrick, 361
Rhone, R. B., 143
Richmond, VA, 16, 28, 33, 274
Riley, Robert, 275, 329
Rishel, Jonathan Lee, 158, 253
Rockey, Gladys & George, 78, 95, 97, 119, 184, 234–35
Rockey, Lee, 114, 119–20, 235
Rockey Road, 47, 65, 78, 94, 112–15, 172–73, 184, 208, 220, 234–35
Rockey, Tom and Freda, 112–13
Rockingham County (NC), viii, 260, 264, 279, 362
Rombach, William, 107, 304, 313, 346
Ronda, NC, 149
Roosevelt, Franklin D., 62, 268, 349
Rosamilia, Charles Jr., 235
Rosecrans, PA, 35, 39–40, 51, 65–66, 80, 94, 96, 101, 109, 146, 186, 222, 291, 362
Rossman, Lee, 130
Roush, Ann, 46, 111
Ruckle, S. E., 143
Runk, Priscilla, 156
Rupert, PA, 143

## S

Salona, PA, 24, 109, 131, 145, 223, 252, 275
Sampson, Anna and Jennie, 143
Sampson, Henry, 140–46, 148, 241, 263, 366
Sampson, John and Mary, 142
Schadt, William "Bucky," 110, 137
Scranton, PA, 116–17, 267–68, 270, 277
Sechrist Riffles, 242
Seiler, Lester, 41, 45, 47–49, 74, 76–77, 85, 93, 109, 127, 143, 252–53, 256–57, 266, 292, 306
Seiler, Raymond, 257
Seiler, Turbit, 45–46, 49, 74, 107, 257

Seitler, Fred, 266
Self, Luther, 42
Selinsgrove, PA, 3, 150
Seven Mountains, 155
Shaffer, Floyd, 89, 375
Shaffer, Harry "Fuzz," 177
Shaffer, Dr. Robert, 49
Shapiro, Lewis, 8
Sheddy, Grace, 307
Shoemaker, Col. Henry, xiii, 126, 148–49, 220, 241, 349, 365–66
Shoemaker, Mrs. W. J., 145
Short Mountain, 232–33
Simcox, Theodore, 234
Slifer, George, 144, 294
Smethport, PA, 4
Smith, George, 45
Snook, Ed, 39–40, 88, 96, 161, 233–34, 253
Snook, Lee, 106, 257
Snook, Lou, 108
Snook, Newton, 161
Snydertown, PA, 130
Sockman, Bill, 231
South Danville (Riverside), PA, 117
Spong family, 372–73
Springer, Charles, John and Kathleen, 228–29
Springer's Corner, 228–29, 360
Spruce Run, 144, 223
Spruce Run Road, 138, 224
Stabley, Adam, 47, 113, 184
Stabley, Teresa, 115
Stamm, Miller, 80, 113, 146–47, 334
Stanley, Isaac, 117
State College, PA, 288, 290, 297, 309, 350–51
Steppe, Charles, 288
Stewart, Samuel, and son Samuel, 241
Stewart-Courtright farm, 58, 164–65, 241–49, 336, 349
Stiver, Bob, viii, 120
Stoltzfus, Isaac, 226
Stone, Richard B., 9, 84, 270
Stradley Hollow, 156, 163, 227
Stubefield, Louise (a.k.a. Mrs. Bohumil Dolezel), 274
Sugar Valley (PA), 24, 39–40, 44, 49, 57, 65–66, 68, 78, 80, 99, 112–14, 117, 131, 137–38, 146–47, 178–80, 182–86, 200, 232–33, 236–38, 291, 312–13, 337–38, 343, 361–62, 379, 381

## INDEX OF PEOPLE AND PLACES 393

Susquehanna River, xi, 2–3, 39, 49, 58, 72, 145, 147, 162, 166, 172–73, 175, 193, 221, 225, 227, 230–31, 234, 239, 241–42, 245–47, 269, 296, 301, 315, 324, 336, 359–60, 364, 375
Swartwood, E. F., 275

### T

Tamarack, PA, 131
Tampa, FL, 265, 278, 303–304, 310
Tangascootac, "Scootac," 1–2, 230, 236, 378
Tate, A. R., 304
Taylor, Leo "Chip," viii, 31, 38, 84, 90–92, 104, 140, 174, 225, 229, 251–54, 283–84, 347, 349
Teeples, Bruce, 346, 365
Ternent, Mark, viii, 77
Thompson, Clair, 126, 145–46, 148, 341
Thompson, Dick, 146, 163, 363
Thompson, L.C., 145
Thompson, Lee, 146, 303
Tibbins, Dr. George, 282, 297–98
Toomes, Blease, 151
Toomes, Cindy Rayle, 29–30, 79, 85, 151, 276
Toomes Run, 96
Torbert, PA, 95, 192, 225
Towanda, PA, 364
Tylersville, PA, 39, 131, 155, 184, 338
Tyson, Bill, 365

### U

Ulmer, David A., 95–96, 295
Ulmer, David S., 95–96
Ulrich, Patricia and Charles, 159, 226
United States Penitentiary, Lewisburg, PA, 267
Uwharrie Mountains (NC), 16

### V

Vermilya, Russell, 105–106
Vogt, George, 41

### W

Wagner, John, 45, 49, 78–79, 137
Wagner, Lee, 158
Wagner, Walt, 174, 177
Walter, Glenn, 150
Wapwallopen, PA, 246
Warrensville, PA, 369
Washburn, Harold "Dutch," 7, 78, 113, 138, 158, 200, 222–23
Watsontown, PA, 82
Weaver, Robert J., 80
Weaver, Yvonne and Steve, 222, 341
Webb, Bud, 252–53, 341
Weidler, Tom, 92–93
Whiskey Run, 234
White, Henry and Julia, 19
White Deer, PA, 118, 310
Whitehead, Judge Harvey, 118
Wilkes Barre, PA, 6, 246, 272, 297
Williams, David Marshall "Carbine," 357–59
Williams, George W., 13–14
Williams, Harry, 159, 250
Williams, Louis, 251
Williams, Luther, 358
Williamsport, PA, xi, 4–5, 8–9, 31, 44, 55–56, 59, 71, 81–82, 88–89, 103, 118, 120–21, 137–39, 147–48, 152–53, 158, 165–66, 169–70, 172, 182, 224, 226–27, 263–64, 266, 269–70, 277–78, 292, 294, 300, 304, 307, 310, 313, 325, 331, 339, 341, 346, 350–51, 354, 363–65, 369, 371–72, 382
Willow Street, PA, 361
Wilson, Jim, 24–25
Woolrich, PA, 147, 229, 239
Worthville, NC, 139
Wortis, Shawn Wolf, 355–56
Wright, Bunny Hyatt, 27, 75, 129, 197
Wyoming, 216, 363
Wyoming, PA, 272

### Y

Yadkin County, NC, 127
Yarrison, Faith, 101, 110–12, 149, 182, 383
Young Woman Creek, 231
Youngman, John C., 166–67, 169, 266, 349–50

### Z

Zanella, Andrew, "Peachy," 2
Zerbst, Warden Fred G., 23

www.ingramcontent.com/pod-product-compliance
Lightning Source LLC
Chambersburg PA
CBHW011406300426
44117CB00018B/2964